HEALTHY HOME KIT

Inspecting for Environmental Hazards

Working with Professionals to Avoid Risks

Cleaning Up Radon, Lead, Asbestos and More!

INGRID RITCHIE, PhD
STEPHEN J. MARTIN, CERA

Real Estate
Education Company
a division of Dearborn Financial Publishing, Inc.

To Edward and Katherine Culver

Publisher: Anita A. Constant
Acquisitions Editor: Christine Litavsky
Managing Editor: Jack L. Kiburz
Senior Associate Editor: Karen A. Christensen
Editorial Assistant: Stephanie Schmidt
Interior and Cover Designs: S. Laird Jenkins Corporation

The creator, author and copyright owner of the following material in *The Healthy Home Kit*, a book, is Ingrid M. Ritchie:

Part 1.   Environmental Hazards and Your Home
Chapter 2, Overview of Environmental Hazards

Part 2.   Contaminants Related to the House Design and Construction Materials
Chapter 3, Radon
Chapter 4, Asbestos
Chapter 5, Lead
Chapter 6, Formaldehyde
Chapter 7, Volatile Chemicals in Construction Materials, Furnishings and Consumer Products
Chapter 8, Moisture

Part 3.   Contaminants from Consumer Products and Activities
Chapter 9, Mold and Other Biological Contaminants
Chapter 10, Contaminants from Furnaces and Other Fuel-Burning Appliances
Chapter 11, Pesticides
Chapter 12, Electric and Magnetic Fields Produced by Power Lines and Household Appliances

The creators, authors and copyright owners of the following materials in *The Healthy Home Kit*, a book, are Ingrid M. Ritchie and Stephen J. Martin.

Published by Real Estate Education Company,
a division of Dearborn Financial Publishing, Inc.

Printed in the United States of America

95 96 97   10 9 8 7 6 5 4 3 2 1

Library of Congress Cataloging-in-Publication Data
Ritchie, Ingrid.
      The healthy home kit / by Ingrid M. Ritchie and Stephen J. Martin.
            p.   cm.
      Includes bibliographical references and index.
      1.   Housing and health.   2.   Sick building syndrome.   3.   House
buying.   4.   Consumer education.   I.   Martin, Stephen John,   1948–
   II.   Title.
RA770.5.R54   1994
613′.5—dc20   94-30835
                                                        CIP

Acknowledgments

The authors gratefully acknowledge the assistance of the following professionals who reviewed selected portions of the manuscript:

Robert Banks, Ph.D.
Robert S. Banks Associates, Inc.
Minneapolis, MN

Lisa Caldwell, RPS
Indoor Air Quality Specialist
Department of Housing and Neighborhood
 Health
Bureau of Environmental Health
Marion County Health Department
Indianapolis, IN

Cheryl Carlson
Enforcement Manager
Air Pollution Control Section
Indianapolis Department of Public Works
Indianapolis, IN

Sabrina Lutz
Indiana Center on Education Policy
Indiana University
Indianapolis, IN

Thomas Pickering
Education Services Coordinator
Metropolitan Indianapolis Board of
 REALTORS®
Indianapolis, IN

Pamela Thevenow, RPS
Administrator,
Department of Housing and Neighborhood
 Health
Bureau of Environmental Health
Marion County Health Department
Indianapolis, IN

Sherri Winters, RPS
Field Supervisor
Department of Housing and Neighborhood
 Health
Marion County Health Department
Indianapolis, IN

Diane Yale
Director of Professional Services
Metropolitan Indianapolis Board of
 REALTORS®
Indianapolis, IN

CONTENTS

List of Figures

Appendix B
How To Use a Respirator and Protective Clothing

Appendix C
Asbestos Removal Procedures

Preface

Imagine buying your dream home—living contentedly with your children, who are playing and attending school in the same neighborhood. One day you become aware that the Environmental Protection Agency (EPA) has placed the industrial facility next to your neighborhood on the "Superfund" list. This means that the land, air or water are contaminated by toxic chemicals. People in the community begin to complain about health problems that might be caused by chemicals leaking from the site. Your property becomes unsalable—even your mortgage company won't foreclose on it. They tell you to forget about repaying the loan because they don't want to become responsible for any of the environmental cleanup of the property. Your life's dream and all your hard work mean nothing. All you can do is sue the developers and all the other parties in the chain of responsibility to regain your financial position and hope that your family's health won't be affected. If you lived in Southbend, Texas, just outside Houston, this happened to your neighborhood. And it continues to happen to others across the country as you read this book.

During the late 1970s, a series of media reports about environmental contamination similar to that in Southbend, Texas, dominated the news and focused our attention on the problem of hazardous chemicals in our environment. We watched helplessly as entire communities such as Love Canal and Times Beach suffered health and economic disaster because of chemicals in their neighborhoods. Now we know that these were not isolated instances.

These large-scale environmental disasters are tragic, but newspaper, radio and television reports also warn of environmental hazards that can affect ordinary homes in communities across the country—homes that are not built on chemical waste dumps or next to industrial complexes. The EPA believes that thousands of people die each year because of environmental conditions found in and around their homes. It is impossible to estimate how many others suffer discomfort and illness related to their homes.

How can you know if your home or a potential property will provide a healthy environment for you and your family? There are, of course, no absolute guarantees, but with a little effort and diligence you can identify many potential environmental hazards related to your property. You can recognize some problems by simply looking at the house and the surrounding area. Environmental testing is needed to identify and confirm other hazards.

The goal of this book is to give you the knowledge to identify and solve potential problems, either by yourself or by hiring qualified consultants, so that you and your family can enjoy a healthy home. Chapter 1 describes some of the environmental concerns in real estate transactions. It gives buyers and sellers an overview of legal issues related to environmental hazards in property transfers, and discusses the professionals and assessments that might be needed to evaluate a property. Chapter 2 explains the different types of nearby hazards that can affect the environmental quality of a home, and gives an introduction to indoor air quality hazards. The chapters in Parts 2, 3 and 4 discuss in detail specific hazards that could affect a home. All of these chapters follow the same format, making them easy to use. A summary chart that identifies the contaminant, sources, testing and ways of reducing exposures introduces each chapter. These topics are discussed in greater detail within the chapter. The chapter concludes with a checklist of questions that will help you identify potentially hazardous situations and sources of contaminants. Finally, at the end of the book are appendixes that contain lists of resources that can provide more information, procedures for using a respirator and protective clothing and procedures for properly removing asbestos and lead from the home.

A list of concerns that once might have included avoiding too much noise or being too close to a major highway has expanded since the 1970s to include many different problems that affect rural, urban and suburban homes; single-family homes and apartments; new and old homes—homes of every type and description.

Living next to dump sites and landfills has never been desirable because of noise, odors and pests. We used to think that living a mile or two away from factories was safe enough and that building housing developments on or near farm fields was an affordable way to achieve the American dream. Years ago, we didn't know that chemicals from these sites could seep through the soil into our drinking water, and even into our houses. We weren't aware that chemical-laden dusts could contaminate the yards in which our children played.

In the past, public officials thought that private well water users had the greatest risk of water contamination problems, and their main concerns were bacteria and nitrates from fertilizers or animal wastes. Public water supplies are assumed to be reliable, safe and free from dangerous chemicals and the threat of disease-causing organisms. The water contamination problems in 1993 that interrupted Milwaukee's water service and made 1,800 people ill, however, once again alerted the public to new contamination problems and weaknesses in the public water supply system.

During the 1970s, scientists discovered that toxic chemicals could also be released into our homes by materials used during construction. Formaldehyde, lead and asbestos have been identified as indoor air contaminants that can lead to a variety of health problems—including an increased risk of developing cancer. Other, more recent, concerns include radon, pesticides, tobacco smoke, molds and chemicals in building materials.

In the face of these concerns, it is clear that we need to know about environmental hazards in and around our homes. Whether we rent or own, we deserve a healthy home for ourselves and our families—one that does not cause discomfort or health problems for the occupants. The information in this book will lead you toward that healthy home.

PART

ONE

Environmental Hazards and Your Home

CHAPTER ONE

Understanding Environmental Concerns in Real Estate Transactions

Perhaps no contemporary issue elicits stronger emotions from property owners than finding unexpected environmental hazards that diminish the enjoyment and use of the property, affect their family's health or cause financial hardship. Every consumer should be aware of these hazards and the potential financial and legal difficulties that can arise from owning a property that has such a hazard. In many instances these hazards do not cause financial ruin or irreversible health effects. Even so, the costs of correcting the problems caused by someone else can be significant, even devastating. Consumers can protect themselves by becoming knowledgeable about their rights and responsibilities before problems arise.

Financial and Legal Issues

Why Are Lenders Concerned?

When a bank or mortgage company loans money for any purpose, it must consider the risks of making the loan. One of these risks is the borrower's ability to repay the loan. But the lender also needs to consider hidden risks related to the property. When you acquire a property through a mortgage, the lender gains a security interest in the property that permits foreclosure if you fail to make the monthly payments. This means that the lender could become an owner of the property and financially responsible for fixing any problems before the property can be sold again.

How Do Environmental Hazards Affect Property Values?

Real and perceived environmental problems can affect the dollar value of real property (land and buildings). The ability to market a property can change drastically when environmental problems are found. In such cases, the appraiser's estimate of the "cost to cure" the problem becomes an important element in determining the marketability of the property. The cost to cure an environmental problem will reduce the appraised market value of the real estate by the amount needed to correct the problem. In extreme cases, the cost of cleanup and correction of the environmental problem can exceed the market value of the property. This is important because the market value determines the amount of money the lender is willing to loan to a prospective buyer.

Sometimes, even after an environmental problem is fixed, the property value still suffers from what appraisers call stigmatization. This term refers to a continuing decline in the value of a property due to an incorrectly perceived environmental problem. Stigmatization can significantly reduce the market value of a property even after a problem has been remedied. If you are considering purchasing a property that might be a "steal," you should evaluate it carefully for existing and past environmental problems that might account for the low price.

Perhaps you are willing to overlook an environmental problem that exists in a property you want to purchase. For example, a farm might have a small dump site that you think can be cleaned out sometime in the future. You are comfortable with the eyesore because it is away from the house and in a part of the property that you will not be using. However, the appraiser who determines the market value of the property for the lender cannot overlook the problem. According to federal banking regulations, the appraiser must consider environmental conditions that are "apparent," or that he or she becomes aware of during the normal research involved in performing the appraisal. The appraiser determines any needed adjustments to the market value based on the cost to correct the problem and other market factors.

In the farm example, the appraiser will consider the potential cost of cleaning a dump area that might also be chemically contaminated and adjust the value of the property accordingly. If the appraised value is below the purchase price, the financial institution may decide that the risk is too large and turn down the loan application or reduce the amount of the loan. Whenever this happens, the buyer should seriously reconsider purchasing the property.

How Does a Lender Know If a Property Has a Problem?

The lender may require certain environmental test results to help make its decision about the loan. Two commonly requested tests are a water quality test for a home with a well and a soil evaluation for a building lot to determine if a septic system is suitable for a property. Other commonly requested procedures include tests for asbestos and lead in older homes.

If the property is being financed through a government-backed program such as the Federal Housing Administration (FHA) or the Department of Veterans Affairs (VA), the lender is required to have an inspection conducted to ensure that the property meets specific minimum property standards. Although this is not an environmental inspection, it can raise certain "red flags" that suggest potential environmental problems.

Who Should Pay for Fixing a Property with an Environmental Hazard—the Buyer or the Seller?

It has been mentioned that environmental hazards affect the desirability and marketability of a property. The costs of correcting minor problems are usually minimal, but the costs of cleaning up serious environmental hazards can exceed the market value the property had before it was contaminated.

In general, it is in the interest of the seller to fix environmental hazards before the property is listed. Buyers may become reluctant to purchase a property if they are told that it contains an environmental hazard. However, the seller might decide to discount the price of a severely contaminated property if the cost of fixing the problem is too great. Even if the price is reduced, buyers may still be unwilling to make an offer to purchase the property.

When a property has an environmental hazard, the buyer has several possible reactions. The buyer can

- walk away from the deal,
- live with the problem,

- assume the cost of fixing the problem,
- accept a discount on the value of the property,
- require the seller to fix the problem, or
- fix the problem after the purchase at the seller's expense as agreed to in the purchase agreement.

The best course of action depends on the hazard and the degree of financial risk the property represents. If the property is heavily contaminated, the buyer should probably walk away from the deal. If the problem is minor, it might make sense to determine a discount and fix the problem later.

An environmental contingency clause helps to reduce the financial risks of the purchase, so the buyer should always include it in the written purchase agreement. This clause can allow the buyer to go back to the seller for help in correcting an environmental hazard, or to back out of an offer to purchase if environmental problems are found during the inspection. The clause can take several forms, depending on whether a problem has been identified. If the property is presumed to be free of hazards, the buyer should require the seller to verify that the property does not have environmental hazards. Figure 1.1 shows an example of a seller's certification that offers only a general statement that the seller has no knowledge of environmental hazards related to the property. The buyer can strengthen the value of the certification by asking the seller to comment on the presence of specific hazards such as asbestos, lead or radon.

Do You Have To Disclose an Environmental Hazard?

If, as a seller, you are asked about the presence of environmental hazards and you have knowledge about them, then the answer is yes. In fact, most states have property disclosure laws that require the seller to tell what they know about the condition of their property—even if the buyer never asks a question.

How To Protect Yourself from an Environmental Legal Problem

Environmental legal issues range from fairly simple to highly technical and complex problems. Some state and local jurisdictions require an evaluation of specific hazards (such as bacteria in well water) under environmental or health regulations before the official transfer of title can take place. Some lending institutions require a disclosure by the seller about the condition of the property, including information about environmental hazards. These are fairly simple issues to resolve. More complicated problems can involve a complex legal document that not only identifies hazards but also assigns legal and financial responsibility to various parties.

FIGURE 1.1.   Sample Seller's Certification of Environmental Hazards

---

SELLER'S CERTIFICATION - ENVIRONMENTAL HAZARDOUS SUBSTANCES

Property Identification:

Address _____

City _____ State _____ Zip _____

Brief Description: _____

_____

_____

_____

Seller Identification:

Name of Owner(s) _____

Address _____

City _____ State _____ Zip _____

Telephone _____

Property Owned From _____ To _____

Seller's Certification:

I do hereby certify that to the best of my knowledge during and before my ownership of the above described property:

a) The property was not used as a dump site or storage facility for hazardous substances.

b) No one has received notification from a federal, state or local government in regard to pending or threatened Superfund or Superlien liability.

c) To the best of my knowledge no environmental hazards have been identified on the subject property.

Exception to above: _____

_____

_____

_____

_____

I (we) do hereby certify that the above information is true to the best of my (our) knowledge and belief.

Date _____ Seller_____

Date _____ Seller_____

FW-70EH   Forms and Worms Inc., 315 Whitney Ave., New Haven, CT 06511   1 (800) 243-4545   Item #115200
National Association of Environmental Risk Auditors

Used with permission of National Association of Environmental Risk Auditors, Bloomington, Indiana.

Each of these requirements is designed to protect the buyer from unexpected problems, but there are no state or federal regulations that require a complete and full property inspection or disclosure for *residential* properties. In the absence of regulatory requirements, *environmental due diligence* is the best protection for a potential buyer.

Environmental due diligence means that the buyer has made all "appropriate and customary" investigations into the past uses and ownership of the property in an effort to determine if the property has an environmental hazard. Environmental due diligence can protect the buyer against potential liability for the cleanup of an environmental problem, providing the investigations take place prior to the purchase of the property.

A buyer can use the *innocent landowner defense* if a purchased property is discovered to have an environmental hazard that should be corrected. The innocent landowner defense demonstrates that the buyer asked the right questions *before* making the purchase. The buyer might be able to shift the cost of any cleanup to previous "potentially responsible parties" (PRPs). PRPs include former property owners, lenders who have previously foreclosed on the property, current tenants and a long list of other potential parties. Using the innocent landowner defense does not mean that a buyer will be able to recover money that has already been invested or paid, but it does protect the buyer from further losses. Identifying responsible parties and recovering costs in cases with severe environmental hazards can be a complicated process.

At this point you may be wondering whether this has anything to do with buying a home. The answer is a resounding "yes!" Although most homeowners are not likely to face a situation of severe environmental hazards, environmental due diligence will help ensure that a prospective buyer knows about potential environmental hazards in the home and makes an informed decision. Further, it should allow the buyer to recover costs associated with fixing undisclosed environmental hazards.

The saying "buyer beware" applies to all real estate transactions. As a buyer, you can protect yourself from legal and financial liability for environmental hazards in two ways: (1) always obtain the advice of competent legal counsel to ensure that the written purchase agreement provides adequate protection against liability if environmental hazards created by previous owners or adjoining owners are discovered, and (2) carefully evaluate a potential property for the presence of environmental hazards.

Professionals and Assessments

Who Are the Professionals?

After making a preliminary examination of the property on your own, you may feel that you need assistance from a professional trained in environmental site assessment. Depending on the problem, you can get help from one or more professionals, including a home inspector, an appraiser, a specialized environmental consultant or an environmental site assessor. Although attorneys and real estate agents are not directly involved in environmental assessments, they also play important roles during the purchase process. The skills and responsibilities of each of these professionals is reviewed below.

The quality of the services provided by each professional depends on his or her knowledge, training and personal ethics. Don't hire a professional without checking references and always ask to see proof of any certifications or licenses the professional claims to have. Verify these credentials by calling the professional organization or government agency that grants the certification or license. Take the time to contact the Better Business Bureau, Chamber of Commerce or Attorney General's office to ask if complaints have been filed against the professional or his or her company.

Attorney. Having competent legal counsel is always a good idea when buying or selling property, but it is especially important if you suspect that a property has an environmental hazard. If you are the seller, an attorney can explain the extent of your potential liability, the information you must disclose and how to disclose such information. The attorney will draft the legal documents that disclose what warranties or representations you are making about the property.

If you are the buyer, an attorney can explain what is considered to be an *adequate appropriate inquiry* into the history and ownership of the property. The attorney will also draft and review legal documents. All these steps will ensure that you meet the requirements of the "innocent landowner defense" paper trail *before you purchase.* Attorneys who specialize in real estate law can be found in the yellow pages of the telephone directory under "Attorneys Grouped by Areas of Practice—Real Estate Law."

Real Estate Agent. Most real estate agents do not have formal training in recognizing and assessing environmental hazards. Agents are advised by their legal counsel to avoid making any representation about the environmental condition of a property. If they do, their comments could partially shift the burden of liability to the agent in the event a problem arises. However, recent case law indicates that the public has a right to expect real estate professionals to exercise due care in obtaining and releasing information regarding the environmental status of a property.

Whenever you work with an agent, it is important to understand whose interests the agent represents. Typically, the agent represents the seller (also called the client) and is called the seller's agent or the listing agent. The agent who represents only the buyer (also called the customer) is called the buyer's agent. With the written permission of both parties, some agents may represent both the buyer and the seller. Most states require agents to disclose whom they represent (this might be done in the form of a brochure or handout at the initial meeting). Agents may have credentials such as the Certified Residential Specialist (CRS) or Graduate, REALTORS® Institute (GRI) certifications offered by the National Real Estate Institute, or other certifications offered by individual states. However, these certifications do not include the ability to recognize environmental hazards. Real estate agents can be found in the yellow pages of the telephone directory under "Real Estate." Agencies that represent the buyer are listed under "Real Estate Buyers' Brokers."

Buyer's and seller's agents should have general information about the history of the neighborhood and potential environmental hazards in the area. An agent might be able to answer the following types of questions:

- Does the area have houses with elevated radon levels?
- Is the area served by an older water system that could be a source of lead?
- Does the area have homes that previously used heating oil stored in underground tanks?
- Is the neighborhood built on a fill area that was formerly a dump site?
- Has the area been flooded?

In addition, the seller's agent may have obtained pertinent information about the environmental condition of the property from the seller at the time of listing. This information must be contained in a seller disclosure form if one is required in the state in which the property is located. The form usually lists information about any negative structural and mechanical features of the house, plus potential environmental hazards such as urea formaldehyde foam insulation, radon, asbestos or lead in paint and water. The disclosure form should be examined carefully to make sure that knowledge of *specific* environmental hazards is included.

The listing agent might also know if the seller has done environmental testing prior to listing the property, but you may need to ask specific questions about those potential hazards that concern you. The aggressive, well-organized agent will have prepared a complete documentation package, approved by the seller, that discloses all such pertinent facts about the property.

When asking questions, remember that the listing agent's client is the seller, not the buyer. Do not automatically assume that an agent will disclose information about environmental hazards or other conditions. The agent is not always required to make disclosures to the prospective buyer unless questioned about them directly, or unless specifically given permission to do so by the seller.

The listing agent does, however, have a responsibility to disclose noted potential environmental hazards to the seller. The agent should recommend that the seller obtain competent legal advice or retain appropriate consultants for technical advice on the situation if a problem is recognized during the listing process.

If necessary, any agent involved in the transaction should be able to refer the buyer or seller to environmental specialists who are qualified to assess the property, or to suggest reputable contractors who might be able to remedy problems that have been found.

Home Inspector. The purchase of a home generally requires an inspection of the property for structural or mechanical defects. This is usually required by the buyer or the lender and is a contingency in the purchase agreement, or in some cases, the mortgage loan commitment. Typically, the home inspector is retained to evaluate the mechanical systems of the home and the general condition of the property. However, this evaluation does not always include looking for environmental "red flags."

Today, many home inspectors are taking additional training courses to enable them to identify and test for potential environmental hazards such as radon, asbestos, lead in paint or water, moisture and mold problems and underground storage tanks for heating oil. A properly trained inspector can also recognize signs of problems outside the home, such as drainage problems, distressed or dying vegetation, chemical contamination and improper septic system operation.

The home inspector's qualifications are limited by his or her training and licenses or certifications held. Buyers and sellers should be aware that there is considerable variability in the quality of home inspectors. For example, the American Society of Home Inspectors (ASHI) is one professional organization that offers a certification for home inspectors. Before receiving this certification, the inspector must pass a written test of his or her knowledge and satisfactorily perform 250 home inspections according to ASHI guidelines. The emphasis of the ASHI certification is on recognizing problems with the mechanical systems, structure and condition of the home. According to the standards of practice for this credential, the inspector is not required to report on pests, underground items, noise, toxic substances or contaminants in the soil, water and air. The ASHI guidelines also exclude determining the effectiveness of any system installed to control or remove hazardous substances.

However, the home inspector might have additional training for the recognition of and testing for environmental hazards. The National Association of Environmental Risk Auditors (NAERA) is a professional organization that offers the Certified Environmental Risk Screener (CERS) or the more advanced

Certified Environmental Risk Auditor (CERA) designation. Home inspectors or others who receive these designations must take courses specifically on environmental hazards, pass a written test of knowledge and submit a demonstration report of their work. Even these designations, however, may not be enough. For example, the federal government and individual states may have specific requirements for the certification of individuals who want to test for radon, lead, asbestos or other contaminants.

Before hiring a home inspector, the buyer should ask for proof of the inspector's knowledge and ability to check for environmental hazards. (You can contact ASHI and NAERA to verify that an individual has those designations—addresses are in Appendix A.) Additional certifications or licenses, if there are any, may be issued by the state or local health or environmental agency. If the state does not require licensing or certification for a specific hazard, the inspector may have been trained through an EPA-approved education program or an association for environmental professionals. Make sure that you understand what the inspector is qualified to do, and ask for and check references.

If you hire a home inspector, you can request a full inspection that includes evaluations of the mechanical, structural and environmental components of the home, or a partial inspection that includes only some of the components. You may need to contact more than one company to obtain a full report. You should consider being present during the inspection, which could take two to four hours to complete. The inspector will write a report with recommendations for further testing or corrective actions if a problem exists. This report is delivered to the person who pays for it (usually the buyer). The average cost of the inspection is $100 to $400 for an evaluation of the mechanical and structural components and another $100 to $250 for an examination of the environmental component of a single family home. Radon testing might be included in the base price for the environmental inspection, but other environmental tests will cost extra. Home inspectors are found in the yellow pages of the telephone directory under "Home Inspection Services."

Although the costs of home and environmental inspection services may seem high, a properly conducted home inspection creates the first line of defense for the buyer. It can result in substantial savings by identifying potential environmental hazards *within* the property before the closing.

Appraiser. Another person who is involved in the real estate transaction and who may be qualified to inspect the property for potential environmental hazards is the appraiser. As part of the federal appraisal standards process, the appraiser is required to comment on negative features of the property that can cause a loss in value. One of the problems that leads to a loss in value is the potential or actual presence of an environmental hazard. Figure 1.2 shows an

FIGURE 1.2.   Sample Appraiser's Calculation

Value of home determined through the steps of the appraisal process:	$100,000
Adjustments made for environmental hazards:	
Radon reduction $3,500	
Lead paint encapsulation 5,500	
Total adjustment	$ 9,000
Adjusted market value of the property	$ 91,000

example of how an appraiser might take environmental hazards into consideration when preparing an appraisal.

The appraiser needs to visually inspect the property to arrive at the valuation and to identify any potential negative features. Once again, this puts the properly trained appraiser in a position to look for some environmental hazards both inside and outside the home. The appraiser's work is similar to that of the home inspector, but the appraiser is required to go a step further. Calculating the value of a property also requires an examination of the external factors surrounding the property that influence the determination of value. Some of the appraiser's work is done through a check of certain property records; in other cases, the appraiser relies on the services of other professionals. Determining the cost of correcting environmental problems requires knowledge and experience that are beyond the training of most appraisers. These estimates are typically provided by environmental consultants, and the appraiser uses this information to determine the marketability and value of the property.

The scope of the hazards the appraiser can evaluate also depends on specialized training in the environmental area. Ask if the appraiser has special certifications, licenses or training in the recognition of environmental hazards, and ask to see proof of this expertise. One example is the Certified Environmental Risk Auditor (CERA) designation granted through the National Association of Environmental Risk Auditors.

A typical home appraisal costs about $200 to $350, and an extra charge of about $200 to $300 could be added to the base fee for a formal environmental assessment. In addition to the standardized residential appraisal report form, the appraiser may use an environmental addendum to cover potential environmental hazards (see Figure 1.3). Because the appraiser has to consider the potential impact of environmental hazards on the value of the property, the appraisal report will provide some indication of potential future liability. The soundness of the environmental addendum really depends on the

FIGURE 1.3. Sample Environmental Addendum

ENVIRONMENTAL ADDENDUM

APPARENT* HAZARDOUS SUBSTANCES AND/OR DETRIMENTAL ENVIRONMENTAL CONDITIONS

Borrower/Client _____

Address _____

City _____ County _____ State _____ Zip code _____

Lender _____

*Apparent is defined as that which is visible, obvious, evident or manifest to the appraiser.

This universal Environmental Addendum is for use with any real estate appraisal. Only the statements which have been checked by the appraiser apply to the property being appraised.

This addendum reports the results of the appraiser's routine inspection of and inquiries about the subject property and its surrounding area. It also states what assumptions were made about the existence (or nonexistence) of any hazardous substances and/or detrimental environmental conditions. **The appraiser is not an expert environmental inspector** and therefore might be unaware of existing hazardous substances and/or detrimental environmental conditions which may have a negative effect on the safety and value of the property. It is possible that tests and inspections made by a qualified environmental inspector would reveal the existence of hazardous materials and/or detrimental environmental conditions on or around the property that would negatively affect its safety and value.

DRINKING WATER

____ Drinking Water is supplied to the subject from a municipal water supply which is considered safe. However the only way to be absolutely certain that the water meets published standards is to have it tested at all discharge points.

____ Drinking Water is supplied by a well or other non-municipal source. It is recommended that tests be made to be certain that the property is supplied with adequate pure water.

____ Lead can get into drinking water from its source, the pipes, at all discharge points, plumbing fixtures and/or appliances. The only way to be certain that water does not contain an unacceptable lead level is to have it tested at all discharge points.

____ **The value estimated in this appraisal is based on the assumption that there is an adequate supply of safe, lead-free Drinking Water.**

Comments _____

SANITARY WASTE DISPOSAL

____ Sanitary Waste is removed from the property by a municipal sewer system.

____ Sanitary Waste is disposed of by a septic system or other sanitary on site waste disposal system. The only way to determine that the disposal system is adequate and in good working condition is to have it inspected by a qualified inspector.

____ **The value estimated in this appraisal is based on the assumption that the Sanitary Waste is disposed of by a municipal sewer or an adequate properly permitted alternate treatment system in good condition.**

Comments _____

SOIL CONTAMINANTS

____ There are no *apparent* signs of Soil Contaminants on or near the subject property (except as reported in Comments below). It is possible that research, inspection and testing by a qualified environmental inspector would reveal existing and/or potential hazardous substances and/or detrimental environmental conditions on or around the property that would negatively affect its safety and value.

____ **The value estimated in this appraisal is based on the assumption that the subject property is free of Soil Contaminants.**

Comments _____

ASBESTOS

____ All or part of the improvements were constructed before 1979 when Asbestos was a common building material. The only way to be certain that the property is free of friable and non-friable Asbestos is to have it inspected and tested by a qualified asbestos inspector.

____ The improvements were constructed after 1979. No *apparent* friable Asbestos was observed (except as reported in Comments below).

____ **The value estimated in this appraisal is based on the assumption that there is no uncontained friable Asbestos or other hazardous Asbestos material on the property.**

Comments _____

PCBs (POLYCHLORINATED BIPHENYLS)

____ There were no *apparent* leaking flourescent light ballasts, capacitors or transformers anywhere on or nearby the property (except as reported in Comments below).

____ There was no *apparent* visible or documented evidence known to the appraiser of soil or groundwater contamination from PCBs anywhere on the property (except as reported in Comments below).

____ **The value estimated in this appraisal is based on the assumption that there are no uncontained PCBs on or nearby the property.**

Comments _____

RADON

____ The appraiser is not aware of any Radon tests made on the subject property within the past 12 months (except as reported in Comments below).

____ The appraiser is not aware of any indication that the local water supplies have been found to have elevated levels of Radon or Radium.

____ The appraiser is not aware of any nearby properties (except as reported in Comments below) that were or currently are used for uranium, thorium or radium extraction or phosphate processing.

____ **The value estimated in this appraisal is based on the assumption that the Radon level is at or below EPA recommended levels.**

Comments _____

Test Version 2c FW-70EZ   © Forms & Worms, Inc. 315 Whitney Avenue New Haven, CT 06511 1-800-243-4545   Item #115050
JANUARY 1991   National Association Environmental Risk Auditors

Used with permission of National Association of Environmental Risk Auditors, Bloomington, Indiana.

FIGURE 1.3.   (*continued*)

USTs (UNDERGROUND STORAGE TANKS)

_____ There is no *apparent* visible or documented evidence known to the appraiser of any USTs on the property nor any known historical use of the property that would likely have had USTs.

_____ There are no *apparent* petroleum storage and/or delivery facilities (including gasoline stations or chemical manufacturing plants) located on adjacent Comments below).

_____ There are *apparent* signs of USTs existing now or in the past on the subject property. It is recommended that an inspection by a qualified UST inspector be obtained to determine the location of any USTs together with their condition and proper registration if they are active; and if they are inactive, to determine whether they were deactivated in accordance with sound industry practices.

_____ **The value estimated in this appraisal is based on the assumption that any functioning USTs are not leaking and are properly registered and that any abandoned USTs are free from contamination and were properly drained, filled and sealed.**

Comments _____

NEARBY HAZARDOUS WASTE SITES

_____ There are no *apparent* Hazardous Waste Sites on the subject property or nearby the subject property (except as reported in Comments below). Hazardous Waste Site search by a trained environmental engineer may determine that there is one or more Hazardous Waste Sites on or in the area of the subject property.

_____ **The value estimated in this appraisal is based on the assumption that there are no Hazardous Waste Sites on or nearby the subject property that negatively affect the value or safety of the property.**

Comments _____

UREA FORMALDEHYDE (UFFI) INSULATION

_____ All or part of the improvements were constructed before 1982 when UREA foam insulation was a common building material. The only way to be certain that the property is free of UREA formaldehyde is to have it inspected by a qualified UREA formaldehyde inspector.

_____ The improvements were constructed after 1982. No *apparent* UREA formaldehyde materials were observed (except as reported in Comments below).

_____ **The value estimated in this appraisal is based on the assumption that there is no significant UFFI insulation or other UREA formaldehyde material on the property.**

Comments _____

LEAD PAINT

_____ All or part of the improvements were constructed before 1980 when Lead Paint was a common building material. There is no *apparent* visible or known documented evidence of peeling or flaking Lead Paint on the floors, walls or ceilings (except as reported in Comments below). The only way to be certain that the property is free of surface or subsurface Lead Paint is to have it inspected by a qualified inspector.

_____ The improvements were constructed after 1980. No *apparent* Lead Paint was observed (except as reported in Comments below).

_____ **The value estimated in this appraisal is based on the assumption that there is no flaking or peeling Lead Paint on the property.**

Comments _____

AIR POLLUTION

_____ There are no *apparent* signs of Air Pollution at the time of the inspection nor were any reported (except as reported in Comments below). The only way to be certain that the air is free of pollution is to have it tested.

_____ **The value estimated in this appraisal is based on the assumption that the property is free of Air Pollution.**

Comments _____

WETLANDS/FLOOD PLAINS

_____ The site does not contain any *apparent* Wetlands/Flood Plains (except as reported in Comments below). The only way to be certain that the site is free of Wetlands/Flood Plains is to have it inspected by a qualified environmental professional.

_____ **The value estimated in this appraisal is based on the assumption that there are no Wetlands/Flood Plains on the property (except as reported in Comments below).**

Comments _____

MISCELLANEOUS ENVIRONMENTAL HAZARDS

_____ There are no other *apparent* miscellaneous hazardous substances and/or detrimental environmental conditions on or in the area of the site except as indicated below:

_____ Excess Noise _____

_____ Radiation + Electromagnetic Radiation _____

_____ Light Pollution _____

_____ Waste Heat _____

_____ Acid Mine Drainage _____

_____ Agricultural Pollution _____

_____ Geological Hazards _____

_____ Nearby Hazardous Property _____

_____ Infectious Medical Wastes _____

_____ Pesticides _____

_____ Others (Chemical Storage + Storage Drums, Pipelines, etc.) _____

_____ **The value estimated in this appraisal is based on the assumption that there are no Miscellaneous environmental Hazards (except those reported above) that would negatively affect the value of the property.**

> ***When any of the environmental assumptions made in this addendum
> are not correct, the estimated value in this appraisal may not be valid.***

Test Version 2c FW-70EZ   © Forms & Worms, Inc. 315 Whitney Avenue New Haven, CT 06511 1-800-243-4545   Item #115050
JANUARY 1991   National Association Environmental Risk Auditors

skill and knowledge of the appraiser. The form in Figure 1.3 underscores the fact that the appraiser is not an expert environmental inspector.

You have a legal right to see the appraisal if you pay for it with "up front" money at the time of the mortgage application and if you request a copy of it in writing. But in practice, getting access to the appraisal may be difficult. In most cases, the appraisal report will be sent directly to the lender. Many times the report, which must be kept in the mortgage loan documents file, may be located in another city where the lender's offices are situated. If the lender feels that a reported environmental hazard is severe enough to warrant attention, the loan may be denied. Should this occur, the lender will discuss with you the reasons for denial and may provide you with a copy of the report to substantiate the decision.

If you are aware that a property has potential problems, you might decide to hire your own appraiser before negotiating on the property. Check with your prospective lender if this appraisal can be used if you decide to purchase the property. If you are going to order an appraisal prior to purchasing a property, you will find appraisers in the yellow pages of the telephone directory under "Real Estate Appraisers." If you are dealing with a lender, they may assign an approved appraiser to your property.

Obviously, the real estate appraiser can play a very important role in the purchase of a property with environmental problems. Currently, there are no federal requirements for a complete environmental inspection in the appraisal of residential properties, but this could change in the future.

Professional Environmental Consultant. There are a variety of environmental consultants with different levels of expertise who may be needed to evaluate or correct environmental hazards. Professional consultants have degrees in specific areas such as hydrology, geology, biology, environmental health, chemistry, industrial hygiene or engineering. In addition, they may have specific training and experience that qualify them for certifications or licenses from governmental agencies or professional designations from recognized professional groups.

Examples of certifications and designations include registered professional sanitarian (RPS), registered environmental health specialist (REHS), professional engineer (PE), certified industrial hygienist (CIH) and certified hazardous materials manager (CHMM). These professionals might also have the Certified Environmental Risk Screener (CERS) or the Certified Environmental Risk Auditor (CERA) designations mentioned above.

Some professionals, such as engineers, sanitarians, environmental health specialists and geologists, must be licensed by federal, state or local jurisdictions in order to work in their fields. Federal and state laws may require additional certifications or registrations in order to perform some types of specialized services, such as lead paint testing and abatement, asbestos testing and removal, pesticide (including termiticide) treatment and abatement, radon testing and removal, soil testing and septic tank removal. (These special requirements are discussed further in the chapters on specific hazards.) Always ask for proof of any certifications, licenses or registrations claimed by the prospective consultant.

Professional environmental consulting firms vary in number of employees, areas of expertise and talents of the individual members. There has been significant growth in this area and the number of consultants offering inspection, testing, laboratory and corrective action services has exploded in recent years. Before hiring a consultant to perform services, verify the qualifications of the *individuals* who will perform the work. Ask for and check references. Make sure that the consultant completes work in a timely manner. This is especially important if the closing depends upon the submission of a report or corrective action (in this case, a penalty clause for failure to deliver on time is another prudent measure). Obtain an estimate of costs and scope of the work, a description of work methods, completion dates for the work and guarantees *in writing*. If extensive testing or corrective actions are needed, a "not to exceed clause" may be needed in the contract to set a ceiling on the potential charges. Professional environmental consultants are found in the yellow pages of the telephone directory under "Environmental & Ecological Services," "Engineers Guide—Environmental," or "Laboratories—Testing."

What Types of Assessments Might Be Needed?

When you hire an environmental consultant to evaluate a home or other property for environmental hazards, you will receive one of several types of reports, depending on the complexity of the property and its potential problems. The simplest report will evaluate one or two specific contaminants at your request. For example, you might ask a consultant to evaluate the radon level or check for molds. In some instances, it may be appropriate to request a site assessment, which is a complete and detailed evaluation of the property.

Preliminary Site Assessment. The least complex and least expensive analysis of a property is a screening evaluation called a *Preliminary Site Assessment* (*PSA*), or *environmental screen*. This type of analysis and report provides a detailed overview of potential environmental hazards based upon a visual analysis of the property and a search of the public records concerning the property. The purpose of this report is to alert the buyer to any potential hazards and to determine whether further investigation into the hazards is needed. Figure 1.4 is an example of an environmental screening form. This is

FIGURE 1.4. Sample Environmental Risk Screening Report

UNIFORM ENVIRONMENTAL RISK SCREENING REPORT

File No.

Client			
Client Address			
Property Address			
City	County	State	Zip
Lender			
Firm Name			
Address			

The undersigned Underwriter/Appraiser/Inspector, acting as Environmental Risk Screener for the client, has made an inspection of the property and the area surrounding the property for the purpose of screening for apparent hazardous substances and detrimental environmental conditions. This report enumerates what inspections and/or test(s) were made and what apparent hazardous substances and detrimental environmental conditions were discovered. This report also contains recommendations for additional inspections and tests.

(The reported results of the inspection and these recommendations are not intended to preclude the client from obtaining a complete hazardous substance and detrimental environmental conditions audit together with the appropriate tests made by a professional hazardous substance and detrimental environmental conditions inspector and/or engineer.)

The following checked items indicate sources used by the undersigned Environmental Risk Screener to perform a screening of the property to discover the existence of apparent hazardous substances and detrimental environmental conditions:

_____ Building Specifications
_____ Historical Aerial Photos
_____ Current Aerial Photos
_____ Title History
_____ Site Survey
_____ Interviews with Local Fire, Health, Land Use or Environmental Enforcement Officials

_____ Neighborhood Zoning Maps
_____ Neighborhood Land Use Maps
_____ List of Commercial Tenants On-site
_____ Verification of Public Water and Sewer
_____ Interviews with Builder, and/or Property Manager
_____ Other _____

ASBESTOS

The following checked items indicate additional specific investigations made by the Environmental Risk Screener.

_____ Dated Building Construction or Rehabilitation Specifications
_____ Engineer's or Consultant's Asbestos Report   _____ Other _____

Below is a summary of my History and Record Check, Field Observation, Available Test Results and my Comments & Recommendations.

Summary of my Field Observations: _____

Known Tests and Results: _____

Comments & Recommendations: _____

PCBs (Polychlorinated Biphenyls)

The following checked items indicate additional specific investigations made by the Environmental Risk Screener.

_____ Utility Transformer Records   _____ Site Survey Transformers
_____ Site Soil and Groundwater PCB Test Results   _____ Other _____

Below is a summary of my History and Record Check, Field Observation, Available Test Results and my Comments & Recommendations.

Summary of my Field Observations: _____

Known Tests and Results: _____

Comments & Recommendations: _____

Page 1

FW 70ES   Test Version   1989 Forms and Worms, Inc., 315 Whitney Ave., New Haven, CT 06511 1(800)243-4545   Item #115100
                4A-3/90   National Association of Environmental Risk Auditors

Used with permission of National Association of Environmental Risk Auditors, Bloomington, Indiana.

FIGURE 1.4. *(continued)*

UREA (Formaldehyde)

The following checked items indicate additional specific investigations made by the Environmental Risk Screener.

_____ Urea-Formaldehyde Foam Insulation Survey _____ Other _____

Below is a summary of my History and Record Check, Field Observation, Available Test Results and my Comments & Recommendations.

Summary of my Field Observations: _____

Known Tests and Results: _____

Comments & Recommendations: _____

LEAD PAINT

The following checked items indicate additional specific investigations made by the Environmental Risk Screener.

_____ Lead Paint Survey _____ Other _____

Below is a summary of my History and Record Check, Field Observation, Available Test Results and my Comments & Recommendations.

Summary of my Field Observations: _____

Known Tests and Results: _____

Comments & Recommendations: _____

DRINKING WATER

The following checked items indicate additional specific investigations made by the Environmental Risk Screener.

_____ Lead in Drinking Water Test _____ Other _____

Below is a summary of my History and Record Check, Field Observation, Available Test Results and my Comments & Recommendations.

Summary of my Field Observations: _____

Known Tests and Results: _____

Comments & Recommendations: _____

AIR POLLUTANTS

The following checked items indicate additional specific investigations made by the Environmental Risk Screener.

_____ Interior Air Test Results _____ Other _____

Below is a summary of my History and Record Check, Field Observation, Available Test Results and my Comments & Recommendations.

Summary of my Field Observations: _____

Known Tests and Results: _____

Comments & Recommendations: _____

FW 70ES   Test Version 4A-3/90   1989 Forms and Worms, Inc., 315 Whitney Ave., New Haven, CT 06511 1(800)243-4545   National Association of Environmental Risk Auditors   Item #115100

FIGURE 1.4.   *(continued)*

The following checked items indicate additional specific investigations made by the Environmental Risk Screener.

_____ Water Utility Records   _____ Gas Utility Records
_____ On-site Radon Test Results   _____ Other_____

Below is a summary of my History and Record Check, Field Observation, Available Test Results and my Comments & Recommendations.

Summary of my Field Observations: _____

Known Tests and Results: _____

Comments & Recommendations: _____

RADON

The following checked items indicate additional specific investigations made by the Environmental Risk Screener.

_____ Oil, Motor Fuel and Waste Oil Systems Reports   _____ Site Tank Survey
_____ Site Soil and Groundwater Test Results   _____ Other_____

Below is a summary of my History and Record Check, Field Observation, Available Test Results and my Comments & Recommendations.

Summary of my Field Observations: _____

Known Tests and Results: _____

Comments & Recommendations: _____

UST's (Undergound Storage Tanks)

The following checked items indicate additional specific investigations made by the Environmental Risk Screener.

_____ Site Soil and Groundwater Test Results   _____ Other _____

Below is a summary of my History and Record Check, Field Observation, Available Test Results and my Comments & Recommendations.

Summary of my Field Observations: _____

Known Tests and Results: _____

Comments & Recommendations: _____

WASTE DISPOSAL

The following checked items indicate additional specific investigations made by the Environmental Risk Screener.

_____ NPL sites which might effect the subject property   _____ State EPA site lists for neighborhoods (within
_____ CERCLIS/HWDMS sites within_____ miles of the   _____ mile radius)
        subject property   _____ Other_____
_____ Site soil and/or groundwater test results: _____

Below is a summary of my History and Record Check, Field Observation, Available Test Results and my Comments & Recommendations.

Summary of my Field Observations: _____

Known Tests and Results: _____

Comments & Recommendations: _____

WASTE SITES

FW 70ES   Test Version 4A-3/90   1989 Forms and Worms, Inc., 315 Whitney Ave., New Haven, CT 06511 1(800)243-4545   Item #115100
National Association of Environmental Risk Auditors

FIGURE 1.4. *(continued)*

ADDITIONAL ENVIRONMENTAL HAZARDS

The following checked items indicate additional sources, tests, investigations and inspections made by the Environmental Risk Screener and not reported in the previous separate sections of this report.

_____ Other _____   _____ Other _____
_____ Other _____   _____ Other _____

Below is a summary of my History and Record Check, Field Observation, Available Test Results and my Comments & Recommendations.

Summary of my Field Observations: _____
_____
_____

Known Tests and Results: _____
_____
_____

Comments & Recommendations: _____
_____
_____
_____

The following is a summary of the investigations, inspections and tests made by and/or considered by the Environmental Risk Screener together with a summary of the Environmental Risk Screener's recommendation: _____

SUMMARY

_____
_____
_____
_____
_____
_____
_____
_____
_____
_____
_____
_____
_____
_____

SPECIAL DISCLOSURE WHEN ENVIRONMENTAL SCREENING IS MADE AS PART OF A REAL ESTATE APPRAISAL

WHEN NO APPARENT HAZARDOUS SUBSTANCES OR DETRIMENTAL CONDITIONS ARE FOUND

_____ 1.   As a result of this inspection, which did not reveal any apparent significant hazardous substances or apparent significant detrimental environmental conditions and based on the undersigned's overall knowledge of the area in which the property is located, the undersigned has elected to make this a "Full Scope" appraisal as defined in the Uniform Standards of Professional Appraisal Practice. The value estimated in this report is based on the assumption that the property is not negatively affected by the existence of hazardous substances or detrimental environmental conditions. Should an inspection or tests made by a professional hazardous substances and detrimental environmental condition inspector and/or engineer reveal the existence of hazardous substances and/or detrimental environmental conditions the value estimates would not be valid.

WHEN ONE OR MORE HAZARDOUS SUBSTANCES OR DETRIMENTAL CONDITIONS ARE FOUND

_____ 2.   Hazardous substance(s) and/or detrimental environmental conditions were found by the undersigned and described in this report. It is assumed that it is possible to remove the hazardous substance(s) and/or eliminate the detrimental environmental conditions. The value estimated in this report is based on the assumption that all hazardous substances and detrimental environmental conditions have been eliminated or rendered harmless.

_____ 3.   The hazardous substance(s) and/or detrimental environmental conditions found by the undersigned and described in this report make it impossible for the appraiser to estimate the value of the property without the collaboration of a professional environmental risk auditor. At the present time, without the needed significant additional information, it is impossible to estimate the value of the property in keeping with the USPAP.

Additional Comments: _____
_____
_____
_____

Environmental Risk Screener   Reviewed by

Signature _____   Signature _____

Name_____ Date _____   Name _____ Date _____

                                                     _____ Did _____ Did not inspect property

FW-70ES   Test Version   1990 Forms and Worms Inc., 315 Whitney Ave., New Haven, CT 06511 1(800)243-4545   Item #115100
            4A 3/90   Approved by National Association of Environmental Risk Auditors

the type of report most commonly used for residential properties. It is the least expensive (about $150 to $250) residential environmental assessment.

The screening consultant will walk through the property to gather visual evidence that might signal potential hazards inside and outside the house. In a residential assessment, the consultant will look for evidence of underground storage tanks, drainage problems, poor groundwater quality, radon, asbestos or lead. The consultant will then look at the adjacent land uses to see if hazardous conditions exist that may affect the property in question.

There is usually no testing for environmental hazards at this point. If the consultant spots signs of a hazard, they will be noted and a comment in the report will suggest further investigation.

The screening consultant might also research the history of the property by interviewing adjacent owners, checking tax and title records and reviewing environmental data related to the property obtained from local agencies, documents such as maps or aerial photographs or other available records. These searches can alert the consultant to potential hazards created by past users or uses of the property. The consultant might ask the seller to complete the seller's certification form discussed above concerning the environmental condition of the property (see Figure 1.1) or an environmental history form (see Figure 1.5).

The consultant then coordinates all of this information into a report. If there are no problems, the investigation is over. If evidence of any hazards is found, the consultant may recommend additional investigations, further testing or corrective actions.

Phase I Environmental Assessment. For a phase I assessment, the consultant will gather the same background information on the property as in the screening assessment. The consultant will search records, examine the interior and exterior of the property and interview the owner and other knowledgeable people such as neighbors. The consultant will also evaluate the surrounding area (usually within one square mile of the property) for nearby hazards.

Figure 1.6 gives an example of a phase I assessment form. This evaluation is more detailed than the screening assessment (see Figure 1.4) because the phase I assessment directly addresses questions required by the Federal National Mortgage Association.

The phase I assessment is likely to include some limited testing for environmental hazards. The most likely tests are for radon, lead and asbestos. The phase I consultant might be qualified to perform some of these tests, or the

FIGURE 1.5.   Sample Environmental History Form

UNIFORM ENVIRONMENTAL HISTORY
Questionnaire and/or Certificate

File No. _____

Property Address _____
City_____ State _____ Zip_____
Name of Person Interviewed _____
Dates of Ownership From _____ To _____
Other Way Familiar With Property From _____ To _____
Interviewer _____ Date _____
Address _____
City_____ State _____ Zip_____
Telephone_____

This form is used to report the results of an interview with the current or former property owner or others familiar with the property about known Hazardous Substances or Detrimental Environmental Conditions on or around the subject property. When signed by the interviewer it becomes their certificate.

#		YES	NO	Comment on all "Yes's"
1.	**ASBESTOS** Are you aware of any asbestos on your property? Pipe covering Heating/Hot water unit covering Tile Siding Other			
2.	Are you aware of any asbestos survey being performed on your property?			
3.	Are you aware of any asbestos tests being conducted on materials from your property?			
	PCBs (Polychlorinated Biphenyls)			
4.	Are you aware of any PCBs on your property?			
5.	Are you aware of any PCBs on neighboring properties that might contaminate your property?			
6.	**RADON** Are you aware of any radon tests made on the property?			
7.	If so, was radon test made more than 12 months ago?			
8.	Were the results over 4 pCi/l? (If so, report actual figures).			
9.	To the best of your knowledge do any properties within one mile have radon levels over 4 pCi/l.			
10.	Are you aware of any evidence that nearby structures have elevated indoor levels of radon or radon progeny?			
11.	Are you aware of any information that indicates the local water supplies have been found to have elevated levels of radon or radium?			
12.	Are you aware of any properties within one mile of your property of any sites that were or currently are used for uranium, thorium or radium extraction or for phosphate processing?			
	UST'S (Underground Storage Tanks)			
13.	Are you aware of any underground storage tanks presently on the property?			
14.	Are you aware of any underground storage tanks which were previously removed from the property, (if so note date).			
15.	Are you aware of any site survey made by a qualified engineer which indicates the property is free of USTs.?			
	WASTE DISPOSAL			
16.	Are you aware of any petroleum storage and/or delivery facilities (including gas stations) or chemical manufacturing plants located within one mile of the property?			

Page 1 of 2

FW-70EQ   Test Version   Forms and Worms, Inc.®   315 Whitney Ave., New Haven, CT 06511   1(800)243-4545   Item# 115250
                3A 1/90   Approved by The National Association of Environmental Risk Auditors

Used with permission of National Association of Environmental Risk Auditors, Bloomington, Indiana.

FIGURE 1.5. *(continued)*

File No.

	#		YES	NO	Comment on all "Yes's"
WASTE SITES	17.	Are you aware of any physical testing (including on-site sampling of soil and groundwater) to determine if the property is free of waste contamination?			
	18.	Do you know if the property was ever used for research, industrial or military purposes?			
	19.	Do you know if the property has ever been occupied by owners or commercial tenants who are likely to have used, transported or disposed of toxic chemicals (e.g. dry cleaners, print shops, service stations, etc.)?			
	20.	Do you know if there is any water provided to the property or from a well or private water company?			
	21.	Do you know if the property or any site within one mile, appears on any state or federal list of hazardous waste sites (e.g. CERCLIS, HWDMS, etc.)?			
	22.	Do you know of any visible evidence or documents that indicate there is or was dangerous waste handling on the property or neighboring sites (e.g. stressed vegetation, stained soil, open or leaking containers, foul fumes or smells, oily ponds, etc.)?			

UREA (Formaldehyde)				
23.	Do you know if the property contains UREA Formaldehyde Foam Insulation? (If yes, note location and amount).			

LEAD PAINT				
24.	Do you know if the property was tested for lead paint?			
25.	Do you have any reason to believe that the property contains lead paint?			

	#				
DRINKING WATER	26.	Do you know if the drinking water was ever tested for lead? (If yes, note date and results).			
	27.	Do you know if any other tests were ever made on the drinking water? (If yes, describe and note results).			
	28.	Do you have any reason to believe there was or is any problem with the quality and quantity of drinking water available at the property?			

AIR POLLUTANTS				
29.	Do you know if the interior air was ever tested?			
30.	Do you have any reason to believe there was or is any problem with the interior or exterior air of the property?			

OTHER ENVIRONMENTAL HAZARDS				
31.	Are you aware of any other hazardous substances or detrimental environmental conditions that effect the property?			

I certify that I have read the answers to the questions on this form and acknowledge that they are accurate to the best of my knowledge and belief.

Signatures — Current or former property owner(s)

______________ Date ______________ Date

______________ Date ______________ Date

Interviewer

Page 2 of 2

FW-70EQ Test Version 3A 1/90

Forms and Worms, Inc.® 315 Whitney Ave., New Haven, CT 06511 1(800)243-4545
Approved by The National Association of Environmental Risk Auditors

Item# 115250

FIGURE 1.6.   Sample Phase 1 Environmental Assessment

PHASE 1 ENVIRONMENTAL ASSESSMENT
Federal National Mortgage Association

File No. _____

REQUIRED FANNIE MAE PROPERTY LOG

Fannie Mae Loan # _____
Property Address _____
_____
_____
Borrower Address _____
_____
_____
Borrower Phone _____
Lender Company Name _____
Individual Lender _____
Environmental Underwriter _____
Individual Environmental
Consultant _____
Firm Name and Address _____
_____
Consultant Phone _____
Date Assessment Completed _____
Assessment Results _____

SUMMARY OF RESULTS AND RECOMMENDATION

1. Phase I Assessment Results (check applicable result for each hazard)

Hazard	Acceptable	Acceptable Requires O&M	Fail	Possible Remedy	Phase II Required
Asbestos	_____	_____	___	_____	_____
PCB	_____	_____	___	_____	_____
Radon	_____	_____	___	_____	_____
UST	_____	_____	___	_____	_____
Waste Sites	_____	_____	___	_____	_____
Other_____	_____	_____	___	_____	_____
_____	_____	_____	___	_____	_____

2. Attach a brief explanation for each hazard requiring a Phase II assessment. List data deficiencies, test results etc., requiring further assessment.

3. Attach a brief explanation for each hazard that is acceptable but requires Operations and Maintenance (O & M) actions. What actions are required and how should they be performed?

4. Attach a brief explanation for each failed hazard that could be corrected with remedial actions. What actions are required and how should they be performed?

5. Other comments:

Signature: _____   Date: _____

INFORMATION CHECKLIST

The following checked items indicate overall sources used by the Field Observer to perform an assessment of the property to determine the existence of apparent hazardous materials and detrimental environmental conditions:

_____ Building Specifications   _____ Neighborhood Zoning Maps
_____ Historical Aerial Photos   _____ Neighborhood Land Use Maps
_____ Current Aerial Photos   _____ List of Commercial Tenants On site
_____ Title History   _____ Verification of Public Water and Sewer
_____ Site Survey   _____ Interviews with Builder, and/or Property Manager
_____ Interviews with Local   _____ Other _____
      Fire, Health, Land Use
      or Environmental Enforcement Officials

2. Asbestos

_____ Dated Building Construction or Rehabilitation Specifications
_____ Report of: Engineer/Consultant/Asbestos
_____ Other _____

3. PCB's (Polychlorinated Biphenyls)

_____ Utility Transformer Records
_____ Site survey of Transformers
_____ Site Soil and Groundwater PCB Test Results
_____ Other _____

Page 1 of 4

FW-70EA   Test Version   ©1989 Forms and Worms, Inc., 315 Whitney Ave., New Haven, CT 06511 1(800)243-4545   Item #115150
          3A-V90   National Association of Environmental Risk Auditors

Used with permission of National Association of Environmental Risk Auditors, Bloomington, Indiana.

FIGURE 1.6. (*continued*)

File No. _____

INFORMATION CHECKLIST (Continued)

4. Radon

_____ Water Utility Records
_____ Gas Utility Records
_____ On-Site Radon Test Results
_____ Other _____

5. USTs (Underground Storage Tanks)

_____ Oil, Motor Fuel and Waste Oil Systems Reports
_____ CERCLIS/HWDMS Results on Neighborhood (within radius of one mile)
_____ Site Soil and Groundwater Tests
_____ Site Tank Survey
_____ Other _____

6. Waste Sites

_____ CERCLIS/HWDMS Results on neighborhoods (within radius of one mile)
_____ State EPA site lists for neighborhoods (within radius of one mile)
_____ Site Soil and Groundwater Test Results
_____ Other _____

7. Additional Hazards

_____ Urea Formaldehyde Foam Insulation Survey
_____ Interior Air Test Results
_____ Lead Paint Survey
_____ Lead in Drinking Water Test Results
_____ Other _____

ASBESTOS

Required Fannie Mae Phase 1 Environmental Assessment questions and signature: YES   NO   UNKNOWN

1. Was the building constructed prior to 1979?   ☐   ☐   ☐
2. Does a site walk through reveal any visible evidence of asbestos?   ☐   ☐   ☐
3. Is there any documented evidence of asbestos?   ☐   ☐   ☐
   Note: If the answer to all three of the above questions is "no", then stop,
          the property is acceptable for asbestos. If the answer to any of the
          questions is "yes" or "unknown", answer the questions below.
4. Is there an asbestos survey by a certified, independent firm performed since 1979? ☐   ☐   ☐
   Note: If the answer to question 4 is "yes", answer the question below.
          Otherwise, stop, a Phase II assessment is required.
5. Did the survey find the building to be free of treated or untreated ACM?   ☐   ☐   ☐
   Note: If the answer to question 5 is "yes", then stop, the property is
          acceptable for asbestos. Otherwise, either the building fails or a Phase
          II assessment is required.
6. Comments of: Underwriter/Appraiser/Inspector _____

7. Phase I Assessment Results (circle one):
   Acceptable   Acceptable Requires O & M   Fail   Fail, Possible Remedy   Phase II Required
8. Signature of: Underwriter/Appraiser/Inspector _____ Date_____

PCBs (Polychlorinated Biphenyls)

Required Fannie Mae Phase 1 Environmental Assessment questions and signature: YES   NO   UNKNOWN

1. Are there any fluorescent light ballasts containing PCBs in the building?   ☐   ☐   ☐
2. Are there any transformers or capacitors containing PCBs anywhere on the property? ☐   ☐   ☐
3. Is there any visible or documented evidence of soil or groundwater contamination from
   PCBs on the property?   ☐   ☐   ☐
   Note: If the answer to all three questions is "no", then stop, the property is acceptable
          for PCBs. If the answer to any question is "unknown", then stop, a Phase II ass-
          essment is required. Otherwise, answer the questions below.
4. (If question 1 above is "yes") Are any of the lights damaged or leaking?   ☐   ☐   ☐
5. (If question 2 above is "yes") Are any of the capacitors or transformers inside
   residential buildings?   ☐   ☐   ☐
6. (If question 2 above is "yes") Are any of the transformers or capacitors not clearly marked,
   well maintained or secure?   ☐   ☐   ☐
7. (If question 2 above is "yes") Is there any evidence of leakage on or around the transformers or
   capacitors?   ☐   ☐   ☐
8. (If question 3 above is "yes") Have PCB concentrations of 50ppm or greater been found in
   contaminated soils or groundwater?   ☐   ☐   ☐
   Note: If the answers to question 4, 5, 6, 7, and 8 are all "no", then the property is
          acceptable for PCBs. Otherwise, the property either fails or requires a
          Phase II assessment.
9. Comments of: Underwriter/Appraiser/Inspector _____

10. Phase I Assessment Results (circle one):
    Acceptable   Acceptable Requires O & M   Fail   Fail, Possible Remedy   Phase II Required
11. Signature of: Underwriter/Appraiser/Inspector _____ Date_____

FW-70EA   Test Version   ©1989 Forms and Worms, Inc., 315 Whitney Ave., New Haven, CT 06511 1(800)243-4545   Item #115150
           2A-9/89   National Association of Environmental Risk Auditors

FIGURE 1.6. *(continued)*

File No.

Required Fannie Mae Phase 1 Environmental Assessment questions and signature:	YES	NO	UNKNOWN

1. Were the results of an EPA approved short-term radon test, performed in the basement within the last six months, at/or below 4 pCi/l or 0.02 WL?
   Note: If the answer is "no" or "unknown", then stop, a Phase II assessment is required. If the answer is "yes", answer the questions below. ☐ ☐ ☐
2. Is there any evidence that nearby structures have elevated indoor levels of radon or radon progeny? ☐ ☐ ☐
3. Have local water supplies been found to have elevated levels of radon or radium? ☐ ☐ ☐
4. Is the property located on or near sites that currently are or formerly were used for uranium, thorium, or radium extraction or for phosphate processing? ☐ ☐ ☐
   Note: If the answer to questions 2, 3 or 4 is "yes", then a Phase II assessment is required. If the answer to questions 2, 3 and 4 is "no", then the property is acceptable for radon. A property may be acceptable for radon with a "unknown" answer for questions 2, 3 or 4 but the underwriter must justify the decision.
5. Comments of: Underwriter/Appraiser/Inspector _____

6. Phase I Assessment Results (circle one):
   Acceptable   Acceptable Requires O & M   Fail   Fail, Possible Remedy   Phase II Required
7. Signature of: Underwriter/Appraiser/Inspector _____ Date_____

(RADON)

Required Fannie Mae Phase 1 Environmental Assessment questions and signature:	YES	NO	UNKNOWN

1. Is there a current site survey performed by a qualified engineer which indicates that the property is free of any UST's? ☐ ☐ ☐
2. Is there any visible or documented evidence of soil or groundwater contamination on the property? ☐ ☐ ☐
3. Are there any petroleum storage and/or delivery facilities (including gas stations) or chemical manufacturing plants located on adjacent properties? ☐ ☐ ☐
   Note: If the answer to question 1 is "yes", and the answers to questions 2 and 3 are "no", the property is acceptable for UST's skip to next section. Otherwise, answer the questions below.
4. (If "yes" to question 3) Have these facilities been maintained in accordance with sound industry standards (e.g. API Bulletins 1621 and 1623; NFPA Bulletins 329, 70, 77 etc.)? ☐ ☐ ☐
   Note: If the answer to 4 is "no", skip to question 7 below. If the answer to 4 is "unknown", the property fails or a Phase II assessment is required. If the answer to both questions 3 and 4 is "yes", answer the questions below.
5. Are any of the tanks more than 10 years old? ☐ ☐ ☐
6. Have any of the tanks that are more than 10 years old not been successfully tested for leaks within the last year using an API approved test? ☐ ☐ ☐
   Note: If the answer to question 6 is "no", answer the questions below. If the answer to question 6 is "yes" or "unknown", the property fails or a Phase II assessment is required.
7. Are there any deactivated UST's on the property? ☐ ☐ ☐
8. (If "yes" to question 7) Were all of the tanks deactivated in accordance with sound industry practices (e.g. API Bulletins #1604 and #2202 or NFPA Bulletin #30)? ☐ ☐ ☐
   Note: If the answer to question 7 is "no", or if the answer to question 8 is "yes" then the property is acceptable for UST's. If the answer to question 7 is "yes" or "unknown" or if the answer to question 8 is "no" or "unknown" then the property fails or a Phase II assessment is required.
9. Comments of: Underwriter/Appraiser/Inspector _____

10. Phase I Assessment Results (circle one):
    Acceptable   Acceptable: Requires O & M   Fail   Fail: Possible Remedy   Phase II Required
11. Signature of: Underwriter/Appraiser/Inspector _____ Date_____

(UST's (Underground Storage Tanks))

FW-70EA   Test Version 2A-9/89   ©1989 Forms and Worms, Inc., 315 Whitney Ave., New Haven, CT 06511 1(800)243-4545
National Association of Environmental Risk Auditors   Item #115150

FIGURE 1.6. (*continued*)

File No.

Required Fannie Mae Phase 1 Environmental Assessment questions and signature:	YES	NO	UNKNOWN

WASTE DISPOSAL FACILITIES

1. Are there results of physical testing (including on-site sampling of soil and groundwater meeting all regulatory standards and sound industry practice) indicating that the property is free of waste contamination and is being operated in an environmentally safe manner? ☐ ☐ ☐
2. Are there any obvious high risk neighbors in adjacent properties engaged in producing, storing or transporting hazardous waste, chemicals or substances? ☐ ☐ ☐
   Note: If the answer to question 1 is "yes" and the answer to question 2 is "no", then stop, the property is acceptable for waste disposal facilities. Otherwise, answer questions below.
3. Was the site ever used for research, industrial or military purposes during the last 30 years? ☐ ☐ ☐
4. Has any of the site space ever been leased to commercial tenants who are likely to have used, transported or disposed of toxic chemicals (e.g. dry cleaner, print shop, service station, etc.)? ☐ ☐ ☐
5. Is water for the building provided either by a private company or directly from a well on the property? ☐ ☐ ☐
6. Does the property or any site within 1 mile, appear on any state or federal list of hazardous waste sites (e.g. CERCLIS, HWDMS etc.)? ☐ ☐ ☐
7. Is there any documented or visible evidence of dangerous waste handling on the subject property or neighboring sites (e.g. stressed vegetation, stained soil, open or leaking containers, foul fumes or smells, oily ponds etc.)? ☐ ☐ ☐
   Note: If the answer to any of questions 2 through 6 are "yes" or "unknown", then either the property fails or a Phase II assessment is required. If the answer to all questions 2 through 6 are "no", then the property is acceptable for waste disposal facilities.
8. Comments of: Underwriter/Appraiser/Inspector _____

9. Phase I Assessment Results (circle one):
   Acceptable   Acceptable: Requires O & M   Fail   Fail: Possible Remedy   Phase II Required
10. Signature of: Underwriter/Appraiser/Inspector _____ Date _____

Required Fannie Mae Phase 1 Environmental Assessment questions and signature:	YES	NO	UNKNOWN

ADDITIONAL HAZARDS

1. Is there any visible or documented evidence of peeling lead paint on the floors, walls or ceilings of tenant or common areas? ☐ ☐ ☐
   Note: If the answer to question 1 is "no", the property is acceptable for lead paint. If the answer is "yes" or "unknown", the property fails. The application may continue, but remedial actions to remove or cover all peeling lead paint must be taken prior to Commitment by Fannie Mae.
2. Do the tenant areas contain Urea Formaldehyde Foam Insulation that was installed less than a year ago? ☐ ☐ ☐
3. (If the answer to question 2 is "yes" or "unknown") Did the current HVAC system meet ASHRAE standards when it was installed? ☐ ☐ ☐
   Note: If the answer to question 2 is "no", or if the answer to question 3 is "yes", then the property is acceptable for UFFI. If the answer to question 3 is "no" or "unknown", then the property fails. The application may continue, but the Lender must demonstrate prior to Commitment by Fannie Mae that the ventilation system currently meets ASHRAE standards.
4. Does the drinking water in the project contain lead at levels above 50ppb? ☐ ☐ ☐
   Note: If the answer to question 4 is "yes" or "unknown", the property fails. Action must be taken prior to Commitment by Fannie Mae to reduce the lead content of the drinking water. Otherwise, the property is acceptable for lead in drinking water.
5. Comments of: Underwriter/Appraiser/Inspector _____

6. Phase I Assessment Results (circle one):
   Acceptable   Acceptable: Requires O & M   Fail   Fail: Possible Remedy   Phase II Required
7. Signature of: Underwriter/Appraiser/Inspector _____ Date _____

FW-70EA   Test Version 2A-9/89   ©1989 Forms and Worms Inc., 315 Whitney Ave., New Haven, CT 06511 1(800)243-4545   Item #115150
National Association of Environmental Risk Auditors

report might include a recommendation to have other specialized consultants do the work.

Once the data are gathered and processed, the phase I consultant will prepare a detailed report. If there are no problems, the investigation is over. In some instances, the consultant will recommend additional tests, corrective actions or a phase II environmental assessment.

Phase II Environmental Assessment. A recommendation for a phase II assessment means there is ample evidence of a significant environmental hazard. The primary purpose of the phase II assessment is to identify the extent of the contamination, identify sources of contaminants and evaluate fully the impact of contamination on the property. This is typically not needed for residential assessments.

Phase III Environmental Assessment. This is the last stage of the environmental assessments, and it includes the corrective action plan for removing the hazard. Further monitoring of the hazard over time might also be needed. If the property requires ongoing work, the cost can be very high. Normally, this level of corrective action is limited to commercial properties. Corrective actions in most residential transactions can usually be handled without this involved procedure.

Assessment Reports. When the assessment is complete, the client receives a final report that details any hazards, provides test results and makes recommendations about future actions. The report should include the sources of information and the quality of those sources. Any disclaimers should be reviewed by a competent attorney before the assessment is used as the basis for making a decision.

Why Bother?

Does it seem that this chapter has overemphasized the importance of checking out environmental problems before a property is purchased? If so, then it has served a purpose. In the past, most people were not concerned about environmental due diligence and liability for environmental hazards. However, the public has become more aware of the health, environmental and economic damages that can result from environmental hazards. In response to these new issues, the legal and real estate professions are expanding their areas of expertise to keep pace with the growing awareness of the rights and responsibilities of buyers and sellers in this arena.

In short, the only protection a buyer has against becoming responsible for environmental hazards created by former owners is to fulfill the requirements of environmental due diligence *before* completing the purchase of a property. If a corrective action is required after the purchase is completed, the new owner will be a *potentially responsible party* and could be required to assume some costs for correcting the problem. Sellers can protect their financial interests by becoming informed about existing hazards and measures needed to make the property marketable.

CHAPTER
TWO

Overview of
Environmental Hazards

In May 1987, nearly 25 miles of New Jersey's beaches were closed because garbage (including medical wastes) was washing ashore. In August of that year, 50 miles of beaches were closed for the same reason.

As reported in A. Nadakavukaren, *Man & Environment: A Health Perspective,* 1990.

In the spring of 1978, a seven-acre rural site about 25 miles south of Louisville was a dump for about 17,000 drums of industrial and toxic waste. Sampling in the area showed that the soil and water were contaminated with about 200 different organic chemicals and 30 metals.

As reported in A. Nadakavukaren, *Man & Environment: A Health Perspective,* 1990.

When Robert and Kathleen Wendt purchased their farm in 1983, Norris Kerkhof owned the grain farm next door. In 1988, Kerkhof added a hog farming operation, and in 1991 planned a $2 million expansion from 55 sows to 480 sows. Kerkhof planned to produce up to 8,000 pigs a year! In their suit, the Wendts claimed that the smell of the pig manure had a serious effect on the health of their asthmatic daughter and aggravated Mrs.

Wendt's sinus condition. In June 1991, a county judge dismissed their case, saying that Indiana's Right to Farm law overrode the Wendt's nuisance claim.

As reported in *Daily Reporter,* Greenfield, Indiana. February 7, 1991; June 29, 1991.

Nearby Hazards

The key phrase in most real estate transactions is "location, location, location." In the past, this meant buying in the most stable, desirable location in the community to protect one's investments. Now this advice includes selecting properties that are free of nearby environmental hazards. After the purchase, homeowners still need to be aware of commercial and industrial developments that could pose an environmental threat to their properties. This chapter gives an overview of some concerns related to the house site, including excessive noise, outdoor air pollution and past and present land use. Other site hazards are discussed in subsequent chapters: radon (Chapter 3), pesticides (Chapter 11), electric and magnetic fields from power lines (Chapter 12), drinking water (Chapter 13) and septic systems (Chapter 14).

Noise

Proximity to highways, airports and shopping centers can be a plus or minus, depending on your outlook. It is convenient to be close to services, but noise and air pollution from traffic, industrial and commercial facilities can cause problems.

More than a nuisance, noise is considered by some health care professionals to be one of the most important stressors of modern times. Noise can contribute to tension, fatigue, hearing loss and deficiencies in attention span. It can also be a contributor to the development of ulcers, high blood pressure and heart disease.

Do you need to measure the noise levels at your property? Most of the time, the answer is "no." It is usually easy to tell if noise is going to be irritating just by listening to it. Noise measurements may be needed when a problem arises, especially from a source outside the home. If you are experiencing high noise levels, contact the local health department or planning agency for help. If they are not responsive, you may need to contact an attorney to determine what can be done about the source of the noise. Noise consulting services can be found in the yellow pages of the telephone directory under "Noise Measurement and Control" or "Environmental and Ecological Services."

Noise is measured in units of decibels (dB). Levels below 40 dBA (the "A" refers to a type of scale) are considered to be comfortable. For comparison, the average house with a stereo playing at a comfortable level will have a noise level of about 30 dBA. The average office might have a level of about 50 dBA.There are no national standards for noise, but some communities have adopted their own standards. A level less than 55 dB is generally recognized as a goal for outdoor residential areas that will protect the public health with an adequate margin of safety. This goal is supported by the U.S. Department of Housing and Urban Development, the Environmental Protection Agency and the Department of Transportation.

Noise levels can be reduced by erecting barriers such as earthen mounds (called berms), wood or concrete walls, or vegetation screens. Careful orientation of a new home so that windows and doors are on the sides of the house that don't face the noise source can reduce indoor levels. Interior construction techniques are also effective in blocking both outdoor sources of noise and interior sources. A common (and aggravating) source of indoor noise is the heating system. This problem can easily be prevented by careful placement of the system and the use of sound-damping construction techniques before the house is built. Even after construction, sound-damping measures can help reduce indoor noise caused by a heating system.

The sound-blocking ability of different construction methods can be measured by comparing sound transmission class (STC) numbers. The STC number is the difference between the sound levels on the side of the wall where the noise is produced and where it is received. Higher STC numbers mean that the method does a better job of blocking noise.

Some typical noise reduction construction techniques include the following:

- Attaching a soundboard under the drywall on each side of the studs
- Using staggered studs or increasing the spacing between studs
- Carefully sealing cracks and edges around the wall
- Reducing window size and increasing the thickness of the glass
- Installing solid wood core doors rather than hollow core doors

When buying a home (or lot), visit the property during the peak traffic hours to get a feel for noise inside and outside of the property. Remember that traffic noise carries for considerable distances. Carefully evaluate noise if the property is within fifteen miles of an airport or within one mile of a major highway or railroad. If you live in a northern climate, noise levels are typically somewhat louder during the winter months when trees and shrubs are bare.

If you are building a home, ask about the STC number of the construction method and what measures are being used to reduce noise. If noise is a special concern, you may need to consult with an architect or noise specialist to get the answers you need in order to reduce noise levels to an acceptable level.

Outdoor Air Pollution

Overall, there have been significant improvements in the quality of the outside air since the 1960s. Even so, air pollution is an important contributor to lung and heart disease throughout the United States. Recent estimates suggest that 2 to 14 percent of deaths nationwide are related to outdoor air pollution. Air pollution also drains the economy because it damages crops (at an estimated cost to farmers of five billion dollars per year) and building materials.

Air pollution is regulated in the United States by the Clean Air Act, which establishes safe levels of contaminants in the outdoor air and safe levels of release (called emission standards) from polluting industries. The quality of outdoor air is monitored through a nationwide network that includes sampling stations in rural and urban areas. There are federal standards for seven pollutants in the outdoor air: particulate matter, sulfur dioxide, nitrogen dioxide, carbon monoxide, lead, ozone and hydrocarbons (see Figure 2.1). Some states have adopted more stringent standards for these contaminants. Even so, there are many areas in the United States that do not meet the national air quality standards. The EPA recently estimated that 150 million people across the United States lived in areas that exceeded at least one air quality standard during 1992. Of these contaminants, ozone was the most widespread air pollution problem; it affected about 45 million people. Are you living in an area that exceeds one or more of the outdoor air quality standards? You can find out if you are living in one of these areas by calling your state or local environmental protection agency (see Appendix A).

In many places, the open burning of leaves and trash and the release of malodors are prohibited by the local health department or environmental agency. Odor regulations are intended to protect the public from annoying smells and harmful chemicals. Because the odor regulations in most places are weak and difficult to enforce, resolving these problems can be a frustrating experience. If you have a problem with odors, first contact the local air pollution control or health agency. Even when regulatory agencies are able to motivate or require a polluter to control odor problems, months may pass before the controls are installed and working properly. If the regulatory agencies are not responsive, consider organizing other concerned citizens to contact local politicians for help. You may need to contact an attorney to help resolve the problem.

In 1986, Congress passed a new law that was intended to give the general public, state governments, industry and environmental groups more power in understanding the magnitude of chemical emissions in their communities. Known as the Emergency Planning and Community Right-to-Know Act, this law created the Toxics Release Inventory (TRI), which started out as

FIGURE 2.1. Regulated Outdoor Air Contaminants

Contaminant	Major Sources	Effects on Human Health and the Environment	Federal Standards to Protect Human Health
Particulate matter, PM-10 (PM-10 particles are very small particles of dust, dirt, soot and smoke that are easily inhaled into the lungs)	Power plants Industries Fires Motor vehicles Wood stoves and fireplaces	Aggravates heart and lung disease Causes eye and lung irritation Decreases visibility Corrodes metals Causes grime on buildings	150 micrograms per cubic meter (24-hour average)[1,2] 50 micrograms per cubic meter (annual average)
Sulfure dioxide	Coal-burning power plants Metal smelters Oil refineries Industrial boilers that burn sulfur-containing fuel	Irritates the eyes and lungs Aggravates existing lung diseases (asthmatics and those with bronchitis or emphysema are especially sensitive) Corrodes metals and stone Damages textiles Is toxic to plants Forms acid rain	0.14 parts per million[3] (24-hour average) 0.03 parts per million (annual average)

[1]One microgram per cubic meter ($\mu g/m^3$) means that one microgram of the contaminant exists in one cubic meter of air; this is a very small unit of measurement (one microgram is the same as one one-millionth of a gram).
[2]A 24 hour average means the concentration is calculated for a period of 24 hours; similarly, 1-hour, 8-hour, quarterly or annual averages are calculated for those periods of time. When a standard includes different time periods for a given contaminant, the numerical value of the standard will be higher for the shortest period of time. This means that standards allow greater exposure to a contaminant for shorter periods of time than for longer time periods.
[3]One part per million (ppm) is a concentration unit that means that one part of the contaminant exists in one million parts of air.
SOURCE: U.S. EPA (1993*a*).

FIGURE 2.1. (*continued*)

Carbon monoxide	The incomplete burning of fuel in motor vehicles, wood stoves, gas stoves and fireplaces	Enters the bloodstream and reduces the amount of oxygen that gets to the body's tissues and organs (people with angina or peripheral vascular disease are most sensitive)	9.0 parts per million (8-hour average) 35.0 parts per million (1-hour average)
Nitrogen dioxide	By-product of fuel combustion by motor vehicles, industries and power plants	Irritates the lower lungs Lowers resistance to respiratory infections	0.053 parts per million (annual average)
Ozone	Produced by reactions that involve volatile chemicals that are released into the air from motor vehicles, dry cleaners, paint shops and other users of solvents	Causes coughing, congestion and chest pain, and reduces lung function (relatively low concentrations can affect healthy adults, children and asthmatics) (Animal studies suggest that long-term exposure can permanently damage the lungs and cause premature aging of the lungs)	0.120 parts per million (maximum daily 1-hour average
Lead	Smelters Lead battery manufacturing or recycling Lead gasoline additives were a major source in the past	Lead affects all of the body's systems Results in damage to the central nervous systems and causes decreases in IQ, mental retardation and behavioral problems (fetuses, infants and children are most sensitive)	1.5 micrograms per cubic meter (averaged quarterly)

a list of 320 chemicals and chemical categories that are released into the air, water and land across the nation. Certain facilities that manufacture, process or otherwise use substances which are listed on the TRI must report to the EPA how much of these toxic chemicals they release into the environment each year. The listed chemicals include pesticides, organic solvents, metals and other compounds that pose serious environmental or health risks, including cancer and birth defects. Recently, the EPA proposed adding another 313 chemicals and chemical categories to the TRI list. About 54 percent of the TRI chemicals are active ingredients in the formulation of pesticides.

Although there are weaknesses with this data base, it does provide communities with valuable information about the sources of toxic chemicals. During 1991, over two *billion* pounds of TRI chemicals were released into the air! Figure 2.2 shows areas that have releases of toxic air pollutants regulated by the Clean Air Act. (Note that this figure does not include releases of toxic chemicals into the land and water, only those into the air.)

How Can You Learn about the Quality of the Air in Your Community? If you live in an urban area, you can keep track of the air quality in your community through a widely used indicator of urban air quality,

FIGURE 2.2.   National Toxic Releases to the Atmosphere in 1990

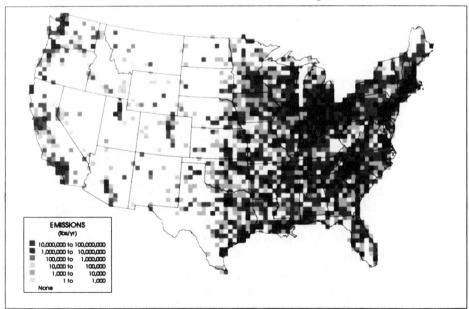

SOURCE: U.S. EPA (1993a).

the Pollution Standards Index (PSI). The PSI is a single number that reflects a combination of contaminants: sulfur dioxide, particulates, ozone, carbon monoxide and nitrogen oxides. A PSI value less than 50 means that the air quality is good, a value between 51 and 100 indicates moderate air quality, and a value over 100 is unhealthy. The PSI is announced during TV and radio newscasts and is also listed in newspapers.

In the past, most of the regulatory emphasis was on very large sources of emissions (major sources), but more information is being developed about smaller sources such as dry cleaners and spray-painting operations. These sources are of concern because many of them release significant amounts of toxic air pollutants. No matter where you live, you can find out what industries in your area release air pollution by contacting your local or state environmental/air pollution agency. The agency will have a record of the sources of air contaminants in your area and will know if each source is meeting the requirements spelled out in its operating permit. The state agency will also have access to the TRI database mentioned above, and you can ask for a list of companies that release contaminants in your area. This list will include the company's name and address, and the names and amounts of chemicals it releases into the air, land or water.

Land Pollution

Before the 1960s, there was little concern about the discharge of chemicals into the air, land and water. During the mid-1970s, the public's attention was drawn to the discovery of land and groundwater contaminated by the uncontrolled releases of toxic materials into the environment. The public's demand for action was followed by the passage of many regulations designed to prevent the abuses of the past. Now, even though new industries must sharply reduce their discharges, many communities and people are affected by problems that were created years ago. Some areas have become corridors of industrial discharges and waste management sites. Abandoned or closed facilities are of special concern because potential environmental hazards might not have been corrected before the property fell into disuse.

The current and past uses of land under a house and of the area surrounding a house should be carefully examined by a prospective homebuyer. Anyone who buys a property that has been used for agricultural or industrial purposes should consider having the site professionally assessed for environmental hazards because the costs of correcting problems can be enormous. A typical investigation includes reviewing aerial photographs of the property to look for hazards, walking through the property and investigating environmental records for evidence of previous problems with the property. Testing for toxic chemicals may be needed, especially if unknown chemicals are discovered at the site. (See Chapter 1 for more information about site assessments.) Even if you are building a home on a lot that was not used for agricultural or industrial purposes, ask the builder or developer where any fill dirt comes from. Most of the time, the fill dirt will not be contaminated, but problems can occur.

Agricultural Land. Pesticides and fertilizers from present and past applications can contaminate the soil, groundwater or surface water. Each time chemicals are applied to the land, some are likely to be carried into the air or washed by rainfall into lakes, streams or the ground. In the past, farmers, who were not aware of the hazards posed by these chemicals, may have dumped unused portions onto the ground. (Farmers also buried other wastes such as garbage, appliances and even cars or tractors.) Some agricultural lands were deliberately used by industrial operators as a cheap way of getting rid of toxic wastes. Even though the contamination occurred decades ago, the land is probably still contaminated because many toxic chemicals linger in the soil for long periods of time.

Another potentially serious problem is proximity to animal feedlots. Waste materials from pigs, fowl, cows and other animals that are concentrated in small areas can cause serious air and water quality problems for surrounding neighbors.

Underground Storage Tanks (USTs). An underground storage tank is simply a tank (and its piping) that is placed either partially (at least 10 percent of its volume) or completely underground. USTs were buried to reduce the potential for fires, explosions and human contact with these hazardous chemicals. Most contain gasoline, diesel fuel or heating oil. These petroleum products contain carcinogens (such as benzene) and other toxic compounds, including toluene, xylene and ethylbenzene.

Commercial USTs have been regulated by the EPA since 1984 under the Resource Conservation and Recovery Act. The EPA's updated regulations require registration and inspection of the tanks, corrosion protection, spill and overflow prevention, leak detection, and removal and clean up when leaks occur. Even older tanks (installed before 1988) must meet provisions for corrosion protection, spill and overflow prevention and leak detection. Some tanks are exempted from the EPA's rules. These include farm and residential tanks holding 1,100 gallons or less of motor fuel intended for noncommercial purposes, tanks on or above the floor of underground areas (such as basements or tunnels), home heating oil tanks, tanks holding 110 gallons of fluid or less, and septic tanks and systems for collecting storm water and wastewater.

Existing and new tanks that are not exempt from the EPA's regulations must comply with federal requirements, including those that deal with leak detection.

The EPA estimates there are about five to six million commercial and residential USTs, and about as many as 25 percent of all USTs may now be leaking. In some areas, the percentage is much higher. For example, in New York, over 50 percent of the USTs are believed to be leaking. Leaks—even small ones—are serious because they can contaminate the surrounding soil and groundwater. For example, as little as one gallon of gasoline can contaminate one million gallons of drinking water. Groundwater is the source of drinking water for nearly half of all Americans. The EPA believes that about 62,000 private water wells and 4,700 public water wells have been contaminated by USTs.

The movement of chemicals from a UST to the inside of a home through openings in the basement or slab foundation can also present problems. Not only are these chemicals toxic when inhaled, they pose a potential explosion hazard if the concentrations build up in the home.

A tank's materials and location may also contribute to problems. Tanks made of bare steel without corrosion protection are the most likely to corrode and leak, but fiberglass tanks also crack and leak. In 1993, the EPA estimated that about 80 percent of USTs were of the bare steel type. The placement of the tank is another risk factor. A tank is highly vulnerable to even the smallest leaks when it is placed in an area where the water table is high or where the soil is sandy or gravelly.

You might suspect a leaking UST if your home has a petroleum odor, or if well water has either a film or sheen on the surface or a petroleum odor. A leaking UST might be responsible for these problems even if your property does not have a tank. Remember that the source could be located away from your home. If you suspect contamination, contact your local health or environmental agency for help.

Even when signs of contamination are not readily apparent, consider hiring a consultant to check the condition of an existing tank if it has not already been checked for leaks. If you are considering buying a home that has an underground storage tank, hire a consultant to check for leaks and to evaluate the condition of the tank *even if* the tank is no longer used. An old tank may contain residual fuels that could leak from the tank as it ages and corrodes. Cleaning up leaks is expensive; costs can range from thousands of dollars for smaller leaks from residential tanks to millions of dollars for leaks from commercial tanks.

Waste Treatment and Disposal Sites (Dumps, Surface Impoundments, Incinerators, Storage, Landfills, Deep Wells and Landfarms). This nation produces a staggering amount of waste—approximately 294 pounds per person per day, which adds up to a total of about 13 billion tons each year; most are industrial wastes. Many of these wastes are toxic. Although the amount of municipal waste produced seems small (about 4.3 pounds per person per day in 1990), these wastes are not negligible because available landfill space is declining. The toxic wastes we produce include:

- Municipal solid wastes—garbage and refuse from our homes, schools and offices
- Industrial wastes—byproducts from manufacturing, mining, coal combustion, and oil and gas production (these wastes do not fit under the technical definition of hazardous wastes)
- Medical wastes—materials from hospitals, universities, medical and dental clinics, laboratories and morgues
- Radioactive wastes—radioactive wastes from nuclear fuel use, weapons production, medical and agricultural uses of radioactive materials, and uranium ore processing
- Hazardous wastes—industrial wastes that meet the legal definition of hazardous (exhibits a toxicity characteristic or appears on a chemical list) and must be stored, transported, processed and disposed of according to special regulations

Where does all of this waste go? In the past, dumping was widespread. Now, the Resource Conservation and Recovery Act (RCRA) of 1976 and other laws governing toxic wastes form the basis of a "cradle to grave" strategy for managing toxic wastes. These efforts should substantially lower the risks associated with the disposal of these wastes, but there is disagreement about the degree of safety that different methods provide. Although current regulations can help ensure safe disposal, these regulations do not address the thousands of problems connected with waste generation. Current environmental regulations address five methods of waste management: reclamation, treatment, incineration, storage and disposal. Even though we now have more protection than ever against the release of toxic wastes into our environment, concerned citizens are protesting the location of waste treatment and disposal sites in their communities. As a consequence, fewer new facilities and expansions of existing facilities are permitted.

The wanderings of a garbage barge named Mobro during the spring and summer of 1987 focused national attention on the NIMBY ("not in my backyard") attitude toward disposal of wastes and the garbage crisis in the United States. The Mobro started in Islip, New York, with over 3,000 tons of commercial trash that was banned from a local landfill reserved for residential refuse. After five months of cruising the Atlantic and Gulf coasts looking unsuccessfully for someone (and someplace) to take the garbage, the Mobro returned to New York where its ripe cargo was finally burned in an incinerator in Brooklyn.

Following basic waste prevention principles can help to reduce wastes and help alleviate disposal problems:

- Buy only products that are really needed
- Purchase products that use minimal packaging that is returnable, reusable or refillable
- Buy products that last longer
- Reuse as many items as possible
- Recycle and compost as much waste as possible

These strategies will help to reduce waste production, make our resources last longer and decrease overall pollution (Figure 2.3 lists some other strategies that have the added benefit of saving money). Even if each of us follows waste prevention strategies, however, toxic wastes will continue to be produced, and these wastes must be properly managed.

FIGURE 2.3.   Household Tips

Reducing Chemical Use and Exposure

- Use less hazardous cleaning products (see Figure 2.8).
- Use pesticides only when absolutely necessary and in the smallest amounts possible (see Chapter 11).
- Don't store gasoline, solvents, pesticides or other hazardous chemicals in the home.
- Use organic methods or integrated pest management to care for your lawn and grow produce (see Chapter 11).
- Buy machine or hand washable clothes; dry clean less frequently.
- Dispose of excess chemicals at a hazardous waste recycling center or hazardous chemical collection day.

Recycle

- Recycle all batteries and use rechargeable batteries if possible.
- Take used car batteries, motor oil, transmission oil and brake fluid to a local auto service center or to a hazardous-waste collection center for recycling.
- Recycle aluminum cans, steel cans, glass, plastics, paper and other materials.
- Give away used clothes or sell them to consignment shops.

Conserve Energy

- Insulate the house, caulk and weatherstrip windows and doors to reduce air infiltration and heat loss and replace drafty windows with energy-efficient ones.
- Buy energy-efficient lights, appliances and cars.

FIGURE 2.3. (*continued*)

- Insulate hot water pipes and the hot water heater; turn down the thermostat on water heaters to 110°F to 120°F.
- During warmer months, use floor and ceiling fans, whole house fans and attic fans to lower air-conditioning needs; each degree increase in the thermostat setting can decrease a cooling bill by 3 to 5 percent.
- During cooler months, dress more warmly and use ceiling fans to distribute heat throughout the house in order to lower heating needs.
- Turn off lights and appliances when they are not in use.
- Consider using active and passive solar heating.
- Design new houses to be energy efficient and take advantage of any features of the lot that can reduce energy needs.

Conserve Water

- No matter where you live, plant trees, shrubs and flowers that are native to the area because these species are hardier and require less water and chemicals for growth. Water in the early morning or evening.
- Install water-saving shower heads and faucet flow restrictors; install water-saving toilets or buy and insert a toilet dam into existing toilets.
- Don't let the water run while brushing teeth, washing or shaving. Don't let the water run when washing dishes by hand.
- Try to wash only full loads of clothes in the washing machine; use the short cycle when possible.
- Try to wash only full loads of dishes in the automatic dishwasher; use the energy-saving cycle.
- Check toilets, faucets and water pipes frequently for leaks and repair them.

Reduce Junk Mail

- You can reduce the amount of junk mail that you get by writing to individual vendors or to Mail Preference Service, P.O. Box 9008, Farmingdale, NY 11735. Let them know that you do not want your name to be sold to large mailing-list companies.

Dump Sites. In the past, wastes were simply dumped on the ground with no regard for potential contamination of the water, air or land. These sites continue to pose serious health and environmental hazards. In some places, entire communities are built on abandoned landfills or dump sites.

In 1980, Congress passed the Superfund law (officially known as the Comprehensive Environmental Response, Compensation and Liability Act) in response to the growing public concern about those contaminated areas. The main purpose of the Superfund is to identify and clean up the most seriously contaminated sites across the nation except for sites involving petroleum, gasoline or radioactive wastes.

The EPA has identified more than 30,000 sites across the United States that are contaminated by chemicals and in need of cleaning. More than 1,270 of the most seriously contaminated sites are on the National Priority List, and approximately 100 sites are added to the list each year (with many more, undoubtedly, still undiscovered). The approximate locations of the National Priority List sites can be seen in Figure 2.4. The process of qualifying a site for Superfund designation and then actually cleaning it up can take many years and millions of dollars. For example, it takes an average of over five years of campaigning and scientific study to have a site placed on the National Priority List, followed by another eleven years (on average) to clean up the site. Some sites that are too contaminated to be cleaned are simply stabilized and covered with dirt, concrete or other material.

FIGURE 2.4.   National Priority List of Hazardous Waste Sites

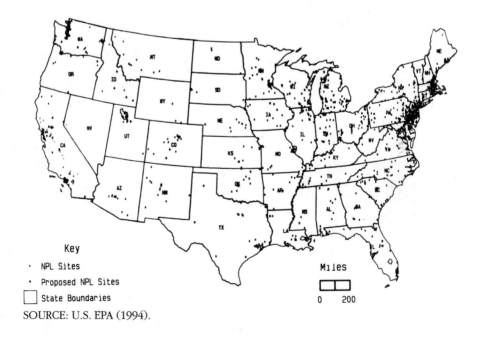

Key

· NPL Sites

· Proposed NPL Sites

☐ State Boundaries

SOURCE: U.S. EPA (1994).

Surface Impoundments. A surface impoundment is simply a hole in the ground that holds liquid or semisolid wastes. Surface impoundments are also known as pits, holding ponds and lagoons. Since a filled impoundment does not have a cover, the wastes it contains can evaporate into the air we breathe. Surface impoundments (especially those used for animal wastes) can produce very offensive odors that can be overwhelming and even toxic. The contained materials can also seep into the ground and contaminate soil and water supplies.

Under newer regulations, however, a surface impoundment must have a bottom liner, a leachate collection system (a system of pipes that collects the chemicals migrating through the impoundment and moves them to a treatment facility) and monitoring wells around the impoundment to monitor the ground-water. About 40 percent of industrial hazardous wastes are treated using surface impoundments.

Incinerators. Incinerators burn and destroy toxic wastes at high temperatures (1600°F or above). Incinerators can burn a variety of materials including medical wastes and animals, as well as toxic chemicals such as polychlorinated biphenyls (PCBs), waste oil, solvents, pesticides and radioactive wastes. Incinerators that burn municipal wastes and industrial toxic wastes can release acid gases, metals and chemicals such as dioxins if the incinerator is not designed and operating properly. Municipal and industrial incinerators are generally watched more carefully by the regulatory agencies than smaller incinerators at hospitals, animal shelters and other facilities. Over the years, contaminants released by any incinerator can build up in neighborhoods in the paths of the emissions. Another problem is the disposal of leftover residues (ash) that might contain toxic metals and other compounds. Incineration is used to manage less than 1 percent of industrial hazardous wastes and 16 percent of municipal solid waste.

Storage. Stored wastes are placed in tanks, drums or piles on the ground. (A surface impoundment is also a type of storage facility.) Storage is a concern because containers (and impoundments) can leak and spill their toxic contents onto the ground, thus allowing them to evaporate into the air or sink into the ground and contaminate groundwater. Precipitation can seep through piles of coal, waste rock produced by mining, and other materials, and wash toxic chemicals into water resources and the ground. Also, tanks and drums that are used for storage without special protection during the summer could rupture if they contain organic chemicals that evaporate easily. Ruptures occur when the tank or drum cannot contain the build up of internal pressure caused by the evaporation of a chemical in the container. Accidents are always a possibility.

Municipal Solid Waste Landfills. Today, about 80 percent of the wastes generated in our communities go to municipal solid waste landfills (formerly called sanitary landfills). The EPA estimates that there are about 6,000 municipal waste landfills across the country. A municipal solid waste landfill is not a dump but a regulated facility that provides a final resting place for the wastes we produce in our communities. A municipal solid waste landfill that is properly located, designed and mangaged should be relatively free of the litter, odors, rodents and water contamination problems usually associated with open dumps.

In 1991, the EPA passed new regulations designed to prevent the environmental contamination problems of the past. Known as the Municipal Solid Waste Landfill Criteria, some of these requirements do not become effective until 1996, and small landfills that process less than 20 tons of waste per day are exempted. In a modern municipal solid waste landfill, the refuse is spread in thin layers and compacted by bulldozers on top of a base material of thick clay and a synthetic liner. At the end of each day, the newly deposited layer of refuse must be covered with six inches of earthen material to reduce problems with litter, rodents and insects. When the landfill is full, a final cover of earthen material two feet deep is placed over the entire area. This land can then be graded and developed into a park, nature area, golf course, baseball field or other recreational area.

Unfortunately, there are many land disposal sites that do not meet modern safety practices. In the mid-1970s, the EPA estimated that 94 percent of 17,000 land disposal sites surveyed did not meet the minimum landfill requirements. Fortunately, most of these sites are no longer used. Even a properly constructed and well-managed landfill can, however, adversely affect surrounding properties. During the landfill's hours of operation, traffic noise, blowing dirt, litter and odors can be troublesome nuisances. Two additional important concerns are the contamination of water and the migration of landfill gases into homes and other buildings.

Water contamination occurs when leachate seeping out of the landfill is contaminated with toxic chemicals. Leachate forms when rainwater moving through the landfill (or any buried material) dissolves chemicals in the waste material. As the leachate carries the chemicals through the landfill and into the surrounding ground, groundwater may become contaminated. Surface water can become contaminated as rainwater carries chemicals on the surface of the landfill to lakes or streams. The synthetic liner and thick clay base material required in the new regulations are intended to prevent leachate from leaving the landfill. However, most landfills do not have liners because their installation was not required until the late 1980s.

As municipal landfills (and dumps) age, bacteria in the soil decompose the organic materials. The decomposition produces gases, including methane, hydrogen sulfide and carbon dioxide, that move through the landfill. The methane and hydrogen sulfide gases are especially dangerous because they can build up in homes to levels that cause an explosion if a spark is present, or lead to asphyxiation. Another problem is that these gases (especially carbon dioxide) can kill shrubs and grasses by smothering their roots. The gas collection system requirements of the new regulations are meant to reduce these problems.

Hazardous Waste Landfills. Hazardous waste landfills are similar to sanitary landfills but, in theory, they provide greater protection against potential leaks and migration of leachate from the landfill site. Regulations passed in 1984 require generators of hazardous waste to treat the waste to make it less toxic before it can be landfilled. Unfortunately, the practice in older landfills was to simply dump the wastes and cover them. These toxic agents (both liquid and gaseous) could easily seep into the ground and eventually contaminate water supply sources.

Deep Wells and Landfarms. Deep wells are just what the name sounds like—deep holes in the ground that contain wastes. Most deep wells are located in Texas and Louisiana and are former oil exploration wells. A little more than 10 percent of all hazardous wastes are disposed of in deep wells. Wastes are first diluted and then placed into deep wells below underground sources of drinking water.

Some wastes (mostly petroleum refinery wastes) can be mixed into the soil in a process called landfarming. Oxygen, microorganisms and nutrients are added to the soil and waste mixture to help break the chemicals down into nontoxic products

What Can Be Done about Nearby Hazards?

The best protections against nearby hazards are awareness of their presence before purchasing a property, and alertness to proposed changes in zoning that might allow hazards to develop once you occupy the property. Spend time driving around both in the immediate neighborhood and in the area within a one mile radius of the property under consideration, and be sure to evaluate the areas where children go to school and play.

Ask questions about potential hazards. Sources of information include the local or state health department, planning agency and pollution control agency. Local agencies are generally more responsive to inquiries and more knowledgeable about their areas than the state agencies. Talk to the real estate agent, the neighbors and the developer (if you're looking at a new property). Another useful source of information is a local newspaper. After you've gathered the answers to your questions, rank the hazards according to the risks they pose to you. Then you can make an informed decision about whether or not to purchase the property.

If you discover a hazard that affects a property you already own, contact the local agency responsible for that problem. Discuss your concerns with the agency's representatives and ask for corrective action. The hazard may be easily remedied, or you may discover that aggressive community action or the assistance of an attorney are needed to accomplish your goals.

Indoor Air Quality Hazards
What Causes Indoor Air Quality Hazards?

Indoor air quality is not a new issue, but until recently, the problems most people faced were limited to combustion products from cooking and heating, and exposure to molds in damp areas of the house.

World War II marked a shift in the types of indoor air quality problems found in residences. After the war, new technologies developed building materials that could be mass-produced cheaply and easily. Synthetic materials such as plastics, new fibers and pressed-wood products replaced traditional materials such as masonry, natural fibers and wood. Personal care products, pesticides and household cleaners entered the market, often as aerosol sprays. More complex cleaning chemicals replaced simpler (and often less toxic) cleaners such as baking soda, vinegar, soap, and lye solutions.

The energy crisis of 1974 and the need to conserve energy led to dramatic changes in the heating and cooling of buildings. The result is that the drafty, uninsulated home or office of the early 1900s has been replaced by a well-insulated and tightly sealed modern structure.

Like people, houses need to breathe in order to stay healthy. The movement of air into and out of buildings is called air exchange, and it occurs under three conditions: when doors and windows are opened, when air passes through cracks and other openings, and when fans are used (see Figure 2.5).

Inadequate air exchange may result in several potentially serious problems. For example, combustion gases produced by a fireplace, wood stove or

FIGURE 2.5.   Air Movement in a House

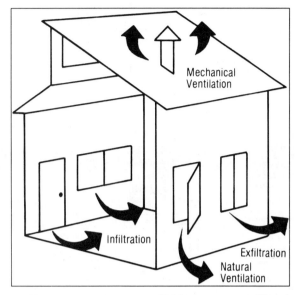

SOURCE: Sandia National Laboratories. 1982. Indoor Air Quality Handbook for Designers, Builders, and Users of Energy Efficient Residences, SAND 82-1773. Albuquerque, NM: Sandia National Laboratories.

other combustion source can reenter a house if there is not enough air in the building. Contaminants can also build up in a tightly insulated house because there are fewer places where fresh outdoor air can enter and replace contaminated indoor air. Moisture can accumulate to levels that favor mold growth and damage the structure. Solutions to these problems include increasing the house's ventilation, reducing sources of moisture and correcting problems with combustion sources.

Indoor air quality depends on many other indoor and outdoor factors that are influenced by our activities. Pollution from factories and cars can drift indoors and increase the levels of sulfur dioxide, ozone, toxic organic chemicals and metals. Some contaminants will settle into the ground, streams or lakes. Once in the ground, contaminants can dissolve in rainwater and move into the groundwater; at this point, chemicals can pollute wells and our drinking water. Contaminants that settle on the ground can enter houses when the wind blows dust indoors or when shoes track dirt indoors.

There are many sources of potential contamination indoors (see Figure 2.6). Cigarette smoke contains many cancer-causing chemicals and is a major source

FIGURE 2.6. Sources of Indoor Air Contaminants

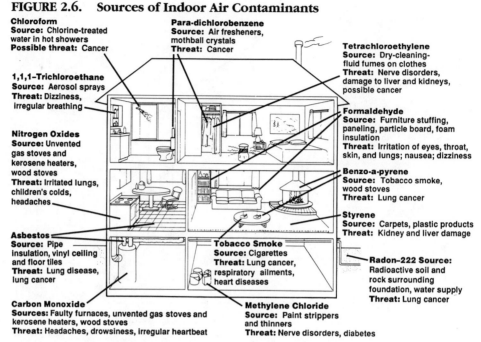

Chloroform
Source: Chlorine-treated water in hot showers
Possible threat: Cancer

1,1,1–Trichloroethane
Source: Aerosol sprays
Threat: Dizziness, irregular breathing

Nitrogen Oxides
Source: Unvented gas stoves and kerosene heaters, wood stoves
Threat: Irritated lungs, children's colds, headaches

Asbestos
Source: Pipe insulation, vinyl ceiling and floor tiles
Threat: Lung disease, lung cancer

Carbon Monoxide
Sources: Faulty furnaces, unvented gas stoves and kerosene heaters, wood stoves
Threat: Headaches, drowsiness, irregular heartbeat

Para-dichlorobenzene
Source: Air fresheners, mothball crystals
Threat: Cancer

Tobacco Smoke
Source: Cigarettes
Threat: Lung cancer, respiratory ailments, heart diseases

Methylene Chloride
Source: Paint strippers and thinners
Threat: Nerve disorders, diabetes

Tetrachloroethylene
Source: Dry-cleaning-fluid fumes on clothes
Threat: Nerve disorders, damage to liver and kidneys, possible cancer

Formaldehyde
Source: Furniture stuffing, paneling, particle board, foam insulation
Threat: Irritation of eyes, throat, skin, and lungs; nausea; dizziness

Benzo-a-pyrene
Source: Tobacco smoke, wood stoves
Threat: Lung cancer

Styrene
Source: Carpets, plastic products
Threat: Kidney and liver damage

Radon–222 Source: Radioactive soil and rock surrounding foundation, water supply
Threat: Lung cancer

SOURCE: G. Tyler Miller Jr. 1994. *Living in the Environment.* 8th edition. ©Wadsworth Publishing Co; Belmont, CA. Used with permission.

of indoor air contaminants. Consumer products such as cleaners and waxes, paints, pesticides, air fresheners and moth repellents release hundreds of chemicals indoors. Personal care products, dry-cleaned fabrics and other furnishings are additional sources. Spray products, especially aerosol cans, are of special concern because the spray is composed of tiny droplets of chemicals that can remain in the air for long periods of time. When breathed, these droplets can go deep into the respiratory tract and cause damage to the breathing tubes and lungs. If you must use a spray, choose a pump sprayer that creates larger-sized particles and be sure that it is used in an area with good ventilation.

The building materials also release many contaminants into houses. Pressed-wood products, vinyl flooring, insulation and carpeting are potential sources of contaminants in new or recently remodeled houses. Glues and adhesives, sealants, plastics and electrical equipment also add chemicals to the indoor air. Wet or moist materials pose additional problems by fostering the growth of mold and other organisms that can cause structural damage or decrease the quality of indoor air. Wood stoves, fireplaces, kerosene heaters, gas cooking stoves and automobile exhaust from attached garages also release contaminants indoors.

Even the weather and climate can influence indoor air quality. For example, wet weather favors the build up of molds and the decay of wood, while hot weather can increase the release of formaldehyde indoors.

Why Should We Be Concerned about Indoor Air Quality?

Because most people spend over 90 percent of their time indoors, indoor air quality is probably more important than the quality of the outside air in determining an individual's overall exposure to air contaminants. Studies conducted by the EPA and other agencies indicate that indoor concentrations of some contaminants are often several times higher than their outdoor concentrations.

Toxic substances can affect our bodies in different ways as shown in Figure 2.7. Some contaminants cause small changes in the body's chemistry that are not significant enough to produce symptoms. Other problems, such as accidental exposure to carbon monoxide from a faulty furnace or improperly used pesticides, can result in serious health problems or death.

Some effects of exposure to contaminates are not life-threatening. They occur almost immediately, but then go away soon after the exposure ends. For example, volatile chemicals released from building materials can cause headaches that get better when one leaves the building. Some indoor air contaminants can temporarily irritate the eyes and upper respiratory tract. Another example of a temporary effect is the discomfort experienced when temperature, humidity, air flow or light levels are not at comfortable levels.

Exposure to a large amount of a toxic substance over a short period of time can result in acute effects that may be life-threatening. For some chemicals, a large dose is actually defined as a small amount of material. For example, ingesting a single taste of some insecticides is enough to kill a grown person because the chemicals are very toxic.

Exposure to low levels of contaminants over a long period can produce long-lasting, chronic effects. For example, a person who works with solvents for refinishing furniture for many months or years could develop liver disease or damage to the nervous system or other parts of his or her body.

Obviously, the severity of the effects experienced vary according to the toxic properties of the contaminant and the length of a person's exposure to that substance. Typically, more serious effects occur when the contaminant is more hazardous and the person's exposure to it is of a longer duration.

Sick Building Syndrome. Sick building syndrome (also called tight or closed building syndrome) describes an illness that afflicts people who work in a building with air quality poor enough to produce health complaints among 20 percent of its occupants. People usually report symptoms such as eye, nose and

FIGURE 2.7.   Body Parts Affected by Toxic Substances

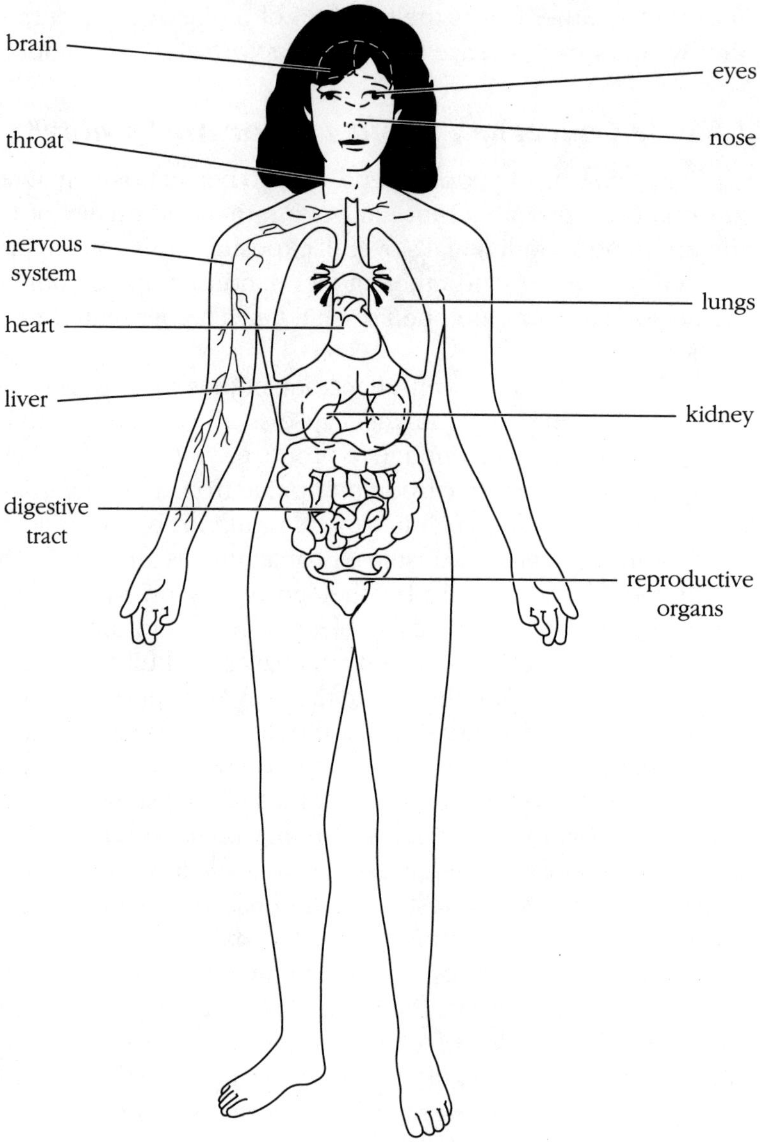

brain

eyes

throat

nose

nervous system

heart

lungs

liver

digestive tract

kidney

reproductive organs

throat irritation, dry skin and mucus membranes, tiredness, headaches and runny noses. Some people may have asthma-like symptoms. Although sick building syndrome probably does not cause death or life-threatening disease, it does cause discomfort, irritation and reduced work efficiency. One characteristic of sick building syndrome is that it is usually difficult for investigators to find a single, specific cause of the problem. However, complaints often decrease when ventilation and temperature problems are corrected.

Multiple Chemical Sensitivity. A relatively new and controversial area of concern is multiple chemical sensitivity, a condition that affects people who may be especially sensitive to chemicals that are common in today's homes and offices. People with multiple chemical sensitivity are sensitive to more than one chemical, and their reactions usually result from small exposures. Common symptoms are joint and muscle aches and pains, frequent respiratory infections, food intolerance, memory loss and a general feeling of not being well.

Multiple chemical sensitivity is difficult to diagnose because of the nature of the complaints and the lack of screening tests. But though there is still some disagreement among doctors and scientists about whether multiple chemical sensitivity is a real condition, the EPA has recognized it as one effect of exposure to chemicals.

How Can We Reduce Exposure to Indoor Contaminants?

A number of common sense approaches will help to reduce exposure to indoor contaminants in your home. Whenever you build or renovate a home, select materials and furnishings that are not likely to cause problems (see Chapters 6 and 7). Make sure that the heating and cooling systems are adequate, and include enough ventilation in the bathroom and kitchen. For your future home, try to select a location that has good air and water quality and when this is not possible, work with local health and environmental agencies to improve conditions.

After you identify hazards, you should realize that some are more serious than others. Rank these hazards according to the risks each entails and the potential cost of correcting each problem. Tackle first those problems at the top of your ranked list. For example, if your house has deteriorating asbestos insulation and asbestos floor tiles in good condition, the insulation should be taken care of first because it obviously poses the largest risk.

As you notice interior environmental problems, you are likely to find that simple measures will lower your general exposure to indoor air contaminants. Switching to less hazardous products and safely using all products and appliances can be easy solutions. Read labels to know what types of ingredients are in the product, and follow directions carefully. Figure 2.8 lists some

FIGURE 2.8.   Alternatives to Hazardous Household Products

Common Household Product	Less Hazardous Alternative
General purpose cleaner and disinfectant	• Dissolve 1/2 to 1 cup of borax in 1 gallon of hot water.
Heavy duty cleaner (for walls, floors and other surfaces)	• Mix 4 tablespoons of trisodium phosphate (TSP) with 1 gallon of hot water (wear rubber gloves). TSP is available at hardware stores and is effective on dirt, grease and some other stains. Be sure to test painted surfaces before applying TSP to them.
Window cleaner	• Combine 1 tablespoon of white vinegar and 1 quart of warm water (some recipes call for 2 to 5 tablespoons of vinegar in 1 quart of warm water). Put the solution into a pump sprayer and wipe treated surface with a clean, absorbent cloth.
Tub and tile cleaner	• Mix together equal parts of warm water and vinegar. Apply to soap film and spots, rinse and wipe dry. • Combine either baking soda or borax with water to form a paste, and add a squeeze of lemon juice. Apply to the surface, rinse and wipe dry.
Drain cleaner	• To prevent clogs, install a drain sieve or hair trap. • To open clogs, use a plunger or metal snake. • To open clogs, pour 1/4 cup of baking soda followed by 1/2 cup vinegar down the drain. Let the mixture sit until fizzing stops, then flush with boiling water.
Mildew remover	• Combine 1/2 cup of vinegar, 1/2 cup of borax and 1 cup of warm water.

FIGURE 2.8.   (*continued*)

Common Household Product	Less Hazardous Alternative
Wood funiture polish and wood floor cleaner	• For furniture, mix 1/2 cup of lemon juice with 1 cup of vegetable or olive oil. Apply with a clean, absorbent cloth and wipe with a second cloth to remove excess. • For wood floors, mix three parts of olive oil with one part of vinegar (or lemon juice). • For wood floors, mix one teaspoon of lemon juice with one pint of mineral or vegetable oil.
Carpet cleaning	• Spot clean with a solution of 1/2 cup of borax and one quart of water. • If commercial cleaning is needed, use water-based steam cleaning whenever possible.
Silver polish	• Clean with a paste of baking soda and warm water. Rinse object well with warm water and dry thoroughly. • Add one tablespoon of baking soda and one tablespoon of salt to boiling water. Drop silver pieces into the water and boil them for three minutes, then remove and polish them with a soft cloth.
Laundry aids	• Instead of fabric softener, try adding 1/4 cup of baking soda to the final rinse. • Try using borax instead of liquid bleach.
Air freshener	• To remove odors, place an opened box of baking soda (several will be needed for a larger space) in a refrigerator or closet. • Sprinkle baking soda or borax in the bottom of garbage pails. • Use pine boughs or sachets of herbs and flowers to scent the air.

frequently used household cleaners and less-hazardous alternatives to these substances. (Chapters 6 and 7 describes how to identify and reduce exposure to chemicals related to building and consumer products and Chapter 11 contains suggestions for reducing exposures to pesticides.) Try to avoid using any chemical product that is applied in spray form (especially aerosol sprays) and products that release chemicals into the air in other ways. Finally, always use chemical products with adequate ventilation!

PART

TWO

Contaminants Related to House Design and Construction Materials

Summary Chart for Radon

Topic	Comments
Description	Radon is a tasteless, odorless and colorless radioactive gas.
Health Effects	Radon causes lung cancer. It is the leading cause of lung cancer death for non-smokers and the second leading cause of lung cancer death for smokers.
Sources	The two most significant sources of radon in most homes are the soil and the bedrock beneath the soil. Water from wells can also be an important source in some areas. Minor sources of radon are some building materials and natural gas.
Testing	Consumers can test for radon themselves or hire consultants to test for radon in the air, soil or water. Short-term and long-term test kits are available from hardware stores, pharmacies and other retail outlets. The EPA has established a guideline level of 4 pCi/L for indoor levels of radon.
Reducing Exposure	Radon reduction methods for homes include increasing the ventilation, sealing cracks and installing radon removal systems. Radon reduction methods for water include aging the water, increasing the amount of air in the water and passing the water over charcoal filters. The efficiency and cost of these systems vary widely.

CHAPTER
THREE

Radon

Dr. Charles Warner, age 35, died in 1993 of small cell carcinoma of the lung, a rare cancer among young adults. Dr. Warner did not smoke. He was not exposed to tobacco smoke at home or work. Mrs. Warner and her husband's cancer specialist believe that radon may be the cause of Charles Warner's cancer and death. As a child, Dr. Warner lived in the same house for over 18 years. His favorite play area was the basement, and his bedroom was above an open well pit. In 1988, his parents measured radon levels over 350 pCi/L in the home.

As reported in *Radon News Digest*, 1993, Vol. 7, No. 3.

What Is Radon and Why Is It a Hazard?

Radon is a colorless, tasteless and odorless gas that results from the natural breakdown (radioactive decay) of uranium and radium in soil, water and rock. The EPA estimates that nearly 1 out of every 15 homes in the United States has radon levels in excess of EPA guidelines, and high radon levels occur in every state (see Figure 3.1).

Breathing radon does not cause headaches, nausea, irritation of the eyes or respiratory tract, asthma or other immediate symptoms. The Surgeon

FIGURE 3.1.   Map of Radon Zones in the United States

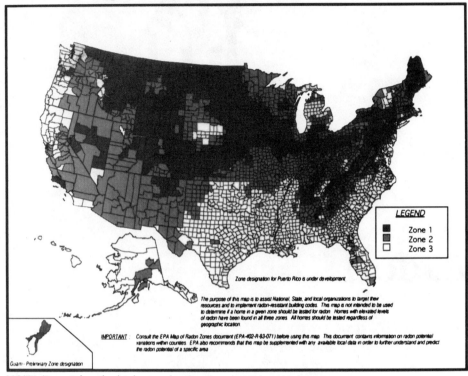

NOTE: Zone 1 has the highest radon levels; zone 3 has the lowest.
SOURCE: U.S. EPA (1994).

General of the United States and the EPA warn that radon is the leading cause of lung cancer deaths in nonsmokers and the second leading cause of lung cancer deaths in smokers. *The risk of lung cancer is especially high for a person who smokes and lives in a home with high radon levels.* The EPA believes that an average of 14,000 lung cancer deaths each year are due to radon, but the number could be as low as 7,000 or as high as 30,000 deaths. According to the 1990 National Safety Council reports, the number of deaths attributed to radon is greater than the number of deaths due to drowning, fires and airline crashes combined.

The EPA believes that although any exposure to radon entails some risk of lung cancer, not everyone who is exposed to radon will get lung cancer. It typically takes many years for cancer to develop after an individual is exposed to a cancer-causing substance. Risk factors vary from person to person. As radon decays, it releases small bursts of energy that can change the genetic structure of the cells. Years later, a tumor can develop in the lungs. Higher radon levels, longer exposures and smoking increase the odds of getting lung cancer. If you currently smoke and are exposed to radon, your risk of getting lung cancer is 20 times greater than the risk for a person who has never smoked and is also exposed to radon. If you are a former smoker exposed to radon, your risk is lower, but it is still eight times greater than the risk for a person who has never smoked.

Figure 3.2 illustrates how the risk of radon-related cancer increases with radon concentration over a *lifetime* of exposure. This table shows what the risk is for a person who spends 18 hours each day exposed to the same radon level for a total of 74 years. The risk for people who live in different houses varies depending on the exposures in each home. Additional exposures at work also have an effect. Small children are especially sensitive to radon and other contaminants because their cells are growing rapidly and their immune systems are not fully developed. Their risk levels may be somewhat greater than those shown in the figure.

Sources

Radon in Air and Water

Radon is released into the environment either from natural sources in the ground or water, or by industrial facilities. Uranium mining in Wyoming and Texas, nuclear weapons production in Colorado and Washington, and phosphate rock mining in Florida contribute to high radon levels in those areas. In most states, however, the soil and geological formations (such as those in the Reading Prong area of Pennsylvania) are the main sources of radon. Some types of building materials (gypsum and concrete) and natural gas can release radon, but these are minor sources of the gas.

Private wells or small community wells supplied by groundwater can be significant sources of radon. Radon gas from the soil or bedrock can dissolve in the water as it seeps through the ground and into wells. Water from a large community well usually has low radon levels because most of the radon will decay before the water reaches individual houses. Surface water supplies from lakes or streams generally have low radon levels.

Water's contribution to indoor radon levels depends on the amount of radon in the water, the temperature of the water and how much water is used. Taking a shower, washing clothes and using a dishwasher are activities that release the most radon from water. Swallowing water with high radon levels could increase the chances of getting cancer, but this risk is believed to be much lower than the risk from breathing air that contains radon.

FIGURE 3.2.   Radon Risks for Smokers and Nonsmokers over a Lifetime of Exposure

Radon Risks If You Smoke			
Radon Level	If 1,000 people who smoked were exposed to this level over a lifetime...	The chance that you'll get cancer from radon exposure is...	WHAT TO DO: Stop smoking and...
20 pCi/L	...about 135 of them could get lung cancer.	...100 times your chance of drowning.	...reduce radon levels in your home.
10 pCi/L	...about 71 of them could get lung cancer.	...100 times your chance of dying in a home fire.	...reduce radon levels in your home.
8 pCi/L	...about 57 of them could get lung cancer.		...reduce radon levels in your home.
4 pCi/L	...about 29 of them could get lung cancer.	...100 times your chance of dying in an airplane crash.	...reduce radon levels in your home.
2 pCi/L	...about 15 of them could get lung cancer.	...2 times your chance of dying in a car crash.	Consider reducing radon levels in your home for measurements between 2 and 4 pCi/L. (Reducing radon levels below 2 pCi/L is difficult.)
1.3 pCi/L	...about 9 of them could get lung cancer.	(average indoor radon level)	
0.4 pCi/L	...about 3 of them could get lung cancer.	(average outdoor radon level)	

NOTE: If you are a former smoker, your risk may be lower. All risks are calculated for a person who spends 18 hours per day for 74 years at the given radon level.
SOURCE: Adapted from U.S. EPA (1992b).

FIGURE 3.2. *(continued)*

Radon Risks If You've Never Smoked			
Radon Level	**If 1,000 people who never smoked were exposed to this level over a lifetime...**	**The chance that you'll get cancer from radon exposure is...**	**WHAT TO DO:**
20 pCi/L	...about 8 of them could get lung cancer.	...the same as your chance of being killed in a violent crime.	...reduce radon levels in your home.
10 pCi/L	...about 4 of them could get lung cancer.		...reduce radon levels in your home.
8 pCi/L	...about 3 of them could get lung cancer.	...10 times your chance of dying in an airplane crash.	...reduce radon levels in your home.
4 pCi/L	...about 2 of them could get lung cancer.	...the same as your chance of drowning.	...reduce radon levels in your home.
			Consider reducing radon levels in your home for measurements between 2 and 4 pCi/L.
2 pCi/L	...about 1 of them could get lung cancer.	...the same as your chance of dying in a home fire.	(Reducing radon levels below 2 pCi/L is difficult.)
1.3 pCi/L	Less than 1 of them could get lung cancer.	(average indoor radon level)	
0.4 pCi/L	Less than 1 of them could get lung cancer.	(average outdoor radon level)	

How Does Radon Get into Homes?

Since radon is a gas, it will move in any unobstructed direction; this explains why it moves more easily through porous soils (such as sandy and gravelly soils) than through tight, clay soils. As radon is released from the ground, it moves into buildings because the air pressure inside a building is lower than the pressure in the soil around the building's foundation. This pressure differential causes the house to act like a vacuum cleaner that draws radon gas into the building through any openings in the foundation.

Some common places where radon enters a home include the following:

- Cracks in basement walls and floors
- Crawl spaces that are open to the basement
- Open sump pumps and drains
- Gaps around service pipes
- Openings where walls and floors join together
- Cracks in floors
- Cavities inside walls

Figures 3.3 to 3.5 show specific places in basement, slab and crawl space foundations that allow radon to enter. Since some of these entry points are not visible, the only way to know if radon is a problem is to test the indoor air. All homes should be tested—new homes, old homes, homes with or without basements, drafty homes, well-sealed homes and even homes with radon-resistant features.

Testing and Understanding the Results

Testing

Testing for radon is easy and affordable. Consumers can purchase low-cost test kits from hardware stores, drug stores and other retail outlets. Costs range from $15 to $100 for one test, depending on whether the homeowner or a consultant places the test kit.

The indoor air should be tested at least once in your home. Consider testing the water for radon if the air levels are high *and* the water source is a private or small community well. Measuring radon in soil is not recommended because interpreting the results is difficult.

When purchasing a test kit look for the phrase "Meets EPA Requirements" or "EPA Listed." This means that the testing device has passed the EPA's proficiency testing program. This provides an assurance (but not a 100 percent guarantee) that the test results will be correct.

If you hire a radon-testing professional, make sure that he or she is an EPA-listed or state-certified radon tester. (Your state radon office [see Appendix

FIGURE 3.3.   Places Where Radon Gas Can Enter Houses with Basements

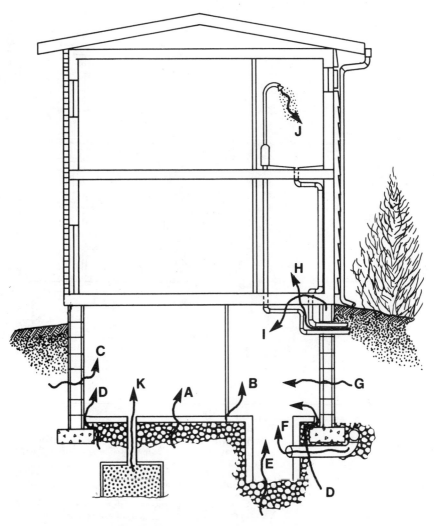

A. Cracks in concrete slabs
B. Cold joint between two concrete pours
C. Pores and cracks in concrete blocks
D. Floor-to-wall crack or French drain
E. Exposed soil, as in a sump
F. Weeping (drain) tile, if drained to open sump
G. Mortar joints
H. Loose fitting pipe penetrations
I. Open tops of block walls
J. Water (from some wells)
K. Untrapped floor drain to a dry well or septic system

SOURCE: U.S. EPA (1988).

FIGURE 3.4.   Places Where Radon Gas Can Enter Houses with Crawl Space Foundations

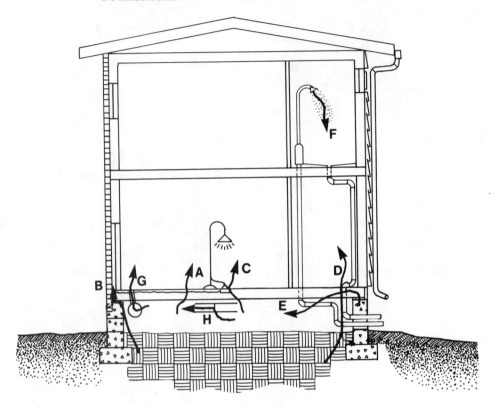

A. Cracks in subflooring and flooring
B. Spaces behind stud walls and brick veneer walls that rest on uncapped hollow-block foundation
C. Electrical penetrations
D. Loose-fitting pipe penetrations
E. Open tops of block walls
F. Water (from some wells)
G. Heating duct register penetrations
H. Cold-air return ducts in crawl space

SOURCE: U.S. EPA (1988).

FIGURE 3.5.   Places Where Radon Gas Can Enter Houses with Slab-on-grade Foundations

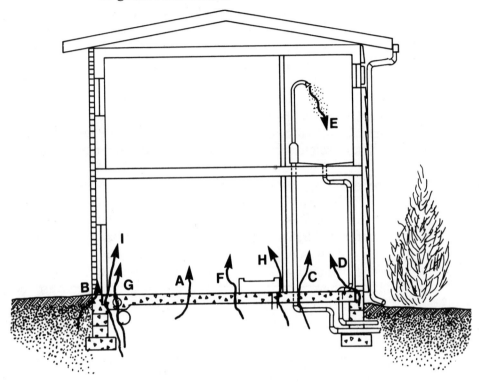

A. Cracks in concrete slabs[1]
B. Spaces behind brick veneer walls
that rest on uncapped hollow-block foundation
C. Loose fitting pipe penetrations
D. Open tops of block walls
E. Water (from some wells)
F. Cold joint between two concrete pours
G. Heating duct registers or sub-slab
cold-air return pipes
H. Hole under bathtub and under commode ring
I. Wall/floor joint

[1]Hairline cracks probably do not contribute

SOURCE: U.S. EPA (1988).

A for a list of federal and state agencies] will have a list of certified testers.) Ask to see the consultant's proof of certification (usually a letter or identification card). This professional should have the skills and knowledge to evaluate your home, and should recommend the best testing method for your home. The radon tester will give you a report with the measurement results, and this person should have the knowledge to analyze and interpret the results.

Do not hire a testing firm that also sells radon reduction services. Be aware that a single firm can also own subsidiary testing and mitigation companies under different names. The state agency responsible for certification may know which companies have the same owners. Ask potential testers for a list of references, and then call those references. Contact the local Better Business Bureau or Chamber of Commerce and ask if any complaints have been filed against the testing firm.

The EPA recommends first conducting a short-term test of the indoor air to get a quick estimate of the radon level, and then doing follow-up testing to confirm the initial results. If you live in an area that has elevated radon levels, this testing strategy will allow you to reduce your exposure to radon more quickly than if you started with a long-term test.

Long-term tests give the best picture of risk because the levels of radon gas in a home can vary significantly depending on the time of day, weather conditions, season, sampling location and amount of air moving into and out of the house. Conducting the test during a week of almost constant rain will result in lower levels because the movement of radon is slowed by the soggy soil. Testing during the summer typically gives lower results than testing during the winter because homes are open more during the warm months, thus making radon buildup indoors less likely than in cold months when doors and windows are usually kept closed. Another important factor that affects short-term or long-term results is the location of the sampler. If it is placed near an obvious radon source (such as a sump), higher levels will be recorded. If the sampler sits next to a frequently used door that opens to the outside, lower radon levels will probably be registered.

Guidelines for Short-term Testing. Short-term testing devices remain in the home for two days to three months. Commonly used samplers are electrets, charcoal canisters and alpha-track detectors (see Figure 3.6). These samplers can give reliable results, but they are not foolproof. Do not rely on any test result that is based on sampling periods less than 48 hours. Increasing the duration of the testing period leads to an increase in the reliability of the results.

Sequential and duplicate testing can also increase the reliability of the results. Sequential testing means following one test by another. Duplicate test-

FIGURE 3.6.   Common Radon Detectors

Used by permission of Landauer, Inc., Radon Detection Products, 2 Science Road, Glenwood, IL 60425-1586.

ing means placing identical testing devices close to one another in the same location. If the test results of sequential or duplicate samplers differ, ask a qualified person for help in interpreting the results. Either of these approaches will increase the cost of testing.

For test periods of only two or three days, close the windows and outside doors at least 12 hours *before* starting the test and keep them closed as much as possible during the test period. Do not perform a short-term test of two to three days during severe storms or when the winds are high.

When the test period is between three days and three months, keep the windows and outside doors closed as much as possible. This is especially important for test periods less than one week.

The following guidelines should be followed when conducting a short-term test for radon:

- Place the sampler in the lowest lived-in level of the home. For example, if the basement is used or is likely to be used for recreation, sleeping or other activities, conduct the test in that area of the house. If the basement is not "lived-in," test on the first floor.
- Place the sampler in a room that is frequently used, such as the living room, family room, playroom or bedroom. Do not place the sampler

in the bathroom, kitchen or utility room. If the kitchen is part of a dining/family room, place the sampler in the dining/family room area.

- Place the sampler at least two to three feet above the floor, ideally at head level. Make sure the sampler has "breathing room" by placing it at least one foot away from other objects. Do not place the sampler in an area that is drafty, hot or humid, and do not place it behind books, picture frames or other objects that will block the flow of air to the sampler.
- Do not move or dust the sampler during the test period. Use a damp cloth to dust the area around it. If the sampler is accidentally dropped, the test may have to be repeated.
- During the test, operate the home's heating and cooling systems normally. (For tests that last less than one week, only operate air-conditioning units that recirculate the air. Do not operate other fans or machines that bring outside air into the house.)
- If there is a radon reduction system in the house, make sure that it is working properly and operating during the test.

After sampling the air for the recommended time, replace the sampler in its original packaging, reseal it and send it to the laboratory. On the package, write the location of the sampler, starting time and date, and ending time and date. The laboratory should send results within two to three weeks.

Guidelines for Long-term Testing. Long-term test kits remain in the home for three months up to one year. Alpha-track and electret samplers (see Figure 3.6) are frequently used for long-term testing. Follow the guidelines for short-term testing and use duplicate samplers. The closed-house guidelines do not apply for long-term testing unless the sampling occurs only during warm months. Lower results are likely during warmer weather unless the doors and windows are kept closed as much as possible.

Real Estate Transactions. About 30 percent of all radon tests take place in conjunction with real estate transactions, and many lenders now require radon testing. Most of these tests are of short-term duration, and when properly conducted, they can alert the buyer to high radon levels. Since these tests are used only for screening purposes, though, the buyer should retest the house after the purchase, preferably with a long-term test.

If the house has a radon reduction system in place, be sure to conduct a radon test to be certain that the system is working properly. Also, ask to see the purchase agreement for the system to determine how much of a warranty is left and whether or not it is transferable to a new owner. You may need the services of a certified radon reduction contractor (see below) if the radon test indicates levels greater than those recommended by the EPA.

Anyone who buys real estate should be alert to the possibility of tampering with short-term tests. Sellers can attempt to lower the radon concentrations by opening windows, sealing the samplers and employing other strategies. Buyers can protect themselves to some extent by asking for tamper-resistant tapes on alpha-track, electret and charcoal samplers. Taping windows shut will also help ensure closed-house conditions. Even these precautions, however, will not prevent all problems.

The most tamperproof testing method for real estate transactions entails the use of sophisticated samplers called continuous monitors. A technician places in the home a monitor that continuously records radon levels. A printout of the results can help the technician spot unusual changes that might occur due to tampering. Motion detectors and proximity detectors can determine if the testing device has been moved, if test conditions have changed or if people are in the room when unusual radon levels occur. Measurements of barometric pressure and temperature can also help identify tampering or other interferences. By comparing the measurements, it is possible to detect problems such as unusual weather conditions, moving the sampler or opening windows. The cost of these testing options is about $300 for a two-day test.

Another type of test that can be useful for real estate transactions involves using the continuous monitor to evaluate specific sources of radon. During the test, the technician samples air from different areas such as a sump or opening between a basement and crawl space. The cost is about $100 to $300 for this test, which is probably most useful in homes with basements. The weakness of a test that looks for sources is that it cannot provide an average radon exposure level. Elevated readings are common when checking for sources, but this does not mean that the average radon level will be high.

Sellers. If you have not tested your home for radon, conduct the test as soon as possible. This will give you time to consider whether or not you want to correct a problem before the sale of your home. Waiting can limit your radon reduction options because the buyer may insist on the most expensive method. Some buyers will agree to a lower selling price in lieu of correcting the problem prior to the sale. If you have radon test results, you should disclose those to the buyer. Some buyers will accept the results, but others might ask for a retest.

Buyers. If the home has been tested for radon, you can decide to accept the results provided by the seller or ask for another test. Do not accept test results from the seller that fail to meet the appropriate guidelines for testing. If you decide that a new test is needed, use a certified radon tester. Make sure that the testing guidelines for short-term tests are followed, and ask for a test that will detect interferences and tampering.

Understanding Results

The amount of radon in the air is measured in picocuries per liter (pCi/L). Sometimes the results will be reported in working levels (WL). One WL is equivalent to 200 pCi/L.

The average indoor radon level in the United States is about 1.3 pCi/L, and the average outdoor level is about 0.4 pCi/L. The EPA believes that currently available control methods can lower radon levels in most homes to below 2 pCi/L.

The EPA has established 4 pCi/L (equivalent to 0.02 WL) as the level at which homeowners should consider taking steps to decrease the amount of radon in their homes. This level is a guideline, not a legally enforceable standard by the government. Although some risk exists at levels below 4 pCi/L, the EPA believes that its guideline provides a good balance between the costs and benefits of radon reduction.

The EPA recommends confirming short-term results before taking actions to reduce radon levels. If the first short-term result is greater than 10 pCi/L, conduct a second short-term test in the same location as soon as possible. If the first short-term test result is between 4 pCi/L and 10 pCi/L, conduct either a long-term test or second short-term test.

When should you take measures to reduce radon levels? The EPA recommends radon reduction when one of the following conditions is met:

- A long-term test result is 4 pCi/L or more
- The *average* of the first and second short-term results in the same location is 4 pCi/L or more

The interpretation of results that are clearly above or below the guideline is easy, but making a decision about a result that is close to the EPA's guideline level can be difficult. Is a long-term result of 3.9 pCi/L safe? Corrective action is still appropriate, even at 3.9 pCi/L, because any amount of radon poses a risk. What does a short-term result of 4.1 pCi/L mean? Because there is uncertainty in the test results, there is roughly a 50 percent chance that the annual average is either above or below the guideline in this example. Whenever short-term testing is used, the greatest chance of error occurs when the test result is in the range of 3 to 5 pCi/L. Be sure to retest if your short-term results fall within this range. If you have questions about test results, contact your local health department or state radon program for help.

Reducing Exposure

A basic principle of radon testing and control is that no two houses are alike, even if they are side-by-side and look the same. Identical houses can have small construction differences or different underlying soils that affect the entry of radon into a house and the effectiveness of control methods.

The best time to control radon is during construction when the costs to do so are their lowest, roughly $350 to $500. The cost of radon control retrofits ranges from $500 to about $3,000, with an average cost of about $1,200. In early 1994, the EPA developed model standards for radon reduction in new construction. As these standards are adopted by model code organizations, buyers of new homes in areas of high radon potential (zone 1 areas shown in Figure 3.1) will probably purchase homes that are fitted with passive radon reduction measures.

Hiring a Radon Reduction Professional

Radon control methods are grouped into two categories: those that keep radon from entering the home, and those that treat contaminated air. The effectiveness and cost of any method depend on the characteristics of each house, the level of radon present, the location and number of radon entry points, and the skill and performance of the person who does the radon reduction work. Skilled homeowners can do some radon reduction projects with good results. Contact your regional EPA office or state agency responsible for radon programs to obtain information about installing radon reduction systems (see Appendix A for addresses).

Hire an EPA-listed or state certified radon reduction contractor to help you decide what to do about an elevated radon level in your house. This professional should have the training and ability to evaluate the radon problem and provide a detailed proposal on how to lower the level. You can expect the contractor to design the radon reduction system, install it according to EPA standards and state codes and ensure that the system works properly.

When hiring a radon reduction contractor, *always check on the experience and reputation of the contractor.* Call your local or state radon office for a list of contractors who have passed the EPA Radon Contractor Proficiency Program or the state certification program (if your state has one). (A contractor who has passed a proficiency test will carry a letter or certification card; ask to see this proof of proficiency.) Ask a potential contractor for a list of references and call them. Contact the local Better Business Bureau or Chamber of Commerce and ask if any complaints have been filed against the contractor. Finally, get more than one estimate if possible.

Once you have decided to hire a contractor, make sure that you understand the scope of the work *and* the type of results that you can expect. Beware of a contractor who promises to eliminate radon because this is not likely to happen. Other information you should understand includes cost, completion date for the work and the level of reduction the contractor will guarantee. Find out if the work includes a monitor to alert you when the system needs servicing. Be sure that you understand what maintenance is needed for the radon reduction and alarm systems. Insist on a written contract that clearly addresses these points.

Finally, remember to test the radon level after the completion of the work. It is a good idea to include retesting as part of the radon reduction contract, but someone other than the contractor should do it. Even if the retest shows an acceptable radon level, test again sometime in the future to ensure that the radon does not return.

Radon Reduction Methods

The cost and effectiveness of radon reduction methods for indoor air and water are summarized in Figure 3.7. Some of these techniques (such as natural ventilation and sealing radon entry points) can be used on all houses, but others are applicable only to specific foundation types.

All Houses. Natural ventilation is a useful step that can be taken immediately to lower radon levels. Opening windows, doors and vents can usually decrease indoor radon levels, but sometimes natural ventilation can depressurize the house and pull even more radon into the home. Opening windows or vents equally on all sides of the house and avoiding the use of exhaust fans can lessen this problem.

A heat recovery ventilator (also called an air-to-air heat exchanger) can be effective. It replaces contaminated indoor air with outdoor air which is warmed or cooled as needed. If the system is not carefully balanced, depressurization can occur and interior radon levels can increase. Heat recovery ventilation is most effective in areas with cold winters and hot summers, and when only moderate reductions in radon levels are needed.

Sealing cracks and openings is a basic part of most radon reduction efforts, but the EPA does *not* recommend the use of this method alone because its effectiveness varies. Finding all of the radon entry points is difficult and as houses settle, new cracks appear. It is difficult to seal the tops of block walls, the spaces between block walls and exterior brick veneer, and openings concealed by masonry fireplaces and chimneys.

A variety of sealing products are available including mortar, urethane foam, polyurethane membranes, waterproof paint, cements or epoxy. Many of these products contain toxic chemicals, and they must be used cautiously and in well-ventilated areas.

Sealing dirt floors in a basement involves excavating the floor and pouring a concrete floor over a bed of crushed stone. This allows another radon reduction system to be installed easily below the slab. A common problem in

FIGURE 3.7.   Comparison of Radon Reduction Methods

Method	Typical Range of a Contractor's Installation Costs	Typical Range of Fan and Electricity Operating Costs and Costs for Heating or Cooling Air	Typical Range of Radon Reduction
Natural ventilation of the house	None ($200–$500 if additional vents are installed)	There may be an increase in energy costs.	Up to 50%
Heat recovery ventilation	$1,200–$2,500	$75–$500 for continuous operation	25%–50% if used for entire house; 25%–75% if used for a basement
Sealing radon entry points	$100–$2,000	None, but there may be some costs for periodic caulking.	Up to 50%
Subslab suction Active Passive	$800–$2,500 $550–$2,250	$75–$175 There may be an increase in energy costs.	80%–99% 30%–70%
Drain tile suction	$800–$1,700	$75–$175	90%–99%
Sump hole suction	$800–$2,500	$100–$225	90%–99%
Blockwall suction	$1,500–$3,000	$150–$300	50%–99%
Natural ventilation of the crawl space	None ($200–$500 if additional vents are installed)	There may be an increase in energy costs.	Up to 50%
House (basement) pressurization	$500–$1,500	$150–$500	50%–99%
Water systems Aeration Activated carbon	$3,000–$4,500 $1,000–$2,000	$40–$90 None	95%–99% 85%–99%

SOURCE: U.S. EPA (1992c).

older homes is a dirt floor in a crawl space connected to a concrete basement. The placement of a tight-fitting cover over the opening can be effective when combined with the sealing of the top of the foundation wall that separates the crawl space from the basement.

Basements and Slab-on-grade Foundations. Radon reduction in these houses typically relies on one of four types of soil suction to draw radon from the soil before the gas can enter the house.

Subslab suction is the most commonly used method for houses with basement or slab foundations. Suction pipes are inserted through the floor into the crushed rock or soil underneath the slab. (An alternative is to insert the pipes below the slab from outside the house.) Passive subslab suction relies on air currents to draw radon from the soil. It may be more effective in cold climates, but it is less effective than active subslab suction that uses fans to pull the radon from the soil. With either method, the radon gas is released away from windows and vents that could pull the radon back into the house.

Drain tile suction relies on existing drain tiles (perforated pipes) that move water away from the foundation. When these pipes are connected to an exhaust fan, the suction draws radon gas away from the house. Drain tile suction works best if the drain tiles completely encircle the house. Floor drains that are connected to a drain tile system can be sealed using water traps as long as the water trap does not become dry.

Sump hole suction can effectively eliminate radon entry into a house from open sump pumps in basements. An exhaust pipe is placed into a tightly capped sump hole and a fan draws radon gas out of the hole.

Blockwall suction and ventilation can be used in houses with hollow block basement walls. Radon gas is drawn away from the block walls or air is blown into the walls to prevent the gas from entering. For this method to be effective, holes (especially those in the top of the blocks) must be sealed. This method is often used with subslab suction.

Crawl Space Foundations. Radon levels can be lowered by naturally ventilating the crawl space. This is accomplished by installing crawl space vents and keeping them open. A major drawback of this method, however, is heat loss through the vents during cold weather.

Used in houses with basements or crawl spaces, house pressurization involves keeping the part of the house that contacts the soil at a higher pressure than the air in the soil. The increased pressure prevents radon and other gases in the soil from entering the house. The first step in this method is to seal any openings between the basement and/or crawl space and the living area. A fan is then used to blow air from inside the living space into the basement or crawl space. Drawbacks include noise and vibrations produced by the fan. A more serious concern is the possibility that combustion gases may be back-drafted into the living space.

Water. The most widely used method for reducing radon in water is to filter the water through a bed of granular activated carbon (GAC). GAC removal works best for moderate levels of radon in water (about 5000 pCi/L). Aeration treatment, a more efficient method of radon reduction than GAC removal, reduces the radon by agitating the water so that it releases the gas. A third, less frequently used, technique is storage of the water long enough to allow the radon to decay naturally.

 Radon Checklist

Questions To Ask	Response	What Does a "Yes" Mean?
All Houses		
Has the house been tested for radon?	Yes No ☐ ☐	The only way to know if radon is present is to test for it. Levels should be reduced to less than 4 pCi/L.
Crawl Space Foundations		
Is the floor of the crawl space exposed soil or gravel?	Yes No ☐ ☐	Radon can travel through the soil or gravel into the crawl space and then into the house through any openings. A secure plastic liner may reduce radon levels.

Questions To Ask	Response	What Does a "Yes" Mean?
Does the crawl space floor have a plastic covering over dirt, and is the plastic covering secure around the perimeter of the floor? Look for the liner under several inches of the pea gravel that is used to secure it.	Yes No ❏ ❏	A secure plastic covering over a dirt base can keep radon from reaching the crawl space air and should be checked periodically.
Does the crawl space have return air heating and cooling ducts? Do the return ducts have any openings? Are there openings for utilities or ducts that go from the crawl space into the house?	Yes No ❏ ❏	Return air ducts could have openings that can draw radon into the house. A house with these ducts may contribute to a high level of radon. Check these for leaks and make sure that all joints are wrapped.
In the crawl space, is there a sump that is not sealed or a dry well?	Yes No ❏ ❏	Any openings in the ground that can allow radon to enter the crawl space and the house should be sealed.
Are there openings for utilities or ducts that go from the crawl space into the house?	Yes No ❏ ❏	Any openings between the crawl space and the house that could serve as entry points for radon should be sealed.
Basement Foundations		
Does the basement have any areas of exposed soil?	Yes No ❏ ❏	Any exposed dirt will provide entry points for radon. If there is an attached crawl space, the seal between the basement and crawl space must be tight. Whenever possible, seal the tops of concrete blocks.

Questions To Ask	Response	What Does a "Yes" Mean?
Does the basement have return air heating and cooling ducts? Do the return air ducts have any openings?	Yes No ☐ ☐	Return air ducts that have openings can draw radon into the house. Check return ducts for leaks and make sure that all joints are wrapped.
Is there a sump that is not sealed or a dry well?	Yes No ☐ ☐	Any openings in the ground that can allow radon to enter the crawl space and the house should be sealed.
Does the basement have standard drains without water traps?	Yes No ☐ ☐	Drains without water traps can allow radon to enter the basement. Install water traps and keep them filled with water.
Do the basement walls and floors have cracks or other unsealed openings?	Yes No ☐ ☐	Any cracks or openings in contact with the soil can allow radon to enter the basement and should be sealed.
Does the basement have a chimney chase?	Yes No ☐ ☐	The chimney chase can provide an opening for radon to enter the rest of the house and can increase the flow of radon by depressurizing the house.
Are there openings for utilities or ducts between the basement and the house?	Yes No ☐ ☐	Any openings between the basement and the house can be entry points for radon and should be sealed.
Is the basement damp or are there signs of recent water damage?	Yes No ☐ ☐	Signs of moisture in the basement mean that radon gas can enter. Waterproofing or dampproofing can reduce radon entry.

Summary Chart for Asbestos

Topic	Comments
Description	Asbestos is a strong, flexible mineral fiber that was often used in buildings. Asbestos has many desirable properties, including fireproofness, resistance to chemicals and good heat and electrical insulating properties.
Health Effects	Asbestos can cause asbestosis and cancer of the lung and lining of the lung. The risk of cancer increases with prolonged exposure, but there is no safe level of exposure.
Sources	Asbestos can be found in insulation around heating pipes and furnaces, plaster, blown-in insulation, vinyl floor tiles and linoleum, roofing felts and tiles, shingles and siding. Houses built before 1973 are likely to contain some asbestos, but it can also be found in some houses built as recently as 1985.
Testing	Obtain the names of qualified testing laboratories from local and state health agencies and hire one of those laboratories to test for asbestos. A material that contains more than 1 percent asbestos by weight is considered to test positive for asbestos.
Reducing Exposure	The EPA no longer recommends removing all asbestos-containing materials. Some materials can be managed in place by building an enclosure around them or by covering the asbestos fibers with a sealant.

CHAPTER
FOUR

Asbestos

In March 1991, Elmer E. Rones died of mesothelioma, a rare cancer of the lining of the lungs that is typically found in industrial workers who have been exposed to asbestos. Rones was a 69-year-old physician who taught at Howard and Georgetown medical schools in Washington, D.C.

His family said that he was exposed to asbestos, but not through an industrial job. They believe that the source of his exposure was asbestos paper that lined a part of the air-conditioning system in his house in Hyattsville, Maryland. The family planned to file suit against the builder of the house and the manufacturer of the asbestos paper.

As reported in *The Indianapolis Star,* May 31, 1992

What Is Asbestos and Why Is It a Hazard?

The word "asbestos" refers to a group of naturally occurring minerals that can separate into fine, strong, flexible fibers. Individual asbestos fibers are not visible without the aid of a microscope because the fibers are very small—up to 1,200 times thinner than a human hair. Asbestos fibers are fireproof, resist chemicals and have good heat and electrical insulating properties. Asbestos fibers were made into yarn, cloth, tape, braided tubes, cement and other materials.

Because of its many desirable properties, asbestos has been frequently used in the past. Buildings in the United States may contain as much as 30 million tons of asbestos combined.

Asbestos is a health concern because breathing the fibers damages the lungs and causes asbestosis, lung cancer and mesothelioma (a cancer of the lining of the lungs or lining of the abdomen that is very rare in individuals who were not exposed to asbestos). These illnesses usually develop 15 to 25 years after exposure to asbestos. People who have been exposed to asbestos and smoke are much more likely than exposed nonsmokers to develop lung cancer and asbestosis.

Although asbestos is present in many buildings across the nation, the risk of exposure varies from structure to structure. In many situations, asbestos is not a serious problem because the material that contains the asbestos is in good condition and not likely to be damaged. Exposed or damaged asbestos is a problem because the fibers can be released into the building air. The technical term "friable" is used to describe material that is easily crumbled or crushed into a powder. Friable asbestos is a serious hazard because disturbing the fibers causes them to enter the air where they can remain airborne for a long time. Since the fibers are not visible, people can inhale them unknowingly.

Nearly 100 years ago, scientists began to learn about the health problems associated with asbestos. The regulation of asbestos, however, did not start until the 1970s, when studies of World War II shipyard workers (who worked with asbestos) and their families provided startling new information about the health effects of asbestos. These studies showed that those workers and their families (who were probably exposed to asbestos fibers on the workers' clothes) were more likely to develop lung cancer and die than people who were not exposed to asbestos. The EPA now lists asbestos as a known human carcinogen based on strong evidence of the ability of asbestos to cause cancer in people.

The federal government regulates asbestos in schools, in the workplace and in the outdoor air. There are no national regulations, however, that govern existing asbestos-containing materials in homes. State governments typically adopt these federal regulations, but some states may have more stringent laws. Some state and local governments regulate the removal of asbestos-containing materials in homes under air quality and waste removal laws.

Many people wonder if they will get cancer if they are exposed to asbestos. This is a difficult question to answer with absolute certainty, but it is possible to make two generalizations. First, exposure to small amounts of asbestos for short periods of time is not likely to cause cancer. Studies show that an individual's chance of developing cancer is greater when the intensity or duration of his or her exposure is increased. Because asbestos is a known cancer-causing agent, however, no level of exposure is completely safe. Second, smoking greatly increases a person's chance of getting lung cancer if he or she works with asbestos.

Sources

Because asbestos has so many desirable properties, there were many ways to use it in buildings. The EPA estimates that friable asbestos is in one out of five apartment buildings that have ten or more rental units, commercial buildings and government buildings.

Houses built before 1973 are likely to have the following types of asbestos-containing materials:

- Insulation around heating pipes and furnaces (this insulation usually looks chalky like plaster or resembles corrugated cardboard, but it could be present in the form of batting or tape around pipes)
- Asbestos-containing plaster that is sprayed or troweled onto walls or ceilings (sprayed ceilings have a texture that looks similar to pop-corn); this plaster is usually white to gray in color unless it has been painted over
- Blown-in asbestos insulation inside the walls or attic
- Vinyl floor tiles, linoleum sheeting and mastic (an adhesive)
- Roofing felts and tiles
- Asbestos shingles and siding
- Other materials listed below

Houses built between 1973 and 1985 could also contain asbestos, but they are not at the same risk as the pre-1973 houses. In these houses, possible sources of asbestos include caulking, putty, mastic, cement, vinyl wallpaper, siding, roofing shingles and felt, joint compound, plaster, stucco, vinyl floor-ing and asbestos floor tiles. If you live in a home built between 1973 and 1985, consider testing any materials that could possibly contain asbestos if they are damaged or if you are thinking about replacing them. Avoid sanding, scraping, sawing, cutting or drilling asbestos-containing materials because these actions release asbestos fibers.

Whether or not an asbestos-containing material is a health threat depends on the condition and the location of the material. Generally, the risk is mini-mal if the material is in good condition, and the risk is greater if the material is damaged or breaking loose. Figure 4.1 lists potential sources of asbestos in the home, activities that release fibers and ways to reduce one's exposure to asbestos.

FIGURE 4.1.   Possible Sources and Control Methods for Asbestos in the Home

Possible Sources	Activities That Release Fibers	Control Methods
Vinyl floor tiles, floor cements and vinyl sheet flooring	Sanding, dry scraping and cutting	Cover old vinyl tiles or sheets with new flooring material
Patching and spackling compounds used before 1977 in patched walls and ceiling joints	Sanding and scraping	Leave alone if in good condition; remove if damaged
Textured paints used before 1978	Sanding, scraping and cutting	Leave alone if in good condiiton; remove if damaged
Troweled on or sprayed on ceilings and walls constructed or remodeled between 1945 and 1978	Sanding, scraping, drilling and impacting	Leave alone if in good condition; remove if damaged
Stove insulation and cement sheets, millboard and paper used to insulate the floors and walls around wood stoves	Normal wear, sanding, scraping, drilling and sawing	Leave alone if in good condition; remove if damaged
Furnace insulation: oil, coal or wood furnaces wrapped with asbestos-containing cement and insulation	Normal aging and wear, updating systems and impacting	Leave alone if in good condition; repair or remove if damaged
Door gaskets in furnaces, ovens and wood and coal stoves	Normal aging and wear	Remove
Hot water and steam pipes installed or insulated between 1920 and 1972 and wrapped in asbestos paper tape or asbestos blanket	Normal aging and wear and impacting	Leave alone if in good condition; repair or remove if damaged
Ceiling and wall insulation installed between 1930 and 1950	Renovations and home improvements	Remove
Appliances, especially hair dryers (recalled in 1979) with asbestos-containing heat shields	Appliances are unlikely to release fibers (except for pre-1980 hair dryers which release fibers during normal use.)	Hire a qualified technician for repair
Roofing, shingles and siding	Scraping, drilling and cutting	Leave alone if in good condition; repair or remove if damaged

Testing and Understanding the Results

If you suspect the presence of asbestos in your home, contact your local health department for assistance. Many departments offer testing services and have knowledgeable staff members who can advise you of your options if asbestos is present. They may also provide you with a list of qualified laboratories and consultants who can test for asbestos and correct problems. These professionals should be certified either by the EPA or your state. Two other valuable resources are the EPA asbestos office in your region and the asbestos program in your state health or environmental protection agency (see Appendix A). The section on reducing exposure provides more information on hiring professionals.

Although the EPA recommends hiring a certified professional for collecting samples for asbestos testing, homeowners themselves can safely collect the samples. Appendix C explains how to safely sample "popcorn" ceilings and cement asbestos board siding. Call your local health agency to obtain instructions for sampling other types of materials.

The number of samples needed depends on the color, texture and location of the materials being tested. If the materials have the same color and texture (smooth or rough), one sample is probably enough, even if the samples come from different places. If the color or texture is different, collect one sample of each different color or texture. It is not possible to know for certain if a material contains asbestos just by looking at it. Be sure, therefore, to test any suspect materials.

The cost of collecting and analyzing a bulk sample is typically between $25 and $50. The most common technique used to identify asbestos requires a microscope test called polarized light microscopy (PLM). This test is not expensive and is appropriate for most residential testing. A drawback to PLM testing is that fibers are occasionally incorrectly identified. More sophisticated methods (such as the transmission electron microscope [TEM]) give test results with greater certainty, but the cost of a single sample analysis can range from $200 to $600.

Regardless of the method used, ask the laboratory two questions: (1) Does the lab use a standard method published by the the EPA or NIOSH (National Institute of Occupational Safety and Health)? and (2) Does it participate in a proficiency testing program? A "yes" to both questions indicates that the laboratory has met minimum federal requirements for testing, and that you can have confidence in the accuracy of the test result. You can contact your local or state agency responsible for asbestos to verify that the laboratory is certified to test for asbestos.

When the laboratory sends the test results to you, you should get more than a "yes" or "no" response about whether or not asbestos was in the sample.

The report should name each type of asbestos present and estimate the percent of the sample by weight that contains that type of asbestos. The most commonly used kind of asbestos was chrysotile or "white" asbestos and the second most common type was amosite or "brown" asbestos. For example, a report might read as follows: "The sample contains 21%±1% chrysotile asbestos." This means that the sample is between 20 and 22 percent chrysotile asbestos. Sometimes, a single sample can contain several different types of asbestos. The report should also identify the names and percentages of any nonasbestos materials that are present in the sample. Be sure to contact the laboratory and ask questions until you understand the report.

When a material contains less than 1 percent asbestos by weight, the test results are negative according to federal guidelines. Positive test results are obtained when the sample contains at least 1 percent asbestos by weight. When the test is positive, the material and its location must be examined to determine if further action is needed.

Reducing Exposure

Safe Management Practices

Asbestos is a health threat only if you breathe (or possibly swallow) the fibers. Deciding what to do about asbestos can be difficult. Since it causes cancer, many people, undestandably, want to get asbestos out of their homes immediately. This may not, however, be the safest or the most economical course of action, and the EPA no longer recommends removing all asbestos. If the asbestos-containing material is in good condition and not likely to be disturbed, leaving it alone may be the best solution.

For example, hot water pipes that have asbestos-containing insulation around them can be left alone if the wrap is in good condition. This also applies to vinyl floor tiles, linoleum floor coverings, roofing shingles and felt, "popcorn" ceilings and asbestos siding if the materials in question are in good condition. Check them for damage and wear two to three times each year. If children live in the home, do not let them play in the area that contains the asbestos.

Remember that damaged asbestos-containing materials can release fibers into the air. The damaged pipe insulation in Figure 4.2 should be repaired because its fibers are likely to become airborne. Asbestos-containing materials can be damaged through physical contact, natural deterioration with aging or water damage.

Problems can be prevented by following safe practices for handling asbestos-containing materials:

- Do not use abrasive pads or brushes in power strippers to strip wax from asbestos flooring.

FIGURE 4.2. **Asbestos-containing Pipe Insulation**

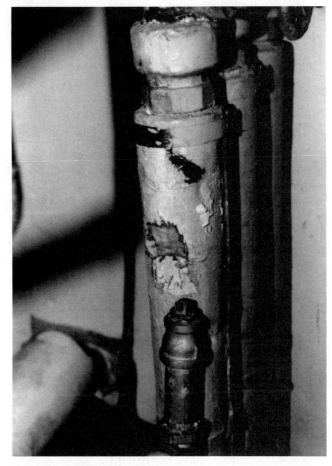

Courtesy of Martha Clark.

- Do not drill, saw or otherwise damage asbestos-containing materials.
- Do not sand or try to level asbestos flooring or its backing (instead, install a new floor covering).
- Do not dust, sweep or vacuum debris that might contain asbestos because doing so will release fibers into the air. (If there is a small amount of material, spray it lightly with water and use damp paper towels to pick up the loose material. Wipe the area at least two times with damp paper towels to remove any remaining contamination. Seal the waste in a plastic bag [use duct tape, not a twist tie], then place the sealed plastic bag into a second bag and seal it in the same manner. If there is a large amount of material, consider hiring a professional to remove it.)

FIGURE 4.3.   Warning Label at an Asbestos Removal Site

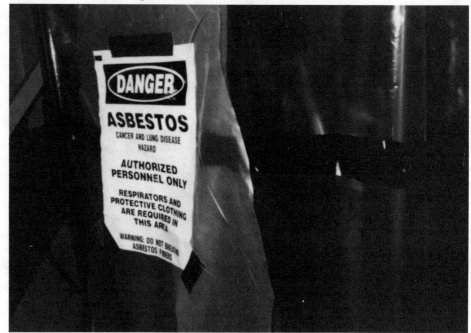

Courtesy of the Puget Sound Air Pollution Control Agency, Seattle, Washington.

Label any materials known to contain asbestos (such as decorative tiles and pipe, boiler or furnace coverings) as well as removal sites so that anyone who comes in contact with the material will know that it contains asbestos (see Figure 4.3).   Look in the yellow pages of your telephone directory under "Safety Equipment & Clothing" or "Asbestos Removal & Abatement Equipment & Supplies" for a list of safety supply stores where asbestos warning labels can be purchased, or contact your local health department or state asbestos coordinator for sources of labels and other safety equipment.

Should the Asbestos Be Removed?

Damaged asbestos-containing material should be repaired, enclosed or removed. Asbestos repair usually requires the sealing (also referred to as encapsulation) or covering of the material. Sealing involves treating the material with a chemical product in order to bind the asbestos fibers together or coat them to prevent the release of the fibers. Sealants are appropriate for some types of damage to pipe, furnace and boiler insulation. Sometimes, the material that contains asbestos may be covered with another material to prevent the release of asbestos fibers into the air. For example, a pipe insulated with asbestos can be repaired by covering it with a protective wrap or jacket.

Asbestos-containing materials may also be confined in a small room or enclosure. This might be a good solution for pipes or a boiler if the insulation is in good condition and the goal is simply to limit access to these areas. Great care must be taken, however, to be sure that the asbestos-containing material is not disturbed during construction of the enclosure.

Removal is an appropriate action if the asbestos-containing material is damaged beyond repair or if the material is likely to be damaged during routine activity. Sometimes a device called a glovebag can be used during the removal of small amounts of asbestos-containing material. The glovebag is a polyethylene or polyvinyl chloride bag-like enclosure that contains the material that is being removed. Glovebag removals require less room preparation and cost less than a removal without the glovebag.

The best way to handle asbestos-containing material varies according to each situation. For example, in a child's basement playroom with hot water pipes that are insulated with slightly damaged asbestos wrap, the best thing to do might be to repair the damage, label the pipes and keep children out of the area. Another alternative would be to repair the damage, label the pipes and enclose them to keep children from accidentally damaging the material. In this situation, removal using a glovebag is possible, but not necessary. If a basement furnace or boiler has an outer jacket of asbestos-containing insulation, a problem is not likely to arise when adults are in the basement if they do not injure the material. Children at play, however, could easily damage the insulation. Possible solutions include repairing any minor damage, labeling the material, keeping children out of the basement and removing or enclosing the material. Removal is necessary whenever major damage exists.

Deciding what to do with asbestos-containing material can be difficult. The best course of action is to ask a professional to examine the situation and make recommendations about possible solutions.

Who Should Test for Asbestos and Correct Problems?

Although it may be expensive, seriously consider hiring a professional *trained in removing and repairing asbestos-containing material* to do any needed work. Since asbestos is a hazardous material, the contractor must have liability insurance, the workers must have special training and waste disposal costs can be high. The cost for a residential removal can easily range from $1,500 to several thousand dollars. Accidental releases are most likely to occur when untrained workers remove or repair asbestos. Therefore, hiring a certified contractor will reduce the chance of spreading asbestos throughout your home.

For example, the improper removal of asbestos-containing mastic used to adhere floor tiles or linoleum to the floor can release fibers directly into the air. Entire houses have been contaminated in this manner. A certified contractor will know that in this situation, an appropriate solution is to install a second floor over the tiles or linoleum rather than removing the mastic by sanding

The EPA and some states train and certify contractors to inspect, test and solve asbestos problems. If you live in a small community, you may have to look in a larger city for qualified contractors. Contact your local health department or state asbestos coordinator for a list of certified contractors. All such contractors must each carry a certification card (or letter) and have insurance coverage.

There are two basic types of asbestos professionals: certified asbestos inspectors and corrective action contractors. Certified asbestos inspectors are trained to inspect homes for asbestos and to collect samples. If asbestos is present, an inspector should provide a written report evaluating the location and condition of the material. The evaluation should include recommendations for preventing additional damage and correcting the problem.

Corrective action contractors are trained to repair or remove asbestos-containing material. They can be general contractors who handle minor or major amounts of various types of asbestos materials, or specialized contractors who are trained to remove or repair asbestos only in isolated parts of a house (such as plumbing systems, roofs or floors). These specialized contractors might not be licensed by a state agency because they do not perform other asbestos-related work.

When hiring a corrective action contractor, ask questions about the repair or removal process and always *ask for references.* Ask to see the contractor's proof of certification and insurance. Stress your concerns about safety to the contractor and become familiar with the proper procedures for asbestos repair and removal so you can be sure they are followed. Check with your local health department or the state agency responsible for asbestos programs to find out if a particular contractor has violated any regulations. Ask the local Better Business Bureau or Chamber of Commerce if there are any complaints against the contractor. Once you decide to employ a contractor, get a *signed* contract that explains the methods that will be used for repair, removal and clean up, as well as estimates for project completion time and the total cost of the work.

After the work starts, a reputable contractor should not allow anyone, even a homeowner, into the work area unless that person is wearing a respirator and protective clothing. If the contractor does not follow the agreed-upon procedures, stop the work immediately and call the local health department for help. Appendix C shows examples of a major removal project in progress.

Do not hire the same firm to evaluate the problem and correct it. Instead, hire one firm to inspect, test and recommend corrective actions and engage a second firm to do the corrective work. (For example, you might want to hire a certified asbestos inspector to monitor the air after the corrective action contractor completes a removal). Get several estimates if possible, although this may be difficult in some parts of the country where services are limited.

If you are unable or unwilling to hire a certified contractor and you decide to repair or remove the asbestos yourself, your local health department or state agency for asbestos programs can help you understand the proper removal or repair methods as well as any regulations that apply to your situation. Although some states allow homeowners to remove asbestos-containing material themselves, other states have restrictions that prohibit or limit the removal or repair of asbestos by individuals without special training in these procedures. Get as much information as you can before you begin. Safe practices for removing cement board siding and spray-on "popcorn" ceilings that contain asbestos are explained in Appendix C. You can request procedures from the Resilient Floor Covering Institute (see Appendix A for the address) for removing sheet vinyl flooring with asbestos backing. Homeowners can also safely remove asbestos from the exteriors (but not the interiors) of convection and forced-air furnace systems. Contact your local asbestos program for information about these removals.

The removal procedures in Appendix C were developed for homeowners by the Puget Sound Air Pollution Control Agency based on EPA guidelines for asbestos abatement contractors. The procedures for removals inside the home, however, do not include the use of a special filtration system to clean the air. If the asbestos-containing material becomes disturbed, it can contaminate the room air. Following these procedures (or similar ones recommended by a health department) will provide protection from asbestos contamination but will not guarantee the absence of contamination because unforseen problems can arise. Improper asbestos removal can contaminate an entire house and in these instances, cleanup can easily cost thousands of dollars. In some cases, however, complete cleanup is not possible, and people who continue to live in the presence of asbestos could suffer dire health consequences (such as cancer) later in life.

 Asbestos Checklist

Questions To Ask	Response	What Does a "Yes" Mean?
Was the home built before 1973?	**Yes No** ❏ ❏	Houses built before 1973 are likely to contain asbestos whereas houses built between 1973 and 1985 might contain asbestos (see below). Houses built after 1985 should be free of asbestos.

Questions To Ask	Response	What Does a "Yes" Mean?
Does the home have insulated heating ducts or hot water pipes? Look for batting, tape, chalk-like plaster or corrugated cardboard wrapping around pipes and ducts. Also check the crawl space ducts.	Yes No ❏ ❏	The insulation might contain asbestos. Test for asbestos right away if the covering is deteriorating and keep adults and children from the area. Ducts in the crawl space are less of a problem, provided the ducts do not have holes or openings that can spread asbestos throughout the home, and the furnace is not in the crawl space. Do not enter a crawl space that has asbestos without using protective respiratory equipment.
Does the home have insulated furnaces or hot water heaters? Look for a chalk-like plaster or corrugated cardboard covering, or batting secured by tape.	Yes No ❏ ❏	The insulation might contain asbestos. Test for asbestos right away if the covering is deteriorating and keep adults and children from the area.
Does the home have plaster that is sprayed on or troweled on walls or ceilings? It might be white to gray in color (unless it has been painted).	Yes No ❏ ❏	The plaster could contain asbestos. Test for asbestos right away if the plaster is deteriorating and keep adults and children from the area.
Does the home have blown-in insulation? Look for insulating material that is white to gray in color in the attic and walls. Remove an electrical outlet cover to check for loose insulation in the walls.	Yes No ❏ ❏	If the asbestos is in the attic or in walls that come in contact with the air ducts, this could be a serious problem. The only way to know if the material is asbestos is to test it. Keep adults and children out of the attic.

Questions To Ask	Response	What Does a "Yes" Mean?
Does the home have vinyl floor tiles or linoleum sheeting?	Yes No ❏ ❏	These floor coverings could contain asbestos. Test for asbestos if the floor coverings are deteriorating or if you want to install new flooring. Be sure to test the mastic that holds the floor covering to the floor. Do not sand these materials.
Does the home have asbestos siding, shingles or roofing that are deteriorating? Are you thinking about replacing these materials?	Yes No ❏ ❏	These materials could contain asbestos. Test them if they are deteriorating or if you plan to replace them.
Does the home have caulking, putty, cement, mastic, joint compound or similar material?	Yes No ❏ ❏	These materials could contain asbestos. Do not drill, sand, cut, saw or scrape them.
Was the home built between 1973 and 1985?	Yes No ❏ ❏	These houses could have asbestos. Potential sources include caulking, putties, mastics, cements, vinyl wallpaper, siding and roofing shingles, roofing felts, joint compound, plaster and stucco, vinyl flooring and floor tiles. Test any material that could possibly contain asbestos if it is damaged or if you plan to replace it.

Summary Chart for Lead

Topic	Comments
Description	Lead is a soft, gray, toxic metal.
Health Effects	Lead affects all of the body's systems, but especially the brain and nervous system. It can result in permanent decreases in IQ levels, behavioral problems and learning problems in both children and adults.
Sources	Lead can be found in paints, varnishes, water, soil and dust. Other sources include some ceramics and toys, art and craft supplies, newspapers and magazines, plastic bags and a variety of materials.
Testing	Hire qualified consultants and laboratories to test for lead in paint, soil and water. (Local and state health agencies can provide names of qualified professionals.) Levels of lead in paint are considered hazardous when they are greater than 0.5% by weight or 1.0 mg/cm^2. A lead measurement of more than 15 ppb in water is considered hazardous. Lead levels in the soil that are greater than 500 ppm are elevated according to EPA guidelines.
Reducing Exposure	The most effective method is to replace lead-contaminated materials with those that do not have lead. Special care must be used, however, to prevent contaminating the house with lead dust when lead-based paint is removed. Another potential solution is to enclose the lead-containing surfaces with lead-free materials. Special housekeeping practices can also reduce exposure until a more permanent solution can be found.

Lead

In 1992, the EPA found that 819 public water systems had high levels of lead, a metal that affects learning and intelligence, especially in children. These systems supply water to about 30 million people. The highest reported level was 484 parts per billion at U.S. Marine Corps Camp Lejeune-Hatnot Pointe, North Carolina, followed by 324 parts per billion at Grosse Pointe Park, Michigan. These levels are much higher than the EPA's level of concern, which is 15 parts per billion.

As reported in *Indoor Pollution News,* May 14, 1993.

The EPA estimates that about 560,000 children have unacceptably high levels of lead in their blood, and that about 680,000 cases of high blood pressure in adult men are related to lead in drinking water.

As reported in *Time,* November 15, 1993.

During 1991, some residents in a westside Indianapolis community, who lived south of an industrial site that housed lead-processing businesses, were told to drink bottled water because their wells were contaminated with lead. Later, during the spring of 1993, the county health workers found that several neighborhood children had elevated lead levels. Karen Elam's 11-year-

*old son had a blood lead level of 97 micrograms of lead per deciliter of blood
and her 13-year-old son had a level of 39 micrograms of lead per deciliter of
blood. Anita Bryson's three sons also tested over the Centers for Disease
Control guideline level of ten micrograms of lead per deciliter of blood. Her
four-year-old son has trouble talking, her seven-year old has a hearing
impairment and her ten-year old has seizures and behaves poorly in school.*

*Karen Elam is very angry because she believes that many children in
the community have learning disabilities, seizures and speech impediments
that are related to lead exposure. Elam and others in the community blame
high lead levels in children on a long-closed lead smelting plant that operated until the mid-1970s. For many years the residents complained about
the pollution coming from the plant, but they had to live with yellow powder
(that contained lead) that used to cake their houses, cars, yards and bodies.*

*Although the community has been exposed to higher lead levels for
many years, it is fortunate because the EPA has given the industrial site
and the neighborhood on a high priority for cleanup. The work, which was
scheduled to begin in the spring of 1994, has been delayed until the summer—prolonging the exposure of children to lead through normal play
activities in their neighborhood.*

As reported in *The Indianapolis News,* May 28 and July 21, 1993 and May 12, 1994.

What Is Lead and Why Is It a Hazard?

Lead is a soft, gray metal known to cause mutations and cancer in laboratory animals. Toxic to many of the human body's systems (even in small
amounts), lead that has been ingested or inhaled can be carried by the bloodstream to all parts of the body.

In the past, most exposure to lead resulted from eating food contaminated
by lead-lined cans. The regulation of food products has greatly reduced the
importance of this source of exposure, but improperly storing foods in ceramicware containing lead can cause isolated cases of lead poisoning. Today,
exposure usally results from breathing or swallowing lead from a variety of
sources. Figure 5.1 shows how children can become exposed to lead (many of
these sources can also affect adults).

Air can become contaminated by lead as a result of industrial activities or
through contact with lead-containing wind-blown dust and dirt. Improper renovations and removals of lead-containing paint can greatly increase the amount
of lead in the air and in household dust. Hobbies such as furniture refinishing
and making stained glass or pottery can contaminate household air if the lead
is heated to high temperatures or if surfaces that contain lead are sanded.

FIGURE 5.1.   Sources of Childhood Lead Poisoning

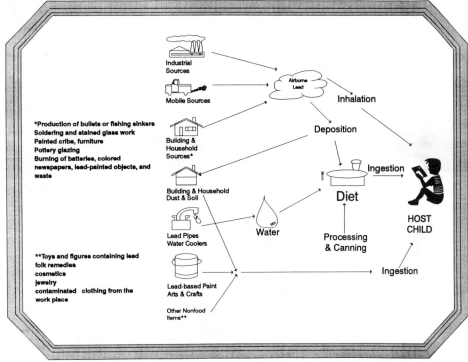

SOURCE: Adapted from U.S. Department of Health and Human Services (DHHS), Centers for Disease Control (1985). *Preventing Lead Poisoning in Young Children.* Atlanta, GA. DHHS: p. 6.

Contamination can also occur as a result of contact with the work clothes of a person who works with lead. Drinking water can be another important source in both newer and older homes.

Lead Poisoning in Children

Although lead can poison both adults and children, it is especially hazardous to the developing brains and nervous systems of unborn and young children. Lead poisoning in children is not a recent phenomenon, and it is one of the most common and preventable pediatric health problems in the United States. Many cases of childhood lead poisoning occur in poor inner city areas, but even children living in affluent homes can get lead poisoning.

Unborn children are at risk because lead ingested by the mother can flow into the unborn child's system through the umbilical cord, even if the mother has not been recently exposed to lead. Lead can build up in the body over the course of a lifetime and during pregnancy, the stored lead is released from the mother's bones into her bloodstream and is then transported to the fetus. Babies born to mothers with higher lead levels are more likely to be premature and have lower birth weights than babies who are not exposed to lead.

Children are more vulnerable to lead poisoning than adults for several reasons:

- Children are more likely than adults to come into contact with lead-contaminated items such as dirt and dust.
- Children are more likely than adults to put into their mouths nonfood items that have been contaminated with lead.
- Children react to lower levels of lead than adults, and children's bodies absorb and retain more lead than adults' bodies.

Most lead poisoning starts slowly and results from the gradual accumulation of lead in the body. Early symptoms are similar to those of a cold or flu and could include headache, tiredness, irritability, constipation, diarrhea, appetite loss, stomachache and occasional vomiting. In some cases, early lead poisoning might not be accompanied by any unique signs or symptoms.

Severely poisoned children might have additional symptoms, including persistent vomiting, clumsiness, muscle and joint pains, weakness and convulsions. Severely poisoned children may suffer kidney damage and serious brain damage, and some them of can become comatose and die.

Lead also affects a child's behavior. At low levels of lead poisoning, a child could exhibit restlessness, a short attention span, impulsive behavior and difficulties with hand-eye coordination. These effects become more severe as the level of exposure increases.

Also of concern is a greater chance of decreased intelligence and impaired neurobehavioral development in children who are exposed to lead, even at low levels. Low levels of exposure can also decrease growth and impair hearing.

The federal government estimates that three to four million children in the United States are poisoned by lead. Based on some scientific studies, children with lead poisoning may be less likely to graduate from high school and more likely to have reading problems, less developed vocabularies, more absenteeism, lower class ranking and problems with attention and fine motor skills.

Has your child been exposed to lead? The only way to know is to have him or her tested at a public health clinic (the cost of the test is usually income-based) or by a private physician (the cost can range from $15 to $60 per test). The test is done by measuring the amount of lead in the blood. According to the Centers for Disease Control, a blood lead level less than 10 micrograms of lead per deciliter of blood (μg/dL) is not considered to be evidence of lead poisoning. Children with blood lead levels of 10 to 14 μg/dl are in a border zone. Simple interventions are used to lower the blood lead level to less than 10

FIGURE 5.2. Lead Poisoning Risk Factors for Children

Does your child

- live in or regularly visit a house built before 1960 that has peeling or chipping paint?
- live in or regularly visit a house built before 1960 that has recent, ongoing or planned renovation or remodeling?
- have a brother, sister, playmate or housemate being monitored or treated for lead poisoning?
- live near a lead smelter, battery recycling plant or other industry likely to release lead?
- live next to a busy roadway?
- live in or regularly visit a house built before 1930 or a house with lead water pipes?

** *If you answered "yes" to any of these questions, your child is at higher risk of childhood lead poisoning. Have your child tested for lead.*

SOURCE: Centers for Disease Control, DHHS (1991).

µg/dL and the children should receive follow up blood lead testing within about three months. Blood lead levels greater than 15 µg/dL require aggressive follow up and interventions to lower blood lead levels. Parents should be especially concerned about testing for lead poisoning if a child fits one or more of the risk factors listed in Figure 5.2. If you have your child tested for lead, ask for a blood lead test that is analyzed using anodic stripping voltammetry (ASV) or atomic absorption (AA) methods, which are more sensitive than the erythrocyte protoporphrin (EP) test that is still used by some physicians.

Lead Poisoning in Adults

The Occupational Safety and Health Administration considers blood lead levels of 40 µg/dL or more to be cause for concern in adult workers, whereas some professional groups and other governmental agencies consider blood lead levels above 25 µg/dL in adults to be hazardous. Adults can be exposed to lead through their work, hobbies that use lead or lead solder, renovation or remodeling activities and other sources. Adults experience symptoms of lead poisoning similar to those in children, with the additional symptoms of memory problems, sleep disturbances and loss of sex drive.

Lead-based Paint
Sources

The most common high-dose source of lead exposure for children is lead-based paint. Prior to 1950, paint (as well as varnishes and other coatings) that contained high levels of lead (up to 50 percent lead) was widely used. After 1950, the lead content of paint decreased and the use of lead-based paint declined. Both exterior and interior lead-based paint, however, continued to be available until the mid-1970s. In 1978, the Consumer Product Safety Commission finally banned the manufacture of paint containing more than 0.06 percent lead by weight for use on interior and exterior residential surfaces, toys and furniture. Lead-based paint is still available, though, for industrial, military and marine applications. If these paints are used in or around homes, they pose potential problems.

Any house built prior to 1980 could have lead-based paint, but houses built before 1950 are at the highest risk. Lead-based paint can be found on almost any interior surface, including walls, ceilings, window sills, doors, radiators, floors, stairs and railings. It can also be found on garages, the exterior of the house, fences and storage sheds.

When lead-based coatings age, they tend to crack in a fairly uniform square-like pattern (see Figure 5.3). (Note, however, that this pattern could also be caused by applying a second coat of paint before the first has dried or by paint that has too much oil or an incompatible pigment or vehicle.) Eventually, the coating flakes and peels away from the surface. Children can ingest lead if they eat the paint chips or chew on coated surfaces. Remodeling or renovation

FIGURE 5.3.   Typical Pattern of Cracking Lead Paint

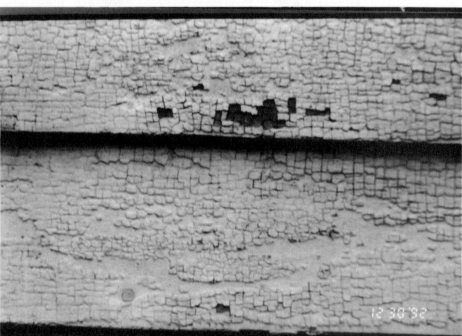

of homes (or other buildings) that are contaminated with lead-based paint is a very important source of lead exposure if the work is not done properly. Children and adults in these homes can absorb lead by eating fallen paint chips or dust, or by breathing lead-containing dust.

Children who live in substandard housing or housing that is being rehabilitated are at the greatest risk of being exposed to lead. The Department of Housing and Urban Development estimates that nationally, about three million tons of lead remain in an estimated 57 million occupied private housing units built before 1980 (about 75 percent of all such housing). Roughly 14 million of these units, occupied by about 3.8 million young children, are estimated to contain lead paint in an unsound condition.

The Residential Lead-based Paint Hazard Reduction Act

Passed in 1992, the Residential Lead-based Paint Hazard Reduction Act (also known as Title X) will require sellers and landlords to disclose the known presence of lead-based paint to their prospective buyers and renters. Purchasers or renters of pre-1978 houses must be given an EPA lead hazard information pamphlet, must have ten days in which to get a lead hazard risk assessment or inspection and must be presented with a sales contract that contains a prescribed "Lead Warning Statement." In addition, the purchaser must sign a statement that verifies that these conditions have been met. These provisions of the Act become effective in 1995; a violation of these provisions could result in significant monetary penalties.

Under Title X, all federal agencies (including the Resolution Trust Corporation) will also have to inspect and abate lead-based paint hazards before the sale and transfer of federally-owned pre-1960 housing. These agencies will also have to notify potential buyers of such housing about the hazards of lead-based paint.

Testing and Understanding the Results

The only way to know for sure if your house or prospective property is contaminated by lead is to test the water, soil, paint or other materials. Your local health department or water utility office can provide information and assistance on sampling. Their representatives will either test samples for you or refer you to qualified laboratories and certified inspectors who can conduct lead testing (see the next section for more information). Qualified laboratories should use either EPA or ASTM methods to test for lead in paint, varnish or other coatings.

There are two basic ways to measure the amount of lead in painted surfaces. One approach is to hire a lead testing company to bring a portable instrument into your home with which the paint on many different surfaces can

FIGURE 5.4.   Sampling for Lead with a Portable Analyzer

be tested. One commonly used portable instrument, an X-ray fluorescence analyzer (XRF) can sample several areas in one visit, provides immediate results and does not disturb painted surfaces (see Figure 5.4). It might take a testing professional two to three hours to inspect a home and measure 30 to 50 samples using an XRF; the cost of this inspection may range from $100 to $200. The unit of measurement used for the XRF and similar instruments is milligrams of lead per square centimeter of surface (mg/cm^2). Measurements taken with the XRF may need to be verified by another testing method.

A second method involves the collection (either by you or by a technician) of paint chip samples which are then sent to a testing laboratory for analysis. The testing cost will depend on who collects the sample and could be in the range of $25 to $50 for each sample. (If you take the samples, the laboratory will provide instructions for proper collection.) Request an atomic absorption (AA) spectrometry test or an inductively coupled plasma-atomic emission (ICP-AE) spectrometry test. The atomic absorption method is more accurate and precise than the XRF method. A positive test for lead is 0.5 percent or more by weight or 1.0 mg/cm^2.

Do not select a laboratory or contractor that uses a screening test kit to test paint, air or water samples. These kits typically rely on a color change to determine if lead is present and there is little information on their reliability and accuracy. Although they are cheaper than laboratory analyses, test kits are usually not very accurate and might not detect low levels of lead that could be harmful.

Reducing Exposure

The presence of lead-based paint in your home does not necessarily mean that you and your family are in immediate danger. Lead-based paint is a health threat only if the lead is inhaled or swallowed. Each case should be evaluated carefully and individually to develop the most cost-effective strategy for ensuring that no one is exposed to lead during the corrective procedures. The best person to judge the seriousness of a health threat posed by lead-contaminated surfaces is a professional who is trained in the removal and repair of lead-containing materials.

Some states have certification programs for training and monitoring professionals who test for and correct lead problems. Contact your local health department or state agency for lead programs to learn more about these regulations. These agencies can provide a list of qualified contractors but if they do not have such a list, refer to the yellow pages of your telephone book under "Lead Removal and Abatement" or under "Environmental and Ecological Services." In a small community, you may have to go to a larger city to locate a qualified contractor.

There are two basic types of professionals who handle lead-contamination problems: lead inspectors and corrective action contractors. Inspectors are trained to inspect homes for lead and to collect samples. If lead is present, an inspector should provide a written report evaluating the location and condition of the material. The evaluation should include recommendations for preventing additional damage and correcting the problem.

Corrective action contractors are trained to repair or remove lead-contaminated surfaces and prevent further contamination of the house. When hiring a corrective action contractor, ask questions about the repair or removal process and always *ask for references*. Ask to see the contractor's proof of certification and insurance. Become familiar with the proper procedures for lead repair and removal so you can be sure that they are followed. Check with your local health department or the state agency responsible for lead programs to find out if a particular contractor has violated any regulations. Ask the local Better Business Bureau or Chamber of Commerce if there are any complaints against the contractor. Once you decide to employ a contractor, get a *signed* contact that explains the methods that will be used for repair, removal and clean up, as well as estimates for project completion time and the total cost of the work.

After the work starts, a reputable contractor should not allow anyone, even a homeowner, into the work area unless that person is wearing a respirator and protective clothing. If the contractor does not follow the agreed-upon work practices, stop the work immediately and call the local health department for help.

Do not hire the same firm to evaluate the problem and correct it. Instead, hire one firm to inspect, test and recommend corrective actions and engage a second to do the corrective work. (For example, you might want to hire a certified lead inspector to monitor the air after the corrective action officer completes a removal.) Get several estimates if possible, although this may be difficult in some parts of the country where services are limited.

If you are unable or unwilling to hire a professional contractor and you decide to repair or remove the lead-contaminated surfaces yourself, contact the local health department or state agency for lead programs to help you understand the proper removal or repair methods as well as any regulations that apply to your situation. Get as much information as you can before you begin. Methods for treating lead in your home are summarized below, and Appendix D gives guidelines for cleaning intact surfaces, removing chips and dust and applying a coating to the surface. Detailed instructions for these and other types of procedures for managing lead-containing materials can be obtained from the National Institute of Building Sciences (see Appendix A for the address).

Removal. Removal of lead-based paint from surfaces is a procedure that permanently removes lead from the home and can be done on-site or at a place away from the house. A skilled homeowner can safely remove lead from small areas, but larger jobs should be left to professionals. Lead-based paint (which is frequently found on doors and trim that are important to the architecture of the house) can be removed from all surfaces in the house. If cost is a factor, a partial removal might be possible. This involves removing lead from surfaces up to a height of about four or five feet—high enough so that children cannot reach the lead-contaminated surfaces. Figure 5.5 shows an example of a lead removal project.

Replacement. Sometimes the most cost-effective solution is to replace lead-contaminated items such as doors, windows and other fixtures with lead-free components. Replacement is a permanent solution that has minimal risk associated with it.

Encapsulation. Encapsulation is a temporary solution that involves covering or sealing lead-contaminated surfaces such as floors, walls, ceilings and some types of trim and pipes. It requires trained workers and routine

FIGURE 5.5.   Lead Removal Project inside a Home

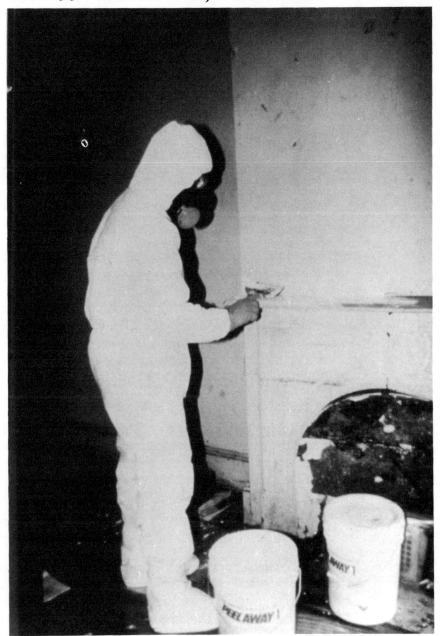

SOURCE: U.S. HUD (1990).

upkeep, but it can be cost-effective for large areas. The covering should be a material that children cannot damage easily. Examples include gypsum board, aluminum, vinyl, plywood, Formica, acrylic sheets, fiberglass, durable carpet, tile and plexiglass. Contact paper and wallpaper that is not vinyl are not acceptable coverings unless all of the lead has been removed.

Housekeeping. If you have lead in or around your home, you will need to clean the floors, walls, window sills and other surfaces regularly and thoroughly to prevent lead from building up in the home. When properly done, cleaning is a time-intensive but effective measure to control lead until more permanent solutions are found.

Do not use a conventional vacuum to remove dust and loose paint chips from the walls, ceilings or any other surfaces. A special vacuum, called a high effeciency particulate air (HEPA) vacuum, is needed for these surfaces because it can trap the small lead dust particles. Furniture, carpets and draperies can be steam cleaned, washed or HEPA vacuumed. You may be able to rent this machine from a tool rental store or borrow one from your local health department. Wetting the surface before vacuuming can lower dust levels. If you do not have access to a HEPA vacuum, wet wipe and mop the exposed surfaces. Use a detergent that has a high content of trisodium phosphate (TSP) and follow the cleaning instructions in Appendix D. After the initial cleaning, the lead-containing surfaces must be wet mopped or wiped daily using the TSP or other effective detergent. This will prevent lead dust from collecting.

In addition to regular cleaning, it is important to prevent the generation of lead-containing dust and to minimize the flaking and chipping of paint. It may be necessary to cover door frames and facings and window sills with masking tape, heavy paper or contact paper. Moving a large piece of furniture against a hazardous wall area can limit exposure to lead from that source. A child's crib or bed should be moved away from unsafe wall areas. If possible, open windows from the top to reduce the possibility of toddlers picking at or chewing on dust or chips that are produced when windows are opened and closed.

To reduce the amount of lead-containing dust and dirt that is tracked into the house, hose off sidewalks, steps, porches and doormats often. Ask everyone to remove their shoes upon entering the house and follow the instructions given below for covering exposed soil.

Make sure that children wash their hands and faces frequently. If your home or neighborhood has elevated lead levels, follow your health department's guidelines for lowering your family's exposure to lead.

Lead in Soil and Dust
Sources

Soil and dust should not be overlooked as important sources of lead. Lead can enter soil and dust from deteriorating or improperly removed lead-based paint, emissions from industrial sources such as smelters and lead battery plants or emissions from leaded gasoline. Even though nearly all of the lead has been removed from gasoline, the undisturbed soil next to roads is still contaminated with lead, and will probably remain so for many more years.

Testing and Understanding the Results

Soil samples are typically collected and sent for analysis to a laboratory that uses either EPA or ASTM methods. Portable instruments can be used to test soils for lead at the site (discussed in the section of this chapter about testing for lead paint). Costs range from $25 to $200 per house, depending on the method and number of samples analyzed.

Lead levels in soil are usually reported in parts per million (ppm); levels greater than 500 ppm are cause for concern according to EPA guidelines. Whether or not corrective action is needed depends on the frequency and severity of exposure to lead in soil.

Reducing Exposure

If you suspect lead in your soil, first have the soil tested and then consider potential solutions. Since lead does not decay or degrade over time, removal is the only permanent solution. Even though it can be expensive, soil removal should be done by a certified lead removal contractor (or a contractor trained in proper removal methods if your state does not have a certification program). Disposal of the lead-contaminated soil must be done according to federal, state and local regulations.

Covering the soil with stones, gravel or grass is another solution. The covering must provide complete coverage, must be maintained and must be secure enough so that children cannot disturb it.

Other strategies that you can follow in order to lower exposure to lead include the following:

- Remove shoes before entering the house
- Hose off sidewalks, steps, porches and doormats
- Make sure that children wash their hands after playing outside in the dirt or snow

- Build a sandbox and fill it with safe, lead-free sand for children
- Plant your garden in a safe, lead-free area away from painted buildings and busy roads, and wash your hands after working in the yard or garden

Water and Plumbing

Sources

Most surface and ground water sources of drinking water have low lead levels, but lead materials in the fixtures, lines and distribution systems can contaminate the water. Some potential sources that are shown in Figure 5.6 include the following:

- Service mains that carry water through streets
- Service lines that carry water from the street to a building
- Lead connectors
- Lead pipes within a building
- Lead-soldered joints in copper plumbing within a building
- Lead-containing brass faucets and other plumbing fixtures
- Lead-containing water fountains and coolers

Neighborhoods settled prior to 1930 are most likely to have service mains, lines and connectors made of lead. However, service lines of lead were installed as recently as 1986. The EPA estimates that there are about ten million lead service lines or connections in the United States. About 20 percent of all

FIGURE 5.6.   The Water Supply System

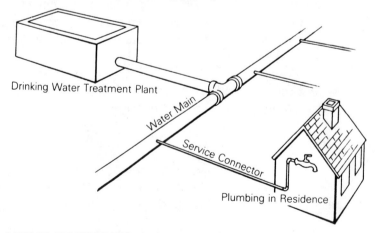

SOURCE: U.S. EPA (1987).

public water systems have at least some lead service lines or connections within their distribution systems.

The composition of drinking water pipes within the house has changed over time. Lead was commonly used before 1930, and galvanized pipes were introduced and used between 1920 and 1950. After 1930, copper pipes joined by lead solder were widely used and more recently, plastic pipes have come into use.

Overall, the major source of lead contamination in drinking water is the lead solder that connects metallic pipes. Slow corrosion of the pipes removes lead from the pipes in a process called *leaching*. New lead solders can release significant amounts of lead into drinking water for up to five years, but they release less lead as they age. Leaching increases when the water is corrosive or soft. Hard water contains minerals that form a protective coating on the inside of the water pipes and keep lead from leaching. Soft water has a low mineral content that does not permit the buildup of such a protective layer. Another factor that increases corrosion and the amount of lead in water is the practice of grounding any part of the electrical system to a metal water supply pipe. Although any electric current traveling through the ground wire will increase the corrosion of lead in the pipes, do not remove the ground wire unless a qualified electrician installs an adequate grounding system.

Lead (and possibly other metals) may be present in your water if any of the following apply to your home:

- Lead pipes—look for a dull gray metal that is soft enough to be easily scratched with a key
- Signs of corrosion—look for frequent leaks, rust-colored water and stained dishes or laundry
- Non-plastic plumbing and fixtures—look for pipes and fixtures that are less than five years old
- Construction before 1930—ask your water utility if the service connectors in your home or area are made of lead
- Wells with submersible brass pumps

Testing and Understanding the Results

Water samples must be collected and sent to a qualified laboratory that uses EPA methods for testing lead. If you collect the sample, use the sample containers provided by the laboratory and follow the instructions exactly (otherwise, the results may not be reliable). The EPA procedure requires both a "first-draw" and a "fully flushed" sample. Be sure that the laboratory you select collects these two types of samples. The first-draw sample is taken from a tap that has not been used for at least six hours and will have the highest level of lead. The fully flushed sample is collected after the water has flushed lead from the pipes and will help to determine if flushing can lower the lead level in water from that tap.

Lead in drinking water is reported in parts per billion (ppb) or micrograms per liter (µg/L). (1 ppb equals 1 µg/L.) The EPA considers a lead level greater than 15 ppb to be elevated.

The amount of lead in plumbing is reported in percentages. Lead levels of concern are more than 8 percent in pipes and pipe fittings and more than 0.2 percent in solders and fluxes.

Reducing Exposure

Regardless of its source, the only way to know if your water contains lead is to test it. If you have a private water supply, check the house for lead drinking water pipes and replace them. Other potential sources include brass fixtures and copper pipes soldered with lead. The EPA advises homeowners with submersible brass pumps to test their well water for lead. If the pump is less than one year old, consider using an alternative water supply until the test result is known.

If you are served by a public water system, contact your supplier and ask if the system contains lead piping and if your water is corrosive. If the answer to either question is "yes," ask what steps the supplier is taking to reduce lead contamination. The EPA requires public water suppliers to test drinking water for lead, and you can ask for the results of testing in your community.

There are several steps you can take to reduce exposure until the source of high lead concentrations is identified and removed.

Water Flushing. *Do not* drink water that has been in contact with your home's plumbing for more than six hours, such as overnight or during the work day. Before using water for drinking or cooking, flush the cold water faucet by allowing the water to run until you can feel that the water has become as cold as it will get. You must do this for each drinking water faucet. (An alternative to flushing is to buy and use bottled water.) Taking a shower or a bath will not flush your kitchen tap. Once a tap has been flushed, you can fill bottles with water and put them in the refrigerator for later use. (Note that flushing may not be effective if you live in a high-rise building with large-diameter supply pipes joined with lead solder.)

Buildings built before 1930 may have service connectors made of lead. Flushing an extra 15 seconds after the water is cool should also flush the service connector. The water that comes out after flushing will not have been in contact with lead pipes or solder long enough to contaminate the water.

Never cook with or consume water from the hot water tap and do not make baby formula with hot tap water because lead dissolves more quickly in hot water than in cold water. If you need hot water, be sure to use water from the cold tap and heat it on the stove or in the microwave.

Before occupying a newly built home, remove all strainers from faucets and flush the water for at least 15 minutes to remove any loose lead solder or flux debris from the plumbing. Periodically check the strainers and remove any accumulation of loose lead.

Plumbing Repairs. Require a plumber (in writing) to use only lead-free materials for repairs or in newly installed plumbing. If the incoming electrical service is grounded to water pipes, do not remove the grounding unless a qualified electrician installs an adequate alternate grounding system. Grounding the electrical system to a metal water supply pipe is done for safety reasons. In addition to accelerating the corrosion of lead in the pipes, it can also cause some of the return current to flow through the pipe and contribute to the magnetic field in a home (see Chapter 12 for more information about this).

Treatment Systems. Treat the water to make it less corrosive by installing reverse osmosis systems, distillation units or calcite filters. Calcite filters should be installed in the line between the water source and any lead service connections or lead-soldered pipes. Carbon, sand and cartridge filters do not remove lead. See Chapter 13 for more information about reverse osmosis systems, distillation units and other types of water treatment devices.

 Lead Checklist

Questions To Ask	Response	What Does a "Yes" Mean?
Painted Surfaces		
Was the home built before 1950?	Yes No ❏ ❏	Any original paint probably has a high lead content.
Was the home built between 1950 and 1980?	Yes No ❏ ❏	Any original paint may still contain lead.
If the home was built before 1980, is the interior or exterior paint peeling, cracking or lifting away?	Yes No ❏ ❏	Damaged paint poses a potential health threat if it contains lead.

Questions To Ask	Response	What Does a "Yes" Mean?
Painted Surfaces		
If the paint is deteriorating, is it cracking in a pattern of fairly uniform squares?	Yes No ❏ ❏	The paint probably contains lead if the home was built before 1980.
Water Supply		
Was the home built before 1930?	Yes No ❏ ❏	The water pipes, main lines and connectors probably contain lead.
Was the home built after 1930?	Yes No ❏ ❏	The water pipes are probably copper joined by lead solder.
Does the home have water pipes that are made of a soft, dull gray metal that can easily be scratched with a key?	Yes No ❏ ❏	The water pipes are probably lead.
Are there frequent leaks, rust-colored water, stained dishes or stained laundry?	Yes No ❏ ❏	Corrosion is occurring and if lead is present it will be leached into the water supply.
Is the plumbing non-plastic and less than five years old?	Yes No ❏ ❏	The pipes may be joined by lead solder. If brass fixtures are present, they may leach lead into the water.
Is the water soft?	Yes No ❏ ❏	Soft water is corrosive and if present, lead may be extracted into the water supply.
Is the electrical system grounded to the water pipes?	Yes No ❏ ❏	Grounding increases the corrosion of metal pipes and solder.

Questions To Ask	Response	What Does a "Yes" Mean?
Does the home have a submersible well pump?	Yes No ❏ ❏	Submersible brass pumps can leach lead into the water.
Location		
Is the home located next to a busy road?	Yes No ❏ ❏	The soil may be contaminated with lead.
Is the home located in the area of a smelter, lead battery plant or other industry that releases lead into the environment?	Yes No ❏ ❏	The soil, air and/or water may be contaminated with lead.
Remodeling and Renovation		
Have the interior and exterior surfaces of a pre-1980 home recently been dry-sanded, heat-treated or otherwise treated to remove paint without testing for lead?	Yes No ❏ ❏	The house may be contaminated with lead if the paint contained lead.

If you answered "yes" to any of the above questions, you should be concerned about the presence of lead. Have the paint, soil, water or dust in and around your home tested for lead.

Summary Chart for Formaldehyde

Topic	Comments
Description	Formaldehyde is a flammable, tasteless and colorless toxic gas.
Health Effects	Formaldehyde causes irritation of the nose and throat as well as tearing and redness of the eyes at low levels. (These effects can occur within a few minutes after exposure to the gas.) At high levels, it irritates the lower airways and results in coughing, chest tightness and wheezing. Formaldehyde can cause other symptoms, and the EPA lists it as a probable human carcinogen.
Sources	Interior building materials such as hardwood plywood, particle board, medium density fiberboard and other pressed wood products release formaldehyde over time. These materials are used as underlayment, cabinets, doors, paneling, flooring and furniture. Formaldehyde is found in carpets, pads and upholstery fabrics. A less common source of the gas is urea formaldehyde foam insulation.
Testing	Hire a professional environmental testing firm to sample for the gas. The sample is collected for periods ranging from 30 minutes to one week. There are no federal standards for formaldehyde in residential indoor air. Levels below 0.1 ppm will protect most people from irritation.
Reducing Exposure	Formaldehyde levels decrease naturally over a period of several years. If levels are high or if people are sensitive to the gas, immediate measures may be needed. A permanent solution involves removing the material that contains the gas. Other strategies include increasing the ventilation and applying a protective coating of urethane, varnish or other sealer to potential sources.
	In newer or recently remodeled homes, steam cleaning with water may be effective on materials that can be cleaned safely with water. Raising the temperature inside the house for a few days may lower formaldehyde levels temporarily (see Chapter 7), but this method has not been proven as an effective way to reduce exposure over a long period of time.

CHAPTER
SIX

Formaldehyde

The family of a nine-year old Baytown, Texas boy, who lived in a mobile home for four years, reached a $570,000 settlement in a product liability suit involving alleged formaldehyde poisoning in their mobile home. The Slaughters' son developed irreversible pulmonary disease presumably as a result of his long-term exposure to the formaldehyde. Other family members developed respiratory problems, but to a lesser degree.

The Slaughters claimed that the manufacturer, Kaufman & Broad Home Systems, Inc., failed to warn them of the hazard and failed to take the needed steps to reduce or eliminate the formaldehyde.

As reported in *Product Safety & Liability Reporter,* Vol. 18, No. 27, July 6, 1990.

What Is Formaldehyde and Why Is It a Hazard?

Formaldehyde is a flammable and colorless reactive gas that belongs to a large family of chemicals called volatile organic compounds (see Chapter 7). It has a characteristic odor that most people can smell at high concentrations. The human body produces formaldehyde naturally as a by-product of metabolism, but not at levels high enough to cause health effects.

Formaldehyde irritates the eyes, nose and throat, and it causes coughing, chest tightness and wheezing. Since many of these symptoms are similar to those that accompany a cold, flu or other respiratory condition, a person who exhibits these symptoms may not know that he or she has an environmental illness. Some people have reported other effects, including nosebleeds, fatigue, headache, problems with memory and concentration, nausea and dizziness. Skin contact with formaldehyde-containing products can cause skin irritation, rash and dermatitis in those who are sensitive.

According to an estimate by the National Research Council, about 10 to 12 percent of Americans might be sensitive to the irritant effects of formaldehyde. In 1987, the EPA classified formaldehyde as a probable human carcinogen. The EPA is updating this classification, however, and the new cancer risk estimates may be lower.

How can you know if formaldehyde might be responsible for your illness? Do you frequently have unexplained colds or one or more of the irritation symptoms listed above? Do you live or work in an area with measured formaldehyde levels above 0.1 ppm? If you answered "yes" to either question, you may be experiencing a formaldehyde-related illness.

You might suspect that your home or workplace contains formaldehyde if it is less than five years old or has been remodeled within the last year. Other potential sources include new furnishings, cars, motor homes and campers. If your symptoms started at about the time one of these sources came into your life, formaldehyde might be the cause. An easy check is to stay away from your home or workplace overnight or for a few days. If your symptoms improve during this time, formaldehyde or other volatile organic chemicals may be present in that place.

The symptoms of formaldehyde exposure and their severity vary according to the concentration of the gas, exposure time and the sensitivity of each person. Some people are very sensitive to low levels of formaldehyde while others may not have any reaction to the chemical at those levels. People who have asthma, existing lung diseases, immune system deficiencies or a general sensitivity to synthetic organic chemicals are likely to be sensitive to formaldehyde. If you believe that this gas might be a problem in your home, discuss your symptoms and formaldehyde test results with your physician.

Sources

Formaldehyde has many uses and is found in numerous items common to most households, including cosmetics, detergents, clothing, food additives, mouthwashes and paper (see Figure 6.1). The major sources of exposure for most people are building materials and furnishings.

The connection between construction materials and formaldehyde-related health effects was first recognized in the mid-1970s, when many people became

FIGURE 6.1.   Potential Sources of Formaldehyde

Types of Products	Common Uses
Pressed wood	Hardwood plywood, particle board, medium-density fiberboard (MDF) and decorative paneling
Insulation	Urea-formaldehyde foam insulation (UFFI) and fiberglass made with formaldehyde binders
Combustion sources	Fireplace and tobacco smoke, automobile exhaust, and natural gas and kerosene fumes
Stiffeners, wrinkle resisters, water repellents and coatings	Floor coverings (rugs, linoleum, varnishes and plastics), carpet backings, adhesive binders, fire retardants, permanent press textiles and wood preservatives
Paper products	Grocery bags, waxed paper, facial tissues, paper towels and disposable sanitary products
Other products	Plastics, cosmetics, deodorants, shampoos, disinfectants, starch-based glues, adhesives, laminates, paints, fabric dyes, inks, fertilizers and fungicides

SOURCE: Adapted from National Resource Council (1981).

ill after their homes were insulated with urea formaldehyde foam insulation (UFFI). The UFFI was sprayed as a foam into the wall cavities of homes and as it cured, formaldehyde gas was released into the living spaces in a process called "offgassing" or "outgassing." Shortly after identifying UFFI as a health threat, scientists discovered that any material made with urea-formaldehyde can release the gas.

Between 1975 and 1981, about 435,000 homes were insulated with UFFI, and there have been many health complaints and lawsuits related to these homes. The Consumer Product Safety Commission banned the installation of UFFI in homes and schools in 1982, but the ban was soon overturned by the courts. Although UFFI is now legally permitted, concerns about safety have curtailed its use. If you have UFFI in your home, and it was installed more than ten years ago, it is not likely to be a problem.

UFFI and building materials that contain formaldehyde release the gas at different rates. The rate of release increases when the temperature and relative humidity are high. The reverse is also true. Less formaldehyde is released when the temperature and relative humidity are low. These factors are important when making decisions about sampling because formaldehyde levels can vary significantly during the day and between seasons. A test conducted on a cold day could indicate formaldehyde levels less than half of one taken during the summer.

Hardwood plywood, particle board, medium-density fiberboard (MDF) and other pressed wood products are the most likely residential sources of formaldehyde. These products are made by combining wood pieces or chips with an adhesive and other chemicals (including urea formaldehyde resins) and pressing them together in hot hydraulic presses. During the last several years, manufacturers of these products have taken steps to reduce the amount of formaldehyde in these products, but it has not yet been eliminated.

In the home, hardwood plywood can be found in decorative wall paneling, furniture, cabinets, doors and flooring. (Softwood plywood also has a variety of applications, but it does not contain formaldehyde.) Particle board is used primarily as underlayment, mobile home decking and to make industrial board. Industrial board and MDF are the main components of many products including furniture and kitchen cabinets.

Manufactured houses and mobile homes are important sources because they typically use more potential formaldehyde-releasing materials than houses built on-site. The Department of Housing and Urban Development (HUD) requires manufacturers to meet a product standard and to warn potential buyers that the home may contain formaldehyde (see Figure 6.2). These regulations, however, do not forbid the use of formaldehyde; therefore, the sales agreement for a manufactured or mobile home should require testing for the gas.

Testing and Understanding the Results

The only way to know for sure if formaldehyde is a problem in your home is to test for it. In some cases, your local or state department of health can test your home free of charge or at low cost, or they may be able to provide a list of testing companies. If not, environmental testing laboratories can be found in the yellow pages of the telephone directory under "Laboratories— Testing" or "Environmental & Ecological Services."

There are two basic methods for short-term testing for formaldehyde. In one, a small sampler containing a liquid or solid chemical is used to collect the air, possibly with the aid of a sampling pump. The sampler is worn or placed in the middle of a room and after collection, it is returned to a laboratory for analysis. A sampler can either be placed by the homeowner (typical cost is $25 to $35) or by the testing company ($50 to $100 or more, depending on the travel time).

FIGURE 6.2.   **Formaldehyde Warning in a
Manufactured Home**

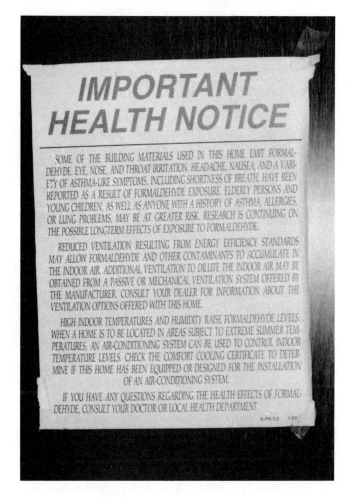

Another testing method involves the use of a portable instrument that produces a continuous record of the variation in formaldehyde levels. Placed in the home by a testing company, this instrument is used to measure the indoor air level or to look for specific sources of formaldehyde (such as kitchen cabinets). Depending on the distance the technician must travel, costs are typically $100 or more.

Both methods can produce accurate results. The recommended sampling time for both methods is at least 30 minutes to one hour in order to determine the average amount of formaldehyde that is present. Samplers that are not attached to sampling pumps might be used for longer sampling times (up to a week). Specific sources of formaldehyde in the home can be identified when the portable instrument is used to collect spot samples from suspect sources such as kitchen cabinets.

Guidelines for Testing

Since formaldehyde levels change during the day, week and season, it is important to have closed house conditions before and during testing. This means keeping doors and windows closed for about 12 hours *before* starting the test. If the test will last less than one day, keep the house closed for the entire test period. If the test lasts longer than one day, keep the house closed as much as possible. If you are purchasing a house, ask the testing company to use motion and pressure detectors (see Chapter 3) to help ensure the accuracy of the test results. If the windows and doors are open, outside air will dilute the formaldehyde released into the house, and the test result will be low. If you are unable to find a testing company that has these detectors, you should retest the house after purchasing it. Consider repeating the test during the summer if the first test is done during the winter months.

When testing your home for formaldehyde, it is important to follow certain guidelines in order to ensure the safety and accuracy of the test.

- There are two strategies for placing the sampler. If you have symptoms that you believe to be formaldehyde-related, put the sampler in a room that seems to make them worse. Otherwise, put the sampler in a room that has the most possible sources of formaldehyde, such as an area that has been recently remodeled, refurnished or recarpeted.
- Place the sampler at least two to three feet above the floor, ideally at head level. Make sure that the sampler is at least one foot away from other objects. Do not place the sampler in an area that is drafty and do not place it behind books, picture frames or other objects that will block the flow of air to the sampler.
- Do not move or dust the sampler, even when the sampling time is more than one day.
- Ask the testing company if the sampling device contains liquid toxic chemicals. Ask for instructions on cleaning up an accidental spill. Even though samplers usually contain only small amounts of liquid chemicals, accidents can occur and it is best to be prepared.

After sampling for the recommended time, follow the testing company's instructions for returning the sampler. You should receive test results within two to three weeks.

Understanding Test Results

Formaldehyde results are usually reported in parts per million (abbreviated ppm) or parts per billion (abbreviated ppb). One part per million is equal to 1000 parts per billion. Low levels of formaldehyde (below 0.03 ppm) are usually present in indoor and outdoor air and are not cause for concern.

Levels below 0.1 ppm are acceptable for most people, but some sensitive individuals could experience symptoms at levels as low as 0.03 ppm. Levels in the range of 0.1 ppm to 0.3 ppm can cause irritation and other symptoms in many people. Levels greater than 0.3 ppm are very likely to cause symptoms in most people. Try to lower the formaldehyde levels if the measured level of formaldehyde is 0.1 ppm or more and if anyone in the home is potentially sensitive.

Sometimes laboratory results are reported as "less than" a specified concentration (abbreviated "<"). This means that the formaldehyde level is below a known amount, but the exact concentration is unknown. Before hiring a testing company, make sure that the testing method it uses can measure a formaldehyde concentration of 0.1 ppm or less. This is important because some members of the household could be sensitive to low levels of formaldehyde.

Reducing Exposure

If formaldehyde is at a level of concern in your home or a prospective property, there are potentially cost-effective solutions. Studies have shown that the passage of time will eventually lower formaldehyde levels by roughly half every 4.4 years. Some people, however, are so sensitive to formaldehyde that they are unable to allow time to take care of the problem. They can reduce symptoms by taking aggressive action to lower formaldehyde levels in the home and work place, and by avoiding many common products that contain formaldehyde.

Removing and Replacing Sources

Removal of formaldehyde sources is the most effective solution, but it can be expensive. Paneling, furniture, cabinets, carpeting and drapes can be removed and replaced with materials that do not contain formaldehyde. Removing UFFI and particle board subflooring may be too difficult and not practical.

When building or remodeling a home, use materials that do not release formaldehyde, such as lumber or metal. If pressed wood products must be used, ask for low formaldehyde-releasing materials.

Treating the Source

Applying urethane, varnish, shellac or special sealers to paneling, ply-wood and particle board can lower the outgassing of formaldehyde from these materials. (Always use these products with adequate ventilation and respira-tory protection as directed by the manufacturer.) In some instances, Formica or other formaldehyde-free material (such as vinyl wallpaper) can provide an effective barrier. These coverings must be applied carefully to all surfaces in order to seal any exposed areas.

There are several possible treatments for UFFI. Sealing cracks in walls and placing gaskets in electrical outlets can reduce points through which formalde-hyde can enter a room. Covering walls with vapor-barrier paint, vinyl wallpa-per or other special coatings can lower the amount of gas that diffuses through the walls.

Washing permanent press fabrics before use and steam cleaning carpets, drapes and upholstery can dissolve formaldehyde and remove it from these materials. However, this will also remove any dirt and water repellent treat-ments. The gas can sometimes be driven off of water-sensitive drapery mate-rials by tumbling the drapes at medium to high heat for about 30 minutes. Before using these options, consider potential damage to the materials.

Another option suggested by research findings is to "bake out" the formaldehyde and other volatile chemicals by increasing the temperature in a new or recently remodeled home for a period of one to several days. Although this option can reduce formaldehyde levels initially, it may not be effective over a long period of time. (See Chapter 7 for more information.)

Some research shows that plants can remove formaldehyde and other chemicals from the air. Spider plants, philodendron (heart leaf, lacy tree and elephant ear varieties), aloe vera and golden pothos are a few types that appear to remove formaldehyde more effectively. Anyone who has mold aller-gies, however, may not be able to tolerate indoor plants.

One method that is *not* recommended is placing containers of ammonia in rooms or in cabinets for varying periods. This practice is not effective and can result in injury if the ammonia fumes overcome someone.

Increasing the Ventilation

Increasing the ventilation indoors is an easy way to lower formaldehyde levels, but this will allow heat to escape and increase energy costs. Heat recov-ery ventilators (also called air-to-air heat exchangers) can lower levels of radon and other contaminants, but there is not enough experience with these systems to determine their effectiveness in removing formaldehyde.

Purifying the Air

Chemical filter systems to reduce contaminants in the air are available. The effectiveness of these systems in removing formaldehyde in homes, however, is unknown.

 Formaldehyde Checklist

Questions To Ask	Response	What Does a "Yes" Mean?
Was the home constructed within the last five years?	Yes No ❏ ❏	New homes can release formaldehyde and other organic chemicals. Test to be sure.
Has the home been remodeled within the last 6 to 12 months with new carpeting, furniture, drapes, paint, vinyl flooring or cabinets?	Yes No ❏ ❏	Newly remodeled homes can release formaldehyde and other organic chemicals. Test to be sure.
Does the home have UFFI insulation? (Look for plugged holes at uniform distances on the exterior of the house or for a spongy material behind electrical outlets.)	Yes No ❏ ❏	UFFI can release formaldehyde into the interior of homes even though it is in the wall cavities. This release is greatest during the first few years after the product has been installed. Test to be sure. Plugged holes on the exterior often (but not always) indicates the presence of UFFI. These openings are also used for other types of insulation that will not release formaldehyde.
Does the home have UFFI insulation that is ten or more years old?	Yes No ❏ ❏	Formaldehyde is not likely to be a problem.

Formaldehyde Checklist

Questions To Ask	Response	What Does a "Yes" Mean?
Is the home a mobile home or manufactured home?	Yes No ☐ ☐	Mobile and manufactured homes may have high formaldehyde levels because of the materials used in construction and the higher ratio of formaldehyde-containing materials to indoor air space. Test to be sure.

Summary Chart for Volatile Chemicals

Topic	Comments
Description	Volatile chemicals are natural and synthetic cornpounds that evaporate readily at room temperature.
Health Effects	Volatile chemicals can affect all of the body's systems. (The respiratory tract, nervous system, kidneys and liver are especially sensitive.) Many of these chemicals are carcinogenic.
Sources	Volatile chemicals are released by many building and consumer products. Examples include wood products, insulation, laminates and other plastics, fabrics and dyes, paints, sealers, varnishes, glues and pesticides. Other sources are elevated outdoor air levels of volatile chemicals and, less frequently, contaminated soil and groundwater.
Testing	Hire qualified laboratories to test for volatile chemicals. Local and state health agencies can provide names of qualified laboratories. Interpreting results of testing for volatile chemicals is difficult.
Reducing Exposure	Whenever possible, use consumer and building products that are fast-drying and water-based. Read product labels, follow safety guidelines and store products containing volatile chemicals outside the living place. Ask the carpet retailer to air the carpet before installation. If possible, clean carpets and upholstery with water-based products. When building a home, discuss the materials with the builder and try to use those that emit lower levels of these chemicals. Whenever indoor air is contaminated by soil or groundwater, professional help will be needed to reduce exposure to volatile chemicals.

CHAPTER
SEVEN

Volatile Chemicals in Construction Materials, Furnishings and Consumer Products

Five years after Glenn and Janice Heacock and their two sons moved into their home in Hammond, Indiana, they began smelling gasoline fumes. At the same time, the family began to have headaches, nausea, bloody noses and eyes, vomiting and nose and throat irritation. Their sons also suffered psychological effects such as depression and wild mood swings.

The smell of the gasoline became worse any time it rained and the groundwater filled the sump pit. Mr. Heacock discovered the cause of the symptoms on September 10, 1990, after one of his sons became ill in the basement. He found gasoline floating on top of the water in his sump pit. He took a jar full of the contaminated water to the fire department, and the family was ordered out of the house because the fire department feared an explosion would occur.

The source of the gasoline in their home was a leaking underground storage tank at the nearby Citgo Quik Mart station. In an attempt to solve the problem, the owners of the station decided not to remove the tank. Instead, a trench was dug around the leaky tank and vapor extractors were installed in the home. The family's problems continued and they filed suit against the station owners. In 1993, a federal court found that Southland Corporation and Citgo, the owners and operators of the station, were negligent and had caused a nuisance. The jury awarded the family $1.5 million.

As reported in *The Indianapolis News,* November 4, 1993.

What Are Volatile Chemicals and Why Are They a Hazard?

Volatile chemicals are compounds that evaporate readily into the air at room temperature. Most are organic (carbon-based) chemicals. Volatile chemicals are emitted from industrial operations, including solvent and degreasing operations, chemical manufacturing, paint manufacturing and some commercial facilities such as dry cleaners and auto body shops. Unburned fuel from transportation sources is another major source of these compounds.

Indoor sources of volatile chemicals include building materials such as wood products, plastics and laminates, insulation and textiles. Volatile chemicals are found in cleaners, paints, sealers, varnishes, glues, pesticides and other consumer and building products.

Other (but less frequent) sources of volatile chemicals indoors are gasoline from underground storage tanks, and chemical contamination from controlled and uncontrolled disposal sites. Chemicals from these sources can enter a house from contaminated soil or well water.

Over 900 organic chemicals have been found in indoor air. Studies by the EPA show that indoor levels of many volatile chemicals are greater than their outdoor levels. This is due in part to the large number of indoor sources of these chemicals and because a house traps the chemicals inside so they cannot escape. Some indoor sources release volatile chemicals over time through a process called "outgassing" or "offgassing."

Volatile chemicals are hazardous because not only may they increase a person's overall cancer risk, but many people also develop irritation symptoms and allergic reactions in response to exposure. Because these chemicals are in the air, most exposure occurs through inhalation, although some volatile chemicals can be absorbed through the skin. Scientists are still learning about potential adverse effects from volatile chemicals, but some effects are known (see Figure 7.1 for a partial listing).

FIGURE 7.1.   Health Effects and Sources of Some Volatile Chemicals Found in Building and Consumer Products

Compound	Health Effects	Sources and Uses
Formaldehyde	Probable human carcinogen, eye and respiratory tract irritant and cause of a variety of low-level symptoms	Hardwood plywood, particle board, medium density fiberboard, pressed wood products and tobacco smoke
Benzene	Carcinogen and respiratory tract irritant	Plastic and rubber solvents, tobacco smoke, paints, stains, varnishes, fillers and gasoline vapor
Xylenes	Narcotic, irritant and hazard to the heart, liver, kidneys and nervous system	Adhesives, joint compounds, caulking compounds, dyes, wallpaper, floor covering, floor lacquer, grease cleaners, shoe dye, tobacco smoke, kerosene heaters, varnish, solvents, enamels, non-lead automobile fuels, pesticides and pharmaceuticals
Toluene	Narcotic and possible cause of anemia	Solvents, solvent-based adhesives, water-based adhesives, edge-sealant, molding tape, wallpaper, joint compound, vinyl floor covering, vinyl coated wall paper, caulking compound, paint, chipboard, emissions from kerosene heaters, tobacco smoke and calcium silicate sheet
Styrene	Narcotic, hazard to the central nervous system and possible human carcinogen	Plastics, paints, synthetic rubber and resins

NOTE: Also see Chapter 11 for hazardous pesticide products.
SOURCE: Ritchie, I. (1991a).

FIGURE 7.1. (*continued*)

Compound	Health Effects	Sources and Uses
Toluene diisocyanate (TDI)	Sensitizer and probable human carcinogen	Plastics, paints, synthetic rubber and resins
Trichloroethylene	Animal carcinogen and hazard to the central nervous system	Polyurethane foam aerosols
Ethyl benzene	Severe eye and respiratory tract irritant and hazard to the central nervous system	Solvents
Methylene chloride (Dichloromethane)	Narcotic, hazard to the central nervous system and probable human carcinogen	Paint strippers and aerosol finishers
Paradichlorobenzene	Narcotic, eye and respiratory tract irritant and hazard to the liver, kidneys and central nervous system	Moth crystals and balls, and room deodorizers
Benzyl chloride and Benzal chloride	Central nervous system irritants and depressants, hazard to the liver, and kidneys, and eye and respiratory tract irritant	Vinyl tiles plasticized with butyl benzyl phthalate
2-Butanone (MEK)	Irritant and central nervous system depressant	Floor and wall covering, calcium silicate sheet, fiberboard, caulking compounds, particle board and tobacco smoke
Petroleum distillates	Central nervous system depressant and hazard to the liver and kidneys	Cleaning products, solvents, paint thinners and paint strippers
4-Phenylcyclohexene	Eye and respiratory tract irritant and hazard to the central nervous system	Synthetic carpet and pads

Low levels of volatile chemicals can cause eye and respiratory tract irritation, fatigue, blurred and double vision, headache, memory problems and depression. Exposure to them over long periods or at high levels can result in other effects, including kidney and liver damage, joint pains, skin irritation and breathing problems. Symptoms of exposure might include dizziness, numbness and tingling in the arms and legs, unsteadiness and irregular heartbeat. Exposure to high levels of some chemicals can even cause death. Sometimes a medical diagnosis is difficult because the symptoms are varied and they may resemble those of the flu.

Testing and Understanding the Results

Routine testing for volatile chemicals is not necessary but testing may be required when an illness indicates exposure to chemicals. When testing is needed, hire a professional indoor air consultant and testing laboratory. A list of testing companies may be obtained by contacting the local health department or by looking in the yellow pages of the telephone directory under "Environmental & Ecological Services" or "Laboratories—Testing."

Some materials (such as carpeting) can be tested by collecting a sample of it according to the laboratory's instructions and sending it to the laboratory for analysis. Sometimes, however, a consultant is needed to evaluate the house and sample the air. Different instruments are available for this testing and some give results immediately.

The unit of measurement for volatile chemicals is typically parts per billion (ppb) or parts per trillion (ppt). One ppb is 1000 times greater than 1 ppt. When hiring a consultant, look for a laboratory that follows EPA methods for collecting and analyzing volatile chemicals in indoor air. These methods can measure very low concentrations of chemicals that can affect some people, but some other methods (including those using portable instruments that give immediate results) cannot measure these very low levels.

Interpreting results for volatile organic chemicals is very difficult because scientists do not know what the safe exposure levels are for most chemicals in indoor air. Sometimes indoor air levels of contaminants are compared to industry standards used to protect worker health and safety. This is not an appropriate comparison, though, because these standards are intended to protect healthy adult workers, not babies, the elderly or people with illnesses. Get help from your physician and local or state health department when interpreting test results.

Sources and Reducing Exposure

Interior and Exterior Construction Materials

It is unlikely that anyone can avoid exposure to volatile organic chemicals in new construction or after extensive renovation projects. Figure 7.2 contains a list of some building materials and whether or not they are likely to release volatile compounds or other chemicals. Over time, the amount of chemicals released will decrease. With some chemicals, acceptable levels might be reached in a few hours but for others, the process could take years. Although materials on the exterior of a house also release chemicals, contamination is not likely to occur indoors if there is an adequate vapor barrier (see Chapter 8 for more information).

The best strategy to reduce exposures is to use fewer products that contain volatile chemicals. Avoid professionals who dismiss your concerns, and recognize that you may have to do most of the research to select safe products because many builders, contractors and sales personnel are not aware of potentially unsafe ingredients in construction materials.

Ask for fast-drying and water-based chemicals and building products whenever possible. (If someone in the household is sensitive to chemicals, test individual products before using them.) If you do the installation, read product labels carefully before beginning the work. Take all "use with adequate ventilation" warnings seriously and use appropriate safety equipment. Contact manufacturers or ask hardware or building supply stores for a "Material Safety Data Sheet" (MSDS) on any product that concerns you. An MSDS is a written explanation about the content, effects and safety precautions needed for chemical products. Contact your local health department for help in understanding information on the MSDS.

Two additional strategies to reduce exposures are increasing ventilation and "baking out" the house. Both methods will increase energy costs temporarily. Supplying extra ventilation for a few months can reduce volatile chemical levels in new houses or areas with recent renovations. Increasing the ventilation is especially important in energy efficient or "tight" houses. Although heat recovery ventilators (also called air-to-air heat exchangers) can lower levels of radon and other chemicals, there is not enough experience with these systems to determine their effectiveness in removing volatile chemicals.

Baking out is a technique that combines increased ventilation with raising the temperature of the house (from 90 to 95 °F) to drive volatile chemicals out of the materials that contain them. Studies show that baking out for a period of several days to two weeks can lower the levels of volatile chemicals. It is not known if baking out is a permanent solution, although some studies

FIGURE 7.2. Building Materials and Volatile Chemicals

Building Component	Materials	
	Likely To Release Volatile Chemicals	**Not Likely To Release Volatile Chemicals**
Roofing	Asphalt shingles, wood shingles (may have preservatives or fire retardant treatments), tar and gravel, and plastic or rubber membranes (the use of a metal foil vapor barrier can reduce the entry of volatiles into the house)	Cement, clay, steel, aluminum, copper and tile
Siding	Wood siding (could have preservatives), vinyl siding, asphalt products, chipboard (waferboard sheathing) and exterior plywood	Metal, and stucco on metal lath
Framing	Laminated lumber	Poured concrete, concrete block, stone, brick and steel
Air and vapor retarders	Vapor retarding paint, sealers and polyethylene sheeting	Untreated building paper, Kraft paper, aluminum foil and paper-backed foil
Insulation	Urea-formaldehyde foam, resin foams (styrene, polyurethane and diisocyanate) and fire retardant cellulose	Glass fiber, mineral fiber and vermiculite (all produce fine dusts if disturbed; use of glass or mineral fiber inside heating and cooling systems can release particles into the room air)
Foundation and sealants	Silicone-based sealants, asphalt-based sealants and wood treated with preservatives	Poured concrete or concrete blocks, brick, stone and cement-based sealant

NOTE: The products that are likely to release volatile chemicals are not hazardous to the same degree and the volatile chemicals will be released at different rates depending on the product and environmental conditions.
SOURCE: Excerpt from *Your Home, Your Health, and Well-Being* by David Rousseau, W.J. Rea and J. Enwright. Copyright © 1988 by David Rousseau. Used by permission of Ten Speed Press. P.O. Box 7123, Berkeley, CA 94707.

FIGURE 7.2. (*continued*)

Building Component	Materials	
	Likely To Release Volatile Chemicals	**Not Likely To Release Volatile Chemicals**
Floor underlayment	Exterior plywood and particle board	Concrete
Subflooring	Exterior plywood	Concrete and solid wood plank
Floor covering	Synthetic and natural fiber carpets and pads, simulated wood made from particle board, and vinyl (hard vinyl may release fewer volatile chemicals and for shorter periods than soft vinyl; adhesives are additional sources)	Concrete and ceramic tile (acrylic additives in mortar, grout and adhesive can release volatile chemicals; dyes and waxes can release volatile chemicals)
Cabinets	Exterior and interior grade plywood, particle board, vinyl imitation wood, veneers, laminates, ceramic tops (contact cement releases volatile chemicals during curing; tile grout and cement are additional sources) and solid wood with backs and shelves of composite materials	Metal (finishes can release volatile chemicals)
Interior wall and ceiling coverings	Prefinished interior paneling, interior plywood and particle board	Plaster on metal or gypsum lath, brick, solid hardwood, gypsum board (gypsum board fillers can release volatile chemicals but hypoallergenic fillers are available), solid softwood paneling and brick veneer (paints or varnishes can release volatiles)

FIGURE 7.2. (*continued*)

Building Component	Materials	
	Likely To Release Volatile Chemicals	**Not Likely To Release Volatile Chemicals**
Adhesives and caulking	Epoxy glues, plastic resin glues, ABS and PVC solvent cements, solvent-based ceramic wall and floor tile adhesive, solvent or latex contact cement, carpet adhesives, construction adhesives and panel adhesives (resin compounds are potential sensitizing agents)	Ceramic tile thin-set mortar adhesive, white glue, yellow glue and wallpaper glue (many wallpaper glues contain fungicide and fire retardants that are volatile)
Sealants	Acrylic sealant, clear silicone (no additives) tub caulk, butyl rubber and polysulfide sealant	
Weatherstripping	Hard vinyl, soft plastic, foamed plastic and neoprene rubber	Felt
Paints, varnishes, oils and waxes	Epoxy paint and varnish (epoxy products are sensitizers), lacquer paint and wood sealer, alkyd oil paint, linseed oil, urethane finish, latex paint, paste waxes, natural oils, mineral oil and natural shellac	Casein paints, special hypoallergenic paints and whitewash
Wall coverings	Paints, ceramic tile (coatings, grouts and adhesives), wood and composite paneling (see paints, adhesives and grout above) and vinyl and self-stick wallpaper	

suggest that the chemical levels could slowly increase (but to lower levels) after the initial baking out. If you want to try baking out, it is best to do this in an unfurnished house because elevated temperatures could damage some materials. Close the windows and doors, and turn up the heat. Do not let the temperature exceed 95°, and do not remain in the house during the baking out. After one to several days, open the windows or turn on the exhaust system to let the contaminated air out of the house and lower the temperature to normal settings.

Chapters 6 and 11 contain additional ways to reduce exposure to formaldehyde and pesticides.

New Carpeting

During the last few years, the safety of emissions from new carpeting has been a topic of debate. The Consumer Product Safety Commission has received numerous complaints from consumers who believe that new carpets are responsible for their health problems. A study by Anderson Laboratories in Deedham, Massachusetts raised additional concerns because some mice died after exposure to emissions from carpet samples.

Other scientists criticized the Anderson study for failing to measure individual chemicals released from the carpet and for not using standard testing procedures. Now the EPA, the Consumer Product Safety Commission, the carpet industry and others are conducting new studies to answer questions of safety.

The chemicals that are released from carpeting come from the carpet itself, the pad installed underneath the carpet and the adhesives used to glue the carpet and pad in place. Carpets are made from natural fibers such as cotton or wool, synthetic materials such as nylon or olefin, or blends of materials. During production, chemicals are used to dye the fibers and to provide stain resistance, static control and mold resistance. The backings used to hold carpets together might contain styrene, butadiene rubber (SBR) latex, polyurethane or polyvinyl chloride. The distinctive smell of many new carpets results from the release of 4-phenylcyclohexene (4-PC) from the SBR latex backing. People can detect this chemical at very low concentrations—as low as one part per billion or less. (Formaldehyde is another outgassing product from carpets and adhesives.) The adhesives used to lay the carpet can release 100 to 1000 times more toxic chemicals than the carpet.

The release of volatile chemicals from carpet varies significantly because carpets differ from batch to batch. So, it is possible to purchase carpet that has high emissions simply because of variations during the manufacturing process.

Also, if the carpet is not completely dry before it is rolled and packaged, mold can grow on the surface.

All of this means that new carpets can release many different chemicals for which the health effects are not completely known. What should a consumer do? This is a difficult question to answer, partially because of the uncertainties surrounding the scientific information. An important consideration is whether or not anyone in the household is allergic to chemicals. If so, the safest course of action may be to forgo the carpet and install hardwood, ceramic or terrazzo. (Unfortunately, these materials are expensive when professionally installed.) Vinyl flooring would not be a good substitute for sensitive people because it also releases volatile organic chemicals.

There are ways to reduce exposure to these chemicals. Ask the carpet retailer to unroll the carpet and air it out for a few days to a week before delivery. Use solvent-free carpet adhesives to lay the carpet. Ventilate the house (by opening windows and using fans to move the air) during installation and as much as possible for at least one to two weeks afterward. Studies suggest that the emissions will decrease the most during the first two weeks after installation, but some volatile chemicals are likely to be released even months after installation.

One action promoted by carpet manufacturers and retailers is to encourage consumers to buy carpets that carry the Carpet and Rug Institute's (CRI) "green label." This is a voluntary program in which participating mills test their products. Buying a "green label" carpet, however, is not a 100 percent guarantee that emissions will be low or gone altogether, and this program has been criticized because a manufacturer can earn the label with minimal testing.

Two other strategies that might help include baking out volatile emissions from the carpet (as described in the section above) or steam cleaning the carpets. The effectiveness of these strategies compared to ventilating the house is not known.

When steam cleaning, make sure that the carpet fibers and dyes are compatible with water. A water-based cleaning solution will probably remove formaldehyde and other water soluble chemicals, but will also remove the soil resistant treatment. If possible, avoid organic solvents because these are volatile and toxic.

Consumer Products

Control the release of volatile organic compounds and other chemicals in your home by purchasing, storing and using products wisely. There are many products that contain and release volatile organic chemicals, including the following:

- Cleaning products
- Furniture polishes
- Paints and varnishes
- Paint and varnish removers and thinners
- Air fresheners
- Moth repellents
- Pesticides
- Plastics
- Hobby and craft supplies
- Dry cleaned clothing

Even cosmetics and personal hygiene products contain volatile organic chemicals. These products are typically used in small quantities and do not cause problems for most people. However, irritation effects and allergic reactions do occur. Avoid the routine use of aerosol sprays because they produce tiny droplets that can be inhaled deep into the lungs. Often, less hazardous substitutes can be used for products containing more toxic chemicals (some suggestions are listed in Chapter 2).

Read labels and avoid using products that contain hazardous chemicals. You can recognize potentially hazardous products by warnings on the label such as "Use in a well-ventilated area," "Caution," "Danger," "Poison" and "Do not breathe vapors." Pesticides (see Chapter 11) and solvents are especially dangerous. These chemicals are the cause of many preventable poisonings each year.

If a hazardous product must be used, make sure that you understand the warning label and carefully follow instructions for using the product. (See the safety tips for solvent products below.)

Store products containing volatile organic chemicals away from the living space. If a secure outdoor storage shed is not available, a well-ventilated area in the garage should be acceptable. Store all chemicals in a secure place if children are in the home.

Solvent Products (Including Paints, Thinners and Strippers).

Any product that contains solvents (such as paints, varnish, stains, thinners, strippers, glues and adhesives) will release the solvent chemicals into the air when used. Products that contain methylene chloride and petroleum distillates are especially hazardous. These chemicals and other solvents affect the central nervous system; products that contain methylene chloride should have a label that warns of a possible cancer hazard. Overexposure to solvents can sometimes cause the heart rhythm to change; this has lead to death for some people. If you have a heart condition, do not use these products.

If you must use solvent products or products with similar hazards, purchase an appropriate respirator from a safety supply store and use it (see Appendix B for instructions on respirator use). Do not use dust masks—they cannot protect you from volatile chemicals! Work outside whenever possible but if the work must be done indoors, make sure that you have adequate cross ventilation. Danger signs of overexposure to toxic chemicals include headache, dizziness, weakness and skipping or irregular heartbeats. If you experience any of these symptoms, leave the area immediately and seek medical attention, especially if you have a skipping or irregular heartbeat or if the symptoms persist.

Dry Cleaned Clothes

Dry cleaning clothes can expose consumers to residues of the several volatile organic chemicals, including perchloroethylene (also known as "perc"), a known carcinogen. The volatile organics used in dry cleaning are hazardous because they can damage the kidneys, liver and nervous system. When clothes are dry cleaned, the garments are immersed in perc and other chemicals to dissolve grease and stains. Next, the garments are spun to dry them; this removes many (but not all) of the chemicals.

Reduce your exposure to perc by asking your dry cleaner to employ a new method of dry cleaning that uses biodegradable soaps. This process still uses perc, but much less than traditional dry cleaning methods. Another strategy is to put the cleaned clothes outdoors for three or more days before bringing them inside. This will help reduce the release of perc but may not eliminate it. If many of your clothes require dry cleaning, consider installing an exhaust fan in the closet to remove contaminated air.

Sources Outside the Home

You can find out if there are sources of volatile chemicals (and other hazardous chemicals) in your community by contacting your local or state environmental or pollution control agency (see Appendix A for addresses).

Any time you detect a chemical odor in outdoor air or water, or observe a sheen or film on top of household water, contact your local health department. Likewise, a gasoline or other chemical odor in the home could be indicative of an outdoor source such as a leaking underground storage tank. These situations require expert help to identify and solve the problem.

Volatile Chemicals Checklist

Questions To Ask	Response	What Does a "Yes" Mean?
Was the home constructed within the last five years?	Yes No ❏ ❏	New homes can release volatile chemicals. Use products that release fewer volatile chemicals whenever possible and provide plenty of fresh air to reduce exposure. Testing may be needed when problems occur.
Has the home been remodeled within the last six months with new carpeting, furniture, drapes, paint, vinyl flooring or cabinets?	Yes No ❏ ❏	Newly remodeled homes can release volatile chemicals. Use products that release fewer volatile chemicals whenever possible and provide plenty of fresh air to reduce exposure. Testing may be needed when problems occur.
Are pesticides, solvents and cleaning chemicals used or stored inside the home?	Yes No ❏ ❏	Minimize the use of these products. Use these products only with plenty of fresh air and store them outside the living area. The preferred location is in a locked storage area away from the house, but a locked, ventilated area in a garage is acceptable.

Summary Chart for Moisture

Topic	Comments
Description	Moisture in the home refers to water that is present as a gas (vapor), liquid or solid (ice).
Health Effects	Too much water can result in the growth of mold, mildew and other biological contaminants. Potential health effects range from upper respiratory tract irritation to life-threatening conditions. (Refer to Chapter 9 for more information about the health effects of mold and other biological contaminants.)
Sources	Sources related to the exterior of the house include improper drainage, problems related to downspouts, air leakage points, missing vapor retarders or improperly installed retarders. A high water table, frequent or heavy rain, poorly operated septic system and flooding also contribute to moisture inside the home. Interior problems include leaking water pipes, poor ventilation, air leakage points and any activity that produces moisture.
Testing	Too much moisture indoors is easy to recognize. Some signs include a damp feeling indoors, mold and mildew, lingering odors and condensation on windows, doors and walls. On the exterior of the house, warped or cracked wood and paint that is peeling, blistering or cracking are signs of potential problems. An easy way to check for excess moisture indoors is to measure the relative humidity. Identify and correct sources of moisture when the humidity is greater than 50 percent.
Reducing Exposure	Correct any problem that contributes to moisture. Some are easy to solve, but others require professional help. There are three basic strategies that are effective: controlling sources of moisture, increasing ventilation and installing vapor retarders or protective coatings.

CHAPTER
EIGHT

Moisture

Between 1970 and 1985, TriState Home Corporation actively built single-family prefabricated houses in Michigan, Minnesota and Wisconsin. These houses had triple layers of insulation and were very tight. A number of these homes had structural problems due to excessive moisture, fungal growth and wood rot. Some residents complained of allergy problems. Health departments in the three states monitored indoor air quality, conducted health studies and looked at ways to relieve the problem.

As reported in *Health and Environment Digest*, February, 1987.

Due to the large number of affected homes, the state of Wisconsin conducted a study to find the cause of the health complaints. An inspection of the homes revealed that TriState had installed vapor retarders both inside and outside of the walls of the homes. Moisture condensed in the space between the vapor retarders, the house walls rotted and mold grew extensively inside the homes. The state of Wisconsin worked with the homeowners to get them low interest loans to fix the houses. Although the homeowners removed the vinyl siding, stripped the outside vapor retarders and installed exhaust fans in the bathrooms, mold problems continued even after the houses dried out. TriState eventually went out of business, and the residents sued the insurance companies.

As reported by Meg Ziarnik, Wisconsin Division of Health, Department of Health and Social Services, Madison, Wisconsin, November 8, 1993.

What Causes Moisture Problems?

Although a house anywhere in the United States can have moisture problems as a result of improper construction and moisture control methods, some areas of the country are more prone to decay problems than others (see Figure 8.1). High outdoor humidity levels along coastal regions cause significant damage from mold and wood rot. Another important cause of moisture problems is winter condensation that occurs in areas where winter temperatures average 35°F or less (see Figure 8.2).

Moisture can be present in homes as gaseous water vapor, liquid water or solid ice. Outside sources of moisture problems include high humidity, precipitation, flooding and standing water. Indoors, there are many sources of moisture; some of these pump a large amount of water into the home (see Figure 8.3). Problems result when the moisture cannot escape to the outside.

Understanding How Water Vapor Moves Indoors

The key to controlling moisture problems is understanding how water vapor moves into and out of a house. Most of the water vapor in a house is carried to the outside by air passing through any cracks or holes in the shell of the

FIGURE 8.1.   Areas in the United States Prone to Wood Decay

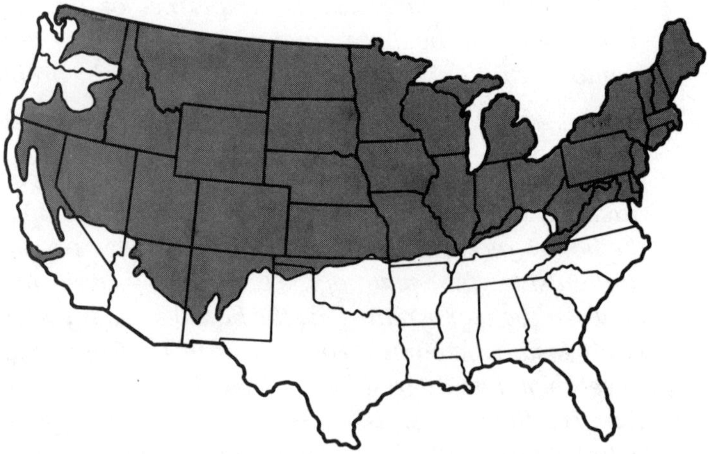

(Adapted from USDA Forest Service Information Bulletin No. 373, USGPO)

AVE. JAN. TEMPERATURES OF 35°F OR BELOW
(AREAS WHERE VAPOR RETARDERS ARE RECOMMENDED)

SOURCE: NCAT (1983).

FIGURE 8.2. **Areas in the United States Prone to Moisture Problems Because of Winter Condensation**

(Adapted from USDA Forest Service General Technical Report FPL-15, 1977)

☐ **HIGH**

▨ **MODERATE**

▨ **LOW**

SOURCE: NCAT (1983).

FIGURE 8.3. **Sources of Water Vapor in the Home**

Source	Amount of Water Vapor Released
Humidifier operating 24 hours	48 pounds in 24 hours
Gas appliances	88 pounds for each 1,000 cubic feet of gas burned
Washing and rinsing an 8 ft × 10 ft room	2.5 pounds
Drying ten pounds of clothes	Ten pounds
Four people living in a home	About three pounds each day

house. Because air naturally moves from higher pressure to lower pressure, air movement is caused by pressure differences between the inside and outside of the house, and by the action of wind on the house. When warm, moist air comes into contact with a cold surface, the water vapor condenses and if the temperature is cold enough, ice forms.

In cold climates, sources of moisture indoors create a higher pressure inside a house than outdoors. The water vapor moves through the walls of the house to the lower pressure outside. Trouble can start when water vapor in the air condenses onto insulation and in wall cavities because if the moisture cannot escape, mold and decay may result.

The reverse of this process occurs in warm, humid climates. In this case, the humidity outside the house causes the pressure to be higher outside. As a result, moist air from the higher pressure area outside of a house moves through any cracks or openings to the lower pressure inside the house. Condensation occurs when the warm, moist outside air contacts the cool surfaces of walls and floors.

Wind also changes the pressure between inside and outside of the house. Typically, the exterior wall on the side of the house that is directly hit by the wind (the upwind side) is under higher pressure than the exterior wall on the opposite side of the house (the downwind side). The wind pushes air through the upwind side and travels out of the house on the downwind side through any cracks or openings. As warm, moist air travels through the house and to the outside, water vapor can condense on the downwind side and result in moisture damage.

Water vapor moves through building materials during a slower process called diffusion, especially after a house has been weatherized. Less heat and moisture can escape a tightly sealed house because there is little air movement. Excess moisture has to go somewhere, so it begins to diffuse through the walls. Pressure differences still control the movement of the water vapor but in a tight house, the pressure is greater inside the house because moisture has nowhere to go. As it moves through the wall materials, the moisture cools and forms liquid water or ice.

Do You Have a Moisture Problem?

If any of the following conditions are present in your home, a moisture problem probably exists:

- Lingering odors
- Dampness
- Humidity greater than 50 percent
- Mold and mildew

- Rotting and decaying wood
- Discolored, warped or cracked wood
- Water-carrying fungus
- Condensation on windows
- Sweating pipes
- Corrosion of metal surfaces
- Water leaks

Testing and Understanding the Results

Routine testing is not needed to recognize moisture problems because the presence of any of the conditions listed above signals problems. Although relative humidity is easy to measure, there is considerable variation in the quality of the readings and inexpensive meters are likely to give incorrect results.

Sources and Solutions Related to the Lot

Drainage problems can result in structural damage from the roof of the house to the foundation, as shown in Figure 8.4. Solutions can range from simple, inexpensive measures to costly, complex corrective actions. It is much easier and cheaper to incorporate drainage control practices during construction than to attempt to correct problems later.

One of the most common causes of drainage problems is improper grading. If the ground slopes toward a house foundation rather than away from it, water and moisture can collect. This problem can be resolved by regrading the ground around the foundation (most building codes require a minimum fall of six inches away from the foundation walls within the first ten feet) or by adding downspouts with extensions to divert the water away from the house.

Actions that are more expensive and aggressive include excavating around the foundation and installing footing drains, a drain tile system and a sump pump to collect and discharge the water away from the foundation. This solution works well if the soil has good drainage but may not be as effective in tight soils, especially if the water table is high. In some areas, the source of the problem is seasonal flooding or runoff and the strategies mentioned above may be ineffective. In these places, houses are often built on stilts.

Heavy vegetation or firewood stacked near the house can reduce ventilation and promote dampness or standing water close to the foundation. Pruning shrubs and trees that are close to the house allows air to flow freely and moisture to evaporate between the vegetation and the exterior walls.

FIGURE 8.4.   Good and Poor Drainage

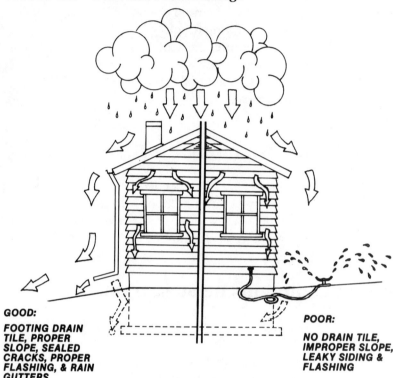

GOOD:
**FOOTING DRAIN
TILE, PROPER
SLOPE, SEALED
CRACKS, PROPER
FLASHING, & RAIN
GUTTERS**

POOR:
**NO DRAIN TILE,
IMPROPER SLOPE,
LEAKY SIDING &
FLASHING**

SOURCE: NCAT (1983).

Sources and Solutions Related to the Exterior of the House

Examine the exterior of the house carefully for signs of mold and moisture damage. Look at the siding, soffits, fascias and gables. Also check the areas below windows, outside of bathrooms and dryer vents, and the roof and flashing. Prevent problems by keeping the exterior of the house in good condition, correcting moisture problems related to the lot and repairing or replacing damaged materials promptly. Chapter 9 explains how to remove mold and mildew from surfaces.

Paint

Mold and mildew typically appear as dark spots or streaks on siding and painted surfaces. Look for peeling, blistering or cracking paint, or dark streaks around a discolored area. Paint in poor condition may simply be a sign of an

FIGURE 8.5. Moisture Problems on Painted Surfaces

Source	Solution
Deteriorating paint on the gable ends of the house as a result of poor ventilation, a lack of insulation or excess moisture in the house.	Add insulation and a vapor retarder to the attic. Increase ventilation in the attic and correct interior moisture problems.
Deteriorating paint on fascia boards and soffits caused by poor drainage, ice dams or inadequate ventilation at the eaves.	Clear debris from roof and gutters. Repair gutters and increase the size or number of gutters. Increase the length of the shingle drip edge or install a new metal drip edge under the shingles that extends at least one-half inch below a butting wood member.
Deteriorating paint below windows on both the exterior and interior.	Seal or replace cracked or deteriorated window sills and the flashing above windows. Seal around exterior window trim.

improper or sloppy application, but always consider the possibility of moisture damage.

Figure 8.5 identifies some common sources of and solutions to paint-related moisture problems. Simply covering a painted surface with new vinyl or metal siding will not correct moisture problems. Further damage can be prevented only by finding and correcting the sources of problems.

Painting contractors have different opinions about the best paint for wood surfaces. Latex paints with vinyl or acrylic polymers provide good protection against moisture problems by breathing and allowing moisture to escape. High luster oil-based paints are the least porous and prevent moisture from escaping. Consult with several paint dealers and contractors to decide what type of product is the best for the job and follow the manufacturer's instructions carefully.

Wood

The visual signs of wet or decayed wood are easy to recognize but not always present. Surfaces that are uneven, warped or sloping may harbor moisture damage. Wet or decaying wood has a dull sound when tapped compared to a clear, sharp sound for dry wood. Decaying wood is soft and breaks easily into short pieces when jabbed with a small screwdriver or similar tool, whereas wood in good condition is hard to pry up and breaks into long slivers. Decayed wood can often be recognized by brown, black, blue, green or steel gray areas of discoloration, and it sometimes has a lighter-than-normal color with dark lines around the discolored area. (The term "dry rot" is somewhat misleading because it is used to describe decayed wood that has become dry. Since decay-causing fungi need moisture to grow, wood which has dry rot was moist at some time.)

Paint does not completely protect wood from moisture because it only coats the surface of the wood. Sometimes, a wood preservative or water repellent should be used to prevent moisture problems and damage. As these products are applied, they soak into the wood and seal the inside. Use preservative and water repellent products cautiously because they contain mineral spirits, turpentine and other toxic synthetic organic chemicals. Preservatives contain toxic fungicides that prevent damage from mold and insects. (Commonly used fungicides are pentachlorophenol [penta] and copper napthanate. Penta is more toxic, but the copper napthanate has an undesirable odor.) Water repellents can be effective in aboveground applications, and preservatives are typically needed below ground.

Pressure treated wood is treated with fungicides and has the additional advantage of being stronger than untreated wood. Use pressure treated wood in belowground areas and where constant wetting occurs. Wood treated with creosote, pentachlorophenol and arsenic compounds, however, should not be used in habitable spaces.

Concrete or Brick Foundations and Exteriors

Look at the foundation for signs of water accumulation and mold growth. Check the crawl space floor for moisture and examine the plumbing for leaks. (Sometimes, running the water for about ten minutes makes moisture easier to detect.) Mold growth on the foundation can appear as black or dark brown spots or streaks on the surface or in cracks.

Another sign of potential mold problems is efflorescence, a white powdery substance composed of minerals that remain on the surfaces of foundations after moisture has moved through the concrete or brick. Also check for concrete, brick or mortar that is crumbling. Both efflorescence and a disintegrating foundation could be caused by moisture that allows mold to grow underneath the exterior shell. Remove efflorescence with the home cleaning solution mentioned in Chapter 9 or buy a commercial solution from a local hardware store.

Sources and Solutions Related to the House Interior

Controlling moisture and increasing ventilation are the keys to preventing mold growth and moisture damage indoors. This section reviews basic practices that will help control moisture in specific areas inside the house.

Controlling Moisture

Condensation. Condensation on interior surfaces (especially windows) during the winter is a common problem that occurs when warm indoor air contacts cool outer walls, windows and doors. Condensation that occurs periodically and for short periods of time is not a cause for concern.

Interior moisture levels vary according to the age of the home and the time of day or year. For example, new homes can have higher-than-average humidity levels for about one year. Some new and older homes have problems only during extremely cold weather; in other cases, condensation occurs only during the morning hours and disappears during the day. These situations are not problematic as long as the water does not run onto the window sash and sills.

Condensation that occurs only when washing and drying clothes, cooking or bathing can be reduced by increasing the ventilation (see suggestions below) to let the moisture out of the house. Leaving the bathroom doors open can sometimes solve condensation problems that result from showering.

Metal windows and doors are particularly vulnerable to condensation problems. Increasing the ventilation, lowering the humidity and buying insulated metal doors and windows are potential solutions. Storm windows do not automatically solve condensation problems during the winter. If a storm window is leaking air, condensation may result when the cold outside air causes the warm inside air to condense onto the glass of the interior window. If the exterior window has condensation, then the inside window is leaking air and the warm, moist inside air condenses onto the colder glass of the storm window. Careful sealing can solve some of these problems but in some cases, new windows may be needed.

Continuous condensation is a serious problem that can have different causes. Occasionally, the problem is the result of simply having too many houseplants; other times, moisture problems may occur because a house has wall insulation but no vapor retarders. Often, condensation occurs only on the north-facing windows because they are colder. Storm windows on the downwind side can have condensation as the wind carries moisture from the upwind side out the downwind side.

Drapes and blinds that keep heat from circulating and loose weatherstripping are common sources of moisture problems around windows. Keeping drapes open can help to increase the circulation of air. Another solution is to check for leaks and weatherstrip and caulk any openings (do the inside first and then the outside). Because storm windows act as air and vapor retarders, be sure to seal interior-side storm windows tightly around all edges. When adding outer storm windows, look for products with weep holes that allow moisture to escape at the bottom. Check existing outer storm windows to be sure weep holes are open and consider installing triple-glazed windows in very cold climates.

There are several steps that you can take to solve a condensation problem. First, eliminate unnecessary sources of moisture: hang laundry outdoors or use a dryer that is vented to the outside, repair leaking faucets and avoid overwatering plants. Do not use evaporative coolers (also known as swamp coolers) in humid, warm climates. An evaporative cooler is a significant source of moisture because as outside air is drawn into the unit, the air passes over water soaked pads. This cools the air, but produces large amounts of interior moisture. Use humidifiers cautiously; avoid using them in new or recently renovated or weatherized houses. Second, increase the ventilation in the house and exhaust humid air by using local exhaust fans or by opening windows slightly for a few minutes each day.

Third, seal from the inside of the house air leaks that come from openings around windows and doors, any cracks or holes in the wall surfaces and any openings where walls, floors and ceilings meet (see Figure 8.6). Also, apply a vapor retarding paint to reduce the diffusion of water vapor through the surfaces and after sealing the inside surfaces, check and seal any potential leaks

FIGURE 8.6.   Areas of the House Where Air and Moisture Leakage Occur

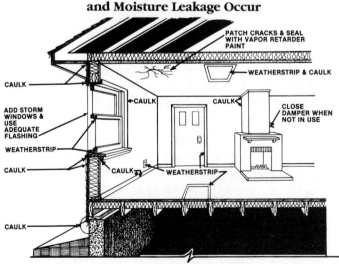

SOURCE: NCAT (1983).

on the outside areas. Finally, if moisture and condensation persist, a dehumidifier may be helpful (see Chapter 10).

Water Damage. If a house has a history of water damage, mold and structural damage are probably present. Flooding, broken pipes and overflows of toilets, sinks or bathtubs can result in mold growth. Signs of trouble are damp or wet wood or gypsum board, and black or dark brown spotting along the length of a wall, floor or ceiling. Look under carpets, vinyl flooring and wood framing to be sure that these materials are in good shape.

Air-conditioning systems are other potential sources of water leaks. If a room air conditioner leaks fluid into the room, check the condensate drain hole, clean the drain if it is plugged and adjust the position (slant) of the cabinet unit if necessary. Central air conditioners can also leak fluid into a room or furnace. If this happens, the condensate drain hole, box or pump could be plugged or clogged and should be cleaned. Make sure that air-conditioning condensation drains to the sewer system or outdoors.

Flooding requires quick and aggressive action because bacteria can begin to multiply within a few hours and fungi within 24 hours. Dry off any moisture or standing water as soon as possible using wet vacuums, if needed. Rinse all surfaces with a 10 percent bleach solution (1.5 cups of bleach to one gallon of water). Be sure to test the surfaces first and if the bleach appears to fade colors or otherwise damage a surface, contact the local health department for alternative disinfecting treatments. Reduce the drying time by opening windows and using fans.

Dispose of wet papers, books and magazines. Carpets, pads, flooring, gypsum board and other materials will likely dry if the water damage is only to a small area. If these materials remain damp or if significant flooding has occurred, remove and replace these materials. Drywall and insulation should be removed up to 12 inches above the water line after a flood because they can act as wicks to draw water up above the original flood line.

If your house has had extensive flooding, you will probably need the help of contractors to determine if it is possible to salvage materials and dry the house. Do not cover any materials that are still damp or moldy with new materials because the mold will resurface. Do not buy a flood-damaged house unless you get an opinion from a contractor who specializes in flooded properties. You could get stuck with a cheap property that might be unusable or expensive to renovate.

Ventilation

Providing adequate ventilation to the living space can solve and prevent many indoor air quality and moisture problems. Adequate ventilation helps maintain comfort and prevents the build-up of indoor contaminants, moisture and odor problems.

There are several sources of guidelines for ventilation in homes. The Council of American Building Officials (CABO) publishes standards for one-and two-family homes. Another organization, the American Society of Heating, Refrigerating and Air-Conditioning Engineers, Inc. (ASHRAE) publishes a model standard for indoor air quality known as ASHRAE Standard 62-1989, *Ventilation for Acceptable Indoor Air Quality.* These professional standards are typically incorporated into state and local building codes. Check local building codes to determine the minimum ventilation requirements in your area for the house and combustion appliances (see Chapter 10 for more information about combustion appliances).

If you are buying a previously occupied home, pay attention to the ventilation system. Some older homes do not have forced-air systems to circulate air throughout the house; in other homes, the ventilation system may not be adequate. If you are building or buying a new home, talk to the builder or heating contractor about the need for adequate ventilation. Recognize that some builders and contractors will not be receptive to your concerns—if you encounter this attitude, find a new contractor.

Kitchens, Bathrooms and Other High-Moisture Areas. Improving the air circulation in all parts of the house by running the furnace blower continuously is a simple solution to many moisture problems that increases the energy costs by only a small amount in most homes. If the home does not have a central forced-air furnace, opening windows or installing a local exhaust fan in high moisture areas is effective. If space is limited, a fan located outside of the high moisture area can help to increase ventilation.

Building codes usually require a bathroom fan that can give one air change every 12 minutes (five air changes per hour), although some ventilation engineers recommend a fan in the bathroom that can give one air change every five to eight minutes. (For example, if the total space in a bathroom is 800 cubic feet [measured by multiplying length by width and height], a fan with a 100 cfm [cubic feet per minute] capability will change the air once every eight minutes.) In the kitchen, a fan that can give one air change every four to five minutes is recommended (15 air changes per hour), but is not required by current model building codes.

Recirculating fans in the kitchen cannot remove moisture and gaseous contaminants. They can remove particulates, but the filters require periodic cleaning. Similarly, infrared heat lamps (with or without blowers) do not remove moisture from the bathroom. Each local exhaust fan must exhaust outside to prevent moisture and contamination problems in other areas. Do not allow local exhaust fans (or clothes dryers) to exhaust to the crawl space, attic, basement or other part of the house interior.

Another device commonly used to increase ventilation and remove moisture in energy efficient homes is the air-to-air heat exchanger. Select these units carefully because some allow moisture and contaminants to pass into the fresh air stream. Smaller room-sized heat exchangers are available, but a central system is probably best because it can provide constant and uniform circulation and ventilation throughout the home.

Crawl Space Ventilation. Ventilation in the crawl space can remove moisture, prevent the growth of mold and lower radon levels. Crawl space vents are easy and inexpensive to install in new or existing houses. They can be formed in the foundation or cut into the rim joists.

In areas with seasonal climatic changes, vents should remain open during the summer and closed during the winter. When a ground cover vapor retarder is not present, though, the crawl space vents should be kept open year around. The vents can usually provide enough ventilation by the natural circulation of the air, but exhaust fans are sometimes needed.

The number of vents needed depends on whether or not a ground cover vapor retarder is in place and on the size of the foundation. Most building codes today specify one square foot of vent area for every 150 square feet of crawl space area. The vents should be at opposite ends of the crawl space, within three feet of each corner of the building and as high up as possible. The total number of required vents could, however, be lowered to one-tenth of the amount required by most building codes if a ground cover vapor retarder is present.

For example, if a house has a 40 foot by 25 foot foundation but no vapor retarder, the area that needs ventilation is 1000 square feet (40 feet × 25 feet). Dividing this area by 150 gives a required vent area of 6.7 square feet. If each vent is .8 square feet, the total number of vents needed is 8.4 (6.7 square feet divided by .8 square feet) which should be rounded up to 9 vents.

The National Center for Appropriate Technology (NCAT) has a different approach to determining ventilation requirements. In the example above, the NCAT method would require twice the number of vents required by most building codes. Many useful publications related to energy concerns can be obtained from NCAT (see Appendix A for the address).

Attic Ventilation. During the summer, heat buildup in the attic can produce temperatures of 150°F or more. During the winter, excess humidity can move through the ceiling and condense in the insulation of a cold attic. Passive vents or exhaust fans can ventilate the attic, but the preferred strategy is natural ventilation because exhaust fans can draw moisture from the structure into the attic. Figure 8.7 shows some examples of good and poor ventilation strategies in the attic.

The type and size of the vents needed depend on the area of the attic space, the climate and whether or not a vapor retarder is present. Four types of vents typically provide natural ventilation in attics: ridge vents, roof vents, under eaves (soffit) vents and gable end vents. Ridge vents give a continuous opening along the ridge line of a pitched roof and allow air (but not rain and snow) to enter the attic. They are very effective and easy to install, only a few inches high and barely noticeable from the ground when covered with shin-

FIGURE 8.7.   Attic Ventilation Strategies

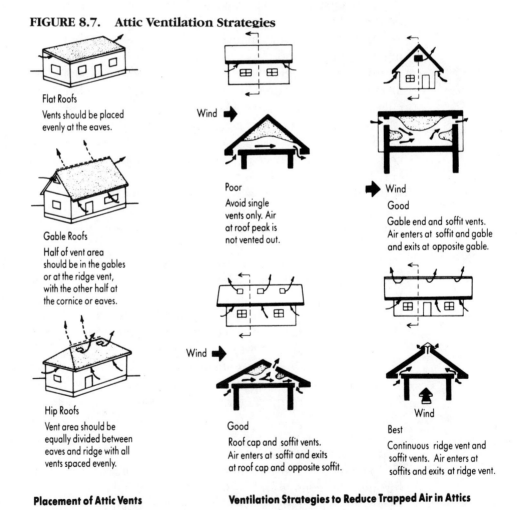

Flat Roofs
Vents should be placed evenly at the eaves.

Gable Roofs
Half of vent area should be in the gables or at the ridge vent, with the other half at the cornice or eaves.

Hip Roofs
Vent area should be equally divided between eaves and ridge with all vents spaced evenly.

Wind

Poor
Avoid single vents only. Air at roof peak is not vented out.

Wind

Good
Roof cap and soffit vents. Air enters at soffit and exits at roof cap and opposite soffit.

Wind

Good
Gable end and soffit vents. Air enters at soffit and gable and exits at opposite gable.

Wind

Best
Continuous ridge vent and soffit vents. Air enters at soffits and exits at ridge vent.

Placement of Attic Vents

Ventilation Strategies to Reduce Trapped Air in Attics

SOURCE: NCAT (1983).

gles. Roof vents are rectangular or circular openings at intervals along the flat portion of the roof. Soffit vents can be present under the eaves either as continuous vents or as separate vent openings. Gable end vents can be rectangular, round or triangular openings.

The best system for naturally ventilating the attic combines ridge vents and soffit vents. (Older homes typically have a system of roof vents and gable end vents, and houses with cathedral ceilings usually rely on a continuous eave and ridge vent installation. In some homes, individual vents are placed in the eaves and near the ridge for each rafter space.) Most building codes require a minimum of one square foot of vent area for every 150 square feet of space that needs ventilation. The required vent area can be reduced when a vapor retarder or other ventilators are present. Check your local building code for specific requirements.

A combination of turbine ventilators and soffit vents is also effective at providing natural ventilation in the attic. Turbine ventilators exhaust air from the attic as the wind drives the turbine blades. A 12-inch diameter ventilator can provide ventilation to 600 square feet of area; a 14-inch unit ventilates about 700 square feet.

When a home has a whole house fan that exhausts into the attic, there must be enough vent space to exhaust the air. An adequate amount is typically one square foot of vent area for each 750 cubic feet per minute (cfm) of fan capacity. All other exhaust fans in the house should vent to the outside and not to the attic. This will prevent air from being forced back inside the living space.

Reducing Moisture Entry

Dampproofing and Waterproofing. Sometimes, dampproofing or waterproofing the basement or crawl space foundation can provide effective moisture control. Unfortunately, these strategies only control symptoms and do not correct underlying problems.

Dampproofing involves putting a coating on interior foundation walls to reduce water seepage into the foundation and can be effective for moderate problems. Some examples of dampproofing products are given in Figure 8.8. Correct preparation of the surface is important. Some of the products contain toxic solvents and other harmful chemicals, and should only be used with adequate ventilation, respirators and protective gloves as directed by the manufacturer (see Appendix B for instructions for testing the fit of a respirator).

Waterproofing involves using a membrane to stop the transport of water and is usually used in new construction (but retrofits are possible). Combined with a sump and pump, properly installed waterproofing can correct many problems, even severe ones. The membrane is typically built up in layers from the edge of the footings to the finished soil line and under the foundation slab,

FIGURE 8.8   Dampproofing Interior Foundation Surfaces

Product	Contents	Advantages	Disadvantages
Ready-mix paints	Hydrocarbon solvent base (mineral spirits) Pigments Portland cement Synthetic rubber binder	Convenient to use Economical Effective	Must be used with adequate ventilation May need more than one coat
Ready-mix latex paints	Water-based Pigments Synthetic rubber binder	Less hazardous, safer, and fewer odors than solvent-based paints Easy to clean-up	May not be the most effective May need more than one coat
Ready-mix solvent-based paints	Solvents Resins Linseed oil Portland cement	Effective	Must be used with adequate ventilation Are difficult to use and clean up May require more than one coat
Two-part epoxy paints	Solvent or water base Epoxy compounds Resins	Usually more effective than most other products	Must be used with adequate ventilation Require careful mixing Cost more than other products May require more than one coat
Portland cement-based powders	Water base Portland cement Lime (calcium hydroxide) Pigment Silica	Reasonably effective Least costly	Must be used with adequate ventilation (silica is carcinogenic) Are difficult to apply due to quick drying time Require careful mixing Can result in staining May require more than one coat

SOURCE: Adapted from NCAT (1983).

FIGURE 8.9.   Exterior Foundation Waterproofing

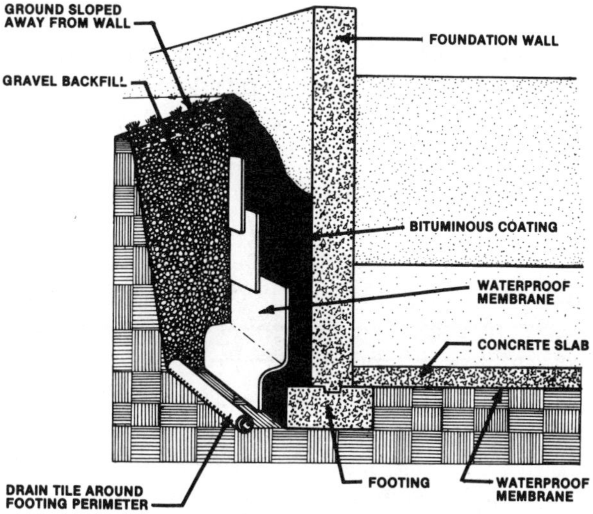

SOURCE: NCAT (1983).

as shown in Figure 8.9. The seams should be carefully sealed. Some examples of waterproofing materials are two-ply hotmopped felts, 6 mil polyvinyl chloride sheeting, or 55-pound rolled roofing. A backfill of crushed gravel should be used, especially in tight soils.

In cold climates, dampproofing and waterproofing in new construction or retrofits should include insulation that is installed on the outside in order to protect the wall or foundation from the freeze-thaw cycle. Rigid insulation such as extruded polystyrene is a good choice.

Placing insulation on the inside walls is not a good idea when moisture problems persist because mold growth and damage to materials will result unless the surfaces are dry. New foundations, concrete floors, uncured masonry and other new construction or remodeling materials can take weeks or even months to dry, especially in tight homes. For this reason, do not insulate a basement interior in a new house or one that has moisture problems until the foundation is dry (this may require the passage of one heating season).

Vapor Retarders. The vapor retarder is a material that can prevent water from moving through it. Correctly installed on the *warm* side, it separates the warm and cold sides of a wall surface and keeps water vapor from condensing on the cold surfaces. The cold side of the wall, floor or ceiling must be covered with a material that can breathe to allow any moisture that is present to escape. A general rule is that the outer skin of the wall should be at least five times more permeable than the vapor retarder to be sure that moisture can escape.

Wall and ceiling vapor retarders are not recommended outside the condensation zone shown in Figure 8.2. In warmer areas, temperature differences are not drastic and a vapor retarder could be on the wrong side for much of the time, resulting in moisture problems.

The permeance, or perm, measures the effectiveness of the vapor retarder. Materials with low perm ratings are better at slowing the movement of moisture. For example, 6 mil polyethylene has a perm rating of .06 and provides good control compared to concrete, which has a rating of 3.2 perm. Effective vapor retarders typically have perm values of .1 or less. Polyethylene films are commonly used because they have perm values between .02 and .08.

The improper placement of vapor retarders can cause rather than solve moisture problems. For example, placing a vapor retarder on the wrong side of a wall surface can increase and trap moisture when the cold side of the wall has a low-perm product and the indoor humidity is high. Examples of low-perm products include vinyl or metal siding, insulating sheathings with foil coverings and low-perm plastics that substitute for building papers that breathe. Low-perm sidings typically have holes that allow moisture to escape, but sometimes these become blocked and trap the moisture.

In colder climates, problems can result in an uninsulated home that has metal siding but no vapor retarder. The use of double vapor retarders and the use of vapor retarders on both sides of a wall can trap moisture and result in extensive damage.

Installing a Vapor Retarder in New Construction. A moisture problem in a recently built house is often caused by an improperly installed vapor retarder. Proper installation is critical and requires attention to detail and careful work. The installer must overlap and carefully seal the seams and all breaks caused by electrical and plumbing fixtures, windows, doors or accidental tears. Any openings can allow moisture to build up and cause damage. The correct way to install a continuous vapor retarder is illustrated in Figure 8.10.

Installing a Vapor Retarder in the Attic. When an attic or ceiling has moisture problems, a common solution is to increase the ventilation. When this does not work, a vapor retarder may be the only solution, assuming that obvious sources of moisture (such as missing or deteriorated flashing) have already been sealed. Vapor retarders in the attic significantly reduce the amount of needed ventilation. Cathedral ceilings and flat roofs are two types of construction that require vapor retarders because there is no attic space for ventilation.

Figure 8.11 shows examples of good installation practices. If an attic has loose fill insulation, a common technique for alleviating moisture problems in that area is to fit strips of polyethylene tightly between the joists. Another approach is to staple batt insulation with attached vapor retarders tightly to the rafters.

FIGURE 8.10.   **Installation of a Continuous Vapor Retarder**

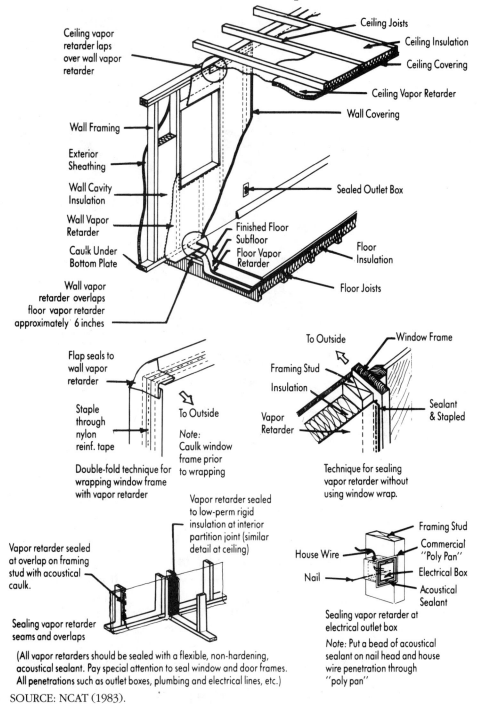

SOURCE: NCAT (1983).

FIGURE 8.11.   Installation of a Vapor Retarder in the Attic

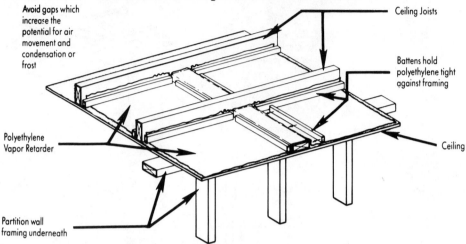

Avoid gaps which increase the potential for air movement and condensation or frost

Ceiling Joists

Battens hold polyethylene tight against framing

Polyethylene Vapor Retarder

Ceiling

Partition wall framing underneath

Polyethylene strips can be installed prior to loose-fill or blown-in attic insulation.

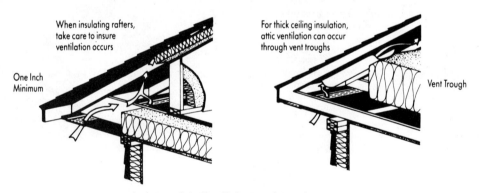

When insulating rafters, take care to insure ventilation occurs

For thick ceiling insulation, attic ventilation can occur through vent troughs

One Inch Minimum

Vent Trough

Insulation work should not block attic ventilation at the eaves.

SOURCE: NCAT (1983).

Installing a Vapor Retarder in the Crawl Space. Moisture problems can occur in all climates when moisture from the soil moves up into the crawl space. Properly fitted ground covers and floor vapor retarders can solve moisture and condensation problems in the crawl space. They are essential when the crawl space is used as an air plenum (see Chapter 10), and they can reduce radon levels.

A vapor retarder (usually 6 mil polyethylene) is usually placed on top of leveled soil and covered with three to six inches of sand or pea gravel. (Check your local building codes for the requirements in your area.) A vapor retarder alone may not solve moisture problems. Therefore, the outside of the foundation should be waterproofed and a drain tile should be installed around the footing to drain away any water that might rise into the crawl space.

A floor vapor retarder can provide added protection, but it should not be used as a substitute for the ground cover vapor retarder. The placement of a floor vapor retarder follows the same principles as wall vapor retarders. In cold climates, the warm side of the floor is the top of the floor, but in warm climates the warm side is the bottom of the floor. Figure 8.12 shows proper installation techniques for warm and cold climates.

FIGURE 8.12.   Installation of a Vapor Retarder in the Crawl Space or Floor

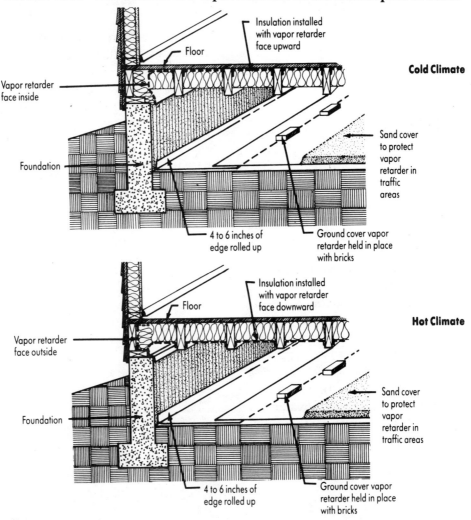

SOURCE: NCAT (1983).

Moisture Problems Checklist

Questions To Ask	Response	What Does a "Yes" Mean?
The House Lot		
Does the ground slope toward the foundation? Does water collect around the foundation?	Yes No ❏ ❏	Moisture can damage the foundation or basement.
Do trees and shrubs crowd the house or foundation?	Yes No ❏ ❏	There may not be enough ventilation between the house and shrubs. In this situation, moisture can collect and result in mold growth and damage.
Does the lot have low spots where water can collect?	Yes No ❏ ❏	Water may not drain away from the house. This could be a sign of potential flooding problems.
Exterior of the House		
Do the exterior walls have warping, peeling or blistering paint? Are there rotted wood surfaces? Are there discolored areas of wood or mold?	Yes No ❏ ❏	These are all signs of potential moisture and structural damage. (Lead-based paint could be an additional problem in older houses—see Chapter 5)
Do concrete or brick foundations have crumbling or efflorescence? Are there water stains? Is any of the wood rotted? Is there evidence of mold?	Yes No ❏ ❏	These are signs of potential moisture and structural damage.

Questions To Ask	Response	What Does a "Yes" Mean?
Is the roofing material peeling or flaking? Is the roof warped? Is flashing around the fireplace or other openings missing or deteriorated? During the winter, does ice accumulate?	**Yes No** ❏ ❏	These are signs of potential moisture and structural damage.
Does the roof have ventilation vents?	**Yes No** ❏ ❏	This is a sign that the attic is ventilated. Check the attic to be sure water is not dripping into the attic around the vents.
Are downspouts missing? If present, do they extend less than six inches from the house?	**Yes No** ❏ ❏	A "yes" to either question could signal problems with water runoff.
Interior of the House		
Is the relative humidity greater than 50 percent?	**Yes No** ❏ ❏	High humidity means the house has too much moisture and not enough ventilation.
Does the house feel damp or smell musty? Do cooking odors linger?	**Yes No** ❏ ❏	These are signs that the house has too much moisture and not enough ventilation.
Is there visible mold or rot on walls, doors or other areas?	**Yes No** ❏ ❏	The house has too much moisture.
Is there evidence of water damage or dampness? (Look for water stains around fixtures in the kitchen and bathrooms, under carpets and on ceilings, other walls and skylights.)	**Yes No** ❏ ❏	There may be structural damage or materials that need to be replaced.

Questions To Ask	Response	What Does a "Yes" Mean?
Is moisture dripping around windows, doors, pipes or other surfaces?	Yes No ❏ ❏	These are signs that the house has too much moisture and not enough ventilation. Pipes may need insulation.
Is there carpeting in the kitchen, bathroom, basement or any room where water is used?	Yes No ❏ ❏	Carpeting in these rooms is a likely place for mold and other microbes to grow.
Basement and Crawl Space		
Is there standing water, dampness or signs of mold in the basement or crawl space?	Yes No ❏ ❏	These are all potential moisture problems that may lead to structural damage.
Do the crawl space and basement have vapor retarders?	Yes No ❏ ❏	Properly installed vapor retarders make it less likely that water can get into the crawl space and basement.
Does the crawl space have vents?	Yes No ❏ ❏	To help remove moisture, vents should be open during warm weather and closed during cold weather.
Do sumps discharge close to the house?	Yes No ❏ ❏	Discharge close to the house can result in water damage in the basement or foundation.
Does the crawl space have debris? Is fiberboard used to make part of the supply or return ductwork in the crawl space?	Yes No ❏ ❏	Debris provides food for microbes. Fiberboard can become wet and grow molds. These problems should be corrected.
Do sumps and drains in the basement and crawl space back up or remove water slowly? (Check by running water in them for five minutes to see if they drain quickly or back up.)	Yes No ❏ ❏	Drains and sumps that do not drain properly can cause water damage. A plumbing contractor may be needed to correct these problems.

PART THREE

Contaminants from Products and Activities

Summary Chart for Mold and Other Biological Contaminants

Topic	Comments
Description	Biological indoor air contaminants include molds (fungi), bacteria and viruses, dust mites, dander, excretions and feathers.
Health Effects	The health effects from biological contaminants range from irritation of the eyes and upper respiratory tract to serious lung diseases. Many of these contaminants result in allergic reactions or a flu-like illness that may include fever. Some illnesses are life-threatening.
Sources	Molds are found in moist, dark, insufficiently ventilated places, such as poorly maintained humidifiers or water-damaged materials. Bacteria and molds grow in and can be dispersed by the heating and cooling system. Hantavirus-associated infections are the result of contact with infected rodents, their excreta or their nests. Dust mites are found in bedding and furniture. Many people suffer allergic reactions to substances produced by dander, feathers and excretions from pets.
Testing	Testing is not always needed because a careful review of sources and symptoms usually identifies the problem. When testing is needed, hire an experienced laboratory to conduct the complex bacteria and fungi testing. Easy to use kits for testing for dust mites are available through pharmacies.
Reducing Exposure	Mold can be eliminated when conditions that favor its growth are prevented by removing excess moisture and increasing ventilation in the home (see Chapter 8). Mold can often be cleaned from materials, but sometimes the only solution is to discard the contaminated material. The best way to prevent infection with hantavirus is to avoid contact with rodents and the places where they live. Rodents must be properly trapped and removed using protective gloves and disinfection. Rodentproofing the home also prevents other diseases transmitted by rodents. The control of dust mites, dander, excretions and feathers relies on cleaning and removing sources of these substances.

CHAPTER
NINE

Mold and Other Biological Contaminants

Meredith Miller moved into her future husband's Lakeside Village condominium unit in January 1983. The unit and adjacent hallway flooded several times from mid-1981 through February 1983 because of plumbing problems. Nine months after moving into the unit, she developed allergies and asthma. An allergist examined her and determined that she was highly allergic to all types of pollens, mold and other substances. But although she had suffered from seasonal hay fever when she lived in the East, she had no history of asthma.

In July 1984, Ms. Miller was hospitalized at Cedars Sinai Hospital in Los Angeles where she was diagnosed with allergies, asthma and an existing heart condition, mitral valve prolapse. After her release, Ms. Miller noticed that the condominium unit smelled musty. She had the unit tested for mold on the advice of her allergist. The results of the testing showed that the unit was infested with mold behind the paneling on the walls and under the carpeting. A microbiologist determined that the mold was caused by the previous flooding.

The Millers tried to get rid of the mold. In the fall of 1984, they removed the paneling, put antifungal paint on the walls, replaced the carpeting with wood flooring and cleaned out the air ducts. In October 1984, Ms. Miller moved back into the unit, but her allergist told her to leave after three days because her allergic reactions were worse than before. Although she did not return to her home, her symptoms continued and worsened. She experienced blurred vision, numbness in her arms and legs, rashes, forgetfulness and confusion.

Finally, in 1986, an allergist discovered that Ms. Miller had a fungal infection and immune dysregulation caused by an untreated fungal infection. Ms. Miller was told that her immune system had been damaged by the long-term fungus infection caused by the severe mold infestation in the condominium. In March 1987, she started gamma globulin infusion treatment for the immune dysregulation and later that year, the asthma attacks stopped.

Ms. Miller sued the condominium owners in court. Although the court agreed that her problems were caused by mold in the condominium, she lost the case because of a legal problem with the statute of limitations.

As reported in *Indoor Pollution News,* May 1, 1992.

What Are Biological Contaminants and Why Are They a Hazard?

Most people know that close contact with other people indoors leads to the spread of colds and flu caused by bacteria and viruses. They are often surprised to find out that other indoor biological contaminants can cause symptoms that range from mild irritations to severe and life-threatening illnesses. Some contaminants, such as molds, pet dander and excretions, feathers and dust mites, can cause both allergic reactions and diseases. According to the World Health Organization, exposure to biological indoor air contaminants at home and work is responsible for a large portion of school and work absenteeism today. Figure 9.1 describes some diseases related to indoor biological contaminants. Because many of the diseases have similar symptoms, their diagnosis can be difficult.

You can protect your household from potential health effects related to biological contaminants by identifying and correcting problems as soon as they arise. Figure 9.2 shows some of the many places in the home that can harbor biological contaminants.

Dust Mites

The house dust mite is a tiny, colorless insect found in many homes. Dust mites like warm, humid conditions. They feed on the skin scales of humans and other animals.

FIGURE 9.1.   Diseases Related to Indoor Sources of Biological Contaminants

Disease	Description
Upper respiratory irritations (URI) and eye irritation *Likely causes: fungi, viruses, dust mites, dander, excretions and feathers*	URI can involve the nose (rhinitis), sinuses (sinusitis) and ears (otitis). Eye problems and URI can be due to infection, allergy, air pollution or air that is too dry or cold. Typical symptoms of rhinitis include itching or sneezing and runny or stuffy nose. Sinusitis often causes pain or fullness in the face and headache. Otitis causes pain in the ear and can affect hearing. Conjunctivitis (an inflammation of the conjunctiva) causes itching, soreness, watering and discharge of the mucous membranes of the eyes. URI are common conditions that can interfere with normal activities.
Pneumonia *Likely causes: bacteria and viruses*	Pneumonia is a serious infection of the lower lung. Indoor air quality does not cause most cases of pneumonia. Legionnaires' disease, however, is a pneumonia occurring mainly in hotels and hospitals that is building-related in about 30 percent of cases. Pneumonia can range in severity from interfering with normal activities to causing death.
Asthma *Likely causes: fungi, dust mites, dander, excretions and feathers*	Asthma occurs when the breathing tubes become irritated and swollen. Breathing becomes difficult and typical symptoms include wheezing and shortness of breath. Asthma is caused or aggravated by many factors, including tobacco smoke, air pollution, emotional stress, exposure to cold and biologic contaminants. Symptoms can start within minutes or hours of entering a contaminated building. Allergic asthma is common and may affect as many as 1 out of 20 people. It can range in severity from interfering with normal activities to causing death.
Allergic alveolitis (hypersensitivity pneumonitis) *Likely causes: fungi, bacteria, excretions and feathers*	Allergic alveolitis is an inflammation of the lower lung that produces breathlessness and results from an allergic reaction to the likely cause. It can begin within 4 to 12 hours of exposure to the contaminant and repeated exposure can result in permanent lung damage. It is an uncommon disease that can range in severity from restricting activities to causing death.

SOURCE: Adapted from World Health Organization (1990).

FIGURE 9.1.   (*continued*)

Disease	Description
Humidifier fever *Likely causes:* *fungi and bacteria*	Humidifier fever is a flu-like illness accompanied by headache and fatigue that begins within four to eight hours after exposure to organisms that are released into the air by contaminated humidifiers. Recovery usually occurs within one to three days. 　　Humidifier fever is an uncommon condition that ranges in severity from interfering with normal activities to incapacitating an individual.
Histoplasmosis *Likely causes:* *fungi*	Histoplasmosis is a flu-like illness that is caused by a fungus in soil that is contaminated with bird droppings. This disease can be fatal.
Allergic bronchopul-monary aspergillosis (ABPA) *Likely causes:* *fungi*	ABPA is a complicated specific form of asthma caused by the fungus *Aspergillus fumigatus* which is very common in soil. 　　Although ABPA is rare, it can result in effects ranging from interfering with normal activities to causing permanent lung damage or death.
Skin conditions (der-matitis, eczema and itch-ing rash) *Possible causes:* *dust mites, feathers,* *dander and excretions*	Dermatitis is an acute or chronic inflammation of the skin caused by physical, chemical or biological agents. Most cases result from physical contact with the contaminant, but can also be caused by airborne particles. Eczema is a chronic skin rash that itches. It reappears throughout life, and biological contam-inants sometimes aggravate this condition. A skin rash that is accompanied by itching, welts and swelling is sometimes the result of exposure to biological contaminants. 　　Skin conditions caused by biological contaminants range in severity from annoying to incapacitating.
Mycotoxicosis *Likely causes:* *fungi*	Mycotoxicosis is a toxic response to products from certain molds. It results in fatigue and inflammation of the heart. 　　Mycotoxicosis is a rare disease that ranges in severity from trivial to incapacitating.

FIGURE 9.2.   Mold and Biological Contaminants in the Home

SOURCE: U.S. Consumer Product Safety Commission and American Lung Association (1990).

Where Biological Pollutants May Be Found in the Home

1. Dirty air conditioners
2. Dirty humidifiers and / or dehumidifiers
3. Bathroom without vents or windows
4. Kitchen without vents or windows
5. Dirty refrigerator drip pans
6. Laundry room with unvented dryer
7. Unventilated attic
8. Carpet on damp basement floor
9. Bedding
10. Closet on outside wall
11. Dirty heating / air conditioning system
12. Dogs or cats
13. Water damage (around windows, the roof, or the basement)
14. Plants

House dust mites are likely to cause eye and upper respiratory tract irritation and asthmatic attacks. Dust mites are responsible for allergic rhinitis, a condition with symptoms of itching, sneezing, nasal stuffiness and a runny nose. Similar symptoms are caused by the common cold and air that is either too dry or very cold. Skin rashes are possible, but less likely, as a result of exposure to dust mites.

Dander, Feathers and Excretions

The excretions of insects such as roaches, carpet beetles, houseflies and bedbugs cause very strong allergic responses in some people. Exposure to domestic animals (particularly cats, but also dogs, rabbits, guinea pigs and birds) can also be important causes of allergic rhinitis and asthmatic attacks. The source of the allergic reaction can be contact with dander or small scales of hair or feathers. Saliva (especially cat saliva) is another potent allergen.

Dander, feathers and excretions cause eye and upper respiratory tract irritation, asthmatic attacks and an inflammation of the lower lung. Some people also develop skin rashes or hives (the medical term for this condition is urticaria).

Bacteria and Viruses

Bacteria and viruses are microscopic organisms that cause many illnesses. These diseases are spread by direct person-to-person contact (through kissing, hugging or touching) or indirectly by inhaling droplets produced by talking, sneezing and coughing or by animal excretions. It is not possible to have homes free of these organisms, even if disinfecting agents are used vigorously. Most of the time, contact with bacteria and viruses does not produce disease, but a person who is already ill or has a damaged immune system can be very vulnerable to their effects.

Other sources of bacteria and viruses include heating and cooling systems, humidifiers and conditions that favor mold growth. Read the section below on molds for more information about sources of and solutions to building-related bacteria.

In 1993, a deadly hantavirus (now called Muerto Canyon virus) that could be transmitted by mice was newly detected and identified in the United States. Although most of the 45 deaths reported during 1993 occurred in the West and Southwest, cases have been diagnosed in eighteen states, including Indiana, Florida, Minnesota and Louisiana. The Centers for Disease Control is also finding indications of other hantaviruses in the United States.

Rodents are also a concern because other diseases can be transmitted by them. For example, bubonic plague is caused by a bacterium that is carried by fleas on rats. When the fleas feed on the rat, the rat can become ill and die. The flea then looks for another host–perhaps a nearby human. Cats and dogs can get the disease from infected fleas or rodents, and they can pass the disease on to humans when they bite, lick or scratch people. The plague does occur in the western states as far east as Texas and as far north as Montana. Although the plague is rarely fatal in people, anyone who lives in an affected area should be alert to the possibility of getting the disease. A person who has been exposed to fleas, rats, dogs or cats, and who suddenly develops fever, chills, headache, nausea and swollen lymph nodes should seek medical treatment immediately.

Farmers, ranchers and others who work with cattle, swine, poultry and birds, and those who have domestic pets are potentially susceptible to other diseases caused by bacteria, viruses and related organisms.

Mold and Mildew

Mold and mildew belong to a group of microscopic organisms called fungi. Fungi can live indoors and outdoors, and most are sustained by organic matter. Molds are a type of fungi that reproduce by releasing tiny seed-like spores into the air that drift until they settle in a new location. Mildew refers to the discoloration produced by the growth of fungi.

Molds are both helpful and harmful. They are used to make cheeses, alcoholic beverages, other foods and important life-saving drugs such as penicillin and streptomycin. When molds grow indoors, however, they can cause problems ranging from irritation to life-threatening pneumonia. Exposure to mold and other fungi sometimes causes illnesses with flu-like symptoms.

House Dust Mites

Testing and Understanding the Results

A simple test kit is available for testing dust mite allergen levels. This test does not count the dust mites but tests the levels of a chemical called guanine found in the dust mite excreta. Each kit contains about 10 tests and is sold in pharmacies for about $15. Contact your pharmacy or an allergist for more information.

There is some uncertainty about what level of dust mites or dust mite allergens poses a risk for most sensitive people. Some people react to dust mite levels above 100 mites per gram of dust or 0.6 milligrams guanine per gram of dust. At these levels, dust mites can cause allergic asthma or worsen an existing asthmatic condition. An amount of mites greater than or equal to 500 per gram of dust may provoke acute attacks of allergic asthma.

Sources and Methods for Reducing Exposure

In North America, the dust mite population increases during the summer when windows are open and ventilation is good. Dust mite levels drop when the relative humidity is below 45 percent and the temperature is less than 68°F. Dust mites are most common in mattresses, carpeting, bedclothes and heavily used upholstered furniture.

Dust mites may be controlled by using dehumidifiers to keep humidity levels below 45 percent. Replacing contaminated materials and frequent cleaning should also be helpful. For example, replace down pillows with synthetic pillows. In some cases, carpeting and upholstered furniture must be replaced with nonfibrous materials. Covering mattresses and box springs with plastic can also reduce exposure to dust mites. When using plastic coverings, remove and wash all bedding weekly in hot water. (A water temperature of 130°F or more kills the mites.) Wash the liners of waterbeds with hot water each week.

Regular cleaning and vacuuming of mattresses, pillows, carpets and other furniture is important. If you are allergic to dust mites, consider wearing a respirator during cleaning or leave the house while cleaning is done. Conventional vacuum cleaners and steam cleaners do not remove the mites because the particles are so small they simply pass through the bag and reenter the air. Special high efficiency particulate air vacuums (HEPA vacuums) are needed. Contact an allergist for help in locating them. (Sometimes they can be rented or borrowed from local health departments.)

Dust mite populations are also controlled by applying chemicals called acaricides to mite-infested materials. These products should be used carefully. If chemical products are applied, they must be removed before allowing pets or children to reenter the area. Residues are very difficult to remove completely from carpets and upholstery. Ingestion of toxic amounts of these chemicals can result in seizures.

Dander, Feathers and Excretions

Testing and Understanding the Results

There are no general test kits for home use to detect pet-related allergens. Many people know the causes of their allergic reactions, but doctors sometimes need to order allergy testing to discover all potential substances that trigger reactions. When excretions from wild or domestic animals and birds cause diseases, medical testing is usually needed to verify the causative organism. The doctor or a public health agency might also collect samples for testing from the home.

Sources and Methods for Reducing Exposures

When animals live indoors, it can be extremely difficult to remove the source of the allergen, especially from carpets, carpet pads and upholstery. The best way to control allergies due to pets is to remove the offending animal and clean the affected area thoroughly. Many of the strategies described for removing house dust mites also work for controlling allergens from animals, birds and other insects.

When purchasing a previously owned home, ask if animals lived indoors and check the inside and outside of the house for signs of cockroaches and places where rodents could enter the house. Piles of wood, trash and other materials provide food and shelter for disease-causing rodents, mosquitoes and a variety of small animals. Read the next section on hantavirus and Chapter 11 on pesticides for more information on controlling rodents.

Urine. A strong smell of urine should make a prospective homebuyer wary. A heavy perfume odor may mean that the owner is trying to mask urine odors, which are very difficult (and costly) to remove. Removal may not be possible if the urine has penetrated porous materials such as wood, carpeting and concrete. Replacing these materials may be the only solution. Avoid using air fresheners to mask odors because some people are also sensitive to the chemicals in those products and the original problem remains. Try cleaning urine stains with a diluted bleach solution of one-half to one cup of bleach per one gallon of water. (Always test a small area of the material to be cleaned with any cleaning solution.) Working in a well-ventilated room, wear latex or rubber gloves and work the cleaning mixture into the stain. Rinse the material with water and allow it to dry completely.

Bird Droppings. One potential source of allergies and disease that is sometimes overlooked is the droppings of birds such as parakeets, poultry, pigeons and starlings. The excreta from birds can cause hypersensitivity pneumonitis (which can be very serious), allergic rhinitis and allergic asthma. Histoplasmosis is a lung and systemic disease caused by inhalation of soil contaminated with fowl droppings. Although it usually occurs in farmers and poultry producers, it can afflict anyone who comes into contact with contaminated soil. Bird droppings can pose a health threat when they are located around the exterior of the house close to windows, air conditioners and air intake pipes. Roosting birds (such as pigeons or starlings) close to your house are a nuisance and pose a health threat. Call your local health department or a private pest control company for help with this problem. There are several control strategies, including the installment of noise alarms, the removal of roosting areas and the use of pesticides.

Hantavirus

Sources

The hantavirus is carried by field mice that are found throughout the United States, usually in rural and semirural areas, but generally not in urban areas. The virus has also been found in a meadow vole in Indiana, and there is evidence that other types of mice and western chipmunks can harbor the virus. The Centers for Disease Control has advised that if the virus is found in one location in a state, it should be presumed present throughout the state.

Infected rodents shed live virus in saliva, feces and urine. People can inhale the virus when droppings, nests or other contaminated areas are disturbed. Infection also occurs if the particles get into cuts or the eyes, but there is no evidence that people can transmit the virus to each other.

According to the Centers for Disease Control, the illness has occurred in people engaged in the following activities:

- Living in dwellings that have rodents
- Occupying previously vacant cabins or other dwellings
- Cleaning barns and other outbuildings
- Disturbing rodent-infested areas while hiking or camping
- Planting or harvesting field crops
- Residing in or visiting areas with rodents

Health Concerns

The hantavirus also causes serious health problems in other parts of the world (mainly the Far East and Scandinavia). In the United States, it has resulted in serious life-threatening respiratory infections and more than half of those known to be infected have died. Infection can occur after only a few minutes of exposure. Symptoms develop about one to two weeks after infection, but the time could range from a few days to up to six weeks. Symptoms initially seem similar to the flu and include high fever, muscle aches, cough and headache. Respiratory symptoms rapidly worsen, however, and the victim can die of respiratory failure as fluid fills the lungs. Anyone who might have come into contact with rodents or their droppings and develops flu-like symptoms should see a physician immediately. Although there is currently no treatment to cure the hantavirus infection, supportive measures can increase the likelihood of survival.

Testing and Understanding the Results

Routine testing for the presence of the virus in rodent droppings and urine is not available to the public. The best protection is to avoid rodents and their excreta, and to follow suggested measures for reducing exposure.

Reducing Exposure

Although the disease is rare in most parts of the country, avoiding contact with rodents and their excreta is the best protection. The Centers for Disease Control has issued precautions and risk reduction measures for households in affected areas. These measures rely on rodentproofing homes (see Figure 9.3), trapping and disposing of rodents safely and cleaning rodent-contaminated areas (see Figure 9.4). Following these commonsense measures will reduce the likelihood of getting hantavirus and other diseases transmitted by rodents.

The Centers for Disease Control has also published precautions for buildings with heavy rodent infestations, workers who are regularly exposed to rodents, and campers and hikers in the affected areas. These guidelines can be obtained by contacting your state health agency (see Appendix A).

Mold

Testing and Understanding the Results

Sampling for molds is not routinely needed because they are usually readily apparent in and around the home, especially in areas with relative humidity measurements above 50 percent. Sampling for molds, bacteria or viruses requires skilled technicians and analysts. Ask testing laboratories if they follow testing guidelines published by the American Conference of Government Industrial Hygienists (ACGIH) Committee on Bioaerosols. Anyone who samples for indoor or outdoor bacteria, viruses and molds should be familiar with these guidelines.

Testing for molds and other fungi requires comparing samples collected from different places inside and outside the house. There are many different types of fungi, and a report of the testing results should include a listing of the types present. This information can help your doctor to diagnose and treat any mold-related health problems that you may be experiencing.

Samples can be collected by wiping surfaces with a cloth that picks up any organisms that are present. At the laboratory, the organisms on the cloth are cultured and later identified. Another way samples are collected is by pumping air

FIGURE 9.3.   Guidelines for Rodentproofing the Home

Seal entryways

- Seal all holes in walls and floors with steel wool or concrete. (Remember that a mouse can fit through a hole 1/4 inch wide–about the size of a small button!) Check around the openings where plumbing and electrical wires enter the house.

Additional sealing measures recommended for rodent-infested areas:

- Create a barrier to entry by placing metal roof flashing around the base of wooden, earthen or adobe dwellings. The flashing should be buried six inches deep into the soil and extend up to a height of 12 inches.
- Place three inches of gravel under the base of stick-built or manufactured homes to discourage rodent burrowing.

Reduce the availability of food inside the home

- Keep food (including pet food) and water covered and stored in rodentproof metal or thick plastic containers with tight-fitting lids.
- Store garbage inside homes in rodentproof metal or thick plastic containers with tight-fitting lids.
- Wash dishes and cooking utensils immediately after use and remove all spilled food.
- Dispose of trash and clutter.

Reduce food and shelter within 100 feet of the home

- Cut grass, brush and dense shrubbery within 100 feet of the home.
- Plant gardens and place woodpiles, compost heaps (which should not contain food scraps) and trash cans at least 100 feet away from the house. Raise woodpiles to at least 12 inches above the ground. Use rodentproof garbage cans (in infested areas these should be raised to 12 inches above the ground).
- Do not leave pet food in feeding dishes.
- Haul away trash, abandoned vehicles, discarded tires and other items that could provide rodents with nesting areas.
- On farms, store grains and animal feed in rodentproof containers. Store hay on pallets, and use traps or rodenticide to keep hay free of rodents. Use raised cement foundations to construct sheds, barns, outbuildings or woodpiles.
- Place spring-loaded rodent traps at likely spots or use an EPA-registered rodenticide approved for outside use in covered bait stations.

FIGURE 9.4.   Safe Elimination of Rodents

Trapping and disposing of rodents

- Before trapping begins, ventilate closed areas or entire buildings by opening doors and windows for at least 30 minutes. (Use an exhaust fan or cross ventilation if possible.) This airing may help remove contaminated particles that are in the air. Leave the area during ventilation and as a precaution, wear a half-mask air purifying respirator with a high-efficiency particulate air (HEPA) filter. Even if a fan is not used, the respirator must be worn if there are dead animals or piles of feces present, or if the structure is associated with a confirmed hantavirus case. (Respirators can be purchased from safety supply houses, and Appendix B contains instructions for using respirators and protective clothing.)
- Seal any openings to the home that are larger than 1/4 inch in diameter.
- Set rodent traps inside the house. (Peanut butter can be used as bait.) Use spring-loaded or snap rodent traps instead of cage traps, or use rodenticide with bait under a plywood or plastic shelter (covered bait station).
- Wear plastic or rubber gloves when removing dead animals.
- Prepare a bleach solution of three tablespoons of bleach mixed with one gallon of water or use a commercial disinfectant. Spray the dead rodent with the bleach solution and put the animal into a plastic bag. Put that bag inside another bag and seal it tightly. Dispose of the double-bagged rodent by placing it into a tightly covered trash container, burying it in a hole two to three foot deep or burning it. Use caution if burning and stay upwind of the burning material.
- Disinfect the traps and any other area that the rodent contacted by spraying them with the bleach solution. Nests, droppings, tainted food and other affected material should be sprayed with the bleach solution, double-bagged and disposed of.

Cleaning rodent-infested areas

- Wear rubber or plastic gloves. If the area is heavily infested, wear coveralls, rubber boots or disposable shoe covers, protective goggles and a half-mask air purifying respirator with a high-efficiency particulate air (HEPA) filter (see Appendix B). *A disposable dust mask is not adequate.* Call the local health department for assistance.
- Spray dead rodents, rodent nests, droppings, foods or other contaminated items with the bleach solution described above or a commercial disinfectant. Soak the suspect material thoroughly and place it in a plastic bag. When cleanup is completed, seal the bag, then place it into a second plastic bag and seal it. Dispose of the bagged material by burying in a hole two to three feet deep or by burning it. If these procedures cannot be used, contact the local or state health department for further assistance.

SOURCE: U.S. DHHS (1993).

FIGURE 9.4. (*continued*)

- Mop floors with a solution of water, detergent and disinfectant, and spray any dirt floors with disinfectant. A second mopping or spraying of floors with a general-purpose household disinfectant is optional. Carpets can be disinfected with household disinfectants or by commercial grade steam cleaning or shampooing. Do not vacuum or sweep dry surfaces before wet cleaning and disinfection.
- Disinfect countertops, cabinets, drawers and other surfaces by washing them with a solution of detergent, water and disinfectant, followed by an optional second wiping down with disinfectant.
- Rugs and upholstered furniture should be steam cleaned or shampooed. If rodents have nested inside the furniture and the nests cannot be decontaminated, the furniture should be removed and burned.
- Launder potentially contaminated clothing and bedding with hot water and detergent. Use rubber or plastic gloves when handling the dirty laundry, and then wash and disinfect the gloves as described above. Machine-dry laundry on a high setting or hang it to air dry in the sun.
- After the cleaning is completed, remove the respirator. Take the cartridges off the respirator and double bag them in plastic. Disinfect the respirator by placing it in a clean container of the disinfectant or bleach solution.
- Any potentially infective waste material (including respirator filters) that cannot be burned or buried deep should be double-bagged in plastic. Contact the local or state health department for instructions on how to handle this waste.

---

through a filter or disk. Any mold that is present in the air will form a deposit on the filter or disk. After the sample is collected, a technician identifies and counts the mold in the laboratory. One type of sampling that is not likely to give good results involves simply setting out a shallow dish (called a petri dish) to collect mold from the air. This type of sampling relies on gravity to deposit the fungi into the dish and misses the smaller fungi in the air. Ask anyone who proposes gravity sampling why he or she wants to use it and seek a second opinion if you are not satisfied with the response.

Sources and Methods for Reducing Exposure

Since molds like moisture, food, darkness and no ventilation, these conditions can help in identifying and solving problems. This section explains where to look for mold and how to prevent its growth inside the house. (See Chapter 8 for information on mold and moisture problems related to the lot and exterior of the house, controlling moisture, increasing ventilation and preventing the entry of moisture indoors.)

Mold can grow on many different items, including wood, paneling, wicker, fabric, leather, carpeting, wallpaper, ceramic tile, concrete and even metal. Molds can grow in basements, attics, crawl spaces, bedrooms, bathrooms, kitchens and in other places such as plant containers. Look for mold where walls join ceilings and floors, areas behind and underneath windows and in poorly ventilated closets. Mold (and mildew) typically appears as black or brown spots or streaks on any of these items, but different colors (such as blue, green or white) are possible (see Figure 9.5).

Existing mold must be eliminated. Simply covering it with paint, stain, varnish or a moisture-proof sealer usually does not work and the mold resurfaces. Do not attempt to clean mattresses, wicker furniture, straw baskets and similar items that contain mold. They cannot be cleaned with conventional methods and should be discarded.

FIGURE 9.5   Example of Severe Mold Growth

Cleaning Moldy Materials. Sometimes it is possible to remove mold from wood and other surfaces. Clean the surface with hot, soapy water or steam and if this does not work, try a noncommercial cleaner or use a commercial product and follow the instructions carefully.

An effective noncommercial cleaner can be made by adding one-half cup of bleach to one gallon of water or by adding one-half cup of vinegar and one-half cup of borax to one gallon of water (other suggestions for bathroom and mildew noncommercial cleaners can be found in Chapter 2). Always test a material to make sure it will not be damaged by the solution. Wash the damaged area with this solution and let the material dry thoroughly. Be sure to use rubber or latex gloves and adequate ventilation when doing the work. If mold stains remain or recur, replace the material.

Bathrooms. The bathroom is one of the most likely areas of the home to have mold and moisture problems, especially if there is no way for the moisture to escape.

Look all around toilets and at the grout around showers and bathtubs for signs of mold and moisture. Remove moldy caulk and clean the surfaces before recaulking. Carefully caulk all seams around tubs, baseboards, sinks and shower doors.

Check for mold on wallpaper as well as the surface underneath the paper. If mold is present, clean or replace the material as needed and cover the walls with an enamel-based paint.

Wipe the surfaces of shower stalls and tubs after each use. Use rubber or latex gloves and *adequate ventilation* when cleaning bathrooms (especially showers) with commercial cleansers that remove mold and scum. These chemicals are corrosive and can damage the skin, eyes and lungs. (If you experience coughing or any eye or respiratory irritation, there isn't enough ventilation.)

Try washing moldy shower curtains in hot, soapy water to clean them, but replace them if mold remains. Tight-fitting shower doors of glass and metal control water better than plastic shower curtains. Doors with hinges are better than sliding glass doors. If you are building a home, consider using a one-piece shower and bathtub stall. Install large tiles rather than small ones to reduce the amount of grout that could become contaminated.

Remove wall-to-wall carpeting and replace it with vinyl flooring or other resilient material. Check the floor underlayment for signs of moisture damage and replace as needed.

Finally, make sure that the bathroom has adequate ventilation. Although operable windows can solve moisture problems, their use is limited for security and other reasons. The best solution is a properly rated fan that exhausts to the outside (see Chapter 10). Always use exhaust fans while showering or bathing.

Kitchens. Problems with moisture and mold can be caused by dripping pipes, appliances and building materials. Look under sinks for signs of mold and rotting wood. Check the refrigerator vegetable bins, drip trays and door gaskets for mold and a slimy liquid that collects around the drain underneath vegetable and fruit bins. Using a hot, soapy solution or a solution of borax or bleach, clean and rinse refrigerators, trash compactors and other areas that have mold.

Carpeting is not a good flooring material in kitchens or dining areas because it is difficult to remove food particles from it completely and it absorbs moisture. Molds grow easily in this environment, and the best solution is to remove carpeting and install vinyl flooring or other resilient material. Check the floor underlayment for signs of moisture damage and replace as needed.

Make sure that the kitchen has adequate ventilation in the form of operable windows or local exhaust fans that vent to the outside (see Chapter 10). Use stove exhaust fans during cooking.

Greenhouses, Pools and Hot Tubs. Greenhouses, indoor swimming pools and hot tubs are excellent places for molds to grow because of the high humidity in these areas. Look carefully for mold growth, standing water and sweating surfaces in these areas. Try cleaning to remove the mold, but remove and replace materials if mold remains.

Because these areas must have adequate ventilation, each should have its own separate ventilation system. It is also important for these areas to have proper floor drainage. Do not use carpeting or floor tiles in these areas. Instead, install vinyl sheeting or other resilient surface.

Basements. Mold and moisture problems in basements are easy to identify but sometimes difficult to correct. Start with low cost solutions and evaluate their effectiveness before trying more expensive methods. Before refinishing a basement, solve any mold or moisture problems and allow surfaces to dry completely (especially before installing carpeting and wallpaper). It is usually prudent to go through a rainy season before finishing a basement in a new home.

Look carefully at basement walls, floors, ceilings and floor joists for signs of mold, water stains or efflorescence on concrete (see Chapter 8). The area around windows and the seams between the floor, walls and ceiling are particularly vulnerable.

If the basement walls, ducting and floor joists are insulated but not completely finished, examine the insulation in a few places for dampness and visible mold growth. Check the condition of the floor joists behind removable ceiling tiles.

Clean any areas that have mold or efflorescence and allow surfaces to dry thoroughly before making additional repairs. Remove materials that cannot be cleaned and remove carpeting and wallpaper from damp basements.

Look for and correct the following signs of moisture problems:

- Moisture leaking into the basement (solutions include dampproofing, waterproofing and installing a perimeter drainage system)
- Floor drains that back up or do not have traps (floor drains must be flushed regularly to prevent water in the trap from becoming contaminated with molds)
- Sumps that back up or do not have covers (a cover will reduce the movement of radon and other gases into the basement)
- Dryers and other exhaust fans that vent into the basement (they should be vented outside)

If basement mold and moisture problems persist, install either a central or portable dehumidifier and maintain it according to the manufacturer's instructions.

Crawl Spaces. Check the crawl space for evidence of mold and moisture problems. Look for mold growth and wood decay around the foundation and floor joists.

If the crawl space has insulated walls, ducts or floor joists, examine the insulation in a few places for dampness and visible mold growth. Replace any moldy insulation and thoroughly clean and dry the materials underneath the insulation.

Look at the crawl space ducts for mold growth around seams and for any openings in the return and supply ducting. Consider replacing fiberboard portions of the ducting system with nonporous materials (see Chapter 10). Also check for and remove loose insulation, wood and paper products in the crawl space because these materials are food sources for growing mold.

Look for and correct the following signs of moisture problems:

- Sweating concrete, dripping pipes and standing water
- A sump that does not work or discharges too close to the foundation
- The lack of a vapor retarder or a vapor retarder that allows water to enter
- No vents or insufficient vents.

Attics. Look for signs of mold and moisture around the roof decking, the joints where the roof and walls join and vent openings. Check for dampness and mold behind insulation. Repair or replace moldy or rotted areas. Make sure that the attic has adequate ventilation or a vapor retarder, if needed (see Chapter 10).

Heating and Cooling Systems. The heating and cooling system can be both a problem and solution to moisture and mold problems. Molds can be carried into the heating and cooling system, and are difficult to remove once established. A properly operating system, however, can effectively remove moisture and prevent molds from growing.

If you live in a cold climate, carefully check for mold and moisture in rooms over unheated garages, closets on outside walls and overhanging areas. These are likely to have problems because of temperature differences and a lack of ventilation. Also look for signs of mold around interior registers, furnace filters and air cleaning devices.

All humidifiers can be sources of microbial contamination, and they should be frequently cleaned and disinfected according to each manufacturer's instructions (see Chapter 10 for guidelines). Mold growth and a film or scum on the water surface can signify potential problems in humidifiers. Also check the sides and bottom of the tank and exposed motor parts. Check in or around the tank for a crusty deposit or slime growth (which has a slippery feel and discoloration that can be red, green or dark colored). The presence of any of these signs means that the humidifier needs to be cleaned and disinfected.

Check water or evaporative (swamp) coolers and heat recovery ventilators regularly for stagnant water and slime growth. Maintain each of these appliances according to the manufacturer's instructions.

Call professional heating contractors for help if the ducts or furnace filters have mold because cleaning these components is difficult. Avoid spraying biocides (chemicals that kill molds) into the system. The effectiveness of these treatments is not known, and these chemicals can cause respiratory problems. If the infestation is severe or ducting is not accessible, the only solution may be to remove or disconnect the ducts or other parts and replace the components as needed. Many problems can be prevented by proper maintenance of the heating and cooling system (see Chapter 10 for guidelines).

Finally, if high outdoor humidity is a seasonal or year-round problem, consider installing either a central or portable dehumidifier which can reduce moisture and help control mold growth, especially in basements. Also, use exhaust fans and wall or window vents to increase ventilation in the crawl space, attic, basement or interior spaces as needed.

Mold and Biological Contaminant Checklist

Questions To Ask	Response	What Does a "Yes" Mean?
Dust Mites, Dander, Excretions and Feathers		
Do you have unexplained allergic symptoms that seem to be related to being in your home?	Yes No ❏ ❏	The problem could be caused by allergens produced by pets, dust mites or mold. (Pollen and grasses are other possible causes that are not considered in this chapter.) Look for potential sources and consult with a doctor about symptoms.
Have bird droppings accumulated on or near the house?	❏ ❏	A heavy accumulation of bird droppings can be a health hazard.
Rodents and Hantavirus		
Is there evidence of mice or rats within the home? Look for droppings inside cabinets and closets, carefully examine the basement floor area and on top of floor joists (if they are accessible) and look for entryways into the home that are more than ¼ inch wide.	Yes No ❏ ❏	Mice and rodents carry many diseases, including hantavirus and the plague. Rodents should be eliminated from the home. Follow the rodentproofing guidelines in this chapter or call the local or state health department for assistance.

Questions To Ask	Response	What Does a "Yes" Mean?
Rodents and Hantavirus		
Is there evidence of mice or other rodents within 100 feet of the home? Potential nesting sites include shrubs, wood-piles and other yard debris.	**Yes No** ❏ ❏	Potential nesting sites and yard debris should be removed. Woodpiles should be raised to at least 12 inches above the ground and food sources should be removed. Follow the rodentproofing guidelines in this chapter or call the local or state health department for assistance.
Molds (see the checklist at the end of Chapter 8 to identify potential moisture problems around the lot, exterior of the house and interior of the house)		
Are there visible signs of mold, rot or discolored areas on wood and other surfaces? Look in all areas of the house including the attic, basement and crawl space. Examine areas covered by insulation.	**Yes No** ❏ ❏	Mold and decay are present. There may be damage to the structure.
Is there carpeting in the kitchen, bathroom, basement or any room where water is used?	**Yes No** ❏ ❏	Carpeting in these rooms is a likely place for mold and other microbes to grow.

Summary Chart for Contaminants from Furnaces and Other Fuel-burning Appliances

Topic	Comments
Description	Combustion-related contaminants are produced by the burning of fuels in vented heating appliances, gas cooking stoves, unvented heaters or other appliances in the house. These contaminants include carbon monoxide, carbon dioxide, water vapor, nitrogen dioxide and a number of other chemicals.
Health Effects	Each year, faulty heating systems cause unnecessary deaths. Combustion contaminants can worsen the health problems of asthmatics and people with heart disease; some contaminants are carcinogenic. Excess water vapor can result in mold growth that affects some people. Tobacco smoke, another combustion contaminant, is the leading cause of lung cancer deaths in the United States.
Sources	Sources of combustion contaminants in the home include vented and unvented heating systems, gas cooking stoves, gas dryers and a variety of hobby and craft activities. Tobacco smoke and unvented appliances also release contaminants directly into the living space.
Testing	It is possible to purchase smoke alarms, gas detectors and carbon monoxide detectors for in-home use. A test for combustion contaminants conducted by a qualified professional can cost between $75 and $100. Acceptable levels of exposure to carbon monoxide are 9 ppm for eight hours of exposure and 35 ppm for one hour of exposure (according to the EPA's outdoor standards). Ask local or state health agencies for help in identifying hazardous levels of other combustion contaminants. Interpreting some tests results requires skilled professionals.
Reducing Exposure	Reduce exposure to combustion contaminants by regularly inspecting and maintaining sources of combustion contaminants. Replace appliance parts in poor condition and correct hazardous conditions. Make sure that there is enough combustion air to burn the fuel efficiently and limit the use of appliances that vent combustion contaminants into the living space. Stop smoking to eliminate the most important source of carcinogenic combustion contaminants in your home.

CHAPTER

TEN

Combustion Contaminants from Furnaces and Other Fuel-burning Appliances

During the winter of 1991 in Prince George County, Maryland, two children died and two adults were hospitalized because of carbon monoxide poisoning. The cause of these deaths was a lack of furnace maintenance and a missing chimney cap. The natural gas furnace vented into a metal chimney. Because the rain cap was missing, water easily got into the chimney and caused the metal to rust and flake. The rust particles accumulated and eventually blocked the chimney. During the same period, the furnace air filter, which was not changed, became clogged and prevented enough air from entering the furnace combustion chamber. As a result, the combustion in the furnace was incomplete and carbon monoxide became a combustion product. Because the chimney was clogged, the combustion gases could not escape through the vent. Instead, they were forced into the furnace room through cracks in the furnace, and leaks in the furnace room ductwork carried the carbon monoxide to all parts of the house.

As reported in *Indoor Pollution News,* November 15, 1991.

What Contaminants Do Furnaces and Other Fuel-burning Appliances Emit and Why Are They a Hazard?

Any appliance or activity that burns fuel is a potential source of combustion contaminants in the home. Natural gas, the most widely used fuel in America, and LP gas are "clean-burning" fuels. Nevertheless, they still break down into hydrocarbons (carbon-containing byproducts), carbon monoxide, carbon dioxide, water vapor and nitrogen-containing compounds. The burning of wood produces these contaminants, other organic compounds and small particles, many of which are carcinogenic. When kerosene, fuel oil and coal burn, all of the above contaminants (plus sulfur dioxide) are produced.

Fuel-burning appliances are responsible for health effects ranging from headaches and respiratory tract irritation to death. Each year, people die after breathing carbon monoxide produced by appliances that do not vent properly or by unvented appliances. Relatively low levels of carbon monoxide can cause flu-like symptoms in healthy people and shortness of breath and chest pain in people with heart disease. Studies also show that children may have more respiratory illnesses when they live in households with combustion sources of nitrogen dioxide. Exposure to sulfur dioxide can cause wheezing, chest tightness and breathing problems.

Some combustion sources pose special concerns because they release contaminants directly into the living space. These sources include tobacco smoke, combustion-related hobby and craft activities, and unvented combustion sources that also release moisture into the home. Too much water vapor is a problem because it condenses onto window frames and sills, and wood and insulation that are not visible, causing water damage and mold.

How can you know if you have health problems related to combustion sources? Consult your physician if you have any of the following symptoms: watery eyes, headaches, dizziness, disorientation, fatigue, sleepiness, nausea, vomiting or shortness of breath. (Facial skin that has a bright cherry-red color is another symptom but it is not always present.) These symptoms could be caused by other health problems such as a cold, flu, allergy or other indoor air contaminant. However, if you are using a combustion appliance and your symptoms worsen at home (when the appliance is in use) and improve when you leave home, a faulty combustion appliance is likely to be the cause of your symptoms.

Smoking

Any discussion of combustion-related contaminants must mention the large impact of smoking on those who smoke and those who breathe the air of smokers. Smoking alone releases over 3,800 contaminants into the air; many of them cause cancer and genetic changes in the body. Smoking is the leading cause of lung cancer in adults and can also lead to heart disease, respiratory problems and aggravation of angina in heart patients. Involuntary smoking is now recognized as an important cause of lung cancer in healthy nonsmokers.

Smoking even affects unborn children. Pregnant women who smoke are more likely than nonsmokers to have premature babies and babies with low birth weights. Both problems make the first months of life more difficult for babies and mothers.

An important finding during the last few years has been that environmental tobacco smoke affects children. Studies show that children who live in households with smokers have more upper and lower lung infections (such as bronchitis and pneumonia) than children who live in smoke-free households. These children also have a slower rate of growth in lung function as the lung matures. It has been suggested that exposure to tobacco smoke in childhood could result in increased susceptibility to developing lung disease in adulthood.

Fire Safety

Every home should have a smoke detector and a fire extinguisher. A general guideline is to place a detector outside of bedrooms and on each floor. In addition, place a detector and a fire extinguisher in any room that has a wood-burning stove. Contact your local fire department for specific recommendations for your home.

To reduce the likelihood of an explosion treat all fuel leaks with extreme caution. If a fuel odor is present, extinguish all sources of flame, open the windows, evacuate the house and call the fuel company from an outside telephone.

Understanding Your Heating System

There are many different types of home heating systems. Homes that are more than 50 years old are likely to have a furnace that uses oil or coal. Radiators that supply hot water or steam heat are common in these homes. (Figure 10.1 shows a typical oil furnace installation.)

Homes built or remodeled during the last few decades are likely to have forced-air systems, but some have radiators that deliver hot water or steam heat. The heating system in a newer home is typically a conventional oil or gas

FIGURE 10.1.   Oil Furnace Installation

Piping Hook-up for Buried Outside Tank

Note: Enough air for combustion must enter
furnace room. Provide 15-square-inch opening
for each gallon of oil burned per hour.

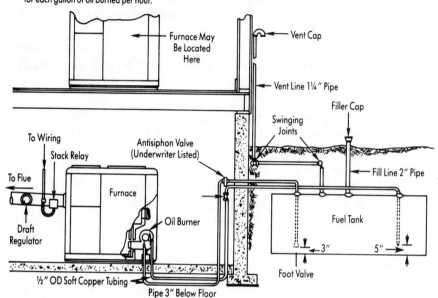

Piping Hook-up for Inside Tank Installation

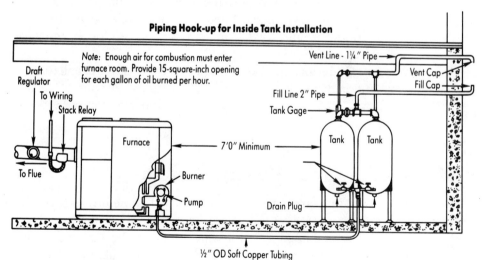

SOURCE: U.S. DHEW (1976, reprinted 1979).

furnace, high-efficiency furnace or electric furnace. (Figure 10.2 shows examples of gas-fired forced-air furnace installations.) Other common heat sources are heat pumps, geothermal systems or solar systems. Some homes have electric strip heating in the ceiling or floors, and houses of all types and ages have fireplaces or stoves for primary and supplemental heating.

FIGURE 10.2.   Typical Gas Furnace Configurations

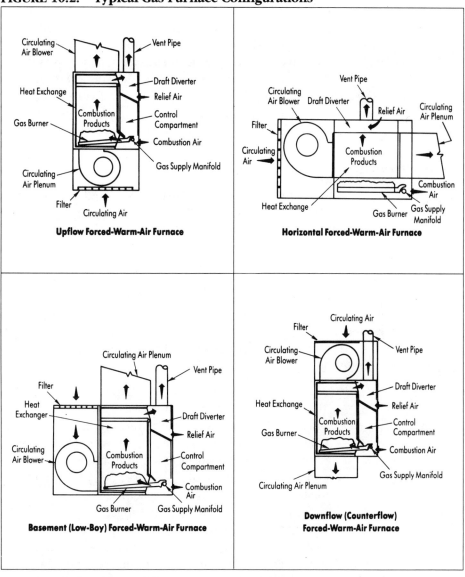

SOURCE: Reprinted by permission of the American Society of Heating, Refrigerating, and Air-Conditioning Engineers, Atlanta, Georgia, from the 1988 *ASHRAE Handbook—Equipment*.

The proper operation and maintenance of any heating system will help it to perform efficiently and extend its life. Follow the manufacturer's instructions or contact a reputable heating contractor to ask for help if no instructions exist. It is especially important to have a heating contractor check fuel-burning furnaces at least once each year before the heating season to be sure that the furnace operates safely and efficiently.

Homes that do not have wall vents or centralized forced-air systems have minimal air circulation unless windows are opened or fans are used. Consider installing a ventilation system to improve air quality and reduce the chance of problems with mold and moisture buildup.

If you have an energy-efficient gas furnace that was manufactured during the late 1970s or early 1980s, contact the Consumer Product Safety Commission (see Appendix A for the address) to find out if your furnace has been the subject of a recall. Some of these furnaces have serious corrosion problems that release carbon monoxide into the living space.

Combustion Air

A fuel-burning appliance must have enough air for efficient combustion. The combustion air usually comes from the room that contains the appliance or from surrounding rooms. Poorly insulated or unweatherized houses usually have enough combustion air because fresh air is constantly pulled into the house through the walls and gaps around the doors and windows, but weatherized and tightly insulated houses may not have enough combustion air. Problems that result from a lack of combustion air include increased heating bills caused by inefficient combustion, deteriorating indoor air quality and safety hazards.

The following are some easily recognizable signs of incomplete combustion in fuel-fired appliances:

- Flames of the wrong color or shape—look at the flame (see Figure 10.3) of the water heater, cook stove, gas wall furnace, kerosene heater or central furnace. A properly burning flame has a blue color without yellow tips and is uniform in shape over all of the burner ports. A sign of incomplete combustion is a light blue flame with yellow tips or a completely yellow flame. An improperly burning flame is not uniform in shape and appears to be reaching out for air. If the color or shape of the flame improves after opening a door or window, another source of combustion air should solve the problem.
- Black soot in or around the appliance—a buildup of soot can extinguish the pilot light in a gas appliance. This is a serious situation. Do not attempt to light the pilot if this occurs. Instead, turn off the gas and call the utility for emergency help from an outside telephone.

FIGURE 10.3.   Flame Tips: Properly Burning (left) and Improperly Burning (right)

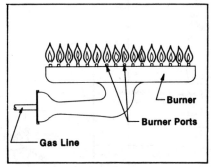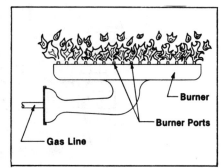

SOURCE: NCAT (1983).

- Corrosion in the appliance vent or flue (the pipe that goes into the chimney or outdoors) and in heat exchangers.
- Condensation on windows or doors.
- Any odor of unburned fuel.

Whenever any of these signs are present, the appliance may need repair, maintenance or additional combustion air. Combustion air can be provided temporarily by opening windows or doors to other rooms, but a better solution is to bring outside air directly to the appliance. A qualified heating contractor can diagnose problems and offer potential remedies. The National Center for Appropriate Technology has useful brochures on this and other energy-related topics (see Appendix A for the address).

Vents, Chimneys and Flues

Vents. A vent is the pipe or duct that carries the combustion gases from the appliance to the chimney or outside air. Appliances that need to be vented should vent to the outside and not to the attic, crawl space or other inside area. The end of the vent should be about 12 inches from windows, doors, air inlets or the ground in order to prevent dirt and combustion gases from blowing into the living space. (When a fan moves air into the house, the vent should be about three feet above this inlet.)

Inside the house, the vent should have an upward slope after it connects to the appliance so gases can escape. A vent that is horizontal or slopes downward does not allow gases to escape to the outside. In most installations, there should be no more than two 90° elbows in the venting system. Ideally, the elbows will not be more than 45°. Figure 10.4 shows a properly vented stove.

FIGURE 10.4.   Properly Installed and Vented Wood Stove

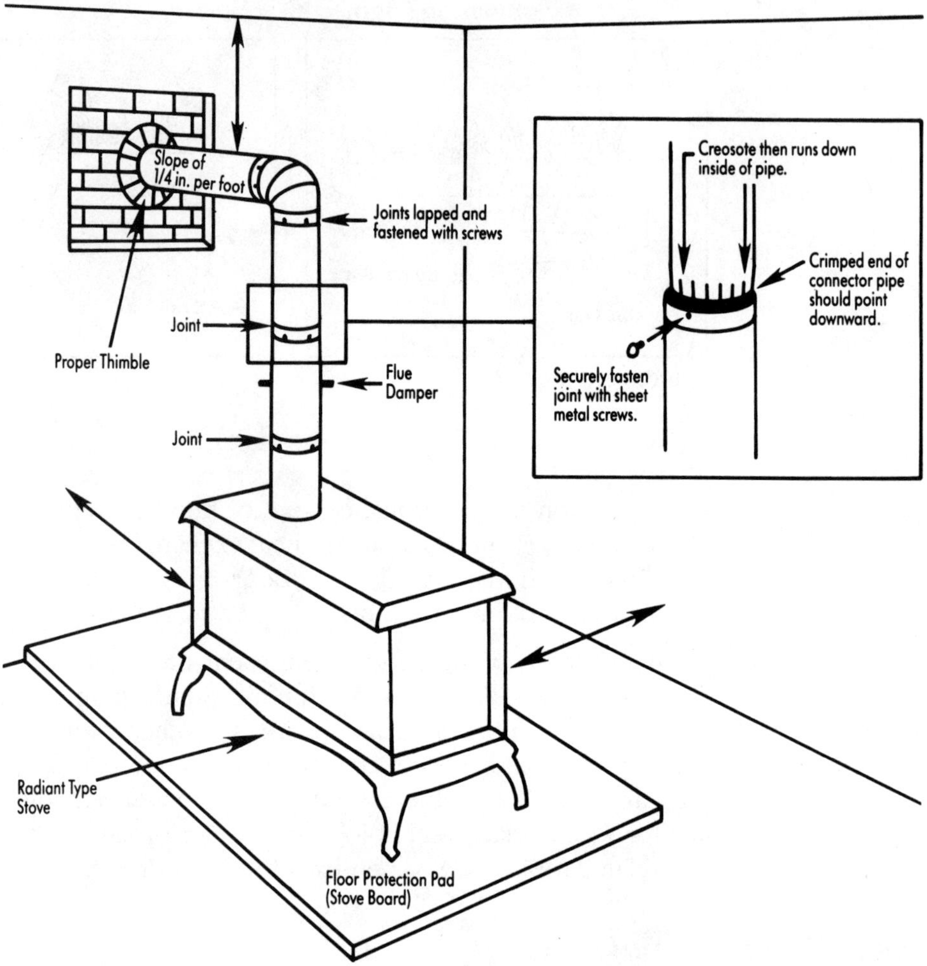

Slope of 1/4 in. per foot

Joints lapped and fastened with screws

Joint

Proper Thimble

Flue Damper

Joint

Radiant Type Stove

Floor Protection Pad (Stove Board)

Creosote then runs down inside of pipe.

Crimped end of connector pipe should point downward.

Securely fasten joint with sheet metal screws.

SOURCE: Jenkins, J. and R. Vacca. "Wood for Home Heating: Safety and Wood Heating Systems." G2936. Madison, WI: Wisconsin Energy Extension Service, 1979.

Draft Hood.   Vented appliances must have a draft hood or backdraft diverter (see Figure 10.5). This is a safety device that prevents dangerous gases from building up in the living area by diluting exhaust gases with air from around the hood. It also keeps a draft from coming down the vent and blowing out the pilot light. A simple test, outlined below, can be performed to determine if a draft hood is working properly. Check the draft hood on each appliance that is connected to the same chimney.

FIGURE 10.5.   Backdraft Diverters and the Draft Hood Test

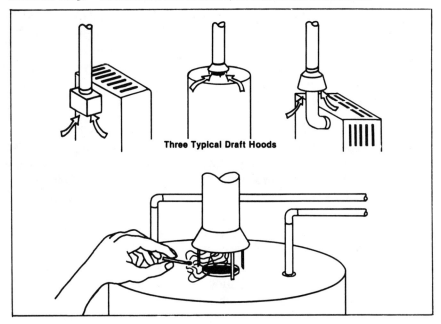

SOURCE: NCAT (1983).

Draft Hood Test

(***CAUTION:*** Before conducting the draft hood test, make sure that there are no gas leaks or fuel odors. Check for gas leaks by applying a soap and water solution to the gas fittings and lines. The appearance of bubbles means that a leak exists. *DO NOT CONDUCT THE DRAFT HOOD TEST IF YOU FIND ANY LEAKS!* Call your local utility for emergency help.)

- Hold a burning cigarette near the inlet of the draft hood as shown in Figure 10.5.
- When the draft hood works properly, the smoke will be drawn into the hood and exhausted out the flue. If the smoke does not flow into the hood, the draft might be inadequate because there is not enough combustion air. Another problem might be debris or something else causing a blockage in the chimney.
- Conduct the test twice, first with the appliance cold and then after the appliance has been operating for a few minutes.

An appliance that has a good draft might still need maintenance or repairs if there are any signs of incomplete combustion. Call a qualified heating contractor for help.

Chimneys and Flues. A chimney is a masonry or concrete structure that carries combustion gases away from the appliance to the outside air. The pipe inside the chimney is called a flue or chimney flue and is usually made of metal or clay. Checking the condition of chimneys and flues regularly can prevent serious problems, and easy-to-perform inspections are described below. If you have any concerns about the installation or condition of the chimney or flue, call a heating contractor for help.

- Check the condition of the inside and outside of the chimney. In masonry chimneys, look for deteriorating mortar between the bricks or stones. Check metal chimneys for rust or holes (a flashlight makes this job easier). Openings should be sealed.
- Look for creosote, a black, tarry substance that has an unpleasant odor. A potential fire hazard, creosote will make black stains along the exterior of the chimney or flue. On interior surfaces, it can appear as bubbles, flakes, curls or as a dry or tacky glaze. Sometimes it forms a pool on the floor. If creosote and soot are more than 1/4 inch thick, have the chimney or flue cleaned by a professional contractor.
- The chimney should have a cap (see Figure 10.6) to keep rainwater, birds and other pests out of the house. Check the condition of the cap at least once each year to prevent the buildup of soot, corrosion, bird's nests and other debris that can cause blockage.
- Check the clearance of the chimney above the roof and make sure it is high enough to prevent backdrafting, a serious condition in which the combustion gases move back down the flue into the appliance rather than exhausting outside the house. Local codes specify the required clearances above the roof. A general rule is that the chimney should be at least three feet above the highest point where it passes through the roof and at least two feet higher than any part of the roof that is within ten horizontal feet of the chimney. Proper chimney placement is illustrated in Figure 10.7. A chimney built inside a house will probably have fewer backdrafting problems than a chimney built along the exterior walls. It is difficult for gases going into exterior chimneys to escape because they are cooled quickly.
- Check how many appliances connect to the chimney. A gas or oil furnace should not connect to a chimney that also serves an appliance that burns solid fuel (such as a wood stove or coal furnace). This type of connection can reduce the draft on the appliances. Whenever two appliances are served by the same chimney, they should be staggered

FIGURE 10.6.   Examples of Chimney Caps

SOURCE: Shelton, J.W. 1979. *Wood Heat Safety.* Garden Way Publishing: Pownal, VT. Used with permission.

FIGURE 10.7.   Proper Chimney Clearances above the Roof

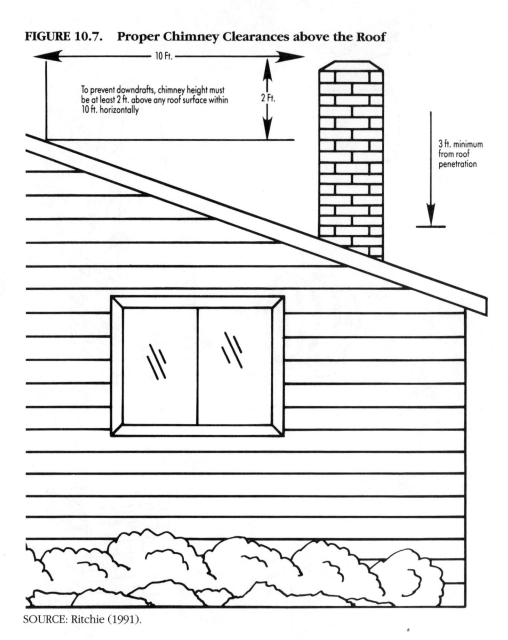

SOURCE: Ritchie (1991).

along the vertical shaft and should not enter the chimney at the same location at the same level. A staggered arrangement prevents fumes from blowing across the chimney and through the second appliance. Some of the problems that can result when more than one appliance connects to a chimney are illustrated in Figure 10.8.

FIGURE 10.8.   Problems Resulting from the Venting of Multiple Appliances Through a Single Chimney

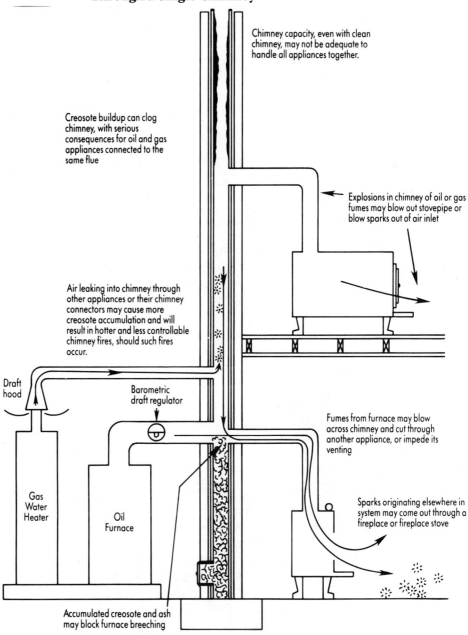

SOURCE: Shelton, J.W. 1979. *Wood Heat Safety*. Garden Way Publishing: Pownal, VT. Used with permission.

Forced-air Delivery Systems

The installation and condition of a forced-air delivery system are the most significant factors that will affect the indoor air quality. Some examples of different types of forced-air distribution systems are illustrated in Figure 10.9. The most important parts of the air delivery system are the supply ducts and registers and the return ducts and registers.

Registers. Warm air supply registers are usually located against outside walls, ideally under windows so that rising warm air from the register meets and warms the cold air by the window. The preferred location for cold air return grills is in or near partition walls, not near cold spaces (such as outside walls). The air must be able to flow into and out of the registers freely. If a register delivers too much air, an air deflector (available in hardware stores) can redirect the air stream.

Ducts. Although sheet metal is the preferred material for both supply and return ducts, most building codes allow the use of alternative materials. One widely used alternative is a flexible duct made of fiberglass sandwiched between layers of plastic. Plastic is acceptable for the return air, but it may not be as desirable for the supply air because the hot air can release organic contaminants from the plastic. Some people may be sensitive to these contaminants. Builders sometimes use the floor joists or wall cavities to form a duct by nailing sheet metal or fiberboard over the openings between the studs in walls or the floor joists. Tightfitting stops of wood or sheet metal are used to seal the ends of the ducts.

Special care must be taken when the crawl space acts as an air plenum. (A plenum is a cavity that acts as a duct.) In this design (see Figure 10.9), the furnace discharges air directly into the crawl space to create a positive pressure that causes warm air to flow upward through open floor registers. Insulating the foundation and crawl space floor will help prevent heat loss. All loose debris must be removed, and the plenum should not have fuel gas lines or plumbing waste cleanouts. Foil-coated fiberboard ducts or gypsum products used as ducts or plenums should not be used in the crawl space because of the possibility of moisture damage to the fiberboard or gypsum.

The crawl space must be made airtight using a properly installed and sealed continuous air and vapor retarder with a permeability rating not greater than one perm. These precautions will reduce the chance of moisture damage and mold growth and also prevent radon gas and other contaminants from entering the crawl space and living spaces in the house.

FIGURE 10.9.   Forced-air Distribution Systems

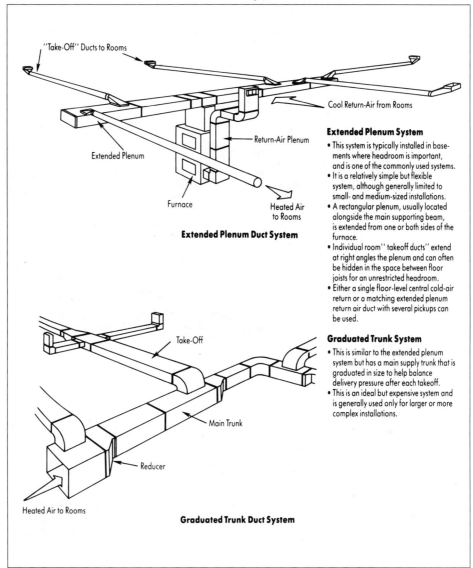

Extended Plenum System

• This system is typically installed in basements where headroom is important, and is one of the commonly used systems.
• It is a relatively simple but flexible system, although generally limited to small- and medium-sized installations.
• A rectangular plenum, usually located alongside the main supporting beam, is extended from one or both sides of the furnace.
• Individual room "takeoff ducts" extend at right angles the plenum and can often be hidden in the space between floor joists for an unrestricted headroom.
• Either a single floor-level central cold-air return or a matching extended plenum return air duct with several pickups can be used.

Graduated Trunk System

• This is similar to the extended plenum system but has a main supply trunk that is graduated in size to help balance delivery pressure after each takeoff.
• This is an ideal but expensive system and is generally used only for larger or more complex installations.

SOURCE: Peter A. Mann, P.A. 1989. *Illustrated Residential and Commercial Construction.* ©1989, Figures 14-11, 14-12, 14-13. Reprinted by permission of Prentice Hall, Englewood Cliffs, NJ.

FIGURE 10.9. (*continued*)

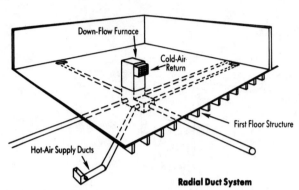

Radial System
- This system requires a `` down-flow'' type of furnace that blows warm air downward to a distribution plenum beneath the floor.
- Individual room supply ducts radiate out from the supply plenum, as shown at the left, and are positioned below the floor joists.
- This system is generally used only in crawl space or slab-on-grade construction, where headroom below the supply ducts is of no concern.
- The cold-air return is usually through a single grille on or near the furnace head.
- In an unheated crawl space the supply ducts must be sealed and well insulated.

Radial Duct System

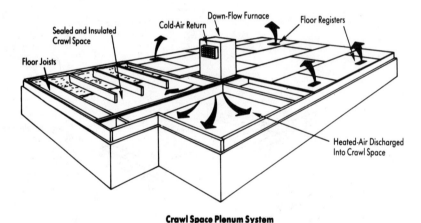

Crawl Space Plenum System

Crawl Space Plenum System
- In this system the crawl space itself is used as a plenum to distribute the warm air to the individual rooms.
- A down-flow furnace is located on the first floor and discharges warm air into the crawl space, where a positive pressure is created. The warmed air then flows upward through the open floor registers into the first-floor rooms. In addition to the connection effect, the floor is warm and rdiates heat. This increases the mean radiant temperature and raises comfort levels.
- Variations in crawl space depth have little effect on the system's overall efficiency, and any type of foundation construction can be used.
- The foundations and crawl space floor must be treated as a fully heated basement and insulated to suit. The crawl space must be made airtight using a continuous and sealed air/vapor barrier.
- System costs are relatively low since no supply ducts are required and overall system efficiency tends to be quite high.

FIGURE 10.9.   (*continued*)

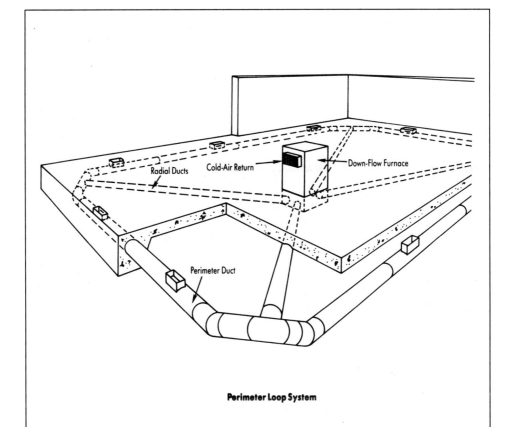

Radial Ducts
Cold-Air Return
Down-Flow Furnace
Perimeter Duct

Perimeter Loop System

Perimeter Loop System

This is similar to the radial system shown opposite with the addition of a perimeter loop connected to the radial supply ducts.

• Supply registers are located in the outer loop at suitable room positions.
• Fewer radial feeder ducts are needed, and the slab perimeter is kept relatively warm provided that the perimeter loop is not insulated.
• The feeders and loop are set in place before the concrete floor slab is poured. Ensure that the ducts are sloped downward toward the supply plenum for the collection of any water that may accumulate in the system.

The radial system can also be used in slab-on-grade construction but tends to result in cold floor areas at the slab perimeter.

Deteriorating or improperly sealed ductwork in a crawl space, basement or slab foundation can degrade indoor air quality. Radon, pesticides and other contaminants can enter the living areas through holes or other openings in the ducts. The solution to this problem is to use nonfibrous material (such as sheet metal) for the ducts and to overlap or tape the joints securely.

All ductwork located in an unconditioned space (such as a basement, attic or crawl space) should be insulated to prevent moisture damage and mold growth. A vapor retarder should cover the insulation when ducts are used for cooling.

Humidifiers and Dehumidifiers

Air that is too dry causes physical discomfort in the form of dry nose, throat, lips and skin. It also increases static electricity and causes furniture and paint to crack. Air that is too humid feels clammy and close and leads to the growth of molds and dust mites (see Chapter 9). When excess moisture becomes trapped inside walls, structural damage can result (see Chapter 8).

Although difficult to do, striking a balance between too much or too little moisture is not impossible. A humidity level between 30 and 50 percent is comfortable for most people and reduces the likelihood of mold and dust mites.

Humidifiers. Humidifiers are usually used to add moisture to the air during the heating season. A centralized humidifier can be built into the central heating and cooling system and used to humidify the entire house. Single rooms can be humidified by small portable units or larger floor units (also called console units).

Each of the following four types of humidifiers adds moisture to the air by a different method:

- Ultrasonic humidifiers that use ultrasonic sound vibrations to create a cool mist
- Impeller or "cool mist" humidifiers that produce a cool mist by means of a high speed rotating disk
- Steam vaporizers that heat water to make steam (a warm mist humidifier is a type of steam vaporizer that cools the steam before it leaves the vaporizer)
- Evaporative coolers that use a fan to blow air through a moistened absorbent material such as a belt, wick or filter (the absorbent material requires periodic cleaning and replacement)

Humidifier use can result in mineral deposits and mold growth in the humidifier itself and in the surrounding area. Slime and mold can grow in standing water. As the water evaporates, mineral deposits and scale form in the humidifier, providing a good place for mold to grow. During operation, any minerals in the humidifier water will be carried into the air along with the moisture, causing a fine white dust to coat furniture and other surfaces. When too much moisture is in the air, mold growth is likely. The ultrasonic and impeller humidifiers seem to produce more mold and mineral problems than the other types of humidifiers.

Mineral deposits can be reduced by using bottled water that is labeled "distilled." Water that is deionized or treated with reverse osmosis will have low mineral levels, but these treatments are not as effective as distillation. Water that is labeled "spring," "artesian" or "mineral" has not been treated to remove minerals.

The following strategies can lessen mineral deposits, slime and mold growth:

- Follow the manufacturer's instructions for cleaning and maintaining the humidifier. (Be sure to unplug units from the electrical socket before changing water or maintaining humidifiers.)
- Do not let the indoor humidity get above 50 percent.
- If the humidifier has a water tank, keep the water clean and do not allow it to stand in the tank for a long time.
- Do not let the area around the humidifier become damp or wet.
- If possible, use low mineral water to prevent scale buildup and the dispersal of minerals in the air.
- Change the water daily in portable humidifiers that have a capacity of less than two gallons. For larger units, change the water as recommended by the manufacturer. Clean the humidifier according to the manufacturer's instructions. If there are none, use a 3 percent solution of hydrogen peroxide on all surfaces that come into contact with the water. Some manufacturers recommend using a diluted bleach solution (usually one-half cup of bleach to one gallon of water). Always rinse well with water before refilling the humidifier.
- Thoroughly clean the humidifier at the end of the season or when the product will not be in frequent use.
- Avoid using antifoulant agents (chemicals that control mold growth) in the water. They may not be effective and can be carried into the air by the water vapor.

Dehumidifiers. Dehumidifiers are usually used during warmer weather and in damp areas to remove extra moisture from the air. To be most efficient, they must be sized correctly according to the area of the house. Performance can be improved by placing the unit in the center of the room to maximize air circulation and closing the room from the rest of the house.

Mechanical dehumidifiers remove moisture by cooling the air and condensing it onto a coil. The condensed water drips into a collection pan or a drain. If the dehumidifier does not empty into a drain, the collection pan must be emptied on a regular basis (usually daily). Mold growth can be a problem when the collected water is not removed promptly or if it saturates other materials. When the temperature falls below 65°F, frost or ice can form. Although some units have automatic defrost cycles, others require manual defrosting.

Avoid chemicals that remove humidity from the air. Some are corrosive and require careful handling and proper disposal.

Air Cleaners

Residential air cleaners can help improve some (but not all) types of indoor air quality problems. Both portable and centralized units are available. Some air cleaners are effective at removing very small particles that can be inhaled deeply into the lungs (such as tobacco smoke, bacteria, viruses, some molds and combustion-related contaminants). Tobacco odors, however, are difficult to remove and often linger even after the smoke particles have been removed.

Air cleaners may not be effective at removing the larger particles that can cause allergic reactions in people (such as pollen, house dust, animal dander and some molds). Larger particles are hard to remove because they usually settle on surfaces in the home before reaching the air cleaner.

The ability of residential air cleaners to remove gases such as formaldehyde and other organic contaminants has not been adequately demonstrated.

There are four basic types of air cleaners for removing particles from the air:

- Mechanical filters that rely on a paper or synthetic material to filter particles
- Electronic air cleaners (such as electrostatic precipitators) that use an electrical field to trap particles; these types of cleaners can produce ozone, a lung irritant

- Ion generators that use static charges to remove particles; they can produce ozone and cause soiling of the walls and other surfaces (this problem is worse for ion generators without collectors)
- Hybrid devices that use two or more of the other removal devices

Performance of Centralized Systems. Only limited information is available on the performance of whole-house in-duct air cleaning systems once they are installed in the home. Manufacturers test these units in laboratory settings that may not reproduce the conditions in a home. Low efficiency filters (such as furnace filters) are evaluated with the weight arrestance test, which measures the ability of the filter to collect a standard synthetic dust. The atmospheric dust spot test is used for medium efficiency air cleaners (both filters and electronic air cleaners) to measure how well a filter reduces soiling. The Military Standard 282 rates the ability of high efficiency air filters (efficiencies above 98 percent) to collect a standard synthetic dust of uniformly small particles.

Whenever you read about one of these test results in the product literature for an air cleaner, keep in mind that the product's performance in your house may not be as good as that given in the literature.

Performance of Portable Systems. There is a rating system available for portable air cleaners that is published by the Association of Home Appliance Manufacturers (AHAM) and the American National Standards Institute (ANSI). This standard rates the clean air delivery rate (CADR) of portable cleaners and measures how much fresh air a unit is delivering. (The fresh air, however, is not 100 percent fresh because some contaminants may not be removed from the air.)

Air cleaners with CADR certification based on the ANSI/AHAM standard are evaluated in terms of the removal of dust, tobacco smoke and pollen. As a general rule the higher the CADR, the less time needed to remove the contaminants from the air. AHAM publishes a useful booklet for consumers that explains the CADR and how air cleaners are rated (see Appendix A for the address). This booklet contains a table of what percentage of particles are removed from the air by cleaners with different CADRs for different room sizes.

The performance of a portable air cleaner improves when it is properly placed. The inlet and outlet of the cleaner must be clear of walls, furniture and other obstructions to the flow of air and the cleaner should be close to specific sources of contaminants.

Guidelines for Purchasing an Air Cleaner. If you are considering purchasing an air cleaner, work closely with a sales representative to determine which product will be best for your situation. There are several important questions to ask before making a decision, including the following:

- How many of the particles can the cleaner remove? As noted above, a claim of 100 percent clean air is not realistic.
- Can the air cleaner handle the volume of air to be cleaned? For example, if you buy a cleaner that handles a small amount of air, say 50 cubic feet each minute, for a room that is 10 feet by 12 feet by 8 feet high (960 cubic feet), it will take about 19 hours for all of the air to be cleaned in this room. A more powerful fan will change the air in the room more quickly.
- What maintenance does the cleaner require?
- How much will it cost to operate the air cleaner? This estimate should include both maintenance and energy costs.
- How much noise does the air cleaner make? Portable air cleaners are noisy, even at low speeds. Listen carefully to these cleaners to be sure that you can live with this distraction.

Avoid air cleaners and chemicals that scent the air. Chemical scents do not clean the air—they add chemicals to it.

Testing and Understanding the Results

Whenever a faulty appliance is suspected of releasing combustion-related contaminants, tests should be conducted to measure levels of carbon monoxide and fuel vapors. Local health agencies or utilities can sometimes do the monitoring; if not, look in the yellow pages of the telephone directory under "Laboratories—Testing" and "Heating Contractors." Hiring a consultant can cost $25 to $100 for a carbon monoxide or fuel test. (Note: If you ever detect a fuel odor, treat it as an emergency. Extinguish all sources of flame, open the windows, evacuate the house and call your local utility immediately from an outside telephone.)

Gas detectors and carbon monoxide detectors have recently become available for home use. They provide an extra measure of safety by giving an audible warning when preset levels of gas are detected. (The gas detectors can detect LP gas [propane or butane] and natural gas [methane].) Purchase detectors that are tested by Underwriters Laboratories and are labelled as "UL listed."

There are several types of do-it-yourself carbon monoxide alarms available for home use. The easiest to use is a battery operated continuous sensor that looks similar to a smoke detector. The battery and sensor need to be replaced periodically (usually once each year). Other types include detectors that are wired into the house and dose monitors that take into account the time of exposure. The cost of these monitors ranges from $50 to about $100. The cheapest detectors are those that rely on a small sensor disk that changes color when high carbon monoxide levels are present. Do not rely on these detectors because even if the disk works correctly, you will not see the color change if you are asleep or don't check the detector.

The level of carbon monoxide that will be harmful to a person's health varies depending on his or her level of physical activity and health status. Once carbon monoxide enters the blood stream, it ties up the hemoglobin, forms carboxyhemoglobin (COHb) and prevents oxygen from reaching the tissues. Another source of increased COHb in the blood is smoking. Nonsmokers typically have COHb levels between 1.2 and 1.5 percent while smokers' levels range from 3 to 4 percent. Heavy smokers could have levels as high as 10 percent.

The EPA considers COHb levels in the range of 5 to 10 percent to be of concern, but levels half this amount can aggravate angina in heart patients. COHb levels in this range can result from breathing levels as low as 15 ppm carbon monoxide for about 10 hours or 50 ppm for 90 minutes.

Carbon monoxide detectors are preset at levels of 100 to 200 or more ppm. They are intended to sound an alarm before the COHb level in a person reaches 10 percent. Although the detectors can prevent asphyxiation, the preset levels may be too high to protect against health effects that occur from exposure to lower levels for longer periods of time.

The EPA has established outdoor standards for exposure to carbon monoxide of 9 ppm for eight hours of exposure and 35 ppm for one hour of exposure. These standards are similar to Canadian and World Health Organization standards for indoor air. Contact your local health or environmental agency for help with identifying standards for other combustion-related contaminants.

Potential Problems and Reducing Exposure to Specific Sources

The best strategy for reducing combustion-related problems with appliances is to maintain and use them properly. Read and follow the instructions for all appliances so you know how they work. This will help you recognize problems and make simple repairs. Be sure to perform maintenance as recommended by the manufacturer (see Figure 10.10 for some suggestions). With

FIGURE 10.10.   Inspection and Maintenance Schedules for Combustion Appliances

Appliance	Inspection Frequency	Maintenance Frequency
Gas forced-air heating systems	Monthly—check air filters Yearly—look at flues and burn chambers for rust and soot	As needed—clean/change filter Yearly (at the start of the heating season)—hire a qualified person to check and clean chimney, clean combustion chamber, adjust burners and check heat exchanger and operation
Gas/oil and water/ steam heating systems and water heaters, and vented kerosene heaters	Twice a year—look at flues and burn chambers for rust, soot and oily residue	Yearly (at the start of the heating season)—hire a qualified person to check and clean chimney, clean combustion chamber and adjust burners and regulators
Unvented kerosene space heaters	Daily (when in use)—look to see that the mantle is properly seated Daily (or before refueling)— look to see that fuel tank is free of water and other contaminants	As manufacturer recommends— check and replace wick Yearly—clean combustion chamber At the end of the heating season—drain fuel tank
Wood/coal stoves	Twice a year—look at flues for rust and soot	Yearly (at the start of the heating season)—hire a qualified person to check and clean seams, gaskets, chimney and connections

SOURCE: Adapted from U.S. EPA, U.S. Consumer Product Safety Commission, and the American Lung Association (1991).

proper care, an appliance will last longer and be less likely to need costly repairs. Hire qualified heating and cooling contractors and other appliance service representatives to install and maintain appliances.

Purchase combustion appliances that meet current safety standards. The appliance should have a label that shows the certification of organizations such as Underwriters Laboratories (UL) and the American Gas Association (AGA). When buying gas appliances, you can save energy and reduce contaminants by buying one with an electronic ignition rather than a pilot light. Make sure heaters are sized correctly for the space to be heated and if you have a very tight house, consider using electric appliances rather than gas appliances that release combustion contaminants directly into the living space.

The remainder of this chapter explains basic problems that occur with vented and unvented appliances and simple solutions to some of these problems. Figure 10.11 lists examples of problems typically encountered with fuel-burning appliances.

FIGURE 10.11.   Possible Problems with Combustion Appliances

Appliance	Fuel	Causes of Problems
Central furnaces, room heaters and gas fire-places	Natural or liquified petroleum gas	Cracked heat exchanger Not enough air to burn fuel properly Defective/blocked flue Maladjusted burner
Central furnaces	Oil	Cracked heat exchanger Not enough air to burn fuel properly Defective/blocked flue Maladjusted burner
Central furnaces and room heaters	Wood	Cracked heat exchanger Not enough air to burn fuel properly Defective/blocked flue Green or treated wood
Central furnaces and stoves	Coal	Cracked heat exchanger Not enough air to burn fuel properly Defective/blocked flue Defective grate

SOURCE: U.S. EPA, U.S. Consumer Product Safety Commission and the American Lung Association (1991).

FIGURE 10.11. (*continued*)

Appliance	Fuel	Causes of Problems
Room heaters and central heaters	Kerosene	Improper adjustment Wrong fuel (not K-1) Wrong wick type or height (if unvented) Not enough air to burn fuel properly
Water heaters	Natural or liquified petroleum gas	Not enough air to burn fuel properly Defective/blocked flue Maladjusted burner
Ranges and ovens	Natural or liquified petroleum gas	Not enough air to burn fuel properly Maladjusted burner Misuse as a room heater
Stoves and fireplaces	Wood and coal	Not enough air to burn fuel properly Defective/blocked flue Green or treated wood Cracked heat exchanger or firebox

Central Forced-air Fuel-fired Appliances

A properly installed central heating system will not endanger indoor air quality or safety. The furnace should not be located in any small, confined space that can draw combustion air away from occupants, and it should not be under a stairway, in a room used as a bedroom or bathroom or in a closet. (There are some exceptions for direct vent furnaces and enclosed furnaces.) Contact a heating contractor to evaluate the adequacy of a particular installation.

Regardless of the type of appliance, the heat inlet registers and cold air returns should be free of carpets, furniture and other obstructions. The venting system should be checked for signs of corrosion and leaks. These problems and any signs of incomplete combustion should be corrected as soon as possible.

Buried fuel tanks (underground storage tanks or USTs) are an additional source of concern (especially in older homes) because they can leak fuel if they deteriorate. If a fuel odor is noticeable in the basement or in the house, a buried fuel tank could be the source. Treat this situation as an emergency and get help from your local utility or health department. Prevent these problems by having the tank inspected and tested regularly and, if necessary, removed. Look in the yellow pages of the telephone directory under "Tank Testing & Inspection" or "Tanks—Removal" to find a contractor trained to work with USTs.

Natural Gas and LP Gas Heaters. These are the most widely used types of central furnaces (see Figure 10.1). Consult the owner's manual for specific details and for advice on the proper operation and maintenance of your unit. Some important guidelines include:

- Make sure that the blower doors are on the furnace securely. Doors that are ajar can allow contaminants to enter the living space.
- Look at the furnace filters (be sure to disconnect the power first). A dirty filter indicates poor maintenance. Replace disposable filters every four to six weeks during the heating season and clean permanent filters by vacuuming or washing them according to the manufacturer's instructions.
- With the power off, look at the burn chamber for lint, soot or rust buildup. Call a heating contractor to clean the furnace if any of these substances are present.
- If possible, examine the flame to see if it is burning efficiently (see Figure 10.3). Natural gas flames should not have yellow tips. LP flames may have some light yellow tipping of the outside part of the flame, but the inside part of the flame should be bright blue. Call a heating contractor if yellow tips exist.

Oil-fired Heaters. An oil furnace is similar to a gas furnace in size, shape and function, but has a different heat exchanger, burner and combustion control system. Figure 10.2 is a diagram of a typical oil-fired heater. The guidelines for oil-fired appliances are similar to those for gas furnaces:

- The presence of any fuel odors, soot, oily residues or other stains in the furnace room suggests that a problem exists. Call a heating contractor for help.

- Have a heating contractor check the location and size of the fuel tank. Tanks that are inside the house must vent to the outside and there should be adequate space between them and boilers, furnaces, stoves or exposed flames.
- Enough combustion air must enter the room. A general rule is to provide 15 square inches of opening for each gallon of fuel burned per hour. (The rate of fuel burning is found on the identification plate on the appliance.)
- Make sure that the blower compartment door fits securely.
- Look at the filters and burner fan. Cleaning is necessary if a heavy coating of soot or oil is present.
- Examine the burner jets. Cleaning is necessary if corrosion or a buildup of soot or rust is present.
- Make sure that the barometric damper is properly lubricated and balanced.

Coal-fired Heaters. Coal-fired appliances are still used and are found mostly in older homes. These appliances include boilers, furnaces and space heaters that look like pot-bellied stoves. Burn coal only in those appliances specifically designed for coal. Contact a heating contractor for guidance in the proper operation and maintenance of these units. Backdrafting can be a problem in coal-fired heaters whenever a full draft is not needed.

Wood-burning Heaters. Some wood-burning appliances are fitted with a gas or oil burner that provides heat when the wood fire goes out or becomes low. Wood-burning central heating appliances require more care and maintenance than furnaces that burn only gas or oil. Indoor air quality and safety problems can result from stoking operations, creosote deposits and draft problems. Contact a heating contractor for guidance in the proper operation and maintenance of these units. Local codes may prohibit these heating appliances.

Space Heaters

Vented Gas or Kerosene Space Heaters. Many older homes use large kerosene or gas room heaters to heat individual rooms or groups of rooms. These appliances usually vent through the chimney and the guidelines for venting them are the same as for the central fuel-fired furnaces:

- The vent should have about 12 to 18 inches of clearance from combustible walls. (Check local codes for exact requirements.)

- Clean the venting system two or three times during the heating season to remove soot and corrosion.
- Consider replacing a gas heater that was made before June 1, 1984. Gas heaters made after this date must have a device that shuts off if the heater is not venting properly.

Unvented Gas or Kerosene Heaters. Unvented space heaters release combustion contaminants directly into the living space, have hot surfaces that can cause burns and are fire hazards. Using heaters according to manufacturer's instructions in well-ventilated areas can reduce, but not eliminate, contaminants. Avoid using unvented heaters but if you must use them, follow the safety tips given in Figures 10.12 and 10.13 and always provide ventilation with outside air when using these heaters.

Vented Wood-burning Stoves. Due to rising fuel costs, many people are turning to wood as their main or supplementary fuel. Fireplaces (with or without inserts) and various types of freestanding stoves are the most common wood-burning appliances.

Because a conventional wood-burning stove has a single combustion chamber that is not airtight, its combustion efficiency is less than that of an airtight stove. An airtight stove is more efficient because it has a second chamber

FIGURE 10.12.   Safety Guidelines for Unvented Gas-fired Heaters

(*Caution: Whenever there is a strong fuel odor, turn off the fuel valve immediately, open the windows, leave the house and call the utility from an outside telephone for emergency service.*)

- If there is no fuel odor, strike a match before opening the gas valve. This prevents the possible buildup of fuel vapor that could easily ignite. To prevent an explosion, ventilate the area before another attempt is made.
- A yellow flame is a sign of incomplete combustion that may lead to an increase in carbon monoxide and particulate levels.
- Always keep a window partially open whenever an unvented heater is in use in order to provide adequate ventilation to reduce contaminant levels and to replace oxygen used for combustion. One inch of open window space for every 10,000 Btu of heater rating is a guideline (equal to roughly four square inches of window opening for every 1,000 Btu of heater rating).
- Never leave a heater unattended while it is in operation and never use it overnight while people are sleeping.

FIGURE 10.13.   Safety Guidelines for Unvented Kerosene Heaters

To minimize indoor air contaminants:

- Use only water clear (K-1) kerosene as a fuel. K-2 kerosene and fuel oil have high sulfur contents and produce high levels of toxic emissions. Never use gasoline because of the risk of explosion and fire hazards and do not use kerosene that is yellow or that has been stored over several months.
- Examine wicks and burners for excessive carbon build up after burning one or two tanks of fuel. Carbon buildup is a sign of incomplete combustion.
- Do not operate the heater in confined areas such as bathrooms and never operate the heater in bedrooms while people are sleeping.
- Size the heater correctly for the space to be heated. A guideline for calculating the approximate needed Btu rating is to multiply the floor area by 28. Consult with a knowledgeable sales representative to find the correct heater size for the space to be heated and avoid heaters that are too large.
- *Always* keep the wick at the proper setting. A wick that is too high or too low can increase emissions.
- *Always* provide adequate ventilation. Do not use heaters in a closed room. Provide outside air for ventilation. Provide at least four square inches of window opening for every 1000 Btu of heater rating.
- Consider other heating options if anyone in the house is ill or has allergies or asthma. Do not use unvented kerosene heaters if there are small children or a pregnant woman in the house.

To minimize safety hazards:

- Do not leave kerosene heaters unattended.
- Be sure that there is adequate clearance between the heater and combustible materials.
- Do not move the heater while it is burning. Turn off the heater if the flame flares or appears uncontrolled. (If you cannot do this, leave the area immediately and call the fire department.)
- Store kerosene in a container labeled "kerosene." (Do not store other types of fuel in this container.) Place the container outside the house in a safe place out of the reach of children.
- Never fill heaters indoors and never add fuel to a heater that is burning or hot.
- Keep children away from kerosene heaters to prevent them from coming into contact with hot surfaces and fuel.
- Check the temperature in rooms with operating heaters to be sure that rooms are not too hot because in small rooms, temperatures can easily reach 100°F or more.

for the combustion of gases that are not burned in the first chamber. Simpler stoves typically have manually-controlled chimney dampers to control the flow of air through or over the fire while more complicated stoves have thermostat-controlled dampers that control the draft.

Improperly installed, maintained or operated wood-burning appliances can create serious safety hazards and problems with indoor air quality. A heating contractor should check the appliance, flue and chimney at least once each year. A properly installed wood-burning stove is illustrated in Figure 10.4.

Installation

- There should be at least 36 inches of space between the sides and top of the stove and combustible materials. The use of a fireproof barrier can reduce the amount of clearances needed. Consult local codes for specific requirements.
- Stoves should not rest directly on carpeting or other combustible material. The floor beneath the stove should be protected with fireproof materials that extend out from the stove at least 18 inches in all directions. Floors made of concrete, clay tile or ceramic do not require fireproofing. Check the condition of any asbestos floor protection and replace damaged or deteriorating floor materials. Ask your local or state health or environmental protection agency how to dispose of the asbestos-containing material safely (see Appendix A).
- Determine if other appliances use the same flue or chimney as the wood stove. An oil or gas appliance should not use the same flue or chimney as a wood or coal appliance. Have a heating contractor correct problems.

Backdrafting

- A smoky odor and fine particulates in the house are signs of backdrafting and incomplete combustion. There are many potential sources of the problem, including blockage in the chimney and a lack of combustion air. Opening a window in the room with the stove or fireplace about one-half to one inch can supply enough combustion air. Contact a heating contractor to evaluate backdrafting problems.
- The guidelines for the clearance of a stove chimney at the rooftop are the same as those for central heating appliances (see Figure 10.7). These clearances will prevent downdrafts in windy weather and roof fires caused by hot flue gases.

Wood Selection and Use

- Open the damper of the stove when adding wood to help the wood burn properly and prevent contaminants from being drawn back into the living area.
- Reduce creosote buildup by using the correct type of wood. Use seasoned hardwood (such as maple, oak and elm) instead of softwoods (such as cedar, fir and pine) which do not burn as hot as and produce more creosote than hardwoods. Resinous woods (such as pine) burn quickly and can be used in *small* amounts for starting fires. Do not use resinous green or wet wood as primary fuel sources, however, because they form more creosote and smoke.
- As a safety precaution, store wood at least 36 inches away from the stove. Do not store more than 25 pounds of wood inside the house at any time.
- *DO NOT BURN* treated wood, railroad ties, plastics, charcoal, metal, tires, trash or other nonwood materials. These release harmful contaminants into the living area when burned.

Stovepipes

- A stovepipe is a single-wall metal pipe that connects the wood stove to the chimney. It should not be used directly as a chimney and it should not go through a ceiling, closet or concealed space. If it goes through any interior combustible material, it must connect to a ventilated thimble.
- The stovepipe connection should be as short and straight as possible to reduce creosote buildup and increase draft. Lengths of about 8 feet are typical, with a rise of about one-fourth inch per foot of pipe. Smoke will leak from the pipe if the joints do not overlap properly. The crimped end should point down toward the stove.
- Look at the connection between the stovepipe and the chimney. Make sure that it is secure and does not leak creosote.
- Check the stovepipe and chimney frequently for creosote buildup (discussed under chimneys and flues above).

Household Appliances

Gas-fired Cooking Stoves. Gas ranges release combustion products directly into the living space. These stoves can produce a significant amount of carbon monoxide and other contaminants in a short time and should not be used as a source of heat.

Because it burns continuously, the pilot light in a gas stove can be an important source of contaminants. Both the pilot light and the burner flames should burn with a well-defined blue flame. The flames should not be yellow. Have the pilot light and the burner flame checked and adjusted by a qualified contractor if they do not appear to burn properly.

- Check the range to be sure there are at least 6 inches of clearance from combustibles at the back and sides of the range and at least 30 inches of clearance from the top. Less clearance is allowable if combustible material is protected by a fireproof material. Check the local building code for specifics.
- If the stove does not have a hood or kitchen vent to exhaust gases from the burners, consider installing one. The end of the hood vent should be outside of the building and not in an attic, crawl space or any area inside the house. A vent hood that recirculates the air does not remove gaseous contaminants.

Gas-fired Water Heaters. Proper venting and installation of water heaters will keep combustion-related contaminants from entering the living space. The venting for the water heater should meet the same guidelines as the venting for a central heating system.

- The water heater should have a properly functioning draft hood.
- The water heater should not be in a bathroom, bedroom, closet or confined space that opens into the bedroom or bathroom.
- If the water heater is in a garage, it should be at least 18 inches above the ground. This clearance will prevent explosions that could occur if gasoline or other flammable liquids spill onto the floor close to the heater.

Gas-fired Clothes Dryers. Gas-fired clothes dryers should vent directly to the outside and not through a chimney or flue. The dryer should not vent into a crawl space, an attic or any area inside the house. Do not use devices that attach to the dryer to provide heat or moisture inside the house. The moisture supply will be uneven, mold growth can be a problem and combustion contaminants can enter the living space. If the air is too dry, use either a central or portable humidifier.

Furnace and Other Fuel-burning Appliance Checklist

Questions To Ask	Response	What Does a "Yes" Mean?
Vented Fuel-fired Heating Appliances		
Is the central-heating appliance located in a small, confined space, under a stairway or in a bedroom, bathroom or closet?	**Yes No** ❏ ❏	These locations are hazardous because combustion contaminants could build up quickly if there are problems with the appliance. There may not be enough combustion air to properly burn the fuel.
Are any of the following signs present: — condensation on windows or other surfaces? — yellow flames that are not uniform in shape? — black soot in or around the appliance or burner assembly? — corrosion in the vent flue or burner assembly?	**Yes No** ❏ ❏	The appliance is not getting enough air for combustion. This will result in higher heating costs and problems with indoor air quality and safety.
Is the draft hood absent on the appliance? Is there a lack of combustion air based on the draft hood test as described under the section on combustion air?	**Yes No** ❏ ❏	A fuel-burning vented appliance should have a draft hood. In the absence of a draft hood, combustion gases may flow back into the house after entering the vent or chimney.
Are the return air ducts deteriorating? (Look for rust and holes.)	**Yes No** ❏ ❏	Deteriorating air ducts can pull contaminated air into the ducts and bring the contaminants to all parts of the home served by the ducts. This is a particular concern for ducts in the crawl space, basement or attic.

Questions To Ask	Response	What Does a "Yes" Mean?
Vented Fuel-fired Heating Appliances		
Is the crawl space used as part of the ducting system?	Yes No ❏ ❏	Radon and other contaminants can enter the living space.
Is fiberboard or cardboard used as part of the ductwork in the crawl space?	Yes No ❏ ❏	Mold can grow on these surfaces and enter the living space.
Vents, Chimneys and Flues		
Are there signs of deteriorating vents and flues? (Look for rust and holes.)	Yes No ❏ ❏	Deterioration is a sign that combustion contaminants can enter the living space.
Do any of the horizontal connections have a horizontal or downward slope in the vent or flue pipes or connections?	Yes No ❏ ❏	Flue pipes and connections must slope upward to enable the gases to escape outdoors.
Does the chimney have signs of wear and deterioration? Is there a buildup of creosote? (Look for a black material on the inside and outside of the chimney.)	Yes No ❏ ❏	A deteriorated chimney or the buildup of creosote are signs of potential problems with indoor air quality and safety.
Does the chimney extend less than three feet above the highest point where it passes through the roof? Is it less than two feet higher than any part of the roof that is within ten horizontal feet of the chimney?	Yes No ❏ ❏	Backdrafting of combustion gases down the flue and chimney into the living space can occur if the chimney does not extend far enough above the roof.

Questions To Ask	Response	What Does a "Yes" Mean?
Vents, Chimneys and Flues		
If there is more than one combustion appliance, do they all connect to the same flue and chimney? Do any connect at the same level?	Yes No ❏ ❏	A yes to the first question means that the draft can be reduced and combustion gases may not be able to go outside. A yes to the second question means that combustion gases can flow from one appliance to the other.
Is the chimney cap missing or in poor condition?	Yes No ❏ ❏	Rainwater, birds and other pests may enter the house through the chimney.
Vented Woodstoves, Fireplaces, Gas Heaters and Kerosene Heaters (see also **Vented Fuel-fired Heating Appliances** and **Vents, Chimneys and Flues**)		
Does the use of a fireplace, woodstove or kerosene heater produce indoor smoke or a fine deposit of ash?	Yes No ❏ ❏	This is a sign of a lack of combustion air and inefficient combustion. Air quality and safety may be adversely affected.
Is the appliance less than three feet away from combustible materials?	Yes No ❏ ❏	A fire hazard exists.
Does the wood-burning stove have a single-wall metal pipe that acts as the chimney?	Yes No ❏ ❏	A fire hazard exists.
Was the gas heater made before June 1, 1984?	Yes No ❏ ❏	Consider replacing the heater. New heaters have safety devices that shut off a heater if it does not vent properly.

Questions To Ask	Response	What Does a "Yes" Mean?
Household Appliances (such as gas-fired cooking stoves, water heaters and clothes dryers)		
Do the flames of pilot lights and burners of these appliances look yellow and poorly defined?	Yes No ❏ ❏	A yellow or poorly defined flame is an indication of incomplete combustion that may produce contaminants in the living space.
Do you use a gas-fired cooking stove for heat?	Yes No ❏ ❏	This is a safety hazard that produces contaminants in the living space.
Does the cooking stove or clothes dryer vent end in any area inside the house?	Yes No ❏ ❏	These vents should exhaust air outside of the house to keep moisture and combustion products from entering the living space.
Is the water heater located in a bathroom, bedroom, closet or other confined space?	Yes No ❏ ❏	This is a safety hazard that could produce unsafe levels of combustion products.
If the water heater is located in the garage, is it less than 18 inches above the floor?	Yes No ❏ ❏	This is a safety hazard that could cause an explosion if a flammable liquid (such as gasoline) spills onto the floor close to the heater.
Unvented Gas or Kerosene Heaters		
Do you use these heaters without opening a window for ventilation?	Yes No ❏ ❏	Unvented heaters are a serious health hazard, especially in tight houses. If you use these appliances, follow the safety guidelines given in Figures 10.12 and 10.13.
All Sources of Combustion		
Is your home missing fire alarms and fire extinguishers?	Yes No ❏ ❏	This is a safety hazard.

Summary Chart for Pesticides

Topic	Comments
Description	Pesticides are chemicals that kill pests. They can remain effective for varying periods of time after application. Many pesticides are volatile chemicals that are released into the air long after they are applied to surfaces.
Health Effects	Pesticides are toxic to people, pets and other organisms. They cause many symptoms and adverse health effects in adults and children as a result of exposure to either high or low concentrations of the chemicals. Pesticides can damage the kidneys, liver, nervous system and respiratory tract. Some pesticides are carcinogenic and some are absorbed through the skin. The long-term health effects of many pesticides are not known.
Sources	People are exposed to pesticides from both proper and improper application of pesticide products. People are often exposed unknowingly in workplaces, public buildings, golf courses, parks, lawns and other areas where people congregate. Exposure also occurs when pesticides contaminate water, soil and materials used by people.
Testing	Hire qualified laboratories to test for pesticides. Local and state health agencies can provide names of qualified professionals.
Reducing Exposure	Use pesticides carefully as a last choice for controlling pests. Keep pests under control by removing food sources, nesting areas and shelter. When using pesticides, use the least hazardous product and the smallest amount possible. Avoid using hazardous consumer products for cleaning and disinfecting.

CHAPTER
ELEVEN

Pesticides

Lawrence and Mary Jane Hannan have a $150,000 home in Indianapolis, but they and their three-year-old daughter are living in a single room of a hotel because a pesticide contaminates their 1,800-square-foot five-year-old home. Their problems started in June 1993 when the couple called Pesco Pest Control Service to eliminate small ants around the fireplace. Their daughter, Kaitlyn, became ill with a cough immediately after the treatment on June 14, 1993 and within a few days, all three family members were ill. Mrs. Hannan and her husband had nausea, headaches and breathing difficulties. Six days after the spraying, Mr. Hannan discovered that his sleeping wife was not breathing properly and took her outside to the patio. They felt better within 30 minutes and decided to leave their house after that experience.

Mrs. Hannan asked the pest company to check its work, but the company claimed that nothing was wrong because the interior of the home did not have a chemical odor. Pesco's insurance company eventually paid to have the house scrubbed down, but the cleaning was not successful. In fact, the cleaning company's sales manager had the same symptoms as the Hannans after spending only 40 minutes in the home and consequently instructed the work crews to wear protective respiratory equipment.

Although the Hannans continue to make mortgage payments they do not know if the house can be cleaned or sold. The Hannans have been unable to salvage any mementos, clothing or furnishings because all of their possessions were contaminated.

As reported in *The Indianapolis News,* October 18, 1993.

What Are Pesticides and Why Are They a Hazard?

Pests are everywhere! Insects chew up our gardens, dandelions crowd our grass, molds damage materials in our homes, termites feed on our houses and mice and rats eat our food. Other examples of pests are cockroaches, fleas, ants, moths, caterpillars, silverfish, mosquitos, bees, wasps and a variety of weeds. More and more, we are turning to pesticides to kill or control these unwanted visitors.

Different types of pests are controlled by various pesticides, including insecticides (insects), herbicides (weeds), fungicides (mold), rodenticides (rodents) and disinfectants (bacteria). Pesticides are toxic to adults, children, pets and other creatures. These chemicals can be harmful to people who are accidentally or unknowingly exposed to them. The potential hazards posed by these chemicals increase as a result of improper use, storage and disposal of these products.

The use of pesticides is widespread. During 1984, Americans used almost 230 million pounds of pesticides for nonagricultural purposes. Home and garden applications accounted for about 29 percent of this total, the annual equivalent of about one-third of a pound of pesticide for every person in the United States. When agricultural pesticides are included in national consumption statistics, pesticide usage in the United States increases to about 8.7 pounds per person per year.

Unfortunately, consumers are casual about handling pesticides. Some people assume pesticides are completely safe because grocery stores, drug stores, and hardware stores sell pesticide products. These people may be lulled into a false sense of security because they do not need special licenses or special protective clothing to use pesticide products. The recent marketing of products with less offensive odors may also cause some consumers to think that the products do not pose hazards or to ignore potential contamination problems. As a result, there are many cases of preventable poisonings each year. (In fact, the second most common cause of childhood poisonings is exposure to pesticides.)

The EPA estimates that about 91 percent of American households use pesticides. The EPA found that less than 50 percent of the participants in a household survey read pesticide labels to learn the proper application procedures and only 9 percent used these products with caution.

Because pesticides are widely used, low levels of these chemicals are present throughout our environments. We are usually not aware of being exposed to pesticides away from our homes. Pesticides are used routinely in schools, day care centers, retail stores, offices and other buildings. Parks and golf courses use pesticides to control weeds and some communities have programs for spraying mosquitos. Sometimes the sprayed chemicals can drift into homes or other buildings. Exposure can also occur when we come into contact with chemical residues in food.

Many uncertainties exist about the safety of pesticides and most people are not aware of the effects of pesticides or the symptoms of exposure. Pesticides enter human bodies by ingestion of food and water, breathing in of air or by absorption through the skin. Most pesticides affect more than one part of the body and produce symptoms that can progress rapidly from mild to fatal. Adverse reactions usually occur right after exposure, but it is possible for them to be delayed. Some individuals are more sensitive than the general population to pesticides (and other chemicals).

Pesticides can irritate the eyes, skin and respiratory tract, and often produce flu-like symptoms (see Figure 11.1 for a list of common symptoms). The mucous membranes and the lining of the respiratory tract are especially sensitive, and pesticides can also damage the heart, kidneys and liver. Some pesticides are sensitizers, which means that an individual's reaction to the chemical will increase in severity with each additional exposure. Many pesticides found in consumer products are classified by the EPA as probable or possible carcinogenic chemicals (see Figure 11.2 for a list of some cancer-causing active ingredients and their uses).

Pesticide Formulations

Pesticides come in different forms, including baits, dusts, bombs, aerosol sprays and dry powders. Some pesticides are sold in solution or as powders that readily mix with water, whereas others are found in products such as slow-release insecticide strips, flea collars and mothballs.

Pesticide products contain both active ingredients that kill the pest or other organisms, and inert ingredients that change the properties of the formulation. (For example, some chemicals help the pesticide to dissolve in a liquid so it can be sprayed.) "Inert" is used here not as a scientific term but as a legal term. The labeling of an ingredient as inert does not mean that the compound cannot adversely affect people or animals. There are about 1200 inert ingredients. Some of them may be more toxic than the active ingredients. Manufacturers do not, however, need to identify inert ingredients on the product label unless the EPA says that the chemicals are very toxic and pose an

FIGURE 11.1.   Symptoms of Pesticide Exposure

Eyes • Irritation • Redness • Swelling	Heart • Shock • High blood pressure • Change in heart rhythm
Respiratory tract • Irritation • Stinging sensation • Swelling • Difficulty breathing • Mucous production	Kidneys and bladder • Incontinence • Damage
Skin • Itching • Redness • Swelling • Blistering • Acne-like condition	Nervous system • Fatigue • Headache • Dizziness • Weakness • Behavioral changes • Decreased vision • Blurred vision • Tingling, numbness and tremors in the arms, legs, hands and feet • Changes in the pupils of the eyes • Paralysis • Coma • Death
Stomach and intestines • Increased saliva • Nausea • Vomiting • Abdominal cramps • Diarrhea	

NOTE: The specific symptoms that result from a given exposure situation will vary from person to person depending on the chemical and the amount of exposure received.

FIGURE 11.2.   Carcinogens in Pesticide Products

Chemical Active Ingredient (product uses)	Consumer Products
Acephate (lawn, turf and ornamentals)	Ortho Orthene Systemic Insect Control and Ortho Isotox Insect Killer
Dichlorvos—DDVP (used to kill insects indoors and in gardens)	Black Flag Ant & Roach Killer, Raid Wasp & Hornet Killer, Bag-A-Bug Gypsy Moth Lure and No-Pest Strips
Permethrin (house and garden insecticides and pet products) Tetramethrin (house and garden insecticides and pet products)	Black Flag Roach Ender, Raid Fumigator Cake and Sudbury Flea & Tick Dip Combat Flying Insect Killer, Raid Flying Insect Killer, Ortho Home & Garden Insect Killer and Raid House & Garden, Formula II
Propoxur (used indoors in ant and roach killers, pet products and mosquito foggers)	Black Flag Ant & Roach Killer, Combat Ant & Roach Instant Killer, Ortho Hornet & Wasp Killer, Sergeant's Flea & Tick Spray and Daltec Flea & Tick Collars
Chlordane (termite control)	(Although cancelled in 1988, products containing this substance may still be stored and should be disposed of properly.)
Dicofol (used for insect and mite control in vegetable gardens and indoors)	Bonide Rose Spray, Ortho Isotox Insect Killer and Pratt Nocolate Insect Spray
Lindane—HCH, BHC (house and garden use, shelf paper, anti-lice shampoos, pet products and termite control)	Kwell Shampoo, Roxo Borerkill, Gro-Well Borer Killer and Ortho Lindane Borer and Leaf Miner Spray
Benomyl (vegetables, ornamentals, lawn and turf)	DuPont Tersan 1991 and Gro-Well Benomyl Systemic Fungicide
Captan (fruit, vegetables, ornamentals, turf, house plants, paints, pet products and human anti-fungal shampoos)	Ortho Tomato & Vegetable Dust, Ortho Orthocide Garden Fungicide, Bonide Rose Spray and Gro-Well Fruit Tree Spray
Chlorothalonil (ornamentals, turf, lawn, paint and grout additive, fruit, vegetables and wood preservative)	Ortho Liquid Lawn Disease Control, Ortho Multi-Purpose Fungicide and Ortho Vegetable Disease Control
Folpet (paints and plastics)	Ortho Phaltan Rose & Garden Fungicide
Maneb (ornamentals and vegetables)	Dexol Maneb Garden Fungicide and Security Maneb Spray

SOURCE: Adapted from Ritchie, I. (1991).

"immediate toxicological concern." Examples of these types of chemicals include carbon tetrachloride, formaldehyde and methylene chloride.

Warning Labels

Pesticide labels contain important information, including the chemical ingredients, symptoms of poisoning and health effects. The label also has instructions for using the pesticide properly and emergency instructions in case of poisoning. All pesticide products have an EPA registration number on the container, and the label must contain signal words that describe the degree of hazard posed by the product as a result of misuse or accidental poisonings.

The word *DANGER* appears on the labels of highly poisonous products that should be used with extreme caution. *WARNING* describes moderately hazardous products and *CAUTION* is used for the least hazardous products. The appearance of the word *CAUTION* on a label does not, however, mean that the product is safe. Follow all safety instructions carefully.

Although hazard labels are important, they do not describe all of the potential hazards related to a product. For example, the labels do not warn consumers of chronic health hazards associated with use of a particular product or about the lack of data on health effects. The labels also do not warn of special hazards to children.

Testing and Understanding the Results

Pesticides can be sampled in air, water or soil, or from different types of materials. Pesticide contamination of the air or materials is usually easy to identify because a history of pesticide use, lingering chemical odors and a recent illness often point to the problem. (It may be more difficult to recognize contamination of the soil or water, but the same warning signs apply.) Sampling may be needed when improper applications are suspected and should always be done to determine if a cleanup is successful.

The chemical analysis of pesticides is complicated and there are no simple screening test kits for pesticides. Ask your local or state health department for help in locating qualified laboratories. Ask if the laboratory uses EPA methods to collect and analyze water, soil and air samples. If samples are collected from the house by wiping surfaces such as kitchen tops, floors, furniture or walls, ask if the laboratory uses standard methods to collect these samples.

Routine sampling for pesticides is not needed but a house should be sampled for pesticides whenever there is a chemical odor indoors and a history of recent termiticide application. If the house has a shallow well or if you are planning to garden, consider sampling for pesticides when there is a history of nearby pesticide use or accidents. Homes in a recently flooded area are at risk because damage to pesticide-related businesses and agricultural operations can result in isolated or widespread contamination.

Pesticide test results are reported in parts per million (ppm), parts per billion (ppb) or micrograms per cubic meter ($\mu g/m^3$). Interpreting pesticide measurements in air and soil can be difficult because guidelines are not available for acceptable concentrations. (Chapter 13 describes safe levels of pesticides in drinking water.) The National Academy of Sciences has recommended air quality guidelines for only four of the most commonly used termiticides in the United States:

aldrin—1 $\mu g/m^3$
chlordane—5 $\mu g/m^3$
chlorpyrifos—10 $\mu g/m^3$
heptachlor—2 $\mu g/m^3$

Contact your local or state health department for help with understanding the results of pesticide sampling.

Sources and Methods for Reducing Exposure

We will never get rid of all pests, but we can coexist with them and reduce the impact they have on our lives. The regular use of pesticides often increases pest problems because pests become resistant to the effects of the chemicals. Two basic strategies can reduce exposure to pesticides and control pests in our homes: 1) the elimination of pests before they become established, and 2) the use of alternative methods of pest control whenever possible. When used together, these strategies form a technique called *integrated pest management* (IPM). Pest control companies that practice IPM rely on nonchemical controls whenever possible but when chemicals are needed, they are applied at optimum times and in the smallest quantities needed to control the pest.

If you plan to hire a pest control or lawn care company, ask if the company practices IPM. If chemicals are recommended for your particular problem, contact your state health or environmental agency and ask about the licensing requirements for companies who do the work you are planning to have done. Federal regulations require pesticide control companies to have a certified pesticide applicator present in the office each day to supervise the work of others who use pesticides classified for restricted use. Although this person is specially trained in the application of pesticides, others who may not have the same training are likely to actually do the work. The requirements for training vary from state to state.

Ask the state pesticide agency if the company you are considering has violated any regulations. Also contact the local Better Business Bureau or Chamber of Commerce and ask if any complaints have been filed against the company.

Before you hire a contractor, ask the following questions:

- Does the company have programs for spot control of pests and non-chemical control methods?
- What chemicals will be used and why? When will the area be safe for you and your family?
- How will the chemicals be applied?
- What are the potential side effects of the proposed chemicals or methods of control? (Ask to see material safety data sheets [MSDS] that describe potential health effects and needed safety precautions. Your local health department or state chemist for pesticides can help you understand this information.)
- Does the company have proof of insurance and a license to operate? (Ask to see both.)
- What guarantees does the company give on its work?

Pay attention to the claims a company makes about its products. The EPA prohibits claiming or advertising a pesticide product to be safe, nonpoisonous, harmless, all natural or nontoxic to humans and pets, and considers these claims to be false and misleading. Any company or product that makes these claims can be prosecuted by law and should be avoided.

Before hiring a company, ask for and call references, and get a written contract describing all terms (including chemicals and application methods to be used) of the work agreement.

Termiticide Applications

Termites are insects that require wood for food. Left unchecked, they can cause extensive damage to houses and other structures. They like damp soil and can build tubes above the ground to a height of about 12 inches to reach a food source. Termiticides are applied to new construction to prevent termite damage and can also be used to control damage in older homes.

Chlordane was widely used until its use was prohibited in 1988 when studies showed it to be carcinogenic. Termiticides used today include chlorpyrifos, permethrin, bifenthrin, cypermethrin and s-fenvalerate. Although some of these chemicals (such as chlorpyrifos) are considered to be safe when properly applied, the long-term health effects from low levels of exposure to these chemicals are not known. Other termiticides (such as permethrin) are possible human carcinogens. Before signing a contract for a termite treatment, make sure that you are satisfied that the least toxic chemical will be used.

Mortgage companies require a termite inspection as a condition of sale, regardless of the age of the house. Local building codes require all new houses to have termite protection for wood that could possibly come into contact with termites. In a new house, the termiticide is usually applied to the soil in a trench around the foundation, but careful construction techniques can also be used to prevent termites from damaging a house. One technique is to install metal shields that project about two inches from the foundation. Another method is to cast sheet metal strips into concrete foundations at joints to prevent termite entry if the foundation settles. When construction techniques are the primary means of protection against termites, regular checks of the foundation and wood are especially important.

In an existing home, termite problems are usually solved by chemical treatments. This may involve drilling holes into the foundation and applying the pesticide into the holes or placing the chemicals into a trench in the soil around the foundation.

Termiticide Contamination. Termiticides can contaminate the indoor air, well water and other materials as a result of unforeseen problems or the use of improper procedures during the application. If odors (even faint ones) linger for more than a few days after a termiticide treatment, call the pest control applicator immediately to remedy the problem. The cause may be an improper application or a structural problem in the house that provides a way for the termiticide to enter the living space.

Contaminated indoor air can be a difficult problem to correct. It can be caused by the seepage of termiticide indoors through poorly sealed injection holes in the basement or foundation, by the spraying of termiticide onto wood rather than into the concrete or soil, or by accidental spills.

Contamination can also occur when a termiticide is accidentally injected into the air ducts. Even when the termiticide is applied correctly, contamination can occur if it is applied in a crawl space or basement that is part of the return air supply system, or if ducts have holes or gaps that would pull the chemical into the air stream.

Potential solutions to ductwork contamination include the following:

* Placing liners into the ducts or replacing small sections of damaged ductwork
* Sealing, removing or replacing the duct work
* Using vents and fans to exhaust contaminated air from a crawl space
* Removing contaminated soil or covering it with a vapor retarder or concrete slab

Wells and drinking water can become contaminated whenever the well is not properly sealed. Shallow wells, dug wells and cisterns are easily contaminated. (Tree roots may channel pesticides into a well.) Termiticides should not be used to treat a house that has a well within the foundation because the potential for contamination is high. Treating a contaminated well is difficult, and the homeowner may have to find a new source of water.

Pesticide Use at Home

Most of our pesticide exposure comes from food residues. Each time we use pesticides, however, higher levels of exposure are possible. To reduce potential exposure, replace synthetic chemicals and pesticides that you use with alternative methods whenever possible (see Figure 11.3 for some suggestions). When pesticides are appropriate, select the least toxic products and use the least amount needed to solve the problem.

FIGURE 11.3.   Noncshemical Pest Control Methods

Pest	Nonchemical Control
Flying insects	Remove insects by hand; vacuum; use a fly swatter or sticky paper coated with a sugar attractant; put screens on windows and doors Dispose of garbage and clean garbage cans regularly; eat or remove overripened fruit; remove moist, uneaten pet food after one hour; clean up manure and cat litter boxes daily
Ants, roaches and blister beetles	Place boric acid and a sugar mixture at strategic points (behind refrigerators, under sinks and ranges, in cabinets, closets and in other places where the insects have been seen) Caulk and seal entry points, including windowsills, thresholds, baseboards, wall shelves, cupboards and sinks Dispose of garbage and clean garbage cans regularly; store all food (including pet food) in sealed containers; don't leave out overnight any food that is not in a sealed container Vacuum up or remove ants by hand and then wipe off countertops or other surfaces with vinegar (several days of treatment should cure the problem)
Rats and mice	Caulk and seal any opening into the house that is greater than 1/4 inch in diameter (see Chapter 9) Remove from the yard any debris or materials that could be used as nests

FIGURE 11.3.   *(continued)*

Pest	Nonchemical Control
Rats and mice	Dispose of garbage and clean garbage cans regularly; place garbage outside in tightly covered, heavy-gauge cans Store all food (including pet food) in sealed containers; don't leave out overnight any food that is not in a sealed container Use Vitamin D3 pellets and spring-loaded traps to kill rodents
Insects and fungi on indoor plants	Wash stems and leaves at the first sign of pests; remove standing water from plant trays; keep humidity levels below 50 percent
Fleas	Vacuum and shampoo floors, carpet and upholstery; launder removable bed and furniture coverings (several aggressive cleanings may be needed) Feed brewer's yeast or vitamin B to pets Wash pets with flea-repellent green-dye soaps; dust pets with powders made from eucalyptus, sage, vetiver or bay leaf
Mosquitos	Remove debris, tires or other items that can collect standing water; correct drainage problems Establish nests and houses for insect-eating birds (such as purple martins) Use screens on all doors and windows
Weeds	Remove by hand; raise mowing height for turf; water turf adequately; mulch shrubs and trees

Every year, children and pets are needlessly poisoned because pesticides are stored in nonpesticide containers (such as beverage bottles) and in easily accessible areas. Follow the safety guidelines in Figure 11.4 for storing, using and disposing of pesticides to prevent accidental contamination and poisonings. Another useful strategy (especially with cleaning chemicals) is to mark products with "Mr. Yuk" stickers and educate children about the hazards of these chemicals. Make sure that emergency telephone numbers are readily available in case an accident occurs.

Especially Hazardous Products. Some pesticide products are especially hazardous and should be avoided. Many of these products contain active ingredients that are known or presumed to be cancer-causing chemicals (see Figure 11.2).

FIGURE 11.4.   Pesticide Safety Tips

Storage

- Store pesticides (other than household disinfectants) in a *locked* cabinet in a well-ventilated utility area or in a garden shed. Avoid storing pesticides in the house because these chemicals can evaporate into the room air over time. As a safety precaution, make sure that household disinfectants (and cleaning chemicals) are stored in a childproof area.
- *Never* store pesticides with or near food, medical supplies or cleaning products. Avoid storing pesticides in basements, especially if flooding is a potential problem.
- Properly discard any pesticides (or other hazardous chemicals) that you have not used during the last six months. Take advantage of a household toxic chemical collection program (such as a Tox-Away Day) if one is sponsored by your community. (If not, follow the guidelines below for disposing of pesticides safely.)

Usage

- Always use the products according to the label directions. *Use protective clothing and respirators* as recommended on the product label. Paper masks are not safe. (See Appendix B for instructions in using a respirator and protective clothing.)
- Keep children and pets away from the area where pesticides are mixed, used or stored.
- Mix or dilute pesticides outdoors. Prepare only the amount needed for each application and do not store extra material. Do not transfer pesticides to nonpesticide containers, even for a short time.
- Follow the label directions for temporarily evacuating the home or lawn area while a pesticide is being applied.
- Never smoke, eat or drink while using pesticides. Keep away from the pesticide product all sources of flame or sparks that may cause explosions.
- Shower and shampoo thoroughly after using a pesticide product. It is very important to wash separately all clothes that were worn while applying a pesticide. (Children have died after absorbing pesticides from clothing that was washed with pesticide-contaminated clothes. Discard shoes and boots that cannot be washed.
- Clean up spills promptly. Do *not* wash spills with water alone. Instead, sprinkle them with kitty litter, sawdust or vermiculite. Sweep the material into a plastic garbage bag, seal it and place the sealed bag into another garbage bag. Seal the second bag and dispose of it with the trash. Call your local or state pesticide agency or poison control center for additional instructions on removing any residues.

SOURCE: Adapted from *Citizen's Guide to Pesticides* (1990).

FIGURE 11.4. (*continued*)

Disposal

- The best way to dispose of a small amount of pesticide is to use it or find a neighbor who can use it. For larger amounts or unused portions, call your local health department or waste management agency for help. Ask if there is a household toxic chemical collection program for pesticides or toxic wastes. If not, use the guidelines below for disposing of less than one gallon of pesticide.
- Make sure that the container is tightly capped. Wrap the container in several layers of newspapers and tie or tape it securely. Place the package into a covered trash can for collection with household wastes.
- Empty pesticide containers are hazardous and should be handled as described above. Do not puncture pressurized containers.
- When you do not have access to waste collection, dispose of the containers by burying them. Crush the empty containers, then bury them at least 18 inches deep in a place away from water sources, gardens and play areas.
- Do *not* burn pesticide containers inside or outside the home. Doing so may produce hazardous fumes, gases or explosions.
- Do *not* pour unused portions of pesticides down the sink! Pesticides can keep septic systems from working properly and can contaminate streams and lakes.

Avoid using **bug bombs** or **foggers**. These products are especially hazardous because people must stay away from their homes until the pesticides dissipate. Some of these products also pose a fire and explosion hazard and should not be used near a source of flame. If you have a serious pest problem, call a professional, discuss your options and select the least hazardous course of action.

Avoid **pest strips**. These products contain DDVP (2,2-dichlorovinyl dimethyl phosphate) as the main ingredient. Also known as dichorvos or *Vapona*, DDVP is classified by the EPA as a possible human carcinogen, and it causes liver and nerve damage in animals. Pest strips slowly release pesticides into the surrounding air, thus contaminating the home. Prolonged exposure to these substances may increase health risks.

Avoid **pest repellents** that are applied to the skin or clothing as sprays, lotions or sticks. Many of these products contain DEET (diethyltoluamide), which is also known by other names, including detamide, metaldephene, MGK and OFF. DEET is absorbed rapidly into the skin and blood system. Do not use DEET on infants or young children. There have been reports of acute poisoning of the nervous tissue in children exposed to DEET-containing products, both through heavy normal use and accidental ingestion. Symptoms of poisoning include headaches, skin irritation and behavioral disorders. Because of these potential effects, adults should use DEET cautiously.

Do not use **flea collars** or **pet sprays** indoors. After a pet has been treated with pesticides, do not let children play with the pet or allow the pet inside the home until the amount of time recommended by the product guidelines has passed.

Avoid **aerosol sprays** and use **hand pump sprays** carefully indoors. Apply sprays only to small areas and do not treat entire walls, floors or ceilings. Do not spray upward into the air because you can easily become contaminated.

Use pesticides in kitchens cautiously. Remove all food, dishes, utensils, food wrappings, pots and pans before treating kitchen cabinets or other areas. Wait until shelves and other surfaces are dry (or cleaned) as directed on the product label before replacing items.

Lawn and Garden Care. A regular program of preventive care can dramatically reduce the need for pesticides in the lawn and garden. Set realistic goals and allow enough time for a maintenance plan to work. Many people become frustrated when nonchemical approaches take time to work.

Make sure that your soil is healthy and has the right pH, acidity or alkalinity, nutrients and texture to grow what you want. Choose disease-resistant grasses and other plants that thrive in your area. Water grass and other plants deeply (but not too often), keep the grass about three inches high and correct thatch buildup.

When pesticides are needed, adhere to all of the safety guidelines given in Figure 11.4. Following the safety tips below will further reduce your exposure:

- Never spray or dust on windy days.
- When spraying pesticides outdoors, close the doors and windows of the home and keep them closed for several hours after spraying. Turn off air conditioners and close any air intakes or vents around the house or crawl space before you apply the pesticide.
- Do not use spray nozzles that deliver a fine mist; a coarse spray is less likely to be inhaled deep into the lungs.
- Cover fish ponds and stay away from wells when spraying or dusting.
- Do not spray nontarget plants; use only the smallest amount of pesticide necessary to do the job.
- Do not spray plants that are in bloom; doing so will kill honeybees.

Pesticides in Food

The Food and Drug Administration sets and enforces standards (called tolerances) to limit the amount of pesticides allowed in commercial food or animal feed used in the United States. This does not mean, however, that these products are free of pesticides. Following the simple steps below can help you to further reduce your exposure to pesticides in foods from the store, garden or the wild:

Commercially Grown Food

- To remove surface residues, rinse fruit and vegetables thoroughly with water, scrub them with a brush and peel them (if possible). (This cleaning will not, however, remove any residue inside the fruit or vegetable.)
- Cook or bake foods to reduce residues of some (but not all) pesticides.
- To remove pesticides (and other chemicals) that concentrate in fat, trim fat from meat, fish and poultry, and discard the fat in broths and pan drippings.
- Whenever possible, buy food that is grown organically without the use of pesticides.

Home-grown Food

- Choose the garden site carefully. Try to pick a location that had limited or no previous chemical use, and put the garden where chemicals from a neighbor's land will not run off onto your garden.
- Build your soil with plenty of organic materials such as compost and manure.
- Select hardy, disease resistant varieties of plants and seeds and plant them at the proper times.
- Use crop and plant rotation to avoid some types of pests.
- Become familiar with integrated pest management methods to reduce the use of pesticides.
- Mulch your garden, shrubs and trees. Use leaves, hay, grass clippings, shredded bark, chipped bark or even seaweed. (Avoid using newspapers and sewage sludge because these contain chemicals that can contaminate your garden.)
- Water adequately.

Food from the Wild

- Contact your local health department or fish and game officials to find out if fish and game restrictions exist because of pesticides or other chemicals.
- When preparing wild game and fish, trim fat and discard the skin to remove as many fat-soluble pesticide residues as possible. To prepare wild plant foods, follow the tips provided for commercial foods.
- Do not gather wild plant foods next to a road, utility right-of-way or hedgerow between farm fields. These sites are likely to be contaminated by pesticides.

 Pesticide Checklist

Questions To Ask	Response	What Does a "Yes" Mean?
If your house has recently been treated with a termiticide or other pesticide, is there a lingering odor indoors?	Yes No ❏ ❏	A lingering chemical odor after a pesticide treatment could mean that the indoor areas are contaminated with pesticides.
Are pesticides other than disinfectants stored inside the home?	Yes No ❏ ❏	These products are a safety hazard. Store pesticides in a locked cabinet in a well ventilated storage area in the garage or away from the house. Store flammable liquids outside the living area and away from an ignition source. Disinfectants and other cleaning chemicals should be stored so that children cannot gain access to the products.

Pesticide Checklist

Questions To Ask	Response	What Does a "Yes" Mean?
Are pest strips used indoors?	Yes No ❏ ❏	Pest strips release pesticides inside the home over time and some of these chemicals are especially hazardous. Use other control options.
Do you use insect sprays or lotions that contain DEET or pesticide insect strips with dichorvos?	Yes No ❏ ❏	These products are especially hazardous. Do not use any product containing DEET on the skin of infants or young children.
Do you spray pets indoors with pesticides or allow pets with flea collars indoors?	Yes No ❏ ❏	Do not apply pesticides to pets indoors. Pest control products for pets can release hazardous chemicals indoors. Use these products cautiously.
Do you have a serious pest infestation problem?	Yes No ❏ ❏	Call a professional for help and select the least hazardous control options. Avoid using bug bombs, foggers or other volatile products indoors.

Summary Chart for Electric and Magnetic Fields

Topic	*Comments*
Description	Electric and magnetic fields are low levels of energy (defined in Europe as 50 Hz and in North America as 60 Hz) that are associated with our use of electric power. They induce electric currents in conductive objects, including people.
Health Effects	The interaction of electric and magnetic fields with biological tissues is still poorly understood. Some scientific studies suggest that living near power lines may increase the chance of contracting some childhood cancers, whereas other studies do not support these findings.
Sources	Electric and magnetic fields are produced by any generation, transmission, distribution and use of electric power. Power lines, transformers, electrical wiring, appliances and any gadgets that run on electricity create these fields.
Testing	Although electric and magnetic fields can be measured using portable meters, electric fields are difficult to measure. Sometimes local electric utilities will provide testing or a list of testing firms.Consumers can rent or purchase equipment to do the test themselves but inexpensive meters are likely to produce questionable results. There are no national standards for acceptable electric or magnetic fields from power lines or other sources.
Reducing Exposure	Replace objects that produce electric and magnetic fields with ones that do not. Limit the amount of time spent next to objects that produce fields and increase the distance between people and the source of the field. Some of these strategies can be used with little inconvenience; others might not be practical because they would cause major disruptions in lifestyle.

CHAPTER
TWELVE

Electric and Magnetic Fields Produced by Power Lines and Household Appliances

The proximity of homes and schools to power lines is affecting house sales all over the country, according to The New York Times. *Monica Bradbury lives 30 feet from one of Con Edison's power lines in Pleasantville. She regularly takes measurements of the magnetic radiation in and around her home, and finds that indoor levels average 36 milligauss. In the article, she says, "There are people on my block who have been trying to sell their houses for two or three years. No matter how low the price, nobody wants them." Ms. Bradbury and other residents asked Con Edison to lower the electric and magnetic fields near their homes. According to Ms. Bradbury, "Basically, they told us there was nothing to worry about."*

Another utility, Niagara Mohawk, was responsive to community concerns and rerouted a power line that was within ten feet of an elementary school near Albany. Magnetic field levels were five to seven milligauss before the line was moved and dropped by 30 to 50 percent after the line was moved.

As reported in *The New York Times,* July 11, 1993.

What Are Electric and Magnetic Fields and Why Are They a Hazard?

Electric and magnetic fields are forms of energy that induce current in surrounding objects, including people. Electric fields are produced by the presence of electrical charges or voltage. Magnetic fields result from the movement of those charges or current flow. The "field" is the area where the electric and magnetic fields exist or exert their influence. The electric and magnetic fields from power generation, transmission, distribution and use are part of a spectrum of electromagnetic energy that is shown in Figure 12.1. Electric and magnetic fields are a consequence of our electrified society and are generated whenever electricity is used.

The terms electromagnetic radiation or electromagnetic field (EMF) are often used to describe electric and magnetic fields associated with our use of electric power. It is actually more correct to refer to these fields as "electric" and "magnetic" fields because their frequencies are so low that they act separately rather than as one form of energy. The energy produced by 60 Hz fields is very weak compared to other types of radiation. Ionizing radiation (for example, from a medical X-ray machine) can break molecular and chemical bonds. Nonionizing radiation (from a microwave oven) can't break chemical bonds, but it can create strong electric currents which cause heating. Electric and magnetic fields from electric power usage are much weaker than the fields in either of these examples.

Most electric power in the United States is generated by 60 hertz (Hz) alternating current (AC), but there are some direct current (DC) lines in Minnesota, California, North Dakota, Oregon, Washington, Vermont, New Hampshire, Massachusetts, Utah and Nevada. Both types of current produce electric fields and magnetic fields. DC lines also produce air ions that have been the subject of past controversy about health and environmental effects.

The current from 60 Hz AC power alternates back and forth 60 times a second, instead of flowing in a straight line like the current produced by DC power lines. Although the energy created by 60 Hz fields is extremely low, it can create a flow of current in our bodies that some scientists believe adversely affects health.

Do the electric and magnetic fields produced by the use of AC electric power cause health problems such as cancer? Scientists do not know the answer and there is currently a great deal of debate about the issue. Over 25 years ago, when scientists first started studying the health effects related to electric power, they believed that electric fields were more important than

FIGURE 12.1.   Electromagnetic Spectrum

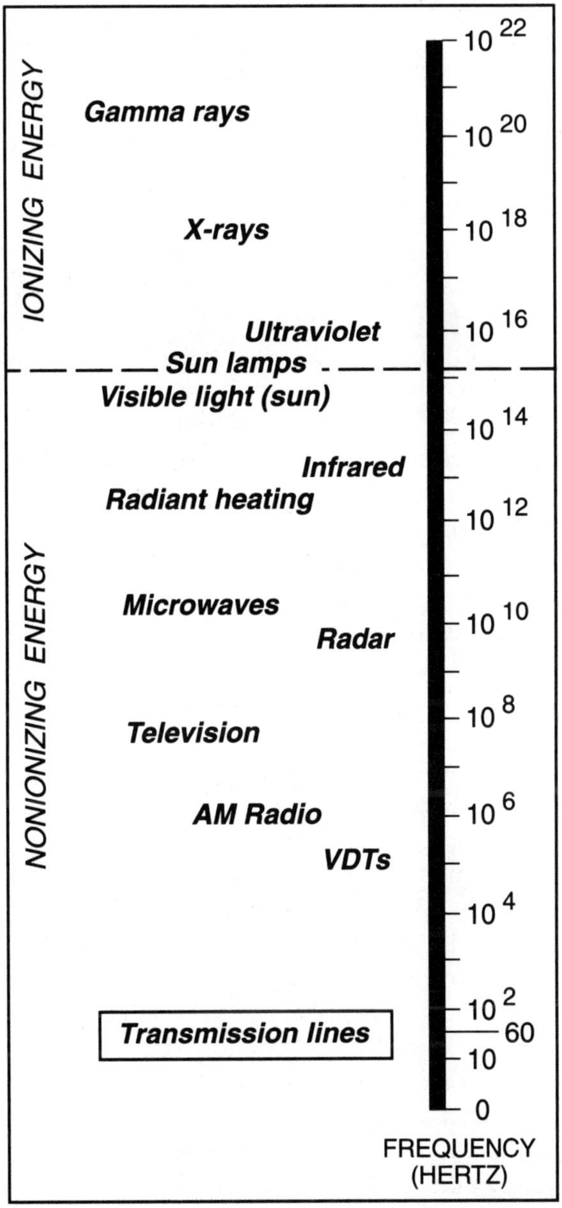

SOURCE: Copyright ©1994. Electric Power Research Institute. EPRI brochure BR 103745 *Electric and Magnetic Field Fundamentals*. Reprinted with permission.

magnetic fields. Since the early 1990s, scientists have also attempted to evaluate the role of magnetic fields.

These studies have tried to identify several types of effects: 1) asymptomatic changes in the basic structure and function of cells, 2) changes that can be felt or measured and 3) changes that produce cancer.

Studies of effects on cells have been conducted primarily on animals exposed to electric fields. Research shows that animals exposed to 60 Hz electric fields experience some changes in behavior, in the nervous system and in the endocrine (hormone) system. Studies of cell and tissue cultures show that some changes occur under exposure to extremely low frequency electric and magnetic fields (up to 300 Hz). It is not clear, though, if electric and magnetic fields cause permanent changes or damage. Even so, these studies are important because they demonstrate that extremely low frequency fields can affect the basic activities of cells and there is concern that damaged cells could develop into other health effects (such as cancer). An important limitation, however, is that scientists do not know how animal or cell studies apply to people who are exposed to extremely low frequency fields.

Some studies of electric utility workers and others show that people can sense the presence of strong electric fields. A person who stands in an electric field of more than about 20 kilovolts per meter (kV/m) is likely to feel a slight tingling sensation. (A field of 10 kV/m can be found under some high voltage transmission lines.) These are very large exposures—over 500 to 1000 times the average electric field exposure that a typical person might receive during his or her day-to-day activities.

One study of magnetic fields revealed that people could not perceive 60 Hz AC magnetic fields that were more than 30 times stronger than those beneath transmission lines. Some studies involving high electric and magnetic fields show that people do experience changes in heart rate, reaction time and hormone levels. The significance of reported effects is not yet established.

For many years, scientists thought that the electric and magnetic fields from power lines and appliances did not have enough energy to cause adverse health effects. The 1979 publication of a study of cancer rates among children in Colorado forced a general reevaluation of those theories. According to the study, children who lived near power lines were two to three times more likely to develop leukemia than children who did not live near power lines. Each year, childhood leukemia from all causes currently strikes about one in 14,000 children.

This study has been followed by some studies that support the original findings and by others that do not. Unfortunately, there have been problems with many of these studies. Some have not adequately considered other factors that could contribute to cancer. Others have examined exposure indirectly (by measuring how far away from lines people live) rather than actually measuring the day-by-day exposure to electric and magnetic fields. These and other weaknesses of the studies make it difficult to understand the relationship between health problems and exposure to electric and magnetic fields from AC power.

The energy created by 60 Hz fields is too low to break chemical bonds in our bodies or to generate much heat. Even so, some scientists believe that these weak fields can cause adverse health effects, and that the explanations of how this happens are different and more complicated than originally thought. Many questions remain unanswered. Exactly how do electric and magnetic fields interact with the body's cells? Are higher level fields more hazardous than lower level fields? Is a continuous exposure to a given field more hazardous than intermittent exposures? Does exposure to fields affect reproduction? Are children and fetuses at greater risk than adults? The electric power industry and federal government scientists are conducting many studies that may answer these and other questions in the future.

Sources

Electric and magnetic fields occur naturally or as a result of generating, transmitting, distributing and using electric power. The earth has a magnetic field that can move the needle of a compass, and thunderstorms produce electric fields. Even our bodies produce electric fields that make our hearts and nervous systems work. However, natural fields do not behave in the same way as alternating current fields generated by electric power.

The process of bringing electrical power into our homes begins when large generating plants produce electricity that reaches our homes through a transmission and distribution system. Transformers along the route increase or decrease the voltage to the proper amount (see Figure 12.2).

The highest electric fields are produced by the high tension (also called high voltage) transmission lines that carry electricity over long distances. These lines carry voltages up to 765 kV. Most of these lines are mounted on tall towers, but some are buried under the ground.

The primary and secondary distribution lines carry electricity at reduced voltages into residential areas. Since the voltage is lower, the fields generated by these lines are usually (but not always) less than those produced by high tension lines. These distribution lines are located close to most homes, and they are likely to be overhead in older neighborhoods, whereas underground lines are common in newer areas. In a home, wires carry the electricity to outlets for lights, machines, radios, television sets and other appliances.

FIGURE 12.2.   Electric Power Distribution System

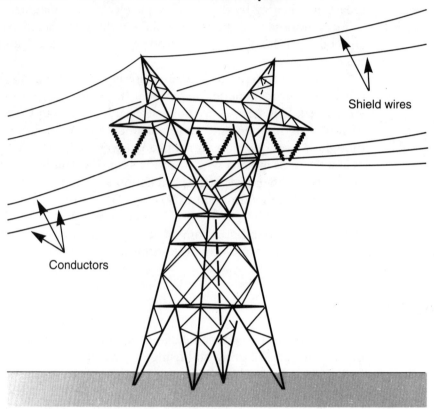

Shield wires

Conductors

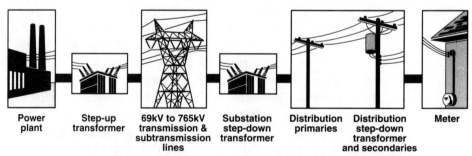

| Power plant | Step-up transformer | 69kV to 765kV transmission & subtransmission lines | Substation step-down transformer | Distribution primaries | Distribution step-down transformer and secondaries | Meter |

SOURCE: Copyright ©1994. Electric Power Research Institute. EPRI brochure BR 103745 *Electric and Magnetic Field Fundamentals.* Reprinted with permission.

Magnetic Field Sources

The unit of measurement for magnetic fields is the gauss (G) or milligauss (mG). One gauss is equal to 1000 milligauss.

When trying to understand magnetic field measurements, it is important to know that many factors determine the amount of exposure that people get in their day-to-day activities. Figure 12.3 shows three examples of the wide variation in magnetic fields that can occur throughout a single day—from up to 0.5 mG when walking outdoors to over 100 mG when traveling on an electric train and using appliances such as an electric blanket. (Magnetic fields from electric blankets can vary widely. Measurements of 0.9 mG for average levels and 2.7 mG for peak levels have been recorded at two inches from newer PTC low-magnetic field blankets. Measurements for ordinary electric blankets have been reported in the range of 12 to 50 mG.) Even though peak exposures occur during the day, the average residential magnetic field background levels (away from appliances) are typically in the range of 0.5 to 1.0 mG according to the Electric Power Research Institute (see Figure 12.3), but some homes can have much higher average levels.

People who work in occupations related to the sources of electrical power are exposed to higher levels of magnetic fields than other workers. For example, workers at power plants and substations could be exposed to 10 to 200 mG or more for different time periods compared to office workers who might be exposed to average levels of 1 to 2 mG. Other examples of workers whose jobs expose them to high levels of magnetic fields include electric arc welders, induction furnace workers and electric railway workers.

Another factor that affects a person's level of exposure to magnetic fields is his or her distance from the source of the fields. Figure 12.4 shows some measurements of magnetic fields at different distances from common appliances in the home. It is clear from these measurements that magnetic field levels drop sharply as one moves away from the source of the field. According to the measurements for a hair dryer in Figure 12.4, the field is ten times lower at one foot from the dryer than at six inches away from the dryer.

In residences, two important sources of background magnetic fields are the distribution lines (lines that bring power to the home) and the grounding systems. When electricity is brought into the home, the neutral wire is grounded at the home (as well as at the distribution transformer). A buried metal water supply pipe near the home's service entrance usually serves as the ground, often resulting in the creation of a source of magnetic field within the house (and also in neighboring houses). Ground currents can also flow through cable television lines, telephone lines, steel concrete reinforcing rods, ground rods and other connections to the ground. The field produced by nearby transmission lines will be relatively uniform in time and space. In

FIGURE 12.3.   Measurements of Magnetic Fields during a Single Day

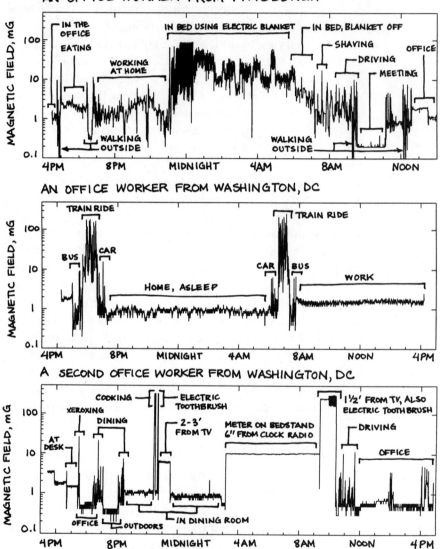

SOURCE: Morgan, G. *Part 2: What Can We Conclude From Measurements of Power-Frequency Fields?* Pittsburgh, Pa.: Carnegie Mellon University. ©1993. Used with permission.

FIGURE 12.4.   Measurements of Magnetic Fields Produced by Different Home Sources

| Sources | Magnetic Field Readings in Milligauss (mG) at Different Distances from Sources | | | |
	6 inches	1 foot	2 feet	4 feet
Bathroom Sources				
Hair dryers				
Lowest	1	-	-	-
Middle	300	1	-	-
Highest	700	70	10	1
Electric shavers				
Lowest	4	-	-	-
Middle	100	20	-	-
Highest	600	100	10	1
Kitchen Sources				
Blenders				
Lowest	30	5	-	-
Middle	70	10	2	-
Highest	100	20	3	-
Can openers				
Lowest	500	40	3	-
Middle	600	150	20	2
Highest	1500	300	30	4
Coffeemakers				
Lowest	4	-	-	-
Middle	7	-	-	-
Highest	10	1	-	-
Crock pots				
Lowest	3	-	-	-
Middle	6	1	-	-
Highest	9	1	-	-

NOTE: These measurements can be used as guides for what you might expect with sources in your house. The measurements come from several different studies and represent the highest, middle and lowest measured values. A dash in the table means that the magnetic field measurement was about the same as the measurements taken before the appliance was turned on.
SOURCE: U.S. EPA (1992b)

FIGURE 12.4. (*continued*)

Sources	Magnetic Field Readings in Milligauss (mG) at Different Distances from Sources			
	6 inches	**1 foot**	**2 feet**	**4 feet**
Dishwashers				
Lowest	10	6	2	-
Middle	20	10	4	-
Highest	100	30	7	1
Food processors				
Lowest	20	5	-	-
Middle	30	6	2	-
Highest	120	20	3	-
Garbage disposals				
Lowest	60	8	1	-
Middle	80	10	2	-
Highest	100	20	3	-
Microwave ovens				
Lowest	100	1	1	-
Middle	200	40	10	2
Highest	300	200	30	20
Mixers				
Lowest	30	5	-	-
Middle	100	10	1	-
Highest	600	100	10	-
Electric ovens				
Lowest	4	1	-	-
Middle	9	4	-	-
Highest	20	5	1	-
Electric ranges				
Lowest	20	-	-	-
Middle	30	8	2	-
Highest	200	30	9	6
Refrigerators				
Lowest	-	-	-	-
Middle	2	2	1	-
Highest	40	20	10	10

FIGURE 12.4.   (*continued*)

Sources	Magnetic Field Readings in Milligauss (mG) at Different Distances from Sources			
	6 inches	**1 foot**	**2 feet**	**4 feet**
Toasters				
Lowest	5	-	-	-
Middle	10	3	-	-
Highest	20	7	-	-
Living/Family Room Sources				
Ceiling Fans				
Lowest		-	-	-
Middle		3	-	-
Highest		50	6	1
Window air conditioners				
Lowest		-	-	-
Middle		3	1	-
Highest		50	6	4
Tuners/Tape players				
Lowest	-	-	-	-
Middle	1	-	-	-
Highest	3	1	-	-
Color TVs				
Lowest		-	-	-
Middle		7	2	-
Highest		20	8	4
Black and white TVs				
Lowest		1	-	-
Middle		3	-	-
Highest		10	2	1
Laundry and Utility Room Sources				
Electric clothes dryers				
Lowest	2	-	-	-
Middle	3	2	-	-
Highest	10	3	-	-

FIGURE 12.4.   (*continued*)

Sources	Magnetic Field Readings in Milligauss (mG) at Different Distances from Sources			
	6 inches	**1 foot**	**2 feet**	**4 feet**
Washing machines				
Lowest	4	1	-	-
Middle	20	7	1	-
Highest	100	30	6	-
Irons				
Lowest	6	1	-	-
Middle	8	1	-	-
Highest	20	3	-	-
Portable heaters				
Lowest	5	1	-	-
Middle	100	20	4	-
Highest	150	40	8	1
Vacuum cleaners				
Lowest	100	20	4	-
Middle	300	60	10	1
Highest	700	200	50	10
Bedroom Sources				
Digital clocks				
Lowest		-	-	-
Middle		1	-	-
Highest		8	2	1
Analog clocks (conventional clockface)				
Lowest		1	-	-
Middle		15	2	-
Highest		30	5	3
Baby monitors				
Lowest	4	-	-	-
Middle	6	1	-	-
Highest	15	2	-	-

contrast, the field produced by ground currents will not be uniform within the house and will vary over time as appliances are used.

Although the house wiring alone is rarely a source of magnetic fields, it can create problems. The knob-and-tube wiring that is present in older homes can create higher magnetic fields (7 mG or more at a distance of only a few feet) because of the arrangement of the wires. Other potential sources of magnetic fields related to the wiring are the use of three-way switches or the grounding of a neutral wire at another site inside the house in addition to the service entrance.

Figure 12.5 shows that magnetic field levels drop off rapidly with distance from power lines. Even so, power lines can contribute to magnetic field measurements indoors because the house does not shield these fields. A comparison of Figures 12.4 and 12.5 shows that being close to some appliances in the

FIGURE 12.5.   Magnetic Fields Measured at Different Distances from Electric Power Lines

Loading of Transmission Line	Maximum Level on Right-of-way	Magnetic Field Readings in Milligauss (mG) at Different Distances from Lines			
		50 feet	100 feet	200 feet	300 feet
115 Kilovolt Line					
Average usage	30	7	2	0.4	0.2
Peak usage	63	14	4	0.9	0.4
230 Kilovolt Line					
Average usage	58	20	7	1.8	0.8
Peak usage	118	40	15	3.6	1.6
500 Kilovolt Line					
Average usage	87	29	13	3.2	1.4
Peak usage	183	62	27	6.7	3.0

NOTE: These measurements were collected by the Bonneville Power Administration. Although they can be used as guides for what you might expect with magnetic fields from similar power lines, you must take measurements to know what the field is around your property.
SOURCE: U.S. EPA (1992b).

home can result in exposure to higher magnetic field levels than being 50 feet from a power line. If you live next to a power line, however, your exposure to magnetic fields is a combination of exposures that result from home appliances and fields from the line. The numbers in both tables are averages from different sources of data and should be used only as guides. The actual values in your home may be different.

Electric Field Sources

As noted above, electric power lines are rated according to the amount of current that flows through the line. The unit that is typically used is kilovolts per meter (kV/m). One kilovolt per meter is a large unit that equals 1000 volts per meter (V/m). Most environmental exposure is measured in volts per meter.

Occupational exposure can vary considerably, depending on the particular work activities being performed. Office workers might experience exposures in the range of 1 to 10 V/m, whereas exposures experienced by electricians, power station workers and electronics workers usually range from 10 to 100 V/m.

Exposures in the home can vary widely depending on the use of electrical appliances and the home's distance from power lines. Typical values are in the 1 to 100 V/m range, but much higher values are possible next to appliances. Figure 12.6 shows some typical examples of electric field strengths around appliances in the home. These levels are generally lower than the measurements of electric fields at closer distances from power lines (see Figure 12.7).

FIGURE 12.6.   60 Hz Electric Field Strengths in the Home

Location	Electric Field Readings in Volts per Meter (V/m)
Broiler	130
Toaster	40
Stereo	90
Hallway	13
Bedrooms	2–8
Electric blanket	100–2000[1]

NOTE: These measurements were taken in the centers of rooms at distances of one foot from the appliances (except the electric blanket).
[1] These are average values for a person using an electric blanket.
SOURCE: Bonneville Power Administration (1989, revised 1993).

FIGURE 12.7.   Electric Field Measurements around Electric Power Lines

Type of Transmission Line	Maximum Level on Right-of-Way	Electric Field Readings in Volts per Meter (V/m) at Different Distances from Lines			
		50 feet	100 feet	200 feet	300 feet
115 kilovolt line	1000	500	70	10	3
230 kilovolt line	2000	1500	300	50	10
500 kilovolt line	7000	3000	1000	300	100

NOTE: These are typical values for Bonneville Power transmission lines. Actual field strengths depend on the design of individual lines and voltage levels.
SOURCE: Bonneville Power Administration (1989, revised 1993).

There are fewer measurements of electric fields than magnetic fields indoors because electric fields are difficult to measure reliably and because past research on low-level exposure to electric fields has not established a correlation between these fields and health problems.

Testing and Understanding the Results

Testing

Special portable instruments are needed to measure electric and magnetic fields. Both types of fields are three dimensional, which means that they can be measured in all directions. Each dimension is called an axis (the plural is axes) and in order to obtain an accurate measurement, readings must be taken in three dimensions: front, side and vertical.

Two types of meters are available for measuring magnetic fields. The least expensive of the two, a single-axis meter, measures only one direction at a time and must be rotated until it is aligned with the field. A three-axis meter can measure all three directions at once and does not have to be rotated in order to obtain accurate readings. Magnetic field meters can be held in the hand because the magnetic field does not change in the presence of a human body (see Figure 12.8).

Electric fields are measured using a meter attached to the end of a large insulating stick. Since the human body is a conducting object, the electric field

Figure 12.8. A Magnetic and Electric Field Meter

SOURCE: Model HI-3604 ELF Field Strength Meter used to measure fields under high voltage transmission line. Photo courtesy Holaday Industries, Inc., 14825 Martin Drive, Eden Prairie, MN 55344, (612) 934-4920.

will vary if the meter is held next to the body. The stick keeps the proper distance between the meter and the person making the measurements.

The focus of current testing efforts is on magnetic fields. Electric fields are difficult to measure, and scientific studies have not established the existence of health problems caused by electric fields in residential settings. Electric utility companies will frequently send trained technicians at no charge to take measurements of magnetic fields in homes or other locations at the request of concerned customers. (If your electric utility cannot provide this service, their staff can probably direct you to a consulting firm.) You could make the measurements yourself by renting a meter ($60 to $100 per week) or purchasing one ($75 to over $500). The EPA Public Information Office (see list of resources) has a list of companies that sell or rent magnetic field meters. Taking accurate measurements, however, requires skill and reliable equipment; inexpensive meters are likely to produce inaccurate results.

Buyers. If you are building or buying a new house and want to have the property or house tested for magnetic fields, you should include the testing as part of the purchase agreement.

If you are concerned about magnetic fields, you may want to examine the distance between the house and substations, transmission lines and distribution lines. If you have children, find out how close their school is to these sources of exposure. Determine if moving to your new location will require you to commute on an electric train. You can use this information (along with test results of magnetic fields and other environmental hazards) to make a decision about whether or not to buy the house.

Guidelines for Testing. The following recommendations for testing magnetic fields (they also apply to electric field measurements) are based on guidelines that have been suggested by the California Department of Health Sciences and the Institute of Electrical and Electronic Engineers. Following these guidelines will provide a good indication of exposure levels at the time the measurements are taken. Because the fields can change over time, levels of exposure can also change. You should still be able to identify sources that contribute the most to your exposures and use this information to make decisions about reducing exposure.

Make sure that you or the person who is taking the measurements understands how to use the equipment. Ask when the equipment's meter was last checked for accuracy. (This calibration should be done at least once each year.)

Make a sketch of the house and yard, and note the location of nearby power lines and places where electrical wires come into the house. Record the results and locations of the readings. After the measurements are completed, you will be able to identify the sources that produce the largest electric or magnetic fields. Keep in mind that different parts of the body will be exposed differently according to the location of the body in relation to the source.

Measurements inside the house

- Leave lights and appliances in their normal on or off positions.
- Take measurements at a height of about three feet above the floor (at waist level). If infants and toddlers are present, take measurements at about one foot above the floor.
- Take measurements at the front door and in bedrooms, the family room, the kitchen or other rooms frequently used by household members. Take measurements near the center of each room away from appliances. Called an *ambient spot* measurement, this provides an estimate of the field due to all sources in the room at a single point in time.
- Take a measurement in the bedrooms eight inches above the center of the bed. (The bedroom is recommended as a testing site because it is an area where most people spend a large portion of their time.)
- Take measurements near an appliance by taking readings at several points along a line away from the appliance with the appliance both on and off. Magnetic field readings near appliances can be difficult to take, and there can be a great deal of variation when readings are repeated.

Measurements outside the house

- Perform measurements at a height of about three feet above the ground (at waist level).
- Starting at one corner of the house, walk away from the outside wall and take readings every six to ten feet.
- If there are electrical wires, transformers or other electrical sources nearby, take measurements every six to ten feet along a line that is perpendicular to the power line or other source.

Understanding Test Results

Although the federal government does not have a standard for electric and magnetic fields related to electrical power, scientific studies suggest that it is important to investigate the effects of these fields. (Some of these studies have used a level of 2 mG to place people into broad exposure categories. This is not a standard and should not be used to determine safe or unsafe levels. This lack of a widely accepted standard makes it difficult to know what test results mean and what actions should be taken.

You can compare the results of measurements in and around your home to reported average background residential magnetic field levels of 0.5 to 1 mG and reported levels in Figures 12.4 and 12.5 to find out if your exposure is at a similar level to that of some other people. Typical background residential electric fields are in the range of 1–100 V/m, and Figures 12.6 and 12.7 can provide comparisons for specific sources.

The states of California, Delaware, Minnesota, Montana, New Jersey, New York, Oregon and Florida have established limitations for the strength of electric fields from high voltage transmission lines. Depending on the line voltage, the electric field limits at the edge of the right of way in these regulations range from 1 to 3 kV/m, whereas limits on the maximum electric field allowed directly in the right of way ranges from 8 kV/m to about 12 kV/m.

Florida, Delaware and New York also have standards for magnetic fields from the lines. The magnetic field levels are limited by utilities in Delaware to 200 mG at the edge of the right of way. Florida's regulations limit maximum magnetic field levels at the edge of the right of way to 150 mG for lines less than or equal to 230 kV and to 200 mG for 500 kV lines, whereas the levels in New York are currently limited to 200 mG. Call your state's Department of Energy to find out what standards (if any) exist in your state.

Reducing Exposure

Because there are no national established health guidelines or standards for magnetic fields, making a decision about some situations can be difficult. At this point, scientific evidence seems to suggest that a possible health hazard exists. Although the risk of childhood leukemia based on the existing studies does not appear to be large when compared to other risks, the scientific data base is not yet complete. New studies could suggest stronger risks, new risks or no risks. Considering the scientific uncertainty, what should you do?

Measured average household levels that are within the background range of measurements for residences nationwide (0.5 to 1 mG) should not cause concern. If average levels are greater than background, a reasonable strategy is to evaluate individual sources and take simple actions (some are suggested below) to reduce your exposure from those sources. (For example, use a quilt instead of an electric blanket.) If measured levels continue to be elevated, consult with your local electric utility to determine if any other measures can be taken to reduce exposure. If magnetic field levels cannot be reduced, you may need to make a decision based on your gut feeling about the nature of the risk. Some people may decide to move or to not buy a particular house are sensible things to do whereas others may think of both of these solutions as overreactions.

There are three basic strategies that can help you to reduce your household's exposure to electric and magnetic fields:

1. Replace sources of electric and magnetic fields.
2. Increase the distances between people and these sources and limit your time around them.
3. Shield sources.

Replacement of sources is a potential solution for inexpensive appliances (such as electric clocks or electric blankets). Whenever you plan to replace an appliance or buy a new house, consider electric and magnetic fields as part of the purchasing decision. View product advertising and sales claims with some skepticism and recognize that you may need to contact the manufacturer or professional organizations to verify claims.

Magnetic and electric fields drop quickly as the distances between the sources and people are increased, as shown in Figures 12.4 through 12.7. Simply moving sources in the home or changing the way you use appliances can help reduce these types of exposure.

Shielding simply means blocking out the electric or magnetic fields by placing an object between the source of the field and people. Electric fields are easily blocked by the walls and roof of a building, trees and shrubs, the ground and other materials (even your skin). A typical house blocks out about 90 percent of outside electric fields.

Magnetic fields, however, can penetrate through most materials, including the ground, wood, air and people. Objects can be shielded from magnetic fields by a special metal alloy called Mu metal, which is very expensive. (For example, the cost of building a Mu metal cabinet to shield a computer would be roughly equal to the cost of the computer.) Use caution when buying appliances and other objects that are advertised as being shielded—most of these claims are false.

Reducing Exposure inside the Home

Exposure to electric and magnetic fields can be higher inside than outside the house. Sources that add to the fields inside the home include the house wiring, appliances and fields that enter from the outside. The following list of suggestions can help you avoid exposure to some sources. The list is not complete, but you can apply these principles to a variety of sources.

- Use regular blankets instead of electric blankets. If you must use an electric blanket, use it to preheat the bed and unplug it when you go to bed. When the blanket is turned off, however, the electric field can remain while the plug is in the socket (even when the blanket is not operating). Consider purchasing a newer model PTC (Positive Temperature Coefficient) low-magnetic field blanket. These blankets have magnetic fields that are 10 to 20 times lower than electric blankets that use older technology.

- Turn off water bed heaters when you go to bed.
- Look for appliances and gadgets in your home that operate with small electric motors that produce strong magnetic fields. (Some examples include electric shavers, hair dryers, electric fans and heaters, microwave ovens and can openers.)

    Reduce your exposure to the fields created by these motors by moving them away from you whenever possible and increasing the separation between your body and the appliance when you use the appliance. For example, move an electric clock so it is at least 2.5 feet away from your bed and do not hold hair dryers next to your scalp.

    Replace electric appliances with mechanical motors. For example, use a wind-up clock or a hand-operated can opener.

- When using video display terminals or watching TV, stay at least 2.5 feet away from the front and at least 3 feet away from the sides and backs of these appliances.
- Laptop computer display screens do not use the cathode ray tube technology that releases fields from videodisplay terminals. The battery packs and chargers that laptops use, however, can produce fields because they are electrical devices. Place these 2.5 to 3 feet away from you.
- Keep beds and cribs away from the electrical service drop and away from walls that contain wiring.
- Consider taking magnetic field measurements if the home contains knob-and-tube wiring or electric strip heating. Depending on the test results, replacement of the wiring may be an option to consider. Distancing family members from these sources might be effective.
- Ask an electrician to check your grounding system if the electrical service drop is a source of high fields. There should be no corrosion or loose wires. Correct any problems. Another strategy is to arrange furniture so that members of the household will reduce their time in high-exposure areas.

Reducing Exposure Outside the Home

- Underground electric distribution lines do produce magnetic fields that are not shielded by the ground. Exposures could be higher or lower than with overhead lines, depending on a number of factors, including how deep the lines are buried, how far away the lines are and how the lines are arranged. Another source of exposure in neighborhoods with buried lines is surface transformers. These are metal electrical boxes that are usually in the front or back yards of some of the houses in a neighborhood. Surface transformers can produce elevated magnetic fields that drop rapidly with distance. Do not let children play on or near those boxes, and consider planting shrubs around them to limit access by children. To prevent accidental shocks, never dig holes if there are possible buried electrical wires without having the utility mark the locations of the wires.

- Overhead electric distribution lines and transformers will create electric and magnetic fields. Do not allow children to climb trees near pole-mounted transformers or near any electrical wires. Besides potential hazards from magnetic fields, the wires pose an obvious electrocution hazard.
- If you are building a house, ask your builder or architect about construction methods and materials that can reduce your exposure to electric and magnetic fields. Recognize, however, that most builders and architects do not have this type of knowledge, and they will need to get more information.

☑ Electric and Magnetic Fields Checklist

Questions To Ask	Response	What Does a "Yes" Mean?
Inside the Home		
Are there appliances or gadgets that operate on small motors? (Examples include electric clocks, microwave ovens, electric stoves and vacuum cleaners.)	**Yes No** ❏ ❏	Small motors that use AC electricity generate electric and magnetic fields. Reduce exposure by limiting the use of these appliances, replacing them or moving them farther away from members of the household.
Are there beds or cribs next to walls that contain electrical wiring or next to places where the wires come into the home?	**Yes No** ❏ ❏	Electric wiring is a source of electric and magnetic fields. To reduce exposure, move beds and cribs away from the wall or service drop entrance.

Questions To Ask	Response	What Does a "Yes" Mean?
Does anyone in the household work with computers at home (or in the office)?	Yes No ❑ ❑	Computers release electric and magnetic fields. To reduce exposure, stay 2.5 to 3 feet away from the screen, sides and back of the computer. Although laptop computer screens do not release magnetic fields, the chargers and power packs do. Stay 2.5 to 3 feet away from them.
Does anyone in the household watch TV or play video games using the TV?	Yes No ❑ ❑	TV sets release electric and magnetic fields. To reduce exposure, limit the amount of time spent watching TV and stay 2.5 to 3 feet away from the screen.
Outside the Home		
Is your house located close to overhead wires or substations?	Yes No ❑ ❑	These are sources of electric and magnetic fields. Consider measuring the fields around your house. Do not allow children to climb trees adjacent to the wires or the poles that contain the wires.
If the electric wires to your house are buried under the ground, are there metal boxes in your yard?	Yes No ❑ ❑	These boxes are transformers that release electric and magnetic fields. Do not allow children to play on or near them and consider planting shrubs around them to provide shielding. Contact your local utility for advice.

Questions To Ask	Response	What Does a "Yes" Mean?
Do your children attend a school that is close to electric transmission lines, substations or similar sources of electricity?	Yes No ❏ ❏	Consider asking the school to measure the fields and discuss your concerns with school officials and the local utility.
Does anyone in your household work at a job where exposure might be high?	Yes No ❏ ❏	Consider talking to management or union representatives about potential exposure and making measurements of levels.

PART

FOUR

Contaminants from Water and Wastewater

Summary Chart for Drinking Water Quality

Topic	*Comments*
Description	Hazardous contaminants in drinking water include bacteria, viruses, protozoa, nitrates, radon, metals, fertilizers, pesticides and other chemicals. Other contaminants affect the taste, odor and quality of the water.
Health Effects	Contaminated water can cause health effects that range from mild stomach and intestinal cramping to severe diarrhea and death. Effects typically last for no more than one or two weeks, but some conditions can last for months or years. There is a growing concern that water contaminants contribute to other health effects, including cancer.
Sources	Important sources of contamination include industrial discharges, runoff from urban areas, improperly located and maintained septic systems, and pesticides and fertilizers from agricultural operations.
Testing	*All Houses.* Potential contamination is possible anytime the water looks, tastes or smells differently than normal. Contact the local health authority or water supplier for help. Testing is probably needed. Test results are typically compared to the national primary and secondary drinking water standards, though some states have stricter standards. Tap water should be tested for lead regardless of whether the supply is public or private. A level less than 15 parts per billion is considered safe. *Public Water Supplies.* Federal regulations require public water suppliers to test the drinking water for contamination periodically. You can get this information by asking the supplier for test results. *Private Water Supplies.* If your water comes from a private surface source or a well, test for bacteria, nitrates and possibly other contaminants. The local health or environmental agency may perform the tests; if not, the agency can provide names of qualified laboratories. The national standards are not enforceable for private water supplies, but they are useful for making comparisons. Some states have standards for contaminants in private water sources.
Reducing Exposure	*All Houses.* If you suspect contamination, use an alternate source of water. Report any unusual conditions to the local health department or drinking water agency (it can advise you regardless of whether your water supply is public or private). Make sure that all fixtures have backflow-prevention devices (see Chapter 14). *Houses with Wells.* Make sure that the well is properly designed, located and maintained. Do not use dug wells because they are easily contaminated. Make needed repairs as soon as possible and always test the water afterwards.

CHAPTER

THIRTEEN

Drinking Water Quality

Seven families who live at Reese Air Force Base in Lubbock, Texas, have wells polluted by trichloroethylene (TCE), an industrial solvent. The EPA's drinking water standard for TCE is five parts per billion. Because measured TCE levels in the wells were as high as 70 parts per billion, the EPA issued a citation of "imminent and substantial endangerment" against the base. The families received bottled drinking water, but the EPA cautioned that the use of tap water for bathing or washing dishes still posed a health threat because any use of the water could release the solvent into the living space.

As reported in *Indoor Pollution News*, July 9, 1993.

In South Bend, Indiana, 29 Hollywood Road residents, two businesses and a church have been on bottled water for nearly two years after chemical contaminants were discovered in their well water. One of the sources of contamination is an old gravel pit (later turned into a landfill) that was used as a dumping ground for industrial wastes and solvents since about 1939. Some contaminants are present in the water at levels that are 250 times the federal drinking water standards. For more than ten years, employees at Casteel General Construction have been drinking coffee from well water with levels of a carcinogen known as cis-1,2 dichloroethylene

(DCE) measured at 1,600 parts per billion, a level 23 times greater than the federally allowed level.

As reported in *South Bend Tribune,* April 5, 1992.

During March and April of 1993, a water parasite, Cryptosporidium, *invaded the Milwaukee water system, which serves 800,000 people. During this period, more than 1,800 people throughout the city sought treatment for severe diarrhea, stomach cramps and fever. One death was officially linked directly to the parasite, and the parasite played a contributing role in five other deaths. Inspectors think that the parasite eluded the filters at the treatment plant. The source of the parasite was finally traced to runoff from slaughterhouse waste that flowed from local rivers into Lake Michigan, the source of the city's water.*

As reported in *Time,* April 19, 1993, and *Indoor Pollution News,* April 16 and May 14, 1993.

Understanding Water Resources

The Water Cycle

Water is one of our country's most important resources. It is essential to life, and Americans rely on safe, clean water for domestic and industrial uses. The water that we drink comes from two basic sources:

1. Groundwater (wells and springs)
2. Surface water (rivers, lakes, streams and ponds)

Rainwater is a third (but minor) source in the United States. About half of our drinking water (96 percent in rural areas and 20 percent in urban areas) and 40 percent of irrigation water comes from groundwater.

Water is naturally purified and recycled in the hydrologic cycle (see Figure 13.1). An understanding of this natural cycling of water can help us understand the problems that occur when we use too much water or pollute existing resources.

When industrial sources release emissions into the air, some of the contaminants stay in the atmosphere and some fall to the ground. When it rains or snows, the water washes the contaminants down to the ground. Some water sinks into the ground and becomes part of a system of underground layers called aquifers. Many people mistakenly think aquifers are underground lakes or rivers. Water does not flow in the ground; instead, it seeps down and fills spaces between sand and rock particles. An area of coarse sand and gravel or a rock layer with many pores and cracks can hold more water than nonporous

FIGURE 13.1.   The Hydrologic Cycle

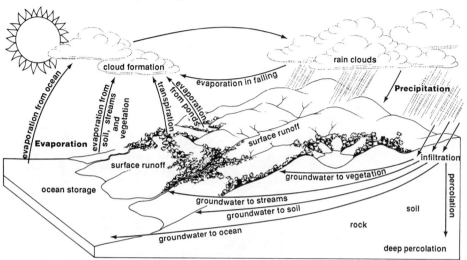

SOURCE: G. Tyler Miller, Jr. *Living in the Environment,* 8th ed. © 1994 Wadsworth Publishing Co., Belmont, CA. Used with permission.

materials such as clay or fine sand. Water moves slower through clay layers than through coarse, sandy layers. Shallow aquifers are most vulnerable to contamination because they are closer to the surface. Unfortunately, they are also the sources of many private water supplies.

As water seeps over and through the ground, it picks up and carries waste materials located on the ground or buried in landfills. Although soil particles and bacteria act as filters to purify the water to some extent, contaminants can remain in the water.

Rainwater that does not soak into the ground moves over the earth's surface, picking up contaminants along the way. Surface runoff degrades the quality of many rivers, lakes and reservoirs. Community water supplies sometimes become contaminated during periods of heavy rain because the water system cannot handle the extra load of incoming rainwater and runoff.

The hydrologic cycle is completed as surface water and moisture in the ground evaporate into the air and form clouds. (At this point, the process begins again.) Vegetation also plays a role in the cycle because plants use water for growth and release water into the atmosphere as they breathe; this process is called transpiration.

As water passes through the hydrologic cycle, it is contaminated by two types of sources. Contaminants that are released directly into the air, ground or water through discharge pipes come from industries known as point

FIGURE 13.2.   Principal Sources of Groundwater Contamination

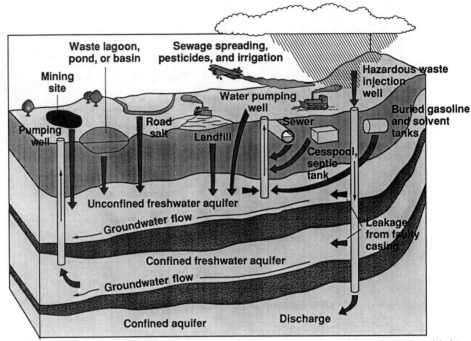

SOURCE: G. Tyler Miller, Jr. *Living in the Environment,* 8th ed. © 1994 Wadsworth Publishing Co., Belmont, CA. Used with permission.

sources. Nonpoint sources generate contaminants over larger areas, often through surface runoff. Examples of these contaminants include septic waste, highway deicing compounds, storm water runoff, runoff from urban areas and agricultural fertilizers and pesticides (see Figure 13.2).

For many years, nonpoint sources were thought to be unimportant. We now know, however, that runoff from urban and agricultural areas causes more degradation of water quality than point sources. Unfortunately, nonpoint sources are more difficult to identify and control than point sources.

Although surface and groundwater contamination exists in every state, the nature of the problems and the degree of contamination vary from region to region. Industrial wastes and urban runoff are important contributors to degrading water quality in all states. The Midwest, northern plains, southern states and some western states have large agricultural bases that generate huge amounts of fertilizer, pesticide and animal waste discharges that can pollute water resources. Many water contamination problems in the coastal states are due to the large petrochemical industrial base and the movement of salt water into fresh water areas. In the Appalachian, mountain and desert states, mining wastes and runoff contaminate waters.

Water shortages have been experienced since 1980 in Colorado, California, Arizona, Nevada, Utah, New Mexico, Oregon and Wyoming. By the year 2000, over two-thirds of the country (mostly western and midwestern states) are predicted to have severe water shortages due to overuse of surface and groundwater resources. When groundwater is overused, the water table drops and land can sink into the ground, resulting in damage to buildings, highways, pipelines and railroad beds, and the intrusion of salt water in coastal areas.

Health Effects of Contaminants

Any water used for domestic purposes should have a good taste and appearance. It should be free of pathogens (disease-causing organisms), chemicals (such as nitrates and nitrites), radionuclides, heavy metals and synthetic organics. Earlier in this century, most water-related diseases were caused by bacteria in the water; each year, thousands of Americans still become ill after drinking water contaminated by bacteria and other pathogens. A more difficult problem now and in the foreseeable future, however, is the possibility that adverse health effects may be caused by drinking low concentrations of chemical contaminants over many years or a lifetime.

Pathogens include bacteria, viruses, protozoans and other disease-causing organisms. Pathogens are generally spread by drinking contaminated water or by hand-to-mouth contact in restaurants, in day care centers or even at home. Sources of pathogens in drinking water are human wastes or wastes from livestock or wild animals. Many waterborne diseases cause diarrhea, cramps and nausea; although people usually recover in a few days to a few weeks, these diseases are sometimes severe and fatal. Pathogens are important because they can affect a person who has consumed only a single drink of contaminated water.

Water is routinely tested for bacterial pathogens using the coliform bacteria as indicator organisms. These bacteria are common in the environment and are generally not harmful. When they are present, though, disease-causing bacteria such as fecal coliforms and *Escherichia coli* are probably also in the water.

Many water suppliers are now testing routinely for two protozoans, *Giardia lamblia* and *Cryptosporidium*, that have caused disease outbreaks throughout the country. Because these organisms can contaminate private and public water supplies that use only disinfection to treat the water, filtering the water before disinfection can effectively remove them. Symptoms of the diseases they cause can be mild to severe and can last for less than a week to months or years.

Nitrate contamination is mainly caused by animal and human wastes, fertilizers and malfunctioning septic systems. The human body converts nitrates into nitrites that can cause a condition known as "blue baby" disease (also called methemoglobinemia). In affected babies, the newly formed nitrites prevent enough oxygen from reaching the babies' tissues. Typical symptoms include bluish, lavender-colored or ruddy-colored skin, or an intermittent bluish color on the mouth, hands and feet. The lack of oxygen can result in shortness of breath.

Blue baby disease is most common in rural farming areas, but it also occurs in suburban and urban areas where wells are closely located to sources of nitrate contamination. Blue baby disease results when babies eat foods or formula made from nitrate-contaminated water. Infants under the age of six months are at greatest risk, and although this disease can be fatal, early diagnosis and use of nitrate-free water usually leads to a rapid recovery.

Long-term exposure to nitrates in drinking water (and food) may cause cancer. Scientists believe that nitrates indirectly cause cancer by forming a potent class of animal carcinogens called N-nitrosoamines. Scientific studies will continue to address this concern.

Radionuclides are naturally occurring radioactive materials. Whenever uranium and radium are present in the ground, there is a chance that these elements or their decay products (such as radon) will contaminate the water. The long-term health consequence of exposure to radon and other radionuclides is cancer. Although some areas of the United States have geologic formations and soils that are more likely to release radon into the groundwater, radon in drinking water typically makes only a minor contribution to indoor radon levels. Hospitals, research facilities, industrial sources, nuclear power and weapons plants, accidental spills and waste disposal operations are other potentially important sources of radioactive materials. Chapter 3 contains more information about radon in water, soil and air.

Heavy metals, such as lead, mercury, cadmium, arsenic, chromium and nickel, occur naturally in soil and rocks. Concentrations of these contaminants are usually very low in surface and groundwater. Contaminants come from many sources, including industrial discharges, runoff from mining and construction activities, incineration by-products, accidental spills, landfills and wastes placed in deep wells. These contaminants can damage the kidneys, liver and nervous system. Lead is of special concern because it is found in the plumbing systems of many homes and in submersible brass well pumps, and it causes health effects at very low concentrations (see Chapter 5 for more information).

Synthetic organic chemicals used in industry, recreation and our homes contaminate water through the direct release of contaminants and runoff. Fertilizer and pesticide runoff from agricultural areas, golf courses, yards and gardens is a large source of these chemicals. Other important sources include industrial discharges, leaking underground storage tanks, urban runoff, chemical spills and improperly managed solid and hazardous wastes.

Many of these chemicals are toxic to the kidneys, liver and other body systems, and some cause cancer and affect reproduction. There are thousands of these compounds in use, but we know very little about most of them. Chapters 7 and 11 have more information about synthetic organic compounds and pesticides.

Federal and State Regulation of Drinking Water Quality

Concern about the safety of drinking water caused the Congress of the United States to pass a law in 1974 (updated in 1986) to protect the quality of public water supplies. This law, the Safe Drinking Water Act (SDWA), requires public water suppliers to routinely test the water they supply and to make sure that it meets the drinking water quality standards established by the EPA. Congress has required the EPA to set standards for 108 contaminants by 1995. (Currently, standards exist for only 84 contaminants.) State governments usually enforce these standards through state health or environmental agencies. Sometimes, states set more stringent requirements for drinking water quality than the federal government.

If a public water system exceeds any of the standards established by the EPA, the water must be treated continuously to make sure that it is safe to drink. The EPA's definition of a public water system is one that provides water to 15 or more households or businesses, or one that provides water to 25 or more people daily for at least 60 days out of the year. Some states include fewer people in their definitions of public water suppliers. Although the SDWA does not regulate private wells or other sources of private water, states and local government units have their own programs to help homeowners protect private water supplies.

Primary Drinking Water Standards. The primary drinking water standards are legally enforceable limits designed to protect public health. Figure 13.3 lists the standards known as the Maximum Contaminant Levels (MCLs) as well as some contaminants and their health effects.

The MCLs are based on the amount of the contaminant a person can consume for a lifetime without experiencing adverse health effects. The MCLs are estimates based on a set of assumptions about a person's weight, the behavior of chemicals in the body and the amount of water a person consumes each day over a lifetime.

FIGURE 13.3.   National Primary Drinking Water Standards

Contaminant	Health Effect	MCL[1]	Sources
Organic Chemicals			
Acrylamide	Probable cancer and nervous system damage	TT[2]	Flocculents in sewage and treated wastewater
Alachlor	Probable cancer	0.002	Corn and soybean herbicide (under review for cancellation)
Aldicarb	Nervous system damage	0.003	Cotton and potato insecticide (restricted in many areas due to groundwater contamination)
Aldicarb sulfone	Nervous system damage	0.002	(Degraded from alicarb by plants)
Aldicarb sulfoxide	Nervous system damage	0.004	(Degraded from alicarb by plants)
Atrazine	Reproductive system and cardiac damage	0.003	Herbicide used widely on corn and noncrop land
Benzene	Cancer	0.005	Fuel from leaking tanks, solvents commonly used in the manufacture of industrial chemicals, pharmaceuticals, pesticides, paints and plastics
Carbofuran	Nervous system and reproductive system damage	0.04	Soil, corn and cotton fumigant/insecticide (restricted in some areas)

[1] In milligrams per liter (mg/L) unless otherwise noted; 1 mg/L is equal to 1 part per million.
[2] TT = Treatment technique requirement in effect.
SOURCES: U.S. EPA (1991).
          40 CFR, part 141 (1992).

FIGURE 13.3. (*continued*)

Contaminant	Health Effect	MCL	Sources
Carbon tetrachloride	Possible cancer	0.005	Cleaning agents, industrial wastes from manufacture of coolants
Chlordane	Probable cancer	0.002	Soil insecticide for termite control, corn and potatoes (most uses canceled in 1980)
2,4-D	Liver, kidney and nervous system damage	0.07	Herbicide for wheat, corn and rangelands
Dibromochloro-propane (DBCP)	Probable cancer	0.0002	Soybean and cotton soil fumigant (canceled in 1977)
p-Dichlorobenzene	Possible cancer	0.075	Insecticides, moth balls and air deodorizers
o-Dichlorobenzene	Nervous system, lung, liver and kidney damage	0.6	Industrial solvent and chemical manufacturing processes
Dichloroethane (1,2-)	Possible cancer	0.005	Used in manufacture of insecticides and gasoline
Dichloroethylene (1,1-)	Liver and kidney damage	0.007	Used in manufacture of plastics, dyes, perfumes, paints and synthetic organic chemicals
Dichloroethylene (*cis*-1,2-)	Nervous system, liver and circulatory system damage	0.07	Industrial extraction solvent
Dichloroethylene (*trans*-1,2)	Nervous system, liver and circulatory system damage	0.1	Industrial extraction solvent
Dichloropropane (1,2-)	Liver, lung and kidney damage and probable cancer	0.005	Soil fumigant and industrial solvent

FIGURE 13.3. (*continued*)

Contaminant	Health Effect	MCL	Sources
Endrin[3]	Nervous system and kidney damage	0.0002	Insecticide used on cotton, small grains and orchards (cancelled)
Epichlorohydrin	Liver, kidney and lung damage and probable cancer	TT[2]	Epoxy resins and coatings, flocculents used in water treatment systems
Ethylbenzene	Kidney, liver and nervous system damage	0.7	Chemical manufacturing, gasoline and insecticides
Ethylene dibromide (EDB)	Probable cancer	0.00005	Gasoline additive, soil fumigant and solvent (canceled in 1984 but limited uses continue)
Heptachlor	Probable cancer	0.0004	Corn insecticide (cancelled in 1983 for all uses but termite control)
Heptachlor epoxide	Probable cancer	0.0002	(Soil and water organisms convert heptachlor to epoxide)
Lindane	Nervous system, liver and kidney damage	0.0002	Insecticide for pest control in seed, lumber and livestock (most uses restricted in 1983)
Methoxychlor	Nervous system, liver and kidney damage	0.04	Alfalfa and livestock insecticide
Monochlorobenzene	Kidney, liver and nervous system damage	0.1	Pesticide manufacturing, metal cleaner and industrial solvent
Pentachlorophenol	Liver and kidney damage and probable cancer	0.001	Wood preservative and herbicide (nonwood uses banned in 1987)

[3]Phase V proposes changing MCL for endrin to 0.002.

FIGURE 13.3.   (*continued*)

Contaminant	Health Effect	MCL	Sources
Polychlorinated byphenyls (PCBs)	Probable cancer	0.0005	Plasticizers and electrical transformers (banned in 1979)
Styrene	Liver and nervous system damage	0.1	Plastic manufacturing and resins used in water treatment equipment
Tetrachloroethylene	Probable cancer	0.005	Dry cleaning chemical and industrial solvent
Toluene	Kidney, nervous system and lung damage	1	Chemical manufacturing, gasoline additive and industrial solvent
Total trihalomethanes (TTHM): chloroform, bromoform, bromodichloromethane and dibromochloromethane	Possible cancer	0.1	(primarily formed when surface water containing organic matter is treated with chlorine)
Toxaphene	Probable cancer	0.003	Cotton and soybean insecticide/herbicide (canceled in 1982)
2-4-5-TP (Silvex)	Nervous system, liver and kidney damage	0.05	Herbicide on rangelands, sugar cane farms and golf courses (canceled in 1983)
Trichloroethane (1,1,1)	Nervous system problems	0.2	Manufacture of food wrappings and synthetic fibers
Trichloroethylene (TCE)	Possible cancer	0.005	Paint stripper, metal degreaser, and waste from disposal of dry cleaning materials and manufacturing of pesticides, paints, waxes and varnishes

FIGURE 13.3. (*continued*)

Contaminant	Health Effect	MCL	Sources
Vinyl chloride	Possible cancer	0.002	Polyvinyl chloride pipes and solvents used to join them, and industrial waste from manufacture of plastics and synthetic rubber
Xylenes	Liver, kidney and nervous system damage	10	Paint and ink solvent, gasoline refining by-product and component of detergents
Inorganic Chemicals			
Arsenic[4]	Dermal and nervous system toxicity effects	0.05	Geological and pesticide residues, industrial waste and smelter operations
Asbestos	Benign tumors	7 MFL[5]	Natural mineral deposits and asbestos and cement pipes
Barium	Circulatory system damage	2	Natural mineral deposits, oil and gas drilling operations and paint and other industrial substances
Cadmium	Kidney damage	0.005	Natural mineral deposits, metal finishing and corrosion products from plumbing
Chromium	Liver, kidney, skin and digestive system damage	0.1	Natural mineral deposits, metal finishing, textile tanning and the leather industry
Copper (action level = 1.3 mg/L)	Stomach and intestinal distress, Wilson's disease	TT[2]	Corrosion of interior household and building pipes

[4]MCL for arsenic currently under review.
[5]Million fibers per liter (MFL), with fiber length >10 microns.

FIGURE 13.3. (*continued*)

Contaminant	Health Effect	MCL	Sources
Fluoride	Skeletal damage	4	Geological sources, drinking water additives, foods processed with fluorinated water and toothpaste.
Lead (action level = 0.015 mg/L)	Central and peripheral nervous system damage, and kidney damage (highly toxic to infants and pregnant women)	TT[2]	Corrosion of lead solder and brass faucets and fixtures and corrosion of lead service lines
Mercury	Kidney and nervous system damage	0.002	Industrial and chemical manufacturing, fungicide and natural mineral deposits
Nitrate	Methemoglobinemia ("blue baby syndrome")	10	Fertilizers, feedlots, sewage and natural occurrences in soil and mineral deposits
Nitrite	Methemoglobinemia ("blue baby syndrome")	1	(Unstable, rapidly converted to nitrate and prohibited in working metal fluids)
Nitrate and nitrite (combined)	(Not applicable)	10	(Not applicable)
Selenium	Nervous system damage	0.05	Natural mineral deposits and by-products of copper mining and smelting
Radionuclides			
Beta particle and photon activity	Cancer	4 mrem/yr[6]	Radioactive waste, uranium deposits and nuclear facilities
Gross alpha particle activity	Cancer	15 pCi/L[7]	Radioactive waste, uranium deposits and geological and natural sources

[6]A rem is a radiation unit of measure that represents the equivalent dose of ionizing radiation to a target organ in the body. A millirem (mrem) is $\frac{1}{1000}$ of a rem.
[7]A picocurie (pCi) is the quantity of radioactive material that produces 2.22 nuclear transformations per minute.

FIGURE 13.3.   (*continued*)

Contaminant	Health Effect	MCL	Sources
Radium 226/228	Bone cancer	5 pCi/L[7]	Radioactive waste and geological and natural sources
Microbiological			
Giardia lamblia	Stomach cramps and intestinal distress (giardiasis)	TT[2]	Human and animal fecal matter
Legionella	Legionnaires' disease (pneumonia), Pontiac Fever	TT[2]	Water aerosols (such as vegetable misters)
Total coliforms	(Not necessarily disease-causing themselves, coliforms interfere with disinfection and can be indicators of organisms that can cause gastroenteric infections, dysentery, hepatitis, typhoid fever, cholera and other illnesses)	(See Note 8)	Human and animal fecal matter
Turbidity	(Interferes with disinfection)	1.0 NTU (nephelometric turbidity unit)	Erosion, runoff and discharges
Viruses	Gastroenteritis (intestinal distress)	TT[2]	Human and animal fecal matter
Other Substances			
Sodium	Possible increase in blood pressure in susceptible individuals	None (20 mg/L reporting level)[9]	Geological sources and road salting

[8]For large systems (40 or more routine samples per month), no more than 5 percent of the samples can be positive. For small systems (39 or fewer routine samples per month), no more than one sample can be positive. All drinking water samples must be free of fecal coliforms and *Escherichia* coli.
[9]Monitoring is required and data are reported to health officials to protect individuals on highly restricted sodium diets.

The standards for most contaminants have a margin of safety built into them. This means an individual could drink slightly contaminated water for short periods without experiencing serious health consequences. There are exceptions to this general rule: water that contains levels of nitrites, nitrates or microbiological organisms that are greater than the MCLs should *not* be used.

Some contaminants do not have MCLs because there is not enough information to determine safe levels of these contaminants. Instead, the EPA regulates them by requiring suppliers to use certain treatment technologies to control them.

Secondary Drinking Water Standards. The secondary drinking water standards in Figure 13.4 are designed to help people identify contaminated water that has poor taste, odor, appearance or some other characteristic that is undesirable but not a health threat. The EPA recommends these standards to states as reasonable goals, but states are not required to enforce them. Some states have, however, adopted their own regulations for some or all of these contaminants.

Testing and Understanding the Results

If you have a private water source, you should have the water periodically tested according to the guidelines given below. Sometimes the state agency responsible for regulating drinking water quality or the local health department will provide testing services at low or no cost, or a list of certified laboratories (or you can look in the yellow pages of the telephone directory under "Laboratories—Testing" or "Environmental & Ecological Services"). Before you hire a testing laboratory, contact more than one to get an idea of cost and how the sample will be collected and analyzed.

Water quality testing professionals can measure very small levels of a wide variety of contaminants in drinking water. Although the unit of measurement for most chemical contaminants is milligrams per liter (mg/L), test results are sometimes given in parts per million (ppm) or parts per billion (ppb). One ppm is equal to 1 mg/L or 1000 ppb. This means that a test result of 0.005 ppm is the same as 0.005 mg/L or 5 ppb.

There are many different water testing methods, but they do not produce the same quality of results. Ask if the laboratory is EPA certified and be sure that the laboratory can detect the contaminant at the level of the MCL. For example, if a laboratory's method can detect the contaminant at 0.20 ppm, but the MCL is 0.10 ppm, find another laboratory. In this case, the first laboratory's method will not tell you if your water is safe because it only detects levels that are two times above the standard. After you select a laboratory, carefully follow their instructions for collecting and returning the sample.

FIGURE 13.4.   National Secondary Drinking Water Standards[1]

Contaminants and Characteristics	Suggested Levels	Effects
Aluminum	0.05–0.2 mg/L	Discoloration of water
Chloride	250 mg/L	Corrosion of pipes and poor taste of water
Color	15 color units	Poor appearance of water
Copper	1 mg/L	Staining of porcelain and poor taste of water
Corrosivity	noncorrosive	Poor appearance of water and leaching of pipe material (such as lead) into drinking water
Fluoride	2.0 mg/L	Dental fluorosis (a brownish discoloration of the teeth)
Foaming agents	0.5 mg/L	Poor appearance of water
Iron	0.3 mg/L	Staining of laundry and poor taste of water
Manganese	0.05 mg/L	Staining of laundry and poor taste of water
Odor	3 threshold odor number	Poor appearance of water
pH	6.5–8.5	Increase in corrosity of water
Silver	0.1 mg/L	Argyria (discoloration of the skin)
Sulfate	250 mg/L	Laxative effect and poor taste of water
Total dissolved solids (TDS)	500 mg/L	Poor taste of water, risk of cardiovascular disease (possibly related to water softness), corrosivity (related to lead levels in water), damage to plumbing and decreased effectiveness of soaps and detergents
Zinc	5 mg/L	Poor taste of water

[1]Secondary Drinking Water Standards are unenforceable federal guidelines regarding the taste, odor, color and certain other nonaesthetic characteristics of drinking water. The EPA recommends these guidelines to states as reasonable goals, but federal law does not require compliance. States may, however, adopt their own enforceable regulations governing these concerns. To be safe, check your state's drinking water rules.
SOURCE: U.S. EPA (1991).

Testing can be expensive. The costs of screening tests are about $25–$35 each for bacteria and nitrate. A test for lead or other metal also costs about $25–$35 for each substance. A scan for some pesticides or synthetic organic compounds might be about $150–$300.

Make sure that the laboratory or an appropriately trained person helps you understand what the results mean. Staff of local or state agencies that are responsible for water issues and the EPA's Drinking Water Hotline are good sources of assistance (see Appendix A). You can compare your test results to the Drinking Water Standards given in Figures 13.3 and 13.4. Your water is contaminated if the results of any tests on your sample of water exceed the standards. Although contaminated water does not always pose an immediate health threat, you can lower your risks by using an alternate source of drinking and cooking water until the problem is corrected. You will need an expert to advise you about treatment options.

Guidelines for Public Water Supplies

The EPA requires public water suppliers to test the water that goes to consumers; you can request a copy of test results from the supplier. If a contaminant exceeds the standards, the supplier is required to tell the appropriate state agency *and* customers. The water supplier can tell customers through a notice in the newspaper, with an announcement on radio or television or by letter. The notice should explain the problem and potential adverse health effects. It should also explain any precautions that consumers should take and what the water supplier is doing to correct the problem.

Sometimes, problems occur after the water leaves the treatment plant. Some (but not all) contaminants leave visible signs, which are described in Figure 13.5. Report these or any unusual color, taste or odor problems to the water utility.

The utility may decide to conduct extra testing or may recommend that you have the water tested. Compare the results of private or public testing to the MCLs. When test results are above the MCLs, problems exist. Suppliers can correct many problems, but sometimes users must wait until a problem corrects itself naturally. In the fall, for example, the supplier may not be able to remove taste and odor problems caused by decaying leaves or algae.

Consider testing the water in your home for lead, especially if you live in a pre-1950 home. Although public water suppliers test for lead, they only test a small number of houses chosen at random.

Most people naturally assume that their water supplier complies with federal regulations and provides safe water. Unfortunately, this is not always true. Public water suppliers have had a poor record of meeting their notification responsibilities.

FIGURE 13.5.   Signs of Water Problems

Sign	Possible Contaminant

Stained clothes and fixtures
    Red or brown
    Black
    Green or blue
	
	Iron
	Manganese
	Copper

Off-color water
    Cloudy
    Black
    Red
    Brown or yellow
	
	Turbidity (bacteria)
	Hydrogen sulfide and manganese
	Iron
	Tannin from plants

Unusual taste and odor
    Rotten egg
    Metallic
 	
    Salty
    Septic, musty, earthy
    Bleach-like
	
	Hydrogen sulfide
	Corrosive water and metals (such as iron and zinc)
	Chloride and total dissolved solids
	Total coliform bacteria
	Chlorine

Pitted fixtures	Corrosive water that increases the water level of metals such as lead and copper
Deposits on fixtures	Hard water

SOURCE: Adapted with permission from *Determining the Quality of Your Drinking Water,* © NSF International, 3475 Plymouth Road, Ann Arbor, MI 48113.

The Natural Resources Defense Council (NRDC) recently published a report that lists thousands of water supply systems that, according to EPA data, violated drinking water laws in 1991 or 1992. Many violations are relatively minor, but the report highlights weaknesses in the water delivery system. You can get copies of this report and information on drinking water quality in your state from the NRDC. (The address is in appendix A.)

The best course of action that a consumer can take is to ask state officials if the supplier has met reporting requirements and if the water quality meets the required standards. If the supplier does not have a good record, make complaints to the supplier and ask state officials for updates on their efforts to force the supplier to comply with regulations. You may want to consider organizing a community action group to make public your concerns.

Guidelines for Private Water Supplies

There are many conditions that should provoke a homeowner to test private water supplies; these include changes in the taste, odor or appearance of the water. It is especially important to test untreated water from a well less than 30 feet deep, a spring, a river or a lake. Consider testing your water if you live in an area with known or suspected industrial pollution, and always test the quality of a new source of water (such as a well or spring) before you use it. There are differences of opinion on how frequently to test water. Here are some guidelines for testing water from a well or spring:

- **Bacteria**—Test at least once each year and anytime you notice a change in the taste, odor or color of the water. Test once each calendar quarter whenever the quality of the water becomes degraded and test for bacteria whenever you suspect that animal or human wastes are entering the well or spring. Also test after periods of significant rainfall, after flooding and after the spring snowmelt.
- **Nitrates**—Test at least once each year, especially if young children or women of childbearing age drink the water. Test whenever there are nearby potential sources of contamination such as farming, gardening and livestock. Whenever bacterial contamination exists, always test for nitrates since the two contaminants can come from the same sources.
- **Radionuclides and radon**—Test the water for radon if you live in an area where elevated indoor levels exist or in an area where groundwater is an important radon source. Test for other types of radioactivity if you live close to industrial sources or waste storage and disposal areas. If contamination exists, additional testing will be needed until the problem is corrected.
- **Lead and other heavy metals**—At least once, test each tap that supplies water for drinking or cooking and repeat tests until any problems are corrected. Testing for lead is also important if you have a submersible brass pump.
- **Synthetic organic chemicals**—Routine tests are not needed unless you live in an area that has known groundwater contamination. Consider testing when potential sources (such as a landfill, military facility, chemical manufacturer, underground storage tank or industrial development) are nearby. Contact your local or state health department or environmental agency for help in identifying the right chemicals for testing.
- **Readily apparent taste, odor, color and staining problems**—Consider testing the water for possible contaminants listed in Figure 13.5 whenever any of these signs are present.

- **Hardness**—Test after the well is installed and any time the hardness seems to be changing. Soft water is corrosive and can accelerate the removal of lead and other metals from the pipes into the water.

Repeat any test result that is greater than the primary drinking water standard and take corrective action if the second test result is greater than the standard. Contact the local or state health department or environmental agency for help with interpreting test results and identifying corrective actions.

Sometimes, testing shows that contaminants are present in low concentrations—below the drinking water standards. This water is safe to drink, but check these contaminants periodically to be sure that the levels remain low.

Reducing Exposure

All Water Supplies

Check the water distribution system to be sure that piping within and outside the home does not contain lead. According to most building codes, the following materials are acceptable for water pipes inside the home:

- Copper pipe or tube
- Galvanized steel
- ABS or PVC plastic (for cold water only)
- CPVC plastic (for hot or cold water)
- Polyethylene (for cold water only)
- Polybutylene (for hot or cold water)
- Other approved equivalents

Make sure that all fixtures have backflow prevention devices and correct all cross connections to prevent contaminated water from getting into the clean water supply (see Chapter 14 for more information).

Use alternative sources of drinking water (such as bottled water or safe water from a friend or relative) if your water becomes contaminated. Bottled water is not a good long-term alternative to fixing a contaminated well or avoiding a problem with a public supply. It costs more than tap water and does not have to meet the same standards as water from public supplies. Sometimes boiling the water is an adequate short-term solution for some contaminants, but *never* boil water that contains nitrates—boiling concentrates the nitrates and hazardous levels can easily result. Sometimes, local governments supply water to residents if there is a regional contamination problem.

Private Water Supplies

In most places, a local health department regulates household wells. The department typically employs a permit system to oversee the placement and construction of wells. After the installation is complete, the health department usually requires a test for bacterial contamination to make sure that the water is safe for consumption. The permit fee often covers the cost of the test for bacteria and might include testing for other contaminants such as nitrates.

If you have a well or are considering constructing one, there are steps you can take to make sure that the water you drink is safe:

1. **Identify potential sources of contamination**. Make sure that the well is at an adequate distance from septic systems, underground storage tanks and other sources of contamination. The required distances will vary depending on the topography of your lot, soil characteristics and other factors. The Council of American Building Officials (CABO) recommends a minimum horizontal distance of 50 feet between water supply wells and a building sewer, septic tank or disposal field. CABO also recommends a minimum distance of 100 feet between the water-supply well and a seepage pit or cesspool. Check local codes for the requirements in your area and ask your local health department or environmental agency for help in identifying and rating potential sources of contamination. The agency responsible for regulating wells may be able to provide you with records about the depth and construction of your well if you do not have this information.

   Protect your well by employing the following safe practices:

   - Store and dispose of household and lawn care chemicals and wastes properly.
   - Apply fertilizers and pesticides to the yard and garden carefully, using minimum amounts of chemicals; do not dispose of excess chemicals on the ground.
   - Check underground storage tanks that hold home heating oil or gasoline periodically to be sure that there are no leaks.
   - Protect the well from the wastes of livestock, pets and wildlife, and use agricultural practices that reduce erosion and prevent surface runoff.

2. **Make sure that your well is properly constructed**. Shallow wells (less than 30 feet deep) are more easily contaminated than deep wells. Contact the agency responsible for regulating wells for records about the depth and construction of your well if you do not have this

information. Consider replacing a shallow or dug well, because they are easily contaminated.

If you plan to install a well, hire a licensed contractor who works in your area. (You can get names of contractors from your state water well contractor licensing agency or in the yellow pages of your telephone directory under "Water Well Drilling and Services.") Ask to see proof of licensing and check the contractor's references. Also ask your local Better Business Bureau, Chamber of Commerce or responsible agency if complaints have been filed against the contractor.

3. **Operate the well properly**. Test the water periodically and make sure that you understand the test results. Always test the water if it looks, tastes or smells different than usual. Test after replacing or repairing any part of the well system, such as the water pipes, pump or the well itself. Correct problems as needed. If you have a new submersible brass pump, the EPA suggests using an alternative water supply until a test for lead is completed.

Well water that is hard (over 300 mg/L of hardness) will cause a buildup of scale in the plumbing pipes. This scale provides a good place for bacteria to become trapped and grow, and can be lessened by treating the water with chlorine once or twice a year.

Home Water Treatment Devices

A home treatment device can solve a variety of problems, but be wary of door-to-door sales representatives who offer to collect and analyze water samples. Because they have products to sell, the results of their tests may include a recommendation to buy their system. It is better to pay a certified laboratory to do the tests. Whenever a laboratory report comes back with a high result, retest the water to confirm the earlier result. Then contact sales representatives about the most appropriate system, and be sure to get more than one opinion.

The EPA does not approve or endorse home water treatment units. It does, however, require the registration of silver-containing filters that might be used in some units. This registration is needed because the silver acts as a pesticide by inhibiting the growth of bacteria. In this case, EPA registration shows that the manufacturer has proven that the silver will not cause adverse health effects when used as directed. (The registration does not mean that the EPA has tested the filter for its treatment ability.)

Before purchasing any water treatment system, check for proof of performance by an independent testing agency. The National Science Foundation, International (NSF) is an agency that tests and certifies the performance of filtering devices. The NSF seal of approval appears on the devices (and the product packaging) endorsed by the organization. Upon request, the NSF will send (at no charge) a list of vendors of different treatment systems for removing contaminants that rates the effectiveness of the equipment. Another source of information is the Water Quality Association. This is an independent, non-profit organization that represents firms and individuals who produce and sell equipment and services that improve the quality of drinking water. It also answers consumer requests for information at no charge. (Addresses for both organizations are given in Appendix A.)

Most home treatment systems are point-of-use (POU) devices that are installed on individual drinking water taps. They are not large enough to treat the water for an entire house or building. Point-of-entry (POE) systems are devices that are installed on the main water line that serves the house. They treat the entire supply entering the house. The most common POE systems remove iron from water or soften the water, but new technologies are becoming increasingly available to reduce other contaminants.

No products on the market can solve all problems. Most cannot reduce or remove exposure to volatile organic compounds that vaporize from hot water in showers or dishwashers. Figure 13.6 provides a list of water treatment options and the common contaminants they can remove. A brief description of each type of water treatment technology follows.

Water Softeners. Water softeners can effectively reduce the minerals that cause the soap deposits of hard water. Units cost around $1000 and can remove iron and lead. They cannot, however, remove radon, nitrates, pesticides or other synthetic organic contaminants.

Water softeners consist of a tank of resin granules that are coated with sodium ions. As water flows through the resin bed, minerals are removed. The dissolved minerals (such as calcium and magnesium) are attracted to the resin bed and exchange places with the sodium. Over time, the resin bed fills up with contaminants that must be removed. This is done by reversing the flow of the softener and flushing common table salt (or potassium salt) through the bed to regenerate it. The collected mineral contaminants are flushed down the drain.

Water softeners can pose a health risk if the salt that is used for flushing enters the drinking water supply. People who are on sodium-restricted diets may want to hook the softener up to the hot water line only. The unsoftened cold water can then be used for cooking and drinking. A reverse osmosis system and a distillation system are other alternatives. These treatment systems remove from the water sodium ions and a broader range of contaminants than water softeners.

FIGURE 13.6.   Treatment Options for Different Water Problems

Water Contaminant (EPA Standards)	Ion Exchange (Cation) Water Softeners	Ion Exchange (Anion)	Activated Carbon Fibers
Synthetic Organic Chemicals			
Atrazine (.003 mg/L)			X
Benzene (.005 mg/L)			X
Lindane (.0002 mg/L)			X
Methoxychlor (.04 mg/L)			X
Trichloroethylene (TCE) (.005 mg/L)			X
Total trihalomethanes (TTHMS) (.1 mg/L)			X
Synthetic Inorganic Chemicals			
Arsenic (.05 mg/L)		X	
Asbestos (7 million fibers greater than 10 microns in length/L)			
Barium (2 mg/L)	X		
Cadmium (.005 mg/L)	X		
Chromium (.1 mg/L)	X		
Fluoride (4 mg/L)			
Lead (.015 mg/L)	X		
Mercury, inorganic (.002 mg/L)			X
Nitrate (10 mg/L)		X	
Radium (5 pCi/L)	X		
Radon (10,000 pCi/L)			X
Bacteria			
Coliform bacteria (1/100 ml)			
Fecal coliform (none allowed)			
Problems Related to Aesthetics			
Metallic taste (caused by iron, manganese, copper oxide or sulfide)	X		
Objectionable taste			X
Soap residue	X		
Scale buildup	X		
Objectionable odor (such as a rotten egg or chlorine smell)			X
Color (reddish brown or black)	X	X	X

NOTE: The table above shows some, but not all, treatment systems that can remove the contaminants checked in each column. The EPA drinking water primary standards are listed next to each contaminant. If the contaminant level in your water is greater than the standard, consider purchasing an appropriate an appropriate treatment system. Ask local water treatment professionals for help with your specific problem.
SOURCE: Adapted by permission of Water Quality Association, P.O. Box 606, Lisle, IL 60532.

FIGURE 13.6. *(continued)*

Solid Block & Precoat Adsorption Filters	Reverse Osmosis	Distillation	Aeration	Disinfection	Oxidation and Filtration	Chlorination
Synthetic Organic Chemicals						
X	X					
X			X			
X		X				
X		X				
X			X			
X			X			
Synthetic Inorganic Chemicals						
	X	X				
X	X	X				
	X	X				
	X	X				
	X	X				
	X	X				
X	X	X				
X	X	X				
	X	X				
	X	X				
X			X			
Bacteria						
		X		X		X
		X		X		X
Problems Related to Aesthetics						
	X	X			X	X
X	X	X				
X					X	
X	X	X			X	X

Filtration. Activated carbon filtration (also called activated charcoal adsorption or carbon filtration) uses specially treated charcoal grains to remove many chemicals such as pesticides, solvents, chlorine compounds and mercury, and related odors and tastes. Carbon filters cannot remove hardness minerals, most heavy metals or bacteria.

The effectiveness of the treatment depends on the size and type of equipment, type and degree of contamination and maintenance of the unit. Activated carbon must be renewed regularly and properly maintained to prevent microbes from growing in the filters. As noted above, some filters are treated with silver to inhibit the growth of bacteria.

Other filtration units are available to remove a variety of contaminants. Sand filters can remove sediment, whereas sand coated with magnesium oxide can remove sediment, iron and manganese. Potassium permanganate can remove iron, manganese and sulfur. Calcite can remove sediment and adjust pH to keep water from being too corrosive.

Reverse Osmosis Systems. Reverse osmosis systems use a membrane to remove contaminants as water is forced at high pressure through the membrane. The material for the membrane can be cellulose, acetate or nylon. Because the membranes eventually become clogged, they must be replaced periodically.

Reverse osmosis systems are best at removing heavy metals such as lead and other inorganic contaminants such as minerals, iron, chloride, fluoride and nitrate. When a carbon filter is added, the system can remove many synthetic organic compounds (such as solvents), pesticide residues and tastes and odors related to these substances.

Although reverse osmosis can remove bacteria and suspended solids, this option is not recommended for this purpose since the membranes are easily clogged. When bacteria and solids are present, the water should be disinfected to kill the bacteria and prefiltered before using the reverse osmosis unit.

The effectiveness of the unit depends on the size and type of equipment, type and degree of contamination, system pressure and maintenance of the unit.

Distillation. Distillation systems boil water to form steam that condenses back into water as it cools. These units kill bacteria and remove dissolved minerals but are not as effective on chlorine compounds and volatile organics such as chloroform and benzene, which reenter the water as the distilled water vapor cools. These systems are slow, require frequent cleaning and can be expensive to operate. The effectiveness of the unit depends on the size and type of equipment, type and degree of contamination and maintenance of the unit.

Drinking Water Checklist

Questions To Ask	Response	What Does a "Yes" Mean?
All Water Supplies		
Does any part of the water distribution system contain lead? (Ask the local water supplier or health department for assistance.)	**Yes No** ❏ ❏	Old houses (pre-1950) are more likely than new houses to have water pipes made of lead, a soft, gray metal that is easy to scratch. Houses built after 1950 could still have lead-contaminated water because of lead in solder and brass fixtures. Regardless of the age of your house, test the water for lead. Lead can cause serious health effects, including problems related to learning and the central nervous system in children, and high blood pressure in adults.
Do you live in an area where radon is a concern in the water? Do you have high radon levels in your home?	**Yes No** ❏ ❏	Both of these are reasons to test for radon in water. Contact your local health department to learn more about radon levels in your area. Radon is believed to increase the risk of cancer.
Does each fixture have a backflow prevention device? (Look for a gap of at least one inch between the rim of the sink and the end of the faucet.)	**Yes No** ❏ ❏	If sinks and other fixtures have backflow prevention devices, dirty water is not likely to flow back into the clean water supply. If these are missing, bacteria and other contaminants can contaminate the water.

Questions To Ask	Response	What Does a "Yes" Mean?
Public Water Supplies		
Are you concerned about the quality of your drinking water? Has the taste, color, odor or any other characteristic of your water changed over time?	Yes No ❏ ❏	Contact your local water supplier for information about the quality of your water. The public water supplier must give you information about the level of contaminants in the water and must tell you if the water is being tested according to EPA requirements.
Private Water Supplies		
Is your well close to a septic system, underground storage tank or other source of contamination (such as fertilizers, pesticides and livestock)?	Yes No ❏ ❏	A well that is too close to one of these sources can become contaminated. Check your local codes for distance requirements in your area.
Is your well water hard?	Yes No ❏ ❏	Hard water can cause a buildup of scales on the inside of pipes, thus providing a good place for bacteria to grow and multiply. Lower the chances of bacterial contamination by treating the water with chlorine once or twice a year.

Questions To Ask	Response	What Does a "Yes" Mean?
Are you considering installing a well or buying a house with a well?	Yes No ❏ ❏	Hire a licensed water well contractor to install your well. Avoid dug wells because they are easily contaminated. Always test the water before purchasing a house with a well and ask a water well contractor to examine the well. Hire a qualified laboratory to do any water tests.
Do you have water test results that are greater than EPA standards and guidelines?	Yes No ❏ ❏	Correct problems as soon as possible. Use an alternative supply of water until problems are corrected. Do not use water that has bacteria or nitrate contamination. Test the water a second time to confirm the first results before buying a water treatment system or taking any other corrective action.

Summary Chart for Household Plumbing and Septic Systems

Topic	*Comments*
Description	Household wastewater contains disease-causing organisms such as bacteria and viruses. Wastewater can also contain high levels of nitrates and other chemicals.
Health Effects	Contact with contaminated wastewater can cause illness in infants, children and adults.
Sources	Household wastewater is used water from kitchens, bathrooms, laundry rooms and other household sources. Problems can result when improperly installed or leaking plumbing fixtures or septic systems allow wastewater to back up in the house or to collect on the ground.
Testing	*All Houses.* Check the plumbing system by running water for several minutes and flushing toilets to determine if the water drains properly. Slow drainage is a sign of potential problems. *Existing Septic Systems.* An improperly functioning system might need a dye test. *New Construction with Septic Systems.* A soil scientist must evaluate the lot size and soil characteristics to determine if a property can support a septic system.
Reducing Exposure	*All Houses.* Check all plumbing fixtures to be sure that each one has a working trap. Correct any problems as soon as possible and limit the use of chemicals that are flushed into the plumbing system. Contact the local health or public works department for help with sewage backup problems related to poor drainage or the public collection system. *Existing Septic Systems.* Do not put materials that do not decompose easily into the tank. Limit the amount of laundry to one or two loads at a time. Check the tank each year and hire a licensed wastewater hauler to clean out the tank every three to five years. *New Construction with Septic Systems.* Hire a licensed professional to design and install the plumbing and septic system.

CHAPTER
FOURTEEN

Household Plumbing and Septic Systems

A 2-year-old girl from the Kenny Brick neighborhood just outside of Albuquerque, New Mexico, may have become critically ill as a result of drinking contaminated well water or playing in sewage. The girl's doctors believe that her symptoms could have been caused by Escherichia coli *bacteria that can be spread through contact with fecal material. As a result of her illness, the child has had her large intestine removed, undergone kidney dialysis and been hospitalized for over one month.*

Health officials believe that about one-third of the 350 to 400 homes in the neighborhood have failing sewage disposal systems that have caused high nitrate levels in the groundwater, sewage odors in water from the wells and the backup of liquid wastes in toilets. The foul smell of sewage fills the air.

The neighborhood was built on clay soil that has become so saturated with sewage that it cannot absorb additional liquid wastes discharged by the septic tanks. Contaminated water (called gray water) can be found throughout the neighborhood. The problem is so severe that even pumping septic tanks two times each month cannot provide relief.

The solution is a $1.6 million construction project to eliminate the cesspools and septic tanks and bring sewers into the neighborhood. Health *officials say this is not an isolated problem and believe that home septic systems are contaminating water throughout the South Valley around Albuquerque.*

As reported in *The Albuquerque Tribune,* October 16 and 18, 1993, and *The Albuquerque Journal,* October 16, 1993.

As reported by Lynette Giesen, Environmental Health Scientist, Bernalillo County Environmental Health Department, November 1993.

What Is Household Wastewater and Why Is It a Hazard?

All houses that have running water must have safe and sanitary systems to remove the used water (called *wastewater* or *domestic sewage*). Wastewater includes water produced by flushing toilets, washing dishes or clothing, bathing and engaging in other day-to-day activities. About 300 gallons of wastewater are produced daily by the average family of four. Most of this water passes through the household plumbing system on its way to final treatment and disposal.

Potential contaminants in household wastewater include bacteria, viruses, protozoa and other disease-causing organisms (pathogens), and nitrates and other toxic chemicals. Anyone who comes into contact with these contaminants can become ill with a severe or life-threatening disease.

Contact with wastewater can occur when a household's plumbing system does not work properly. Potential problems include improper plumbing traps, backflow, clogged drains and wastewater backup (which may be caused when the wastewater removal system does not work properly).

The Household Plumbing System

The household plumbing system is composed of several separate systems that bring water into and remove wastes from the home (see Figure 14.1). The water supply system brings water into the home through pipes that carry hot and cold water and are typically one inch or less in diameter. The source of the water could be a private well or a public water supply (see Chapter 13 for information on drinking water quality).

The drainage system consists of a network of pipes that collect used water from fixtures and eventually carries the used water outside of the home. The vent piping system connects to the drainage system, but it carries air, not water. The heart of the drainage and vent piping systems is the soil stack, a large pipe (about four inches in diameter) that runs from the house sewer connection straight up through the roof. The upper part of the soil stack is called the main vent and is left open to the air. All plumbing fixtures close to the stack drain

FIGURE 14.1.   Household Plumbing System

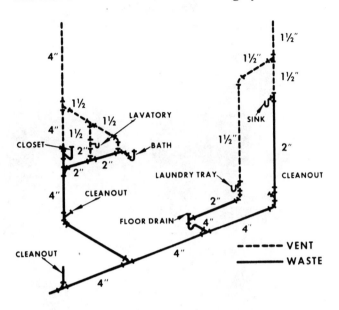

SOURCE: U.S DHEW, 1976 (reprinted 1979)

directly into it. A sink or other fixture that is located away from the soil stack may drain into a smaller vertical pipe called a waste stack that connects to the house sewer and runs through the roof of the house. The upper ends of the stacks are open to make sure that the sewage drains properly, water stays in the traps and sewer gases can escape the house. At the base of the soil stack there is an accessible opening for removing obstructions called a cleanout plug.

The household plumbing system is completed by a pipe called a building drain that connects the soil stack to the house sewer. The house sewer runs from the outside of the house to the public sewer system and treatment plant or to an on-site system (such as a septic tank). The sewer line usually has a cleanout plug outside of the house.

The household plumbing system must be installed according to strict building codes. The codes have changed over time, however, and practices that were once allowed may not be acceptable today.

Sources of Problems and Methods for Reducing Exposure

Plumbing Traps. All fixtures in the house should be equipped with plumbing traps to keep sewer gases from entering the living area. A trap can

**FIGURE 14.2a.   Plumbing Traps—Example of
Permitted U-trap**

SOURCE: U. S. DHEW, 1976 (reprinted 1979).

be either separate from the fixture or built into it. The typical trap on a sink or
basin is a U-shaped section of pipe that has about two to four inches of water
in it (see Figure 14.2). As long as water fills the bottom of the U, the pipe is
closed and gases cannot pass through it. The water that stays in the toilet bowl
serves the same purpose.

    If there are sewer odors in the home, check the trap to be sure that it has
enough water and look for S-shaped traps. Check local building codes to see
if S-shaped traps are allowed—even if they are permitted, consider replacing
them, because they are difficult to seal and ventilate properly. The main vent
and the waste stack could also be sources of odors and should be checked for
obstructions.

FIGURE 14.2b. **Examples of S-traps That Are Not Permitted in Most Building Codes**

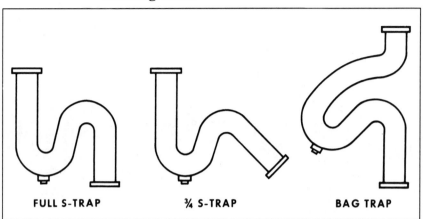

FULL S-TRAP   ¾ S-TRAP   BAG TRAP

Sometimes a "glugging" sound occurs right after a fixture empties. The noise is caused when extra air is sucked down the pipe with the wastewater. This is an indication that the venting system is inadequate and that there may not be enough water in the trap to keep sewer gases out of the living space. Try to reseal the trap by pouring a cup of water into the trap just after the noise stops.

Backflow. Backflow is the flow of contaminated water or other unwanted materials into the drinking water system. Backflow can be attributed to several conditions, including loss of the water seal in the trap, vent pipes that are too small or improperly installed, negative pressure in the plumbing system or cross connections (which are any physical connections or arrangements between the drinking water supply and another piping system that could result in a flow from one system to the other).

The most common backflow prevention devices are air gaps that prevent a cross connection between the water supply pipes and a sink or basin. There should be a gap of at least one inch between the end of the faucet where water exits and the rim of the sink (see Figure 14.3) to keep wastewater from entering the clean water supply when the sink overflows. Figure 14.3 also shows a sink that does not have an air gap. This problem is typically found in older homes with original fixtures.

Vacuum breakers are backflow-prevention devices that are required at any water-supply outlet with a hose connection or at outlets that could be submerged and are not protected by air gaps. Vacuum breakers are installed on hose bibb outlets, some solar or storage tanks and some plumbing fixtures.

FIGURE 14.3.   Sinks and Backflow Protection

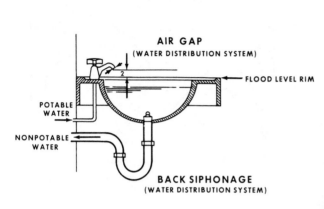

SOURCE: U. S. DHEW, (1976, reprinted 1979).

Another example of a cross connection is shown in Figure 14.4. Here, waters from a city system and a private polluted well are connected by a valve. Contaminated water can enter the clean water supply if the valve is open or leaking or if negative pressure is created in the city water system.

Wastewater Backup. Any time wastewater enters the living space, a potentially serious problem exists that requires prompt action and thorough cleanup. The immediate threat is the transmission of disease from handling contaminated materials, but the growth of mold and deterioration of building materials are additional concerns. (Some tips for cleaning flooded areas are given in Chapter 8.) If you have wastewater backup problems, also contact your local health department for instructions specific to your particular situation.

There are some wastewater backup problems that buyers can recognize when they are evaluating a property. However, sometimes wastewater overflows are simply unpreventable acts of nature. Some of the most frustrating experiences occur in floodplain areas where backup problems are typical during periods of heavy rain. Although flood insurance covers financial losses,

FIGURE 14.4.   Example of a Cross Correction

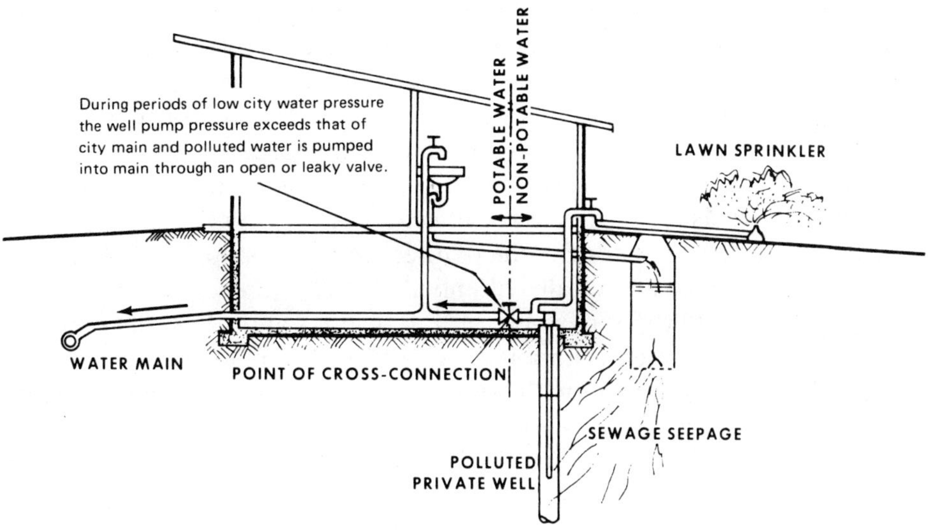

During periods of low city water pressure the well pump pressure exceeds that of city main and polluted water is pumped into main through an open or leaky valve.

POTABLE WATER | NON-POTABLE WATER

LAWN SPRINKLER

WATER MAIN   POINT OF CROSS-CONNECTION

SEWAGE SEEPAGE

POLLUTED PRIVATE WELL

SOURCE: U. S. DHEW (1976, reprinted 1979).

personal items are not easily replaced and the cleanup can be overwhelmingly unpleasant. Carefully consider the purchase of a home in these areas.

Rapid residential growth in an area can cause serious backup problems if needed sewer pipe replacements are not made. (For example, growth in the suburbs can adversely affect older residential areas en route to the treatment facility.) Another cause of periodic backup problems in entire neighborhoods is a pump failure in a lift station or overloading of the lift station.

A seasonal high groundwater table could cause periodic backup problems in homes that are served by private sewage disposal systems. Many communities have problems only during periods of heavy rain when public sewers that handle both domestic and storm wastewater get overloaded. Backup problems due to rainwater seepage (called infiltration) into the sewer pipes also occur in communities with separate sanitary sewers that are old and deteriorating.

Buyers can protect themselves against these hazards to some extent by asking the local health department or public works department if there is a history of wastewater backup in the neighborhood they are considering.

Clogged Drains. The most common cause of clogged drains is simply the accumulation of grease, hair and solid objects that won't dissolve in water.

When a sink drain or toilet is clogged, first try using a plunger. Empty most of the water, but leave enough to cover the rubber end. If the plunger does not unclog the drain within five minutes of effort, try using a plumber's snake (also called a cleanout auger) that can be purchased at a plumbing or hardware store. This tool is made of flexible metal in different lengths, and it is pushed into the drain to loosen and break up the clog. (A similar tool is used to unblock a sewer line.) Consult a book on home repairs when using these tools to maximize the effort and minimize the mess. The main stack rarely clogs, but none of the fixtures above the stoppage will drain if it does clog. In this situation, call a plumber!

Proper cleaning of any buckets and tools that come into contact with wastewater is important to prevent potential diseases. Wash interior contaminated surfaces with hot soapy water, followed by a rinse with a diluted bleach solution of 1.5 cups of bleach to one gallon of water. (Test a small area to be sure that the bleach will not harm any surfaces.) Wear rubber or latex gloves and use adequate ventilation.

Whenever you consider buying a house, always check the drains. This can be done easily and quickly. Simply turn on each water faucet and shower head and flush each toilet. If the water moves slowly, problems exist. Before signing a contract, call a plumber for an opinion about the problem and remedy.

Septic Systems

About 25 percent of all Americans use on-site septic systems for the disposal of household wastewater. Although a properly designed, located and maintained septic system can adequately treat household wastewater, malfunctioning systems pose serious problems, including the following:

- Contamination of groundwater and wells that supply drinking water
- Contamination of nearby lakes and streams
- Pooling of wastewater on the property

Designated Function of a Septic System

A septic system has two main parts (see Figure 14.5): the septic tank and the absorption field (also called the drainfield). The septic tank is a large storage tank that is typically buried in the ground at some distance from the house. The wastewater is partially broken down by bacteria as it drains into the tank and separates into three layers. The top layer is a scum that contains grease and

FIGURE 14.5.   Household Septic System

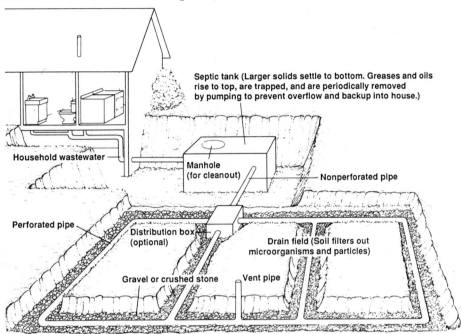

Septic tank (Larger solids settle to bottom. Greases and oils rise to top, are trapped, and are periodically removed by pumping to prevent overflow and backup into house.)

Household wastewater

Manhole (for cleanout)

Nonperforated pipe

Perforated pipe

Distribution box (optional)

Drain field (Soil filters out microorganisms and particles)

Gravel or crushed stone

Vent pipe

SOURCE: G. Tyler Miller, Jr. 1994. *Living in the Environment,* 8th ed. © 1994 Wadsworth Publishing Co., Belmont, CA. Used with permission.

lightweight solids that float. The middle layer contains water, detergent, solids suspended in the water and dissolved materials. About half of the solids and scum are broken down by the bacteria into a liquid and gas. The remaining solid material settles to the bottom of the tank and over time, the settled sludge and scum fill the tank.

Each time wastewater flows into the septic tank, an equal amount of liquid (called effluent) is forced through a network of pipes (also called a finger system) out the other end of the tank and into the absorption field (the part of the ground that receives and filters the effluent). Bacteria in the soil digest the solids and potential disease-causing organisms as the effluent trickles into or evaporates from the soil.

PVC pipes with drainage holes are typically used for the drainfield. (State and local specifications may allow the use of other materials, such as clay or concrete tile). One common drainfield design involves placing the pipes into gravel-filled trenches, but other designs (such as above grade systems) are available to overcome problems with space, ground slope and soil type.

Sources of Problems and Methods for Reducing Exposure

Buying a House with a Septic System. Before you buy a house with a septic system, learn as much as you can about the drainage of the lot. Contact the local agency that handles the permits for septic systems, and ask about drainage problems in the neighborhood and if a drawing of the septic tank and absorption field is available. Another source of flooding information is the county or regional soil and water conservation district office.

If possible, look at prospective homes during the rainy season. Whenever the ground has moisture, it is more difficult for the absorption field to process the wastewater. Water collecting in low areas or ponding on the lot can be a sign of trouble. A problem definitely exists if you know that the source of the collected water is the drainfield.

Buying a Lot and Installing a Septic System. Before you buy land that requires a septic system, get a professional opinion from a soil scientist or health department to determine if the site is suitable for a septic system.

State and local governments regulate the design and location of septic systems. You must have a permit (usually issued by the local health department) to install a septic system. The permit application typically involves two steps:

1. The department will ask for a soil test. In some areas, the local health department staff will collect a soil sample and determine if the soil is adequate for a septic system. In other areas, the home-owner must hire a soil scientist to check the soil and location to determine how much waste the soil can process. Sometimes, the soil test might include a percolation test to measure how fast water drains through the soil. (Many health departments no longer accept the percolation test.)
2. The health department might ask for a copy of the house plans in order to determine the proper size of the septic system. The home-owner then has a system designed according to the minimum requirements of the local health department. The completed design is submitted to the health department for approval.

Construction can begin after the health department approves the plan. To minimize the likelihood of problems, hire a licensed septic system installer to do the work. During construction, the health department staff will perform an inspection to make sure the work is done properly. When problems occur, the health department can delay the installation schedule until any problems are resolved to the department's satisfaction.

System Design and Location. The septic tank and absorption field must be large enough to process the wastes generated by the household. The minimum capacity required by most building codes for a septic tank ranges from 750 gallons for a single-family home with one or two bedrooms to 1500 gallons for a home with five or six bedrooms.

A good location for a septic tank is one that has the right soil, the proper slope and enough land for the absorption field. The septic tank and absorption field should never discharge directly or indirectly into rivers, streams, creeks, ponds or lakes. The best soil is a combination of sand, silt and clay. Soil that has too much clay can push the wastewater to the surface if it drains too slowly. Sandy soil can let the wastewater pass through too quickly. This means the bacteria might not be filtered out before passing on to groundwater. Routinely wet soils are not suitable because the moisture in the soil will keep the wastewater from seeping through the ground. Septic systems are not suitable for floodplain soils.

Septic systems are not suitable where the ground slopes more than 12 to 15 percent or where there is less than 24 inches of soil between the surface and an impermeable layer. The ideal slope for the installation of a septic system is about 2 to 6 percent. Sometimes, hillside designs (step-down systems) can be used with steep slopes, but they are more costly and harder to install than regular systems. Whenever the water table is too close to the surface, the wastewater can be pushed to the surface of the ground, or it can migrate more easily to contaminate groundwater. State and local codes may have somewhat different specifications for acceptable ground slope and soil depth.

The lot must be large enough to accommodate the absorption field and meet separation requirements to water supplies, streams, buildings and other structures. Absorption fields that are too small may not have adequate capacity for the daily loading rate. Figure 14.6 shows the minimum recommended distances between the parts of the septic system and other structures developed by the Council of American Building Officials (CABO) for its model code for one-family and two-family homes. Local codes may differ and some counties require a minimum lot size (usually five acres) for new septic systems. To prevent damaging or blocking the distribution lines for the absorption field, do not build structures or plant trees over the septic system. Also, downspouts and gutter drains should be drained away from the field.

System Operation and Maintenance. Although the septic system is usually constructed below ground, the system should not be installed and forgotten. Proper maintenance and operation are necessary to avoid problems that might require the replacement of the system. The following precautions will help ensure a healthy system.

FIGURE 14.6.   Minimum Distances Between the Parts of the Septic System and Other Structures

Structure	Building Sewer[2]	Septic Tank	Disposal Field
Building or parts of the building[3]	2 feet	5 feet	8 feet
Water supply well	50 feet[4]	50 feet	50 feet
Stream	50 feet	50 feet	50 feet
Large tree		10 feet	
Seepage pit or cesspool		5 feet	5 feet
Disposal field		5 feet	4 feet[5]
Domestic water line	1 foot	5 feet	5 feet
Distribution box			5 feet

[1]These guidelines come from the *CABO One And Two Family Dwelling Code;* local and state regulations may be different.
[2]The building sewer is the pipe that carries sewage from the collection point to the public or private sewer or individual sewage disposal system.
[3]This includes covered or uncovered porches and steps, roofed patios, carports, covered walks, covered driveways, breezeways and similar structures.
[4]The distance for metal pipes can be reduced to 25 feet when approved piping is used.
[5]Add an additional two feet for each added foot of depth that is more than one foot below the bottom of the drain line.
SOURCE: *CABO One And Two Family Dwelling Code.*©1992, Council of American Building Officials 5203 Leesburg Pike, Falls Church, VA. Adapted with permission.

All household wastewater should go into the septic tank. Many people mistakenly think they are saving their tanks by letting laundry wastewater bypass the septic tank. In some households, for example, laundry water is released directly onto the ground. Sometimes the laundry water is routed to a sump pump that discharges to the ground. (Because the sump pump does not treat the water, this practice has the same effects as a direct discharge.) With a few precautions, a system that is properly designed, located and maintained will be able to process all household wastes. Bypassing the tank can contaminate the soil and surface and groundwater, and is a violation of state and local codes.

Another common practice that should be avoided is discharging water from the sump pump to the septic system. This will overload the system and is also a violation of state and local codes. In an area without sewers, water from the sump pump should be discharged to a drainage ditch far enough away from the house to not recirculate back to the foundation.

In a new septic tank, bacterial action will occur naturally as the tank receives wastes and it is not necessary to add a "starter" product to the tank to begin the process. Although a properly operating septic system can handle normal amounts of detergents, bleach, toilet bowl deodorizer and cleaner, drain cleaner and other household chemicals, limiting the use of these products will help protect groundwater.

Do not add the following materials to the septic system: grease, coffee grounds, ground wastes from a garbage disposal, disposable diapers, sanitary napkins, paper towels, facial tissue and cigarette butts. They do not decompose easily and can build up in the tank and plug the inlet or the soil absorption field.

Doing the laundry can add a large amount of water to the tank in a short amount of time. Minimize problems by using phosphate-free detergent and washing only full loads of laundry. Spread the washing out over an entire week by not washing more than one to two loads on a single day. Do not wash during or right after a heavy rain. Other water conservation strategies include repairing leaky faucets and toilet tanks, and using water-saving models of devices such as faucets, toilets and showerheads.

Check the tank once each year to determine if it needs cleaning (or hire a licensed waste hauler to do this). A septic tank usually requires pumping every three to five years, but in some cases more frequent pumping is needed. (Do not enter the septic tank, because it contains toxic and flammable gases that can be lethal.)

A dye test should be conducted on an existing septic system if drainage problems are suspected. During this test, a harmless dye is added to sources of wastewater (such as toilets, washing machines or sinks). The dye becomes part of the effluent and can be seen wherever the wastewater goes. Therefore, if colored water is seen in a ditch, it means that the effluent is directly or indirectly being discharged into this ditch.

Signs of a malfunctioning Septic System. Look for the following signs to determine if potential problems exist:

- Wastewater odors outside the home may indicate the presence of a nearby discharge source or pooled septic system effluent. Odors inside the home may mean that a wastewater plumbing line is clogged, a drain trap is working improperly or a vent stack is plugged.

- The presence of lush grass and spongy soil over the absorption field means that the soil is filled to capacity with effluent.
- Pooled or ponded "gray" water over the absorption field is usually a sign of a malfunctioning septic system.
- Sluggish or backed up drains may indicate a clogged sewer line, full tank or saturated absorption field.

 Household Plumbing Septic System Problem Checklist

Questions To Ask	Response	What Does a "Yes" Mean?
Plumbing System and Traps		
Do you notice a "glugging" sound when you use fixtures?	Yes No ❑ ❑	A dry trap could be the cause. Flush water after the sound stops. (If the sound does not stop, contact a plumber.)
Are there any fixtures with S-shaped traps or no traps?	Yes No ❑ ❑	S-shaped traps can allow the backflow of wastewater and sewer gas odors. Replace these traps with U-shaped traps and install U-shaped traps on any fixture that does not have a trap.
Are there any fixtures without air gaps?	Yes No ❑ ❑	Fixtures without air gaps should be corrected because they do not stop contaminated water from flowing into clean water.
Have you had a problem with a cross connection or been told that a cross connection exists?	Yes No ❑ ❑	Eliminate these connections to prevent potential water contamination.

Questions To Ask	Response	What Does a "Yes" Mean?
Septic System		
Is flooding a problem on your lot?	Yes No ❑ ❑	Flooding indicates that the soil does not drain quickly. Septic systems are likely to have problems in these areas.
Does there appear to be good surface drainage on the lot?	Yes No ❑ ❑	Good surface drainage will assist in the proper function of the septic system.
Does the ground slope away from the house?	Yes No ❑ ❑	Ground that slopes away from the house assists in the drainage of rainwater. Slopes of 2 to 6 percent are suitable for septic systems. (Lots with greater slopes may be suitable with special absorption field designs.) A lot with a very steep slope or a lot with ground that slopes into the house is not suitable for septic systems.
Is the drainfield outlined by lush green grass? Does the lot have an odor typical of wastewater? Is the ground spongy even if there has not been a recent rain?	Yes No ❑ ❑	A "yes" to any of these questions means that the absorption field may not be working properly. Ask a qualified professional to examine the situation.

| Is the septic system more than ten years old? | **Yes No** ❏ ❏ | With good installation and care, the average life span of a septic system can be 15 to 20 years. This average depends on many factors. When a home that you are considering buying has a septic system that is more than ten years old, have the system checked by a qualified professional before you purchase the home and ask to see the previous owner's maintenance records. |
| Has it been more than five years since the septic system was pumped? | **Yes No** ❏ ❏ | Septic systems usually require pumping every three to five years. Regular and frequent pumping prevents early failure of the septic system. |

Appendix A

Information Sources

Environmental Protection Agency Regional Offices

EPA Headquarters
401 M Street. SW
Washington, D.C. 20460

EPA Region 1
JFK Building
Boston, MA 02203
(CT, MA, ME, NH, RI, VT)

EPA Region 2
26 Federal Plaza
New York, NY 10278
(NJ, NY)

EPA Region 3
841 Chestnut Street
Philadelphia, PA 19107
(DC, DE, MD, PA, VA, WV)

EPA Region 4
345 Courtland Street, NE
Atlanta, GA 30365
(AL, FL, GA, KY, MS, NC, SC, TN)

EPA Region 5
77 W. Jackson Boulevard.
Chicago, IL 60604-3507
(IL, IN, MN, OH, WI)

EPA Region 6
1445 Ross Avenue
Dallas, TX 75202-2733
(AR, LA, NM, OK, TX)

EPA Region 7
726 Minnesota Avenue
Kansas City, KS 66101
(IA, KS, MO, NE)

EPA Region 8
One Denver Place
999 18th Street, Suite 500
Denver, CO 80202-2405
(CO, MT, ND, SD, UT, WY)

EPA Region 9
75 Hawthorn Street
San Francisco, CA 94105
(AZ, CA, HI, NV)

EPA Region 10
1200 Sixth Avenue
Seattle, WA 98101
(AK, ID, OR, WA)

State Health, Environment or Natural Resource Agencies

Alabama

Environmental Management Department
1751 Congressman W.L. Dickinson Drive
Montgomery, AL 36130
205-271-7700

Alaska

Environmental Conservation Department
410 Willoughby, Suite 105
Juneau, AK 99811-1795
907-465-2600
(contains Environmental Health and
Environmental Quality divisions)

Arizona

Health Services Department
1740 W. Adams
Phoenix, AZ 85007
602-542-1024

Environmental Quality Department
3033 N. Central
Phoenix, AZ 85012
602-257-6917

Arkansas

Health Department
4815 W. Markham
Little Rock, AR 72205-3867
501-661-2111

Pollution Control and Ecology
Department
P.O. Box 8913
Little Rock, AR 72219
501-562-7444

California

Health Services Department
714 P Street
P.O. Box 942732
Sacramento, CA 94234-7320
916-322-2040

Environmental Protection Agency
555 Capitol Mall, Suite 235
Sacramento, CA 95814
916-445-3846

Colorado

State Health Department
4300 Cherry Creek Drive
Denver, CO 80222-1530
303-692-2000

Natural Resources Department
1313 Sherman Street, Room 718
Denver, CO 80202
303-866-3311

Connecticut

Health Services Department
150 Washington Street
Hartford, CT 06106
203-566-2038

Environmental Protection Department
79 Elm Street
Hartford, CT 06106
203-424-3001

Delaware

Health and Social Services Department
Public Health Division
Jesse Cooper Building
P.O. Box 637
Dover, DE 19903
302-739-4701

Natural Resources and Environmental
Control Department
89 Kings Highway
P.O. Box 1401
Dover, DE 19903
302-739-4403

District of Columbia

Public Health Commission
1660 L Street, NW
Washington, D.C. 20036
202-673-7700

Public Works Department
2000 14th Street, NW, 6th Floor
Washington, D.C. 20009
202-939-8000

Florida

Health and Rehabilitative Services Department
1317 Winewood Boulevard
Building E, Room 227
Tallahassee, FL 32399-0700
904-487-1111

Environmental Protection Department
Office of the Secretary
3900 Commonwealth Boulevard
Tallahassee, FL 32399-3000
904-488-4805

Georgia

Human Resources Department
Public Health Division
2 Peachtree Street NW
Room 7-300
Atlanta, GA 30303
404-657-2700

Natural Resources Department
205 Butler Street SE, Suite 1252
Atlanta, GA 30334
404-656-3500

Hawaii

Health Department
1250 Punch Bowl Street
P.O. Box 3378
Honolulu, HI 96801
808-586-4400

Land and Natural Resources Department
P.O. Box 621
Honolulu, HI 96809
808-587-0404

Idaho

Health and Welfare Department
450 W. State Street, 10th Floor
P.O. Box 83720
Boise, ID 83720-0036
208-334-5500

Environmental Quality Division
1410 N. Hilton
Boise, ID 83706-1290
208-334-5840

Illinois

Public Health Department
535 W. Jefferson Street
Springfield, IL 62761
217-782-4977

Environmental Protection Agency
P.O. Box 19276
Springfield, IL 62794
217-782-3397

Indiana

Health Department
1330 W. Michigan Street
P.O. Box 1964
Indianapolis, IN 46206
317-633-8400

Environmental Management
Department
100 N. Senate Avenue
P.O. Box 6015
Indianapolis, IN 46206-6015
317-232-8162

Iowa

Public Health Department
Lucas State Office Building
Des Moines, IA 50319
515-281-5605

Natural Resources Department
Wallace State Office Building
Des Moines, IA 50319
515-281-5385

Kansas

Health and Environmental
Department
Landon State Office Building
900 SW Jackson Street, Suite 620
Topeka, KS 66612
913-296-1522

Kentucky

Human Resources Cabinet
Health Services Department
275 E. Main Street
Frankfort, KY 40621
502-564-3970

Natural Resources and Environmental
Protection Cabinet
Environmental Protection Agency
Fort Boone Plaza
18 Reilly Road
Frankfort, KY 40601
502-564-2150

Louisiana

Health and Hospitals Department
Public Health Services Office
P.O. Box 60630
New Orleans, LA 70160
504-568-5054

Environmental Quality Department
P.O. Box 82263
Baton Rouge, LA 70884-2263
504-765-0741

Maine

Human Services Department
State House Station 11
Augusta, ME 04333
207-287-2736

Environmental Protection Department
State House Station 17
Augusta, ME 04333
207-287-2811

Maryland

Health and Mental Hygiene Department
201 W. Preston Street
Baltimore, MD 21201
410-225-6860

Environment Department
2500 Broening Highway
Baltimore, MD 21224
410-631-3000

Massachusetts

Public Health Department
150 Tremont Street
Boston, MA 02111
617-727-0201

Environmental Affairs,
Executive Office
100 Cambridge Street, 20th Floor
Boston, MA 02202
617-727-9800

Michigan

Public Health Department
3423 N. Logan Street
P.O. Box 30195
Lansing, MI 48909
517-335-8022

Natural Resources Department
P.O. Box 30028
Lansing, MI 48909
517-373-2329

Minnesota

Health Department
717 Delaware Street SE
P.O. Box 9441
Minneapolis, MN 55440-9441
612-623-5460

Pollution Control Agency
520 Lafayette Road N
St Paul, MN 55155
612-296-7301

Mississippi

Health Department
P.O. Box 1700
Jackson, MS 39215-1700
601-960-7634

Natural Resources Department
Pollution Control Bureau
P.O. Box 10385
Jackson, MS 39209
601-961-5100

Missouri

Health Department
P.O. Box 570
Jefferson City, MO 65102
314-751-6001

Natural Resources Department
P.O. Box 176
Jefferson City, MO 65102
314-751-4422

Montana

Health and Environmental Sciences
Department
Cogswell Building
P.O. Box 200901
Helena, MT 59620-0901
406-444-2544

Nebraska

Health Department
301 Centennial Mall S.
P.O. Box 95007
Lincoln, NE 68509
402-471-2133

Environmental Control Department
P.O. Box 98922
Lincoln, NE 68509-8922
402-471-2186

Nevada

Human Resources Department
505 E. King Street, Room 600
Carson City, NV 89710
702-687-4400

Conservation and Natural Resources
Department
123 West Nye Lane
Carson City, NV 89710
702-687-4360

New Hampshire

Health and Human Services Department
6 Hazen Drive
Concord, NH 03301-6505
603-271-4331

Water Supply and Pollution Control Commission
6 Hazen Drive
P.O. Box 95
Concord, NH 03302-0095
603-271-3503

New Jersey

Health Department
John Fitch Plaza, CN 360
Trenton, NJ 08625
609-292-7837

Environmental Protection Department
401 E. State Street, CN 402
Trenton, NJ 08625-0402
609-292-3131

New Mexico

Health and Environment Department
1190 Street Francis Drive
Santa Fe, NM 87503
505-827-2613

New York

Health Department
Environmental Health Center
II University Place
Albany, NY 12203-3313
518-458-6400

Environmental Conservation Department
50 Wolf Road
Albany, NY 12233
518-457-3446

North Carolina

Environment, Health and Natural Resources
Department
P.O. Box 27687
Raleigh, NC 27611
919-733-4984

North Dakota

Health & Consolidated Laboratories
Department
Environmental Health Section
600 E. Boulevard
Bismark, ND 58505
701-224-2374

Ohio

Health Department
246 N. High Street
Columbus, OH 43266-0588
614-466-2253

Natural Resources Department
1930 Belcher Drive
Building D3
Columbus, OH 43224
614-265-6877

Oklahoma

Health Department
1000 NE 10th Street
P.O. Box 53551
Oklahoma City, OK 73152
405-271-4200

Pollution Control Department
1000 NE 10th Street
Oklahoma City, OK 73152
405-271-4688

Oregon

Human Resources Department
Health Division
800 NE Oregon, Suite 21
Portland, OR 97232
503-731-4000

Environmental Quality Department
811 SW 6th Avenue
Portland, OR 97204
503-229-5395

Pennsylvania

Health Department
P.O. Box 90
Harrisburg, PA 17108
717-787-6436

Environmental Resources Department
Office of the Secretary
P.O. Box 2063
Harrisburg, PA 17105-2063
717-787-2814

Rhode Island

Health Department
3 Capitol Hill
Providence, RI 02908
401-277-2231

Environmental Management Department
9 Hayes Street
Providence, RI 02908
401-277-2771

South Carolina

Health and Environmental Control Department
2600 Bull Street
Columbia, SC 29201
803-734-4880

South Dakota

Health Department
445 E. Capitol Avenue
Pierre, SD 57501
605-773-3361

Environment and Natural Resources
Department
523 E. Capitol Avenue
Pierre, SD 57501
605-773-3151

Tennessee

Health Department
Tennessee Tower
312 8th Avenue N., 9th floor
Nashville, TN 37247-0101
615-741-3111

Environment and Conservation Department
L & C Tower
401 Church Street, 21st Floor
Nashville, TN 37247
615-532-0104

Texas

Health Department
1100 West 49th Street
Austin, TX 78756-3199
512-458-7375

Natural Resource Conservation
Commission
12100 Park 35 Circle
Austin, TX 78753
512-239-1000

Utah

Health Department
Bureau of Environmental Health Services
288 N. 1460 W.
P.O. Box 16660
Salt Lake City, UT 84116-0660
801-538-6856

Environmental Quality Department
Office of the Executive Director
168 N. 1950 W.
Salt Lake City, UT 84116
801-536-4402

Vermont

Health Department
108 Cherry Street
P.O. Box 70
Burlington, VT 05402
802-863-7280

Natural Resources Agency
Environmental Conservation Department
Center Building
103 S. Main Street
Waterbury, VT 05671
802-241-3600

Virginia

Health Department
Main Street Station
P.O. Box 2448
Richmond, VA 23218
804-786-3561

Natural Resources Office
9th Street Office Building, 7th Floor
202 N. 9th Street
Richmond, VA 23219
804-786-0044

Washington

Health Department
1112 Quince SE
Olympia, WA 98504
206-586-5846

Ecology Department
P.O. Box 47600
Olympia, WA 98504-7600
206-407-6000

West Virginia

Health and Human Resources
Department
Public Health Bureau
State Capitol Complex
Building 3, Room 519
Charlestown, WV 25305
304-348-2971

Division of Environmental Protection
#10 McJunkin Road
Nitro, WV 25143-2506
304-759-0515

Wisconsin

Bureau of Public Health
1414 E. Washington Avenue, Room 227
Madison, WI 53703
608-266-3681

Natural Resources Department
P.O. Box 7921
Madison, WI 53707
608-266-2121

Wyoming

Health Department
117 Hathaway Building
Cheyenne, WY 82002-0710
307-777-7656

Environmental Quality Department
122 W. 25th Street
Cheyenne, WY 82002
307-777-7938

Additional Sources of Information

Chapter 1

The American Society of Home Inspectors
(ASHI), Inc.
85 W. Algonquin Road, Suite 360
Arlington Heights, IL 60005-4423
708-290-1919

ASHI is a nonprofit professional association that provides testing and certification services for home inspectors. ASHI can verify by mail or by telephone whether or not an individual home inspector is certified through this organization. It can also provide a copy of its standards of practice that lists the areas covered by the inspector.

National Association of Environmental Risk
Auditors (NAERA)
4211 E. 3rd Street
Bloomington, IN 47401
812-333-0077

NAERA is a nonprofit professional association that provides testing and certification services for individuals who perform environmental assessments. NAERA can verify by mail or by telephone whether or not an individual auditor is certified through this organization.

Chapter 2

The following materials are available at no charge from:

The EPA's RCRA Hotline
1-800-424-9346 or TDD 800-553-7672 (hearing impaired)
(In Washington, D.C. 703-412-9810 or TDD 703-412-3323)

Household Hazardous Waste: Steps to Safe Management
The Consumer's Handbook for Reducing Solid Waste
How to Set Up a Local Program to Recycle Used Oil
Recycle
Recycling Used Oil: 10 Steps to Change Your Oil
Recycling Works! State and Local Solutions to Solid Waste Management Problems
Used Dry Cell Batteries: Is a Collection Program Right for Your Community?
Household Hazardous Waste Management: A Manual for 1-Day Community Collection Programs

Other resources:

U.S. EPA
Information Access Branch
Public Information Center (PIC)
401 M Street, SW, PM-211B
Washington, D.C. 20460
202-260-7751

Provides information and referrals on environmental issues. Also provides *Access Express*, a quick reference guide to major EPA information sources.

Human Ecology Action League (HEAL)
P.O. Box 49126
Atlanta, GA 30359-1126

HEAL is a nonprofit volunteer organization of people affected by or concerned about environmental conditions that are hazardous to human health. HEAL publishes and sells educational materials on a variety of issues related to chemical sensitivity.

U.S. Consumer Product Safety Commission
Chemical Hazards Program
5401 Westbard Avenue, Room 419
Bethesda, MD 20207

CPSC Product Safety Hotline
    1-800-638-CPSC
Teletypewriter for the hearing impaired
    Outside Maryland 1-800-638-8270
    Maryland only 1-800-492-8104

Reviews complaints regarding the safety of consumer products and takes action to ensure product safety. CPSC has informational brochures available at no charge on a number of consumer-home issues.

Your local Lung Association, or
The American Lung Association
1740 Broadway
New York, NY 10009

Provides consumer information on indoor air and outdoor air quality, conducts smoking cessation programs and provides information on respiratory illnesses.

Chapter 3

The following materials are available from:

U.S. EPA
Information Access Branch
Public Information Center (PIC)
401 M Street, SW PM-211B
Washington, D.C. 20460

> *Home Buyer's and Seller's Guide to Radon*
> *Radon in Schools*
> *Radon: A Physician's Guide*
> *Consumer's Guide to Radon Reduction*
> *Radon Technical Support Document*
> *A Citizen's Guide to Radon (2nd edition)*
> *Radon Reduction Techniques for Detached Houses*
> *Radon-resistant Residential New Construction*
> *Removal of Radon in Household Water*

Other resources:

The EPA's Safe Drinking Water Hotline
1-800-426-4791

A toll-free information service for radon and other contaminants in drinking water.

Chapter 4

The following materials are available from:

U.S. EPA
Information Access Branch
Public Information Center (PIC)
401 M Street, SW PM-211B
Washington, D.C. 20460

> *Asbestos Fact Book*
> *Asbestos in the Home: A Homeowner's Guide*
> *Guidance for Preventing Asbestos Disease among Auto Mechanics*

Other resources:

American Industrial Hygiene Association
Support Services Department
2700 Prosperity Avenue, Suite 250
Fairfax, VA 22031-4307

The American Industrial Hygiene Association (AIHA), a professional group of industrial hygienists, provides (at no charge) lists of certified asbestos consultants and laboratories that test for asbestos. The laboratories and individuals have special training and skills needed to identify and analyze asbestos.

Resilient Floor Covering Institute
966 Hungerford Drive, Suite 12-B
Rockville, MD 20850

The Resilient Floor Covering Institute provides at no charge a brochure on safe procedures for removing vinyl floor coverings. Send a self-addressed stamped envelope to their address.

Chapter 5

The following materials are available from:

U.S. EPA
Information Access Branch
Public Information Center (PIC)
401 M Street, SW PM-211B
Washington, D.C. 20460

> *Lead and Your Drinking Water*
>
> *Fact Sheet No. 14: Lead Paint Poisoning*
>
> *Lead Leaching from Submersible Well Pumps*

Other resources:

The EPA's Safe Drinking Water Hotline
1-800-426-4791

This is a toll-free information service for all water quality problems, including lead.

National Lead Information Center
1-800-LEAD-FYI

This is a toll-free information service that covers all aspects of lead contamination.

National Sanitation
Foundation, International
3475 Plymouth Road
Ann Arbor, MI 48105

This organization provides information on treatment units for lead and other contaminants in drinking water.

Water Quality Association
P.O. Box 606
Lisle, IL 60532

This organization provides information on treatment units for lead and other contaminants in drinking water.

Frandon Enterprises, Inc.
P.O. Box 300321
Seattle, WA 98103

This company sells kits for testing ceramicware for lead.

SKC, Inc.
RD1 #395 Valley View Road
Eighty Four, PA 15330

This company sells kits for testing ceramicware for lead.

National Institute of Building Sciences (NIST)
1201 L Street, N.W., Suite 400
Washington, D.C. 20005
202-289-7800

NIST has developed a work practices manual for removing and managing in-place lead-containing materials. Copies are available to the public for a charge.

Chapter 6

The following material is available from:

U.S. Consumer Product Safety Commission
Washington, D.C. 20207

An Update on Formaldehyde

Chapter 7

The following material is available from:

U.S. EPA
Information Access Branch
Public Information Center (PIC)
401 M Street, SW PM-211B
Washington, D.C. 20460

Carpet and Indoor Air Quality

The following material is available from:

Consumer Information Center
Department 620-Y
Pueblo, CO 81009

Indoor Air Quality and New Carpet—What You Should Know

Chapter 8

The following material is available from:

National Center for Appropriate Technology
3040 Continental Drive
P.O. Box 3838-3838
Butte, MT 59702

Moisture and Home Energy Conservation

Chapter 9

The following materials are available from:

U.S. EPA
Indoor Air Quality Information
Clearinghouse
P.O. Box 37133
Washington, D.C. 20013-7133

Use and Care of Home Humidifiers
Biological Pollutants in your Home

The following materials are available from:

American Lung Association
1740 Broadway
New York, NY 10019

Home Control of Allergies and Asthma

The following materials are available from:

National Center for Appropriate Technology
3040 Continental Drive
P.O. Box 3838
Butte, MT 59702-3838

Moisture and Home Energy Conservation

Chapter 10

The following materials are available from:

U.S. EPA
Indoor Air Quality Information
Clearinghouse
P.O. Box 37133
Washington, D.C. 20013-7133

> *Combustion Appliances and Indoor Air Pollution*
>
> *Use and Care of Home Humidifiers Fact Sheet*
>
> *Residential Air Cleaners Fact Sheet*
>
> *Residential Air-Cleaning Devices: A Summary of Available Information*

The following materials are available from:

U.S. Consumer Product Safety Commission
Washington, D.C. 20207

> *On the Side of Safety...Caution! Choosing and Using Your Gas Space Heater*
>
> *What You Should Know about Space Heaters*
>
> *What You Should Know about Kerosene Heaters*

The following materials are available from:

National Center for Appropriate Technology
3040 Continental Drive
P.O. Box 3838
Butte, MT 59702-3838

> *Heat Recovery Ventilation for Housing—Air-to-Air Heat Exchangers*
>
> *Introducing Supplemental Combustion Air to Gas-Fired Home Appliances*

The following materials are available from:

Association of Home Appliance Manufacturers
(AHAM)
20 North Wacker Drive
Chicago, IL 60606

> *AHAM Consumer Guide for Room Air Cleaners*

For further information on in-duct air cleaner standards, contact your heating and cooling contractor, or:

Air-Conditioning and Refrigeration
Institute (ARI)
1501 Wilson Boulevard, 6th Floor
Arlington, VA 22209

Chapter 11

The following materials are available from:

U.S. EPA
Information Access Branch
Public Information Center (PIC)
401 M Street, SW PM-211B
Washington, D.C. 20460

> *Pesticide Fact Book*
> *Pesticide Safety Tips*
> *Citizen's Guide to Pesticides*

Other resources:

Bio-Integral Resource Center (BIRC)
P.O. Box 7414
Berkeley, CA 94707

BIRC has information on the least toxic alternatives to pesticides and specific pesticide problems.

Rachel Carson Council, Inc.
8940 Jones Mill Road
Chevy Chase, MD 20815

This organization has information about pesticides and lawn care.

National Pesticide
Telecommunications Network
1-800-858-7378
(In Texas: 806-743-3091)

This is a toll-free, 24-hour pesticide information service.

County cooperative extension offices

These offices have information on lawn care and landscaping, including plant selection, pest control and soil testing. Look in the telephone directory under county or state government.

Natural Resources Defense
Council
40 West 20th Street
New York, NY 10011

This organization publishes information on pesticides and other toxic chemicals, including a publication on pesticides in children's food.

Chapter 12

The following materials are available from:

U.S. EPA
Information Access Branch
Public Information Center (PIC)
401 M Street, SW PM-211B
Washington, D.C. 20460

> *Electric and Magnetic Fields from 60 Hertz Electric Power: What Do We Know about Possible Health Risks?*
>
> *Questions and Answers about Electric and Magnetic Fields (EMFs)*
>
> *EMF in your Environment*

The following brochures are available from:

Carnegie Mellon University
Department of Engineering and Public Policy
Pittsburgh, PA 15213
Attention:EMF Brochure

> *Measuring Power of Power Frequency Fields (part 1) ($2.50 per copy)*
>
> *What Can We Conclude from Measurements of Power Frequency Fields (part 2) ($3.00 per copy)*

All orders must be prepaid. Make checks payable to Carnegie Mellon University.

Chapter 13

The following materials are available from:

U.S. EPA
Information Access Branch
Public Information Center (PIC)
401 M Street, SW PM-211
Washington, D.C. 20460

> *Drinking Water from Household Wells*
>
> *Home Water Treatment Units: Filtering Fact from Fiction*
>
> *Lead Leaching from Submersible Well Pumps*

Other resources:

State drinking water offices

The drinking water office is usually located in the Health or Environmental Protection Department of state government and is often called the Public Water Supply Program. Consult the blue "government pages" in your local phone book in larger urban areas; in smaller communities, contact the local health department. Appendix A also has a list of state health and environmental agencies.

U.S. EPA Safe Drinking Water Hotline
1-800-426-4791
(In Washington, D.C, 202-382-5533)

The EPA provides copies of federal drinking water regulations, information on health effects of specific contaminants and other information related to drinking water.

National Resources Defense Council (NRDC)
NRDC Publications
40 West 20th Street
New York, NY

NRDC recently published *Think Before You Drink: The Failure of the Nation's Water System to Protect Public Health.* This report provides information on problems with our public water supply system. For a copy of the report send $7.50 plus $1.45 shipping and handling to the NRDC address. You can purchase a copy of drinking water information about your state by sending $10 plus $1.45 shipping and handling for each state summary.

Water Quality Association
P.O. Box 606
Lisle, IL 60532

The Association provides information on water purification equipment and testers to consumers at no charge.

National Sanitation Foundation, International
3475 Plymouth Road
Ann Arbor, MI 48105

The Foundation tests and certifies the performance of filtering devices, and provides consumers with an information packet at no charge.

The Freshwater Foundation
2500 Shadywood Road
Box 90
Navarre, MN 55392

The Foundation provides information on groundwater protection, private water and wastewater systems and other environment-related topics. It charges a small fee for publications.

The National Rural Water Association
P.O. Box 142B
Duncan, OK 73534

The Association provides technical publications, training and technical assistance to small water systems and rural water districts.

The National Drinking Water Clearinghouse
West Virginia University
P.O. Box 6064
Morgantown, WV 26506-6064

The services of the Clearinghouse are intended for communities of less than 10,000 people and those who work with them. It provides publications, databases, referrals and educational products.

Chapter 14

The following material is available from:

The Freshwater Foundation
75 W. County Road 6
Wayzata, MN 55391

Understanding Your Septic System

Appendix B

How To Use a Respirator and Protective Clothing

You can purchase respirators (and other safety supplies) from safety supply stores. These are listed in the yellow pages of the telephone directory under "Safety Equipment & Clothing" or "Asbestos Removal & Abatement Equipment & Supplies." If you have difficulty locating a source of safety equipment, contact your local health department for help.

- Do not use a respirator if you have heart or lung problems. Wearing a respirator makes your heart and lungs work harder. Instead, hire a contractor to do the work.
- Do not attempt to wear a respirator if you have a beard or long sideburns. Facial hair will prevent the respirator from sealing properly. Shave cleanly before putting on the respirator.
- Do not wear contact lenses with a half-mask respirator. Contaminants (such as solvents) can penetrate the contacts.
- Ask the vendor to give you a preliminary qualitative fit test when you purchase the respirator.

A respirator must fit properly so that it can prevent asbestos fibers or other substances from contaminating the air you breathe. When you purchase your respirator, ask the vendor to help you select a respirator that fits your face shape (respirators come in different sizes and the styles can vary slightly). Be sure that the respirator is an approved NIOSH-MSHA respirator. Tell the vendor what type of work you are doing and let him or her recommend the type of cartridge you need. The cartridges can filter out particles and gases, and are color-coded for specific contaminants. For example, the color purple is for asbestos and black is for organic vapors. Purchase enough cartridges to allow you to use new cartridges each day you work.

- Read the instructions that come with your respirator and carefully follow the instructions for putting it on. Practice putting it on and taking it off before you actually use it.
- Screw the filters or cartridges into the threads on the mask. They should be snug, but not too tight. Put on the respirator. Be sure that the straps are positioned properly. Bottom straps should wrap around the base of the head; upper straps around the upper part of the head. Do not make the straps too tight.
- Check the fit each time you use the respirator. The fit tests are easy to do and will let you know if air is leaking into the respirator. If you change the adjustment of the respirator after you do these tests, repeat the tests.
- Use a new cartridge or filter each time you start to work. This usually means that you will change the filter or cartridge before each day of work. The filters or cartridges purify the air as you breathe. When you exhale, the air leaves the mask through the exhalation valve.
- Leave the work area to replace the filter or cartridge whenever signs of leakage are present. These include smelling the contaminant or difficulty in breathing.
- You will be able to talk while you are wearing the respirator, but the sound will be muffled.
- *Do not remove the respirator once you are in the work area. Do not eat, drink, smoke, chew gum or chew tobacco while you are wearing a respirator or working around hazardous chemicals and materials. Doing so will expose you to the contaminant.*
- If you are wearing protective clothing and a respirator, dress in the following order:

  1. Put on disposable coveralls
  2. Put on foot coverings if they are separate from the suit
  3. Tape the ankles (tape pants over foot coverings if they are separate)
  4. Put on the respirator and check the fit
  5. Put on the head covering, if any, over the respirator straps
  6. Put on the gloves, if any
  7. Tape the wrists if the gloves are worn outside the suit

Caution: Wearing a respirator and protective clothing places stress on your body. If you experience any signs of heat stress, contact medical help immediately. These include muscle cramping, profuse sweating, weakness, headaches, dizziness and rapid pulse. Hot, dry skin, confusion, unconsciousness and delirium are medical emergencies.

Note: When working with caustic or organic chemicals such as solvents and pesticides, ask the local health department or safety supply store to tell you what type of protective gloves are needed. Some chemicals can be absorbed through the skin, and special materials are needed for different chemicals. The following section provides pictures and instructions on how to wear a half-mask respirator and how to test it to ensure a proper fit.

FIGURE B.1.   How To Wear a Half-mask Respirator and Perform Fit Tests: Putting on the Mask

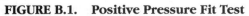

FIGURE B.1.   Positive Pressure Fit Test

FIGURE B.1.   **Negative Pressure Fit Test**

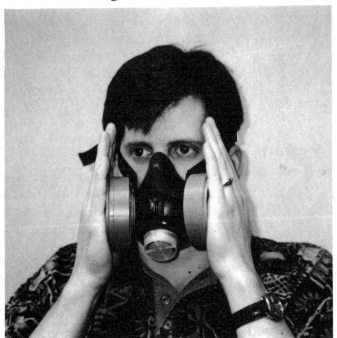

Positive Pressure Test

Cover the exhalation valve with your thumb or the palm of your hand, as shown in Figure B.1. At the same time, gently exhale into the mask for about five seconds. The fit is secure if the facepiece bulges slightly but no air leaks out of the mask. If air leaks out of the mask, change the position of the facepiece and readjust the tension of the elastic straps. Repeat the positive pressure test until you get a tight seal.

Negative Pressure Test

Cover the cartridges or filters with the palms of your hands, as shown in Figure B.1. This may seem awkward at first. Make a good seal, but do not push too hard on the filters, because too much pressure can change the way the mask fits. Gently inhale and hold your breath for about five seconds. The mask should collapse slightly. If air does not leak into the mask the fit is secure. If the mask leaks air, change the position of the facepiece and readjust the tension of the elastic straps. Repeat the negative pressure test until a tight seal is obtained.

Note: Once you adjust the mask, you must repeat both positive and negative pressure tests. Do not make an adjustment and then complete only one of the tests.

Appendix C

Asbestos Removal Projects for Homeowners

Words of Caution

Check with the local health or environmental agency that is responsible for asbestos programs to determine if you, as a homeowner, can legally remove asbestos-containing materials. If you are allowed to remove the material, find out if you need a permit and ask about any regulations that apply to your situation. Some states have special requirements for disposing of asbestos-containing materials. Some states allow homeowners to remove asbestos-containing materials, but prohibit the homeowner from paying other noncertified people to do the work. Be sure that you understand your legal responsibilities.

The following removal procedures are intended to help homeowners minimize health risks associated with do-it-yourself asbestos removal projects. It should be understood, however, that removing asbestos from your home can be dangerous. Some release of asbestos fibers into the air is unavoidable and there are no known safe levels of asbestos exposure.

No set of instructions can address all possible situations that a homeowner might encounter in an asbestos removal project. These procedures address the most likely issues involved in removing asbestos-containing spray-on popcorn ceilings and cement asbestos board siding. If carefully followed, these procedures will allow you to remove the asbestos-containing material safely. Be sure to read each procedure carefully until you understand the steps involved and have a copy of the procedure with you while you are doing the work.

These procedures were developed by the Puget Sound Air Pollution Control Agency. The Agency assumes no liability or responsibility for injuries, illnesses or related health problems arising from your performance of an asbestos removal project. You assume all risk involved.

Common sense dictates that unique and particularly challenging projects should not be undertaken by the homeowner. In such cases, it would be prudent to avoid the possibility of asbestos contamination by abandoning the do-it-yourself approach and hiring a certified asbestos abatement contractor.

Background Information

The Work Will Be Difficult

It is important to note that even under the best circumstances, home-owner-performed asbestos projects can be both physically demanding and potentially dangerous.

- Breathing through a respirator is more difficult than normal breathing and places additional stress on the heart and lungs.
- Protective clothing can be hot and uncomfortable.
- Work spaces become very humid due to the water used in wetting the asbestos.
- Eye protection often reduces visibility.
- Caution must be taken with wiring and electrical power especially when water is used to wet the asbestos.

Understand that as a homeowner, you do not have the equipment, materials and experience of an asbestos abatement contractor. Unlike contractors (who have special machines with high-efficiency filters to remove fibers from the work place air), you have few, if any, "backups" if something goes wrong.

Protective Equipment and Clothing

Before beginning any removal project, you'll need to obtain the following items:

- **Respirators.** Use half-face, dual cartridge respirators, each equipped with a pair of high-efficiency particulate air (HEPA) filters (color-coded purple). One respirator is required for each person working within the containment area. Appendix B contains instructions on how to test the fit of the respirator and use the protective clothing.

- **Coveralls.** Several pairs of disposable coveralls with built-in booties should be purchased. Oversized coveralls make it easier for workers to move. One pair will be needed for each entry into the containment area, and every time a worker leaves a containment area during a removal, coveralls should be wetted and disposed of in sealed asbestos disposal bags.
- **Rubber boots.** These are highly recommended so that coverall booties do not wear through. Rubber boots can be washed off as needed during the removal and after the work is completed.
- **Eye protection.** Each person performing removal work should be equipped with a pair of nonfogging goggles or safety glasses.
- **Gloves.** Durable, disposable rubber or latex gloves should be worn by each person working within the work area. Every time a worker leaves a work area during a removal project, these gloves should be disposed of in properly sealed asbestos disposal bags. A new pair of gloves should be donned with each reentry into the containment area.

Basic Rules

- **Worker protection.** Each worker must wear protective clothing in the work area.
- **Wetting.** Wetting is critical to successful asbestos fiber control. Before, during and after removal, asbestos-containing material should be thoroughly wetted with water in order to keep asbestos fibers out of the air. Once removed, asbestos debris should be kept wet until packaged and sealed for disposal.
- **Containment.** You will need to contain your asbestos debris by constructing a plastic containment around the materials you wish to remove. This is accomplished by covering walls and floors within the project room or rooms with plastic in order to ensure that all debris is captured and remains on plastic sheeting during the removal process.

How To Remove Spray-on "Popcorn" Ceilings Properly

Before You Begin

Are You Sure That Your Ceiling Contains Asbestos? Not all spray-on "popcorn" ceilings contain asbestos. To know for sure, submit "popcorn" samples for laboratory analysis either to a local health agency or private laboratory. Laboratories are listed in the yellow pages under "Asbestos—Consulting and Testing," and the cost for most analyses is minimal.

You can safely take samples of "popcorn" ceilings that are in good condition without using a protective respirator, but if you would be more comfortable wearing one or if the ceiling is damaged, see Appendix B. Removals must be done while wearing a respirator.

Use a spray bottle containing water mixed with a few drops of liquid detergent to wet thoroughly three or four small ceiling areas. Using a putty knife, take a composite sample by carefully scraping about one square inch of "popcorn" from each wetted area into a self-sealing plastic bag. Follow the laboratory's instructions for submitting the sample. If the laboratory results are negative (meaning that less than 1 percent asbestos was found in the sample), take two additional samples to confirm the analysis.

If you decide not to check for asbestos, assume that the ceiling is contaminated and treat it accordingly.

If Your Ceiling Does Contain Asbestos, Are You Sure That You Want To Remove It? Remember, asbestos is a problem only if fibers are released into the air. Asbestos-containing spray-on "popcorn" ceilings that are in good repair and not being disturbed will not release asbestos fibers. In such cases, the safest, easiest and least expensive option may be to leave it alone. Sometimes, it is possible to work around asbestos without removing it. For example, "popcorn" ceilings that are in good condition can usually be painted (spraying is recommended). Be aware, however, that painting these ceilings may prevent you from safely removing the asbestos in the future. Do-it-yourself removal is highly dependent on your ability to wet thoroughly the material before disturbing it, and painting can seal the "popcorn" material, making it difficult or impossible to wet.

The Work May Cause Damage. These procedures can result in damage to walls and ceilings. Duct tape can discolor wood paneling, tear wallpaper and remove paint and texture. Water can stain walls and using metal scrapers on wetted plasterboard ceilings can result in tearing of the plasterboard paper.

If Your Ceiling Has Been Painted . . . If your "popcorn" ceiling has been painted, you may not be able to penetrate the paint with water to wet the asbestos-containing material. Thorough wetting is critical for preventing the release of asbestos fibers during removal. Try one or more test areas to determine if you can penetrate the paint layer to wet the material thoroughly.

You can safely do this wetting test on material in good condition without using a protective respirator, but if you would be more comfortable wearing one or if the material is damaged, see Appendix B. Use a plastic spray bottle containing a teaspoon or less of liquid detergent (wetting agent) in water. Spray the water over a few square inches of ceiling, allowing 15 to 20 minutes for the water to soak into the "popcorn." Respray several times during this period, then carefully scrape off the material with a small putty knife, catching the debris on a piece of sheet plastic held in your hand. Carefully examine the removed "popcorn" material for wetness.

Dispose of the debris by carefully wrapping it in the plastic, sealing it with duct tape and placing it in the garbage. If the removed "popcorn" was not thoroughly wet, try increasing the number of spray applications, the amount of wetting agent used and the soaking time in order to determine the best way to achieve the maximum wetting of your spray-on material. If, after trying various spray procedures, you are unable to get water through the paint in order to saturate the "popcorn" to the ceiling substrate, *do not undertake this project.* Leave the ceiling alone or hire an asbestos abatement contractor to do the work. If you remove this ceiling dry, you will contaminate your home with asbestos and expose yourself and your family to high concentrations of airborne asbestos fibers that can remain in your home indefinitely.

Removal Procedures

Basic Rules. Remember the three basic rules of working with asbestos:

1. Wear protective clothing
2. Keep the asbestos wet
3. Use proper containment

Personnel and Supplies

Workers. It is recommended that three workers perform the job. Two should perform the work and a third should be standing by outside the work area in order to provide water, tools and other supplies as needed while work is in progress. This will minimize the need for removal workers to remove and replace disposable clothing with each exit and entrance to the work area.

Protective Clothing and Equipment. Before beginning your project, make sure that you have the protective clothing listed in the *Words of Caution.* Appendix B gives instructions for testing the fit of the respirator and using the protective clothing.

Tools and Supplies

- **Tank sprayer (2–3 gallons).** This will be your means of wetting "popcorn" ceiling materials.
- **Liquid dishwashing detergent.** Mixed at one cup per five gallons of water for best results in wetting.
- **Wallboard taping or "putty" knives.** The best sizes for scraping off "popcorn" ceiling materials have four- to six-inch blades.
- **Polyethylene sheeting.** This will be used to create containment areas. You will need enough 2 or 3 mil sheeting to cover 1.5 times the area of the walls and enough 6 mil sheeting to cover three times the area of the floors in the work area. A knife or scissors is needed to cut the sheeting.
- **Asbestos waste disposal bags.** These bags will be used for containing asbestos-contaminated debris and materials. The bags should be sized 33 inches by 50 inches and made of 6 mil polyethylene. Each should be preprinted with required asbestos warnings. Assume that you will need at least four bags per 100 square feet of removed material.
- **Duct tape.** You will need numerous rolls to build the containment area and seal waste disposal bags.
- **Clean disposable rags.** A large supply should be on hand for assorted removal and cleanup purposes.
- **Bucket.** You will need this for washing tools at the end of the project.
- **Encapsulants.** These could be latex primer or an approved latex asbestos-sealing product. They will be used for encapsulating areas after "popcorn" materials have been scraped off.

Note: All asbestos-specific equipment and materials can be purchased at safety supply stores listed in the yellow pages of the telephone directory under "Asbestos Removal & Abatement Equipment & Supplies."

Prep Work

First Things First

1. Post signs warning any drop-in friends, family and other visitors of the work taking place.
2. Remove all furniture from the room(s) where the "popcorn" removal is to take place.
3. Turn off heating/air-conditioning systems and tape all light switches in the *off* position.

4. Turn off electrical power to all ceiling light fixtures in the project area and then remove them. After removal, seal exposed wires with electrical tape. Be careful not to disturb the "popcorn" material during these activities.

5. Remove any smoke alarms or other devices attached to or near the ceiling, once again being careful not to disturb "popcorn" material.

Build a Containment Area

1. Throughout the area of the house where the "popcorn" ceiling is being removed, cover the floors with 6 mil polyethylene plastic sheeting. Place the sheets so that they overlap room edges by about a foot. Run the extra foot of sheeting up each wall and tape the edges there securely. Make sure that there is plenty of excess plastic—*do not* pull it tight—so that the plastic won't pull away from the walls when you're working near room corners and edges. Tightly seal all seams between pieces of sheet plastic with duct tape. If "popcorn" is to be removed from rooms that are joined by halls or spaces where no removal is to take place, lay 6 mil plastic sheets on the floor between containment areas in order to create a path on which to walk.

2. Hang 2 or 3 mil polyethylene plastic sheeting on the walls within approximately one inch of the ceiling, forming a tight seal with duct tape. Make sure that the sheets overlap and extend to the floor. Seal all wall seams with duct tape. To minimize damage to wallpaper, consider using slender finishing nails to secure a piece of screen molding to the top of the wall and taping the plastic wall sheets to the wood strip.

3. Lay a second layer of 6 mil plastic on the floor. In larger rooms, install the second layer in pieces of 100–120 square feet. Lay the plastic in a loose, overlapping manner *without* using tape or adhesives.

4. Construct plastic "isolation" walls with plastic in doorways or room openings, if necessary, to separate the work area from the rest of the house.

5. If there is a door to the outside within the containment area, make this your point of entry and exit to the work area. Open the door and seal the doorway with 6 mil plastic. Create an entrance/exit through the plastic by cutting a five to six foot vertical slit in the plastic, and then taping a floor length plastic flap over on the inside of the containment area. Then lay down a sheet of 4 to 6 mil polyethylene outside the

door. At minimum, have a water spray bottle, clean wet rags, a bucket and an asbestos waste disposal bag at this location. If there is no exit door to the outside within the containment, create an entrance/exit within the house—either through a door or through an "isolation" wall as described above. Lay down a sheet of 4 to 6 mil polyethylene outside the door and, as a minimum, have a water spray bottle and an asbestos waste disposal bag at this location.

6. Once you've completed the plastic containment, make sure that the entire area where the removal is to take place is isolated with polyethylene sheeting. The only exposed surfaces within the containment should be the ceiling and about an inch or less of wall below the ceiling. This ensures that all asbestos material is contained during removal.

7. Windows may be opened for ventilation. However, air pollution regulations require that there be no visible emissions to the outside air. Construct and tape an oversized plastic flap or canopy over the inside of each open window (or take other precautions) to ensure that no debris passes through windows.

Wet the Ceiling

1. You should be able to wet a ceiling in good condition safely without wearing the respirator and protective clothing; however, you may be more comfortable putting these on before you begin the wetting. Wear the respirator if the ceiling is damaged, Appendix B contains the instructions for putting on safety equipment. Then proceed with Step 2.

2. If your "popcorn" ceiling was painted, use the wetting process determined to be successful in earlier tests. Apply the water plus wetting agent with the tank sprayer (see Figure C.1). However, if the testing procedures for wetting described earlier failed to penetrate the paint and thoroughly saturate the "popcorn" to the ceiling substrate, *do not proceed.* Leave the ceiling alone or hire an asbestos abatement contractor to do the work.

3. If your "popcorn" ceiling was never painted, spray the ceiling with liquid detergent and water using the tank sprayer. Mix liquid detergent with the water at a ratio of one cup to five gallons. Spray the "popcorn" material several times and *ensure that the "popcorn" is thoroughly wet before removal.* Spray-on "popcorn" material is very porous and absorbs a lot of water. Thorough wetting will keep asbestos fibers out of the air.

FIGURE C.1.   Wetting and Scraping the "Popcorn" Ceiling

Courtesy of Puget Sound Air Pollution Control Agency.

FIGURE C.1.   (*continued*)

4. Wait 15 to 20 minutes for the water to penetrate thoroughly.

Note: If someone outside the containment area is not available to refill sprayers, you may need a hose with automatic shutoff at the entrance to the plastic enclosure for refilling the tank sprayer(s).

Test for wetness. Those who will enter the containment area to test for wetness and removal should put on respirators, disposable coveralls, and other protective clothing outside the containment area while standing on the entrance/exit plastic. (See Appendix B.)

Once inside the containment area, test for wetness by scraping off a few inches of ceiling material. If it is thoroughly wet to the gypsum board or other underlying ceiling substrate, you can begin the removal. If the material is not thoroughly wet, reapply water (with detergent) and allow time for it to soak into the "popcorn."

Again, if you find you are unable to wet this material thoroughly, *do not proceed!* Use a certified asbestos abatement contractor to perform any additional work.

Note: If you must leave the plastic containment area during the project, wet and remove protective equipment and clothing while standing on the plastic just outside the entrance/exit to the work area. Place coveralls and gloves in a waste disposal bag. Then step off of the plastic. Upon returning, put on new coveralls, gloves, and the respirator.

Removing the "Popcorn" Ceiling

1. Cushion ladder legs by wrapping them with rags or a similar material, to keep them from tearing the plastic sheeting on the floor.
2. Using four- to eight-inch putty or wallboard taping knives, thoroughly scrape the spray-on "popcorn" material from the ceiling, allowing the debris to fall onto the plastic sheets below (see Figure C.1).
3. Wipe any remaining residue off with clean wet rags. Refold and change rags frequently so that you are wiping with a clean surface; otherwise, the remaining asbestos material will be smeared around but not removed. If the ceiling beneath the material is painted, wet wiping is very effective. With unfinished Sheetrock, wiping is helpful but is less effective. Don't try to rinse contaminated rags; dispose of them in an asbestos waste disposal bag.
4. Use clean rags to wet wipe the exposed portion of the wall between the top of the duct tape and the ceiling.

5. *Keep the plastic on the floor and the walls damp at all times by spraying it periodically to prevent any debris from drying and becoming airborne.*

Note: If your spray-on "popcorn" ceiling was applied as part of the original construction, the ceiling was likely never finished for painting. Thus, even if you did no damage during the "popcorn" removal, you will probably need to refinish or retexture the ceiling before painting. Under no circumstances should you sand ceilings after removal of sprayed-on "popcorn" material. Doing so will release asbestos fibers into the air.

Cleanup

Remove Debris from the Floor

1. After you've removed all of the "popcorn" ceiling material in one room within the containment area, wet wipe any debris from the plastic on the walls and then carefully fold and roll up the top layer of loose plastic sheets on the floor to contain fallen debris.
2. Double bag the folded plastic (along with the ceiling debris it contains), using premarked asbestos waste disposal bags. The top level of floor plastic was put down in 100–120 square-foot sections, and plastic plus wetted "popcorn" on this square footage will be quite heavy and may be all you want to carry in a single, double-bagged container. Make sure that all contaminated wipe rags are also placed inside these bags. Follow this process for each subsequent room.
3. After removing all asbestos material from the project enclosure, thoroughly wipe down all tools and ladders with clean wet rags. Place tools in a bucket or plastic bag for more thorough cleaning later and dispose of rags as asbestos debris.
4. Before you remove any plastic sheets that are taped to the walls and floor, encapsulate those ceiling areas from which "popcorn" material has been removed. Roll or spray these areas with a latex primer paint or an approved latex asbestos encapsulant. In spite of your best efforts to remove the asbestos fibers, some fibers may remain on the ceiling. These asbestos fibers will be encapsulated by the paint primer or other spray application. Any future ceiling finishing work *should not involve sanding these surfaces.*

Remove Plastic Containment

1. Spray the plastic on the walls and floors with water one last time, making sure that any visible asbestos debris is thoroughly wet.

2. Beginning at the point most distant from your containment area entrance/exit, remove all plastic. First, peel the plastic off of the walls and lower it onto the floor. Then, carefully roll up the plastic on the floor, taking care to keep all debris contained within the plastic. Work backwards towards your exit and stay on the plastic flooring at all times during this process. In larger rooms, you may need to bag the wall plastic separately in order to avoid creating a bundle of plastic too large to bag. Roll and fold the plastic sheeting toward you while remaining on the plastic.

3. Place each roll of contaminated plastic inside asbestos waste disposal bags. Do not attempt to reuse the plastic.

4. Place each bag of asbestos debris into a second, clean bag, carefully securing each by twisting the tops, bending the twisted part over and securing with duct tape.

Decontamination

1. Make sure that you dismantle and bag the containment area in such a way that the last remaining piece of plastic is the plastic sheet you placed on the floor outside what was formerly the entrance/exit to the containment area.

2. While standing on this last piece of plastic sheeting, spray yourself with water to wet down any asbestos debris/fibers on the outside of your respirator and disposable coveralls.

3. Remove boots. Double bag them in asbestos waste disposal bags for disposal or, should you want to keep them, remove any gross accumulations of "popcorn" material and set them aside on the plastic sheet for further cleaning.

4. Remove your disposable gloves and coveralls by peeling them off and turning them inside out as you remove them. Step off of the last plastic sheet.

5. Remove respirators and take out the filters. Discard the filters with other asbestos waste. Using clean wet rags, wipe down your respirator, goggles, tools used in the removal and, if you elect to keep them, your boots. Place your respirator, goggles and tools in the bucket and your boots in a plastic bag for washing later.

6. Double bag remaining debris, cleaning rags, other disposable items and the last plastic sheet in properly labeled asbestos disposal bags. Tightly seal each bag with duct tape. Use wet rags for any further cleanup. *Never attempt to vacuum or sweep up asbestos debris*. This will cause any fibers present to become airborne in your house.

7. Take a shower.

Disposal

1. Follow the disposal instructions of your local asbestos agency.
2. All debris must be properly packaged for disposal by double-bagging your debris inside labeled 6 mil bags designed specifically for asbestos disposal. Alternatively, you may double wrap the debris in 6 mil polyethylene sheeting, seal seams with duct tape and affix the standard asbestos warning labels.

How To Remove Cement Asbestos Board Siding Properly

Before You Begin

Are You Sure That Your Siding Contains Asbestos? Submit a small sample for laboratory analysis. Laboratories are listed in the yellow pages under "Asbestos–Consulting and Testing," and the cost of an analysis is minimal. To take a sample, wet and break off a small piece of siding (about one square inch) and place it inside a self-closing plastic bag. You do not need to wear a respirator or protective clothing when taking this sample.

If, for some reason, you decide not to check your siding for asbestos content, assume that it contains asbestos and treat it accordingly.

If Your Siding Does Contain Asbestos, Are You Sure That You Want To Remove It? Remember, asbestos is a problem only if its fibers are released into the air. Unless cement asbestos board siding is disturbed, it will not release asbestos fibers; therefore, the safest, easiest and least expensive option may be to leave it alone.

Sometimes, it is possible to work around asbestos without removing it. If asbestos-containing siding must be disturbed as part of a remodeling project, however, then removal may be your only option.

Removal Procedures

Basic Rules. Remember the three basic rules of working with asbestos:

1. Wear protective clothing
2. Keep the asbestos wet
3. Use proper containment

Personnel and Supplies

Workers. Although it is possible for one person to do a siding removal job, the task can be more effectively carried out by two workers. With two workers, one can concentrate on carefully removing pieces of siding while the other keeps materials wet and packages debris as it is generated.

Protective Clothing and Equipment. Before beginning your project, make sure that you have the protective clothing listed in the *Words of Caution.* Appendix B gives instructions for testing the fit of the respirator and using the protective clothing.

Tools and Supplies

- **Garden hose.** A hose, equipped with an automatic shutoff nozzle, will be needed to supply water at the entrance to the work area.
- **Water sprayer.** A pint spray bottle or garden pump sprayer will be used to wet asbestos-containing materials.
- **Liquid dishwashing detergent.** This will be mixed with water to produce best results when wetting asbestos.
- **Removal tools.**
  - A pry bar for lifting nails (a bar equipped with a blade at least two inches wide is best)
  - A nail puller or nailhead cutter
- **6 mil polyethylene sheeting.** This will be used to cover a six-foot strip of ground at the base of the walls from which siding is being removed and to create a transition zone for entering and exiting the work area. Other uses may include wrapping containers of removed siding if pre-marked asbestos waste disposal bags are not used for this purpose. A knife or scissors is needed to cut polyethylene sheeting
- **Debris containers.** Cardboard boxes, burlap bags or other sturdy containers will be needed to help keep the sharp edges and corners of siding debris from puncturing plastic bags. Perforated plastic containers of asbestos will not be accepted by waste disposal sites.
- **Asbestos waste disposal bags.** If removed siding is to be bagged rather than wrapped, assume that you will need a dozen bags per 100 square feet of removed siding. If siding is to be wrapped rather than bagged, disposal bags may be needed only for daily disposal of sheet plastic ground cover, disposable coveralls, gloves, etc. You will need asbestos warning labels for wrapped debris.
- **Duct tape.** Several rolls should be purchased for sealing disposal bags or wrapped debris.

Note: All asbestos-specific equipment and materials may be purchased from a safety equipment vendor listed in the yellow pages of the telephone directory under "Asbestos Removal & Abatement Equipment & Supplies."

Prep Work

As you prepare to remove the siding, remember that your safety objective is to keep asbestos fibers out of the air by minimizing breakage, keeping the siding wet and containing all debris.

1. Post signs warning any drop-in friends, family and other visitors of the work taking place.
2. To the extent that landscaping and terrain will allow, lay a six-foot wide strip of 6 mil sheet plastic along the side of the house where removal is to occur. Try to work in the shade so that wetted siding will remain wet.
3. Create an entrance/exit "transition" zone to the work area by laying down an additional six-foot by six-foot piece of sheet plastic in a convenient location next to the plastic strip along the wall. Keep a plastic disposal bag at this point.
4. Thoroughly hose down about 50 square feet of siding.
5. Mix approximately one teaspoon of liquid dishwashing detergent with water in the pint spray bottle or about a half cup of detergent in a garden pump sprayer.
6. Put on a pair of disposable coveralls as well as gloves, goggles, boots and respirators equipped with HEPA filters according to the instructions in Appendix B.

Removing the Siding

1. Remove pieces of siding by pulling nails or cutting nail heads so as to minimize breakage. If necessary, carefully lift siding pieces with the pry tool to expose nail heads (see Figure C.2).
2. If siding should begin to crack or crumble, immediately wet the cracked or broken areas with the pint spray bottle or garden pump sprayer.
3. Wet the back side of each piece of siding as it is removed.
4. Carefully lower removed siding to the ground. *Do not throw or drop it. Breakage releases asbestos fibers!*
5. Keep all debris on the plastic strip at the base of the wall and keep it wet until packaged and sealed.

Note: Once removal work begins, do not leave the plastic without first removing disposable coveralls and other protective equipment at the "transition zone." Each reentry onto the plastic will require putting on the respirator and a new pair of coveralls and gloves.

FIGURE C.2.   **Removing Cement Asbestos Board Siding**
(above; broken siding; below; prying to expose nails)

Courtesy of Puget Sound Air Pollution Control Agency

FIGURE C.2. (*continued*; above; pulling out nails; below left; removing siding; below right; disposal)

Clean Up

1. Load wetted debris and other contaminated materials into sturdy containers like cardboard boxes or burlap sacks. If cardboard boxes are used, line each box with 6 mil polyethylene and leave enough excess plastic to cover the debris and seal with duct tape. Boxes should then be wrapped in one more layer of 6 mil plastic or inserted into a single premarked asbestos waste disposal bag.
2. Double bag or double wrap other filled containers in 6 mil asbestos waste disposal bags. Twist the top of each filled bag, bend the twisted part in half and seal it closed with duct tape. If containers are to be wrapped rather than bagged, use 6 mil polyethylene plastic and make sure that all seams are sealed with duct tape. Put an asbestos warning label on each sealed package.
3. At the end of each work shift, rewet any debris on the strip of plastic next to the wall. While continuing to stand on the plastic strip next to the wall where the removal is being done, double-bag or wrap all debris as described above. Then wrap or roll up the strip of plastic along the wall, working your way back to the entrance/exit "transition zone" strip of plastic. Step onto the transition zone plastic and double-bag or wrap the last of the strip plastic.

Decontamination

1. Upon reaching your designated entrance/exit, step onto the six-foot by six-foot square of plastic. While standing on this last piece of plastic sheeting, spray yourself with water in order to wet down any asbestos debris/fibers on the outside of your respirator and disposable coveralls.
2. Remove your boots, disposable gloves and coveralls by peeling them off and turning them inside out as you remove them. Step off of the last plastic sheet.
3. Take off respirators and remove their filters for disposal. Wash off and wipe down the tools used in removal, along with your respirators, goggles and boots. Move each item off of the plastic as it is cleaned.
4. Double-bag the remaining debris and disposable items in properly labeled asbestos disposal bags or double-wrap them in 6 mil plastic sheets. Tightly seal each bag or package with duct tape. Never attempt to vacuum or sweep up asbestos debris; this will cause any fibers present to become airborne in your house. Use wet rags for any further clean up.
5. Take a shower.

Disposal

1. Follow the disposal instructions of your local asbestos agency.
2. All debris must be properly packaged for disposal by double-wrapping it in 6 mil polyethylene and sealing it with duct tape. The most common way to accomplish this is to double-bag your debris inside prelabeled 6 mil bags designed specifically for asbestos disposal. Alternatively, you may double-wrap your debris in 6 mil sheet polyethylene, seal seams with duct tape and put standard asbestos warning labels on the wrapped debris.

Appendix D

Lead-based Paint Removal Projects for Homeowners

These guidelines apply to the in-place removal of lead using one of the acceptable methods listed below. They are based on the Department of Housing and Urban Development guidelines for correcting lead-based paint problems in public and Indian housing. The guidelines give instructions for cleaning surfaces, removing lead-based paint, applying coatings and disposal of wastes. If you simply want to remove windows, trim or doors, proper removal steps are still needed, but they are not as extensive. Some guidelines follow at the end of the removal procedures. Contact your local health department or the National Institute of Building Sciences (see Appendix A for address) for further information and other procedures.

Words of Caution

Check with the local health or environmental agency that is responsible for lead programs to determine if you, as a homeowner, can legally remove lead-containing materials. If you are allowed to remove the materials, find out if you need a permit and ask about any regulations that apply to your situation. Be sure that you understand your legal responsibilities.

The following guidelines are intended to help homeowners reduce the health risks associated with a do-it-yourself lead removal project. It should be understood, however, that removing lead from your home can be dangerous. Read these procedures carefully before you begin the work. The guidelines will lower the chance of accidental contamination of your home, but no set of instructions can consider all possible situations that can happen. To learn more, contact your local health or environmental agency before you start working.

Common sense dictates that unique and particularly challenging projects should not be undertaken by the homeowner. In such cases it would be prudent to avoid the possibility of lead contamination by abandoning the do-it-yourself approach and hiring a certified lead abatement contractor.

Background Information
The Work Will Be Difficult

It is important to note that even under the best circumstances, homeowner-performed lead projects can be both physically demanding and potentially dangerous.

- Breathing through a respirator is more difficult than normal breathing and places an additional stress on the heart and lungs. Hire a certified contractor if you have a heart or lung condition.
- Eye protection often reduces visibility.
- Caution must be taken with wiring and electrical power.

Understand that as a homeowner, you do not have all of the equipment, materials and experience of a lead abatement contractor.

Protective Equipment and Clothing

Before beginning any removal project, you'll need to obtain the following items:

- **Respirators.** Use half-face, dual cartridge respirators, each equipped with a pair of high-efficiency particulate air (HEPA) filters (color-coded purple). If chemical products are used during the removal, additional cartridges may be needed; ask the vendor for advice. Respirators provide little protection if they do not fit properly, so ask the vendor to check the fit. One respirator is required for each person working within the containment area. Appendix B contains instructions on how to test the fit of the respirator.
- **Coveralls.** You can do the work in your own work clothes, but you may want to purchase several pairs of disposable coveralls with built-in booties. Oversized coveralls make it easier for workers to move.

One pair will be needed for each entry into the containment area. If you use your own clothing, purchase disposable booties; these can be removed each time you exit the workplace, thus reducing the chances of spreading lead-containing dust. Every time a worker leaves a containment area during a removal, coveralls should be wetted and disposed of in sealed plastic disposal bags. Work clothes should be removed and placed in a bag. Wash these clothes separately from the family laundry using a high phosphate detergent (if allowed in your community).

- **Eye protection.** Each person performing flooring removal work should be equipped with a pair of nonfogging goggles or safety glasses.
- **Gloves.** Durable, disposable rubber or latex gloves should be worn by each person working within the work area. These should be removed each time a worker leaves the work area and a new pair of gloves should be donned with each reentry into the containment area. If you are working with chemical products, gloves made of other materials may be needed.

Are You Sure that There Is Lead?

Make sure that the surface actually contains lead by taking a sample and having it analyzed. Contact your local health department or state agency responsible for lead programs for help with collecting and analyzing samples; the cost is minimal.

Taking a sample usually involves removing paint chips. This can be done by using a razor blade utility knife and shaving off a one-inch-long, 1/8-inch-wide sliver. If there are multiple layers of paint, make sure that you remove all of them. Be sure to remove any chips that fall to the floor or onto a sill and dispose of them. Wet-wipe any dust that collects. Place the sample into a self-sealing plastic bag or empty film canister for delivery to the lab. You do not need to wear a protective respirator when collecting the sample.

If a technician collects samples, a portable instrument might be used to sample multiple areas in the home.

Cleaning Procedures

This procedure is appropriate for cleaning lead-containing surfaces prior to removals, and replacement or general cleaning of lead-containing surfaces.

Required equipment includes wringer buckets, squeegee sponge mops, spray bottle, rags, paper towels and different sizes of hand sponges. A scraper or putty knife may be needed. Use protective plastic sheeting to catch debris if scraping is needed.

Surfaces in Good Condition

1. Wash the surfaces using a detergent that has a high phosphate or trisodium phosphate (TSP) content. Look for products that have more than 5 percent trisodium phosphate, complex sodium phosphates or phosphorus as phosphates. Automatic dishwasher detergents such as Calgon and Spic and Span are examples of acceptable products. Wear waterproof gloves and tight-fitting goggles whenever you use these detergents because they are very irritating to the skin and eyes. If high-phosphate detergents are not available in your area, ask the local health department or safety supply store for other recommendations.

   Wash vertical surfaces from top to bottom. Wash ceilings and floors a section at a time. As the water becomes dirty, change the detergent solution. After washing, rinse the surfaces with fresh water using the same pattern as for washing, and change the rinse water frequently.
2. Repeat the wash and rinse cycle.
3. Use paper towels to absorb excess water on the polyethylene or surfaces, and place towels in disposal bags. You may need to absorb water with sponges or rags and wring them out into a bucket if the water puddles on protective sheeting.

Deteriorated Surfaces

1. Deteriorated surfaces result in paint chips and contaminated debris. Prepare the area, use protective clothing, and follow disposal guidelines given in the section on removal.
2. Use a putty knife or scraper to remove paint that is chipped or curling. Remove only the loose paint until the paint that remains is well-adhered to the surface. Collect the paint chips and place them in disposal bags.
3. Follow the wash and rinse directions given in *Surfaces in Good Condition*.

Removal Guidelines
Basic Rules

Breathing lead dust and ingesting paint chips can cause brain damage and other health effects. Children, women of childbearing age, pregnant women and nursing mothers should not be present during the work. They can return only after all the cleanup is done.

Wear protective clothing. *Do not use paper dust masks—they are not safe. DO NOT eat, drink, smoke, chew gum or chew tobacco during removal and cleanup.* If you do, you could expose yourself to lead. Wash hands and face before doing any of these activities.

Carefully follow the manufacturer's instructions on any paint removal products. These products may be toxic and can cause harm if used improperly. Follow label directions on the products. If you do not understand the directions, call your local health department for assistance.

Removal Methods for Indoor Areas

The following methods are acceptable removal methods:

1. Wire-brushing or dry-scraping alone with the aid of a nonflammable solvent or abrasive compound that does not contain methylene chloride
2. Hand-sanding or machine-sanding with a machine equipped with a HEPA filter vacuum to feather edges and prepare the surface for repainting or sealing
3. Controlled, low-level heating with elements that do not exceed temperatures of 1,000 degrees Fahrenheit

The following methods are *not* acceptable removal methods. The use of any of these methods can generate lead dust or fumes and toxic chemicals that can harm you:

1. Power-sanding without a HEPA filter vacuum
2. Heating with elements or guns that reach temperatures above 1,000 degrees Fahrenheit
3. Applying compounds that contain methylene chloride
4. Torch or flame burning
5. Applying potassium- or sodium hydroxide-based solutions that are not in paste form
6. Dusting, sweeping or using conventional vacuum cleaners to remove lead-containing material

Removal Methods for Exterior Areas

The following methods are acceptable removal methods:

1. Abrasive blasting using a wet-misting technique or vacuuming system
2. Wire-brushing or dry-scraping alone or with the aid of a nonflammable solvent or abrasive compound that does not contain methylene chloride
3. Hand-sanding or machine-sanding with a machine equipped with a HEPA filtered vacuum to feather edges and prepare the surface for repainting or sealing
4. Controlled, low-level heating with elements that do not exceed temperatures of 1,000 degrees Fahrenheit.

The following methods are *not* acceptable removal methods. The use of any of these methods can generate lead dust or fumes and toxic chemicals that can harm you and contaminate the area outside your home.

1. Power-sanding without a HEPA filtered vacuum
2. Heating with elements or guns that reach temperatures above 1,000 degrees Fahrenheit
3. Applying compounds that contain methylene chloride or other toxic organic chemicals
4. Torch or flame burning
5. Applying potassium- or sodium hydroxide-based solutions that are not in paste form
6. High pressure spraying without containment underneath
7. Using a conventional vacuum cleaner (the dust will be blown out of the collection bag)

Supplies

- **Polyethylene sheeting or drop cloths.** This will be used to cover exposed areas in the workplace and to double-wrap painted surfaces that are waste materials. You will need enough 2 or 3 mil sheeting to cover 1.5 times the area of the walls and enough 6 mil sheeting to cover 3 times the area of the floors in the work area. A knife or scissors is needed to cut the sheeting.
- **Duct tape.** Several rolls should be purchased for building the containments and sealing waste disposal bags.
- **Cleaning equipment.** Plain or wringer buckets (two), mops, rags, different sizes of hand sponges and paper towels. A large supply of rags

and sponges should be on hand for precleaning, removal and final cleaning purposes.

- **6 mil polyethylene disposal bags.** These will be used to remove waste materials.
- **Two-by-fours.** These may be needed to hold containment sheeting or to erect a vertical containment for exterior removals.
- **Removal tools.** Ladder, putty knife or paint scraper, utility knife, spray bottle or garden spray (depending on the size of the job).
- **HEPA vacuum.** This vacuum, if available, will allow you to vacuum lead-containing dust safely. If you do not have access to a HEPA vacuum, use wet-wiping and mopping.
- **Fan.** A fan may be needed to provide adequate ventilation if chemical products are used.

Prepare the Area

Indoor Areas

1. Post signs warning any drop-in friends, family and other visitors of the work taking place.
2. Clear the area of any movable items such as furniture and boxes. Cover any remaining items with two layers of plastic and seal with heavy-duty tape (duct tape works well). (Ideally, wall-to-wall carpeting should be removed from the area and later replaced.)
3. Seal the room that contains lead from the rest of the house and the outside by following the next steps carefully. First, turn off the heating and air-conditioning system and fans. Second, cover all air duct openings with plastic and secure them with tape. Use two separate layers. Covering air ducts is especially important in preventing lead dust from contaminating the entire house.
4. Set up the containment area by putting plastic sheeting or drop cloths in the work area to catch any paint chips. Be sure the coverings do not have holes or openings. Use plastic sheeting rather than drop cloths if water will be used during the cleaning or removal.

   If you are not going to remove lead from the floor, it must be covered with drop cloths (only if water is not used) or plastic sheeting. The covering must be lapped and sealed in order to prevent any lead-containing materials from reaching the floor. Tape the cloth or plastic about six inches up the walls.

Hang polyethylene plastic sheeting on the walls within approximately one inch of the ceiling, forming a tight seal with duct tape. Make sure the sheets overlap and extend to the base of the floor or to the baseboards if they are the surface to be removed. Seal all wall seams with duct tape. To minimize damage to wallpaper, consider using slender finishing nails to secure a piece of screen molding to the top of the wall and then taping the plastic sheets to the wood strip.

Prepare one room at a time and put a second layer of protective covering on the floor first.

5. Create an access to the work room by taping polyethylene sheeting to the doors. Tape one layer of polyethylene to the door casing and floor. Cut an opening in the center of the plastic a few inches from the floor (you should be able to easily pass through the opening). Reinforce the opening with tape as needed. Place polyethylene on the floor going from the opening to the outside of the house. Tape a second layer of polyethylene to the top of the door casing. Let it hang to the floor, and do not tape the sides and bottom.

6. If you are using chemicals, keep the area well ventilated by opening windows and placing a fan blowing out in one of them.

Outdoor Areas

1. Post signs warning any drop-in friends, family and other visitors of the work taking place.
2. Be sure to close windows and doors before removal begins. Cover any duct or vent openings with plastic and seal them with two layers of tape.
3. Place plastic sheeting or drop cloths as close to the building foundations as possible. Be sure that drop cloths do not have holes or openings.

  - **Preparation for dry removal.** Extend the drop cloths or plastic sheeting out from the foundation a distance of 3 feet for each story that will undergo the lead removal. Make sure that the sheeting extends at least 5 feet but not more than 20 feet from the building. Weight the sheeting at the foundation and along the edges and seams. If the wind speed is more than 15 miles per hour or the debris is being carried beyond the ground sheeting, you will need to build a vertical containment (two-by-fours covered with plastic sheeting) around the project.

- **Preparation for wet removal.** Follow the guidelines for dry removal. Be sure that the edge of the plastic sheet is wide enough to catch any liquid runoff, and raise the outside edge of the sheet (two-by-fours work well) to trap the liquid wastes. Where seams occur, seal them with tape and raise the edges onto two-by-fours. Add a new section of plastic sheeting as needed.

Put On Protective Clothing and Equipment. Put on a respirator equipped with HEPA filters and protective clothing as instructed in Appendix B. If you are using chemicals, you also need protective gloves and cartridges for organic chemicals or corrosive chemicals, depending on the product you are using.

> **Note:** If you must leave the work area during the project, wet down and remove your protective equipment and clothing while standing on plastic just inside of the entrance/exit to the work area. This will prevent you from carrying lead dust into other areas. Upon returning, put]new coveralls just outside of the entrance to the workplace.

Removal of Paint

1. Follow the instructions for preparing the work area.
2. Remove the lead-containing paint using one of the acceptable methods.

    If you are scraping to remove the paint, scrape all the way down to bare wood. Mist the area to be removed with water or detergent solution prior to scraping.

    If you are using chemical methods, follow the manufacturer's instructions carefully.
3. Dispose of the debris. Mist surfaces with water before sweeping up debris. Smaller amounts of solid waste should be collected and placed into double plastic bags which you should then seal with strong tape. Larger amounts of waste can be stored in larger containers, provided they are secure.

    Wrap large debris (such as doors, windows and trim) in plastic that was not used during the removal. Seal the plastic with tape and dispose of the debris properly.

    If there is too much water to be absorbed with paper towels, liquid wastes can be sponged, pumped, vacuumed or bailed into spill-proof and leakproof containers.

4. Spray the polyethylene sheeting that is taped to walls or to other surfaces with a fine mist of water in order to prevent disturbing any dust. These materials are contaminated wastes, and must be handled carefully. First remove the upper layer of plastic from the floor. Working from the edges to the middle, fold it upon itself in order to trap any remaining dust inside. Place the plastic sheeting into double plastic bags and tape them securely. Leave the second layer of floor containment in place; this will be removed after the final cleaning.

5. Wash with TSP detergent and rinse all surfaces according to the cleaning procedure above. Surfaces that have been stripped of lead-based paint will be coated with a residue of dust that is nearly invisible and difficult to remove.

    If a HEPA vacuum is available, use it on all accessible surfaces. Wet-wipe or mop as appropriate and HEPA vacuum again.

    Remove excess water as discussed in Step 2 under the *Cleaning of Surfaces in Good Condition*.

6. Beginning at the point most distant from your containment area entrance/exit, remove all plastic. First, peel the plastic off the walls and lower it to the floor. Then, carefully roll up the plastic on the floor, taking care to keep all debris contained within the plastic. Work backwards towards your exit and stay on the plastic flooring at all times during this process. Roll and fold the plastic sheeting toward you while remaining on the plastic. Place each roll of plastic inside double plastic bags and tape them securely.

7. Remove your protective clothing in the work area and wipe your shoes off with a wet rag. Wash any work clothing separately from the rest of the family laundry. Wash your hair and body with soap and water at the end of each workday.

If the above steps are followed carefully, the area should be clean, but the only way to know for sure is to test the surfaces. This can be done by collecting wipe samples and having a laboratory analyze them. Contact a qualified laboratory for help with this sampling.

Waste Disposal

1. Contact your local department of health or environmental protection to find out if special requirements apply.

2. If there are no special disposal requirements, follow the above collection and bagging procedures and dispose of the wastes at the local landfill. *Do not* dispose of liquid or solid wastes that are not contained.

Do not simply dump materials into areas that are not contained; doing so will contaminate yourself or others.

Painting and Sealing Abated Surfaces

The final step in the removal project is to paint or seal the cleaned surfaces. After the surfaces are completely dry, prime the surfaces and repaint or seal with a clear polyurethane. Seal vinyl tile or linoleum with an appropriate wax. Seal concrete floors with a concrete sealer.

Covering Lead-Containing Surfaces

Acceptable coverings for lead-based paint must be durable and not easily damaged by children. Such coverings include gypsum board, aluminum, vinyl, plywood, Formica, acrylic sheets, fiberglass, durable carpet, tile or Plexiglas™.

Do not use contact paper or wallpaper that is not vinyl unless all of the lead-based paint is removed first.

1. Follow the procedures for cleaning the surfaces and preparing the work area.
2. Fasten the covering material securely onto the surface to be covered. Make sure that the covering material is secure at the corners where edges come together (such as floor, wall and ceiling joints). Any method such as nailing, cementing or gluing can be used, providing that the surface will not be disturbed by a small child or normal wear and tear.

   Use particular care when sealing the edges of sheet metal with molding or caulk.

   When covering exterior surfaces, be sure that all seams and junctions of old and new material are sealed with siliconized latex or similar caulk. If any edges are left open and unsealed, lead dust can enter the room.
3. Remove the waste materials and dispose of them according to state or local regulations. Perform the final cleaning and then remove the protective sheeting from the floors or walls.

SOURCE: U.S. Department of Housing and Urban Development (HUD). *The HUD Lead-Based Paint Abatement Demonstration (FHA)*. Vol. II. Appendices I–P. Washington, D.C.: HUD, Office of Policy Development and Research, 1991.

References

Preface

Aeppel, T. "Superfund site spawns a spate of litigation, though not a cleanup." *The Wall Street Journal* (9 February 1994).

Chapter 1

Appraisal Institute. *Statement of Purpose*. Chicago: Appraisal Institute, 1993.

Cain, D., Indiana Certified General Appraiser, Real Property Evaluation, Inc. Personal communication, Indianapolis, Ind., 22 April 1994.

Customer Education Group. *The Appraisal Guide*. CT068L10/92. Washington, D.C.: Fannie Mae, 1992.

Customer Education Group. *Basics of Sound Underwriting*. CT058L03/92. Washington, D.C.: Fannie Mae, 1992.

French, W. B., Martin, S. J. and T. E. Battle. *The Guide to Real Estate Principles, Practices, and Licensing Examinations*. 6th ed. Englewood Cliffs, N.J.: Regents/Prentice Hall, 1992.

Guide to Environmental Risk Management. San Diego, Calif.: Vista Environmental Information, 1993.

The American Society of Home Inspectors (ASHI), Inc. *The Standards of Practice and Code of Ethics*. Arlington Heights, Ill.: ASHI, 1993.

Chapter 2

Indiana Department of Environmental Management and Indiana Recycling Coalition. *You Can Cut It! A Complete Guide to Reducing Indiana's Solid Waste at the Source*. Indianapolis, Ind.: Indiana Department of Environmental Management, 1993.

Lavelle, M. "The Minorities Equation." *The National Law Journal* 15(3): S2 (21 September 1992).

Miller, G. T. *Living in the Environment*. 8th ed. Belmont, Calif.: Wadsworth, Inc, 1994.

Nadakavukaren, A. *Man & Environment.: A Health Perspective*. 3rd ed. Prospect Heights, Ill.: Waveland Press, Inc, 1990.

Ritchie, I. *Introduction to Indoor Air Quality: A Self-Paced Learning Manual*. EPA/400/3-91/002. Washington, D.C.: U.S. Environmental Protection Agency, Office of Air and Radiation, 1991.

U.S. Department of Housing and Urban Development. *The Noise Guidebook*. HUD-953-CPD. Washington, D.C.: U.S. Department of Housing and Urban Development, Office of Planning and Development, 1985.

U.S. Environmental Protection Agency. *National Air Quality and Emissions Trends Report, 1989.* EPA-450/4-91-003b. Research Triangle Park, N.C.: U.S. Environmental Protection Agency, Office of Air Quality Planning and Standards, 1991.

U.S. Environmental Protection Agency. *National Air Quality and Emissions Trends Report, 1991.* Research Triangle Park, N.C.: U.S. Environmental Protection Agency, Office of Air Quality Planning and Standards, 1992.

U.S. Environmental Protection Agency. *National Air Quality and Emissions Trends Report, 1992.* EPA-454/R-93-031. Research Triangle Park, N.C.: U.S. Environmental Protection Agency, Office of Air Quality Planning and Standards, 1993a.

U.S. Environmental Protection Agency. *Criteria for Solid Waste Disposal Facilities. A Guide for Owners/Operators.* EPA/530-SW-91-089. Washington, D.C.: U.S. Environmental Protection Agency, Solid Waste and Emergency Response, 1993b.

U.S. Environmental Protection Agency. "UST Program Fact Sheets. Overview of the UST Program." EPA 510-F-93-007. U.S. Environmental Protection Agency, Solid Waste and Emergency Response, 1993c.

U.S. Environmental Protection Agency. *EPA Environmental News.* "EPA announces proposed rule to expand the Toxics Release Inventory." (January 6). Washington, D.C.: U.S. Environmental Protection Agency, Communications, Education, and Public Affairs, 1994.

U.S. Environmental Protection Agency. *Addition of Certain Chemicals; Toxic Chemical Release Reporting; Community Right-to-Know.* 40 CFR part 372. Washington, D.C.: U.S. Government Printing Office, 1994.

Wagner, T. *In Our Backyard: A Guide to Understanding Pollution and Its Effects.* New York, N.Y.: Van Nostrand Reinhold, 1993.

Chapter 3

Federal Register. *Environmental Protection Agency Model Standards and Techniques for Control of Radon in New Residential Buildings; Notice.* Vol. 59, No. 54: 13402–13416, 1994.

U.S. Environmental Protection Agency. *Radon-Resistant Residential New Construction.* EPA/600/8-88/087. Washington, D.C.: U.S. Environmental Protection Agency, Research and Development, 1988.

U.S. Environmental Protection Agency. *Technical Support Document for the 1992 Citizen's Guide to Radon.* EPA 400-R-92-011. Washington, D.C.: U.S. Environmental Protection Agency, Office of Air and Radiation, 1992a.

U.S. Environmental Protection Agency. *A Citizen's Guide to Radon (2nd edition).* 402-K92-001. Washington, D.C.: U.S. Government Printing Office, 1992b.

U.S. Environmental Protection Agency. *Consumer's Guide to Radon Reduction.* 402-K92-003. Washington, D.C.: U.S. Government Printing Office, 1992c.

U.S. Environmental Protection Agency. *Home Buyer's and Seller's Guide to Radon.* 402-R-93-003. Washington, D.C.: U.S. Government Printing Office, 1993.

Chapter 4

Federal Register. *Asbestos-Containing Materials in Schools; Final Rule and Notice.* FR 52: 41826–41905, 30 October, 1987.

Puget Sound Air Pollution Control Agency. *Asbestos Removal Procedures for Home Owners: How to Properly Remove Sheet Vinyl Flooring with Asbestos Backing*. Seattle, Wash.: Puget Sound Air Pollution Control Agency, 1993.

Puget Sound Air Pollution Control Agency. *Asbestos Removal Procedures for Home Owners: How to Properly Remove Cement Asbestos Board Siding*. Seattle, Wash.: Puget Sound Air Pollution Control Agency, 1993.

Puget Sound Air Pollution Control Agency. *Asbestos Removal Procedures for Home Owners: How to Properly Remove Asbestos from the Exteriors of Convection and Forced-air Furnace Systems*. Seattle, Wash.: Puget Sound Air Pollution Control Agency, 1993.

Puget Sound Air Pollution Control Agency. *Asbestos Removal Procedures for Home Owners: How to Properly Remove Spray-On "Popcorn" Ceilings*. Seattle, Wash.: Puget Sound Air Pollution Control Agency, 1993.

U.S. Environmental Protection Agency. *Asbestos in Buildings: A National Survey of Asbestos-Containing Friable Materials*. Washington, D.C.: U.S. Environmental Protection Agency, Office of Toxic Substances, 1984.

U.S. Environmental Protection Agency. *Guidance for Controlling Asbestos-Containing Materials in Buildings*. EPA 560/5-85-024. Washington, D.C.: U.S. Environmental Protection Agency, Office of Pesticides and Toxic Substances, 1985.

Chapter 5

Centers for Disease Control, U.S. Department of Health and Human Services. *Preventing Lead Poisoning in Young Children*. Atlanta, Ga.: Centers for Disease Control, 1991.

U.S. Environmental Protection Agency, Office of Water. *Lead and Your Drinking Water*. OPA-87-005. Washington, D.C.: U.S. Government Printing Office, 1987.

Residential Lead-Based Paint Hazard Reduction Act of 1992. Public Law 102-550. 28 October 1992.

U.S. Department of Housing and Urban Development. *Lead-based Paint: Interim Guidelines for Hazard Identification and Abatement in Public and Indian Housing*. Washington, D.C.: U.S. Department of Housing and Urban Development, Office of Public and Indian Housing, 1990.

U.S. Environmental Protection Agency. *Environmental Fact Sheet. Lead Leaching from Submersible Well Pumps*. EPA 747-F-94-001. Washington, D.C.: U.S. Environmental Protection Agency, Office of Prevention, Pesticides, and Toxic Substances, 1994.

Chapter 6

National Resource Council. *Indoor Pollutants*. Washington, D.C.: National Academy Press, 1981.

Ritchie, I. *Introduction to Indoor Air Quality: A Reference Manual*. EPA/400/3-91/003. Washington, D.C.: U.S. Environmental Protection Agency, Office of Air and Radiation, 1991a.

Ritchie, I. *Introduction to Indoor Air Quality: A Self-Paced Learning Manual*. EPA/400/3-91/002. Washington, D.C.: U.S. Environmental Protection Agency, Office of Air and Radiation, 1991b.

World Health Organization (WHO). *Environmental Health Criteria 89. Formaldehyde*. Geneva, Switzerland: WHO, 1989.

Chapter 7

Levin, H. (editor). "Carpets and indoor air." *Indoor Air Bulletin* 2(6):4–14, 1992.

Ritchie, I. *Introduction to Indoor Air Quality: A Reference Manual.* EPA/400/3-91/003. Washington, D.C.: U.S. Environmental Protection Agency, Office of Air and Radiation, 1991.

World Health Organization (WHO). *Indoor Air Quality: Organic Pollutants.* EURO Reports and Studies 111. Copenhagen, Denmark: WHO, 1987.

Chapter 8

Council of American Building Officials (CABO). *CABO One and Two Family Dwelling Code.* Falls Church, Va.: CABO, 1992.

National Center for Appropriate Technology (NCAT). *Moisture and Home Energy Conservation.* Butte, Mont.: NCAT, 1983.

Ritchie, I. *Introduction to Indoor Air Quality: A Reference Manual.* EPA/400/3-91-003. Washington, D.C.: U.S. Environmental Protection Agency, Office of Air and Radiation, 1991.

Chapter 9

Council of American Building Officials (CABO). *CABO One and Two Family Dwelling Code.* Falls Church, Va.: CABO, 1992.

Ksiazek, T. G. Chief, Diagnostic and Immunochemistry Section, Special Pathogens Branch, Centers for Disease Control. Atlanta, Ga., letter to State Epidemiologist dated 18 February 1994.

Ritchie, I. *Introduction to Indoor Air Quality: A Reference Manual.* EPA/400/3-91-003. Washington, D.C.: U.S. Environmental Protection Agency, Office of Air and Radiation, 1991.

U.S. Consumer Product Safety Commission (CPSC) and American Lung Association. *Biological Pollutants in Your Home.* CPSC and American Lung Association, 1990.

U.S. Department of Health and Human Services (DHHS). "Hantavirus infection—southwestern United States: Interim recommendations for risk reduction." *Morbidity And Mortality Weekly Report.* Vol. 42, No. RR-11. Atlanta, Ga.: U.S. DHHS, 1993.

World Health Organization (WHO). *Indoor Air Quality: Biological Contaminants.* WHO Regional Publications. European Series No. 31. Copenhagen, Denmark: WHO, 1990.

Chapter 10

Council of American Building Officials (CABO). *CABO One and Two Family Dwelling Code.* 1992 Edition. Falls Church, Va.: CABO, 1992.

National Center for Appropriate Technology (NCAT). *Introducing Supplemental Combustion Air to Gas-fired Home Appliances.* DOE/CE/15095-7. Butte, Mont.: NCAT, 1983.

Ritchie, I. *Introduction to Indoor Air Quality: A Reference Manual.* EPA/400/3-91/003. Washington, D.C.: U.S. Environmental Protection Agency, Office of Air and Radiation, 1991.

U.S. Department of Health, Education and Welfare (DHEW). *Basic Housing Inspection.* HEW Publication No. (CDC) 80-8315. Atlanta, Ga.: U.S. DHEW, 1976 (reprinted 1979).

U.S. Environmental Protection Agency, Consumer Product Safety Commission, and the American Lung Association. *Combustion Appliances and Indoor Air Pollution.* Washington, D.C.: U.S. Government Printing Office, 1991.

U.S. Environmental Protection Agency. *Indoor Air Facts. No 8. Use and Care of Home Humidifiers.* Washington, D.C.: U.S. Environmental Protection Agency, Air and Radiation, 1991.

Chapter 11

Consumers Union. *What EPA Knows about the Risks of Home Use Products Containing 50 Common Active Ingredients.* Mt. Vernon, N.Y.: Consumers Union, 1987.

Morgan, D.P. *Recognition and Management of Pesticide Poisonings.* 4th ed. EPA-540/9-88-001. Washington, D.C.: U.S. Environmental Protection Agency, Office of Pesticide Programs, 1989.

Ritchie, I. Introduction to Indoor Air Quality: A Reference Manual. EPA/400/3-91-003. Washington, D.C.: U.S. Environmental Protection Agency, Office of Air and Radiation, 1991.

U.S. General Accounting Office. *Nonagricultural Pesticides: Risks and Regulations.* GAO/RCED-86-97. Washington, D.C.: U.S. General Accounting Office, 1986.

U.S. Environmental Protection Agency. *Citizen's Guide to Pesticides.* 4th ed. 2OT-1003. Washington, D.C.: U.S. Environmental Protection Agency, Office of Pesticides and Toxic Substances, 1990.

U.S. General Accounting Office. *Lawn Care Pesticides: Risks Remain Uncertain While Prohibited Safety Claims Continue.* GAO/RCED-86-97. Washington, D.C.: U.S. General Accounting Office, 1990.

Chapter 12

Bierbaum, P.J. and J.M. Peters (editors). *Proceedings of the Scientific Workshop on the Health Effects of Electric and Magnetic Fields on Workers.* DHHS (NIOSH) 91-111. Cincinnati, Ohio: U.S. Department of Health and Human Services, 1991.

Bonneville Power Administration. *Electrical And Biological Effects of Transmission Lines: A Review.* Portland, Oreg.: U.S. Department of Energy, Bonneville Power Administration, 1989 (revised 1993).

Electric Power Research Institute, Inc. (EPRI). *Exposure Assessment Fundamentals.* Palo Alto, Calif.: EPRI, 1992.

Electric Power Research Institute, Inc. (EPRI). *Electric and Magnetic Field Fundamentals.* Palo Alto, Calif.: EPRI, 1994.

Electric Power Research Institute, Inc. (EPRI). *Occupational EMF Exposure Assessment.* Palo Alto, Calif.: EPRI, 1994.

IEEE Magnetic Fields Task Force. "A protocol for spot measurements of residential power frequency magnetic fields." Presented at the IEEE/PES 1992 Summer Meeting of IEEE

Power Engineering Society. Seattle, Wash., July 12–16, 1992. Paper 92-SM 460-6-PWRD, 1992.

Morgan, G. *Electric and Magnetic Fields from 60 Hertz Electric Power: What Do We Know about Possible Health Risks?* Pittsburgh, Pa.: Carnegie Mellon University, Department of Engineering and Public Policy, 1989.

Robert S. Banks, Associates, Inc. *Electric and Magnetic Fields: Summary of Developments. 1991–1992 Supplement.* Washington, D.C.: Edison Electric Institute, 1993.

U.S. Environmental Protection Agency. *Questions and Answers about Electric and Magnetic Fields (EMFs).* 402-R-009. Washington, D.C.: U.S. Environmental Protection Agency, Office of Radiation and Indoor Air, 1992a.

U.S. Environmental Protection Agency. *EMF in Your Environment.* 402-R-92-008. Washington, D.C.: U.S. Environmental Protection Agency, Office of Radiation and Indoor Air, 1992b.

Wertheimer, N. and E. Leeper. "Electrical wiring configurations and childhood cancer." *American Journal of Epidemiology* 109(3): 273–284, 1979.

Chapter 13

Code of Federal Regulations (CFR). *National Primary Drinking Water Regulations.* 40 CFR, part 141. Washington, D.C.: U.S. Government Printing Office, 1992.

Council of Better Business Bureaus, Inc. *Consumer Information Series. Tips on...Water Quality Improvement.* Publication No. 24-236 (reprinted 1990). Arlington, Va.: Council of Better Business Bureaus, Inc., 1988.

Miller, G. T. *Living In The Environment.* 8th ed. Belmont, Calif.: Wadsworth, Inc., 1994.

Ripley, P.J. and B.S. Murdock. *Environmental Issues in Primary Care.* Minneapolis, Minn.: Minnesota Department of Health, 1991.

Salvato, J.A. *Environmental Engineering and Sanitation.* New York, N.Y.: Wiley-Interscience, 1972.

The Council of American Building Officials (CABO). *CABO One and Two Family Dwelling Code.* Falls Church, Va.: CABO, 1992.

The Freshwater Foundation. *Water Filters: Their Effect on Water Quality.* Navarre, Minn.: The Freshwater Foundation, 1985.

U.S. Environmental Protection Agency. *Drinking Water from Household Wells.* EPA 570/9-90-013. Washington, D.C.: U.S. Environmental Protection Agency, Office of Water, 1990.

U.S. Environmental Protection Agency. *Citizen Monitoring: Recommendations to Household Well Users.* EPA 570/9-90-006. Washington, D.C.: U.S. Environmental Protection Agency, Office of Water, 1990.

U.S. Environmental Protection Agency. *Home Water Treatment Units: Filtering Fact from Fiction.* EPA 570/9-90-HHH. Washington, D.C.: U.S. Environmental Protection Agency, Office of Water, 1990.

U.S. Environmental Protection Agency. *Is Your Drinking Water Safe?* EPA 570/9-91-005. Washington, D.C.: U.S. Environmental Protection Agency, Office of Water, 1991.

U.S. Environmental Protection Agency. *Environmental Fact Sheet. Lead Leaching from Submersible Well Pumps.* EPA 747-F-94-001. Washington, D.C.: U.S. Environmental Protection Agency, Office of Prevention, Pesticides, and Toxic Substances, 1994.

Chapter 14

Council of American Building Officials (CABO). *CABO One and Two Family Dwelling Code.* Falls Church, Va.: CABO, 1992.

Daniels, G. *Home Guide to Plumbing, Heating, Air Conditioning.* Danbury, Conn.: Grolier Book Clubs, Inc., 1976 (reprinted 1989).

Franzmeier, D.P., J.E. Yahner, G.C. Steinhardt, and D.G. Schulze. *Understanding and Judging Indiana Soils.* West Lafayette, Ind.: Purdue University Cooperative Extension Service, 1989.

Marion County Soil and Water Conservation District. *Marion County Residential Guide for Soils, Drainage, and Erosion Control.* Indianapolis, Ind.: Marion County Soil and Water Conservation District.

Salvato, Joseph A. *Environmental Engineering and Sanitation.* 2d ed. New York, N.Y.: Wiley-Interscience, 1972.

The Freshwater Foundation. *Understanding Your Septic System.* Wayzata, Minn.: The Freshwater Foundation, 1986.

U.S. Department of Health, Education and Welfare (DHEW). *Basic Housing Inspection.* HEW Publication No. (CDC) 80-8315. Atlanta, Ga.: U.S. DHEW, 1976 (reprinted 1979).

Index